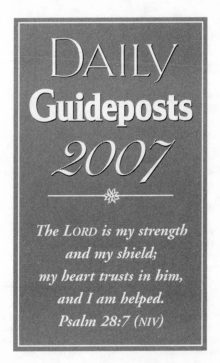

DAILY
Guideposts
2007

The LORD is my strength
and my shield;
my heart trusts in him,
and I am helped.
Psalm 28:7 (NIV)

GuidepostsBooks™
New York, New York

Daily Guideposts, 2007

ISBN 0-8249-4707-X

Published by GuidepostsBooks
16 East 34ᵗʰ Street
New York, New York 10016
www.guidepostsbooks.com

Distributed by Ideals Publications, a Guideposts company
535 Metroplex Drive, Suite 250
Nashville, Tennessee 37211

ACKNOWLEDGMENTS

Every attempt has been made to credit the sources of copyrighted material used in this book. If any such acknowledgment has been inadvertently omitted or miscredited, receipt of such information would be appreciated.

All Scripture quotations, unless otherwise noted, are taken from *The King James Version of the Bible*.

Scripture quotations marked (AMP) are taken from *The Amplified Bible*, © 1965 by Zondervan Publishing House. All rights reserved.

Scripture quotations marked (JB) are taken from *The Jerusalem Bible*, © 1966, 1967 and 1968 by Darton, Longman & Todd Ltd. and Doubleday & Company, Inc. All rights reserved.

Scripture quotations marked (MSG) are taken from *The Message*. Copyright © 1993, 1994, 1995, 1996, 2000, 2001, 2002 by Eugene H. Peterson.

Scripture quotations marked (NAS) are taken from the *New American Standard Bible*, © The Lockman Foundation, 1960, 1962, 1963, 1968, 1971, 1972, 1973, 1975, 1977. Used by permission.

Scripture quotations marked (NEB) are taken from *The New English Bible*. Copyright © The Delegates of the Oxford University Press and the Syndics of the Cambridge University Press 1961, 1970.

Scripture quotations marked (NIV) are taken from *The Holy Bible, New International Version*. Copyright © 1973, 1978, 1984 International Bible Society. Used by permission of Zondervan Bible Publishers.

Scripture quotations marked (NKJV) are taken from *The Holy Bible, New King James Version*. Copyright © 1997, 1990, 1985, 1983 by Thomas Nelson, Inc.

Scripture quotations marked (NLT) are taken from the *Holy Bible*, New Living Translation. Copyright © 1996. Used by permission of Tyndale House Publishers, Inc., Wheaton, Illinois 60189. All rights reserved.

Scripture quotations marked (NRSV) are taken from the *New Revised Standard Version Bible*. Copyright © 1989 by the Division of Christian Education of the National Council of the Churches of Christ in the U.S.A. Used by permission. All rights reserved.

Scripture quotations marked (RSV) are taken from the *Revised Standard Version of the Bible*. Copyright © 1946, 1952, 1971 by Division of Christian Education of the National Council of Churches of Christ in the U.S.A. Used by permission.

Scripture quotations marked (TLB) are taken from *The Living Bible*. Copyright © 1971 by Tyndale House Publishers, Wheaton, IL 60187. All rights reserved.

"Great Is Thy Faithfulness" © 1923. Renewed 1951 Hope Publishing Co., Carol Stream, IL 60188. All rights reserved. Used by permission.

"Do the part of it you love to do . . ." quoted in February Reader's Room is copyright © 2005 by Cecelia McLeod.

Brian Doyle's photo by Jerry Hart. Edward Grinnan's photo by Julie Skarratt. Rick Hamlin's photo by Lilly Dong. Roberta Messner's photo by Jan D. Witter/Camelot Photography. Roberta Rogers' photo by John S. Rogers. Elizabeth Sherrill's and John Sherrill's photos by Gerardo Somoza. Van Varner's photo by Steven Boljonis.

Cover photograph by Carr Clifton
Cover design by Marisa Jackson
Interior design by David Matt
Design adaptations by Holly Johnson
Artwork by Gail W. Guth
Indexed by Patricia Woodruff
Typeset by Planet Patti Inc.
Printed and bound in the United States of America

TABLE OF CONTENTS

TABLE OF CONTENTS

F ROM THE VERY BEGINNING of the story of God's dealings with His people, the journey has been a rich sign and symbol of the spiritual life. God makes a covenant with Abraham, who responds by journeying out of the idolatry of Ur of the Chaldees; Joseph's involuntary journey to Egypt results in the deliverance of his brothers and his father Jacob; God calls the children of Israel on a journey from bondage in Egypt through the desert to the land of promise; Mary and Joseph journey to Bethlehem to bring forth the infant Redeemer; and Jesus journeys to Jerusalem and beyond, to the very gates of death, to put humankind back on the road to God.

As it was for God's people, so it is for every one of us: Our life is a walk with God, in Whom "we live, and move, and have our being" (Acts 17:28), and Who gives us the grace we need to meet all the challenges our journey may bring. Sometimes the journeys that we take with God are travels that move us across the country or around the world, on a vacation that shows us God's glory in the beauty of His creation; on pilgrimages to places hallowed by the footsteps of generations of believers; on a trek to a new place where we're called to live, work and witness. Sometimes they're journeys we take without leaving our hometown, when we make a visit of reconciliation to an estranged friend; as we struggle through the dark valley of illness or bereavement; when we move through the years with a beloved spouse; as we watch a child grow up; when we find ourselves suddenly transported to a joyful new place in our relationship with God.

But wherever we are, however we travel, our journey has one ultimate goal: to share in the abundant life of the One Who is our Creator, Redeemer and Companion. And so our theme for *Daily Guideposts,* 2007 is "Strength for the Journey." Our family of fifty-nine writers will be your special traveling companions throughout the year, sharing some of the ways God has strengthened them for their own life-journeys.

Come with us to discover the light of healing pouring from the open door of a church, follow a faithful caregiver on a 2,500-mile journey to discover the true meaning of service, listen to a testimony of faith at the Great Wall of China and find a new perspective on the meaning of marriage in a visit to an art museum. We'll take you all over the world, from the mountains of Spain to the deserts of Arabia. We'll give you glimpses of God, Who travels with us in the melody of a hymn, the imagination of a four-year-old, the kindness of a stranger, and the courage and grace of a centenarian.

As always, we've got some extraordinary destinations on our itinerary. At the beginning of every month in "Lessons from the Journey," Elizabeth Sherrill shares some of the things a lifetime of travel has taught her about our spiritual journey. And at the middle of the month, Roberta Messner takes you in search of "God-finds," the special people God puts into our lives as signs of His love and blessing.

In January, Isabel Wolseley will be your traveling companion on a once-in-a-lifetime voyage to the icy, unspoiled beauty of Antarctica. During Holy Week, Roberta Rogers takes you to Jerusalem to walk the road past Calvary to an encounter with the risen Lord. In May, follow Edward Grinnan as he confronts the workaday worries we all have to deal with and finds a renewed trust in the Lord. Join Marilyn Morgan King in June as she discovers the grace God gives us in even the most painful journeys. In August, you'll take a very special mountain excursion with John Sherrill aboard an old-fashioned steam train. And in December, Daniel Schantz will show you the simple things that make the road to Christmas a journey to joy.

If you've traveled with us before, you'll be glad to see old friends like Van Varner, Marion Bond West, Fred Bauer, Patricia Lorenz, Scott Walker, Fay Angus and Oscar Greene. And you'll meet two new members of our family: Rebecca Ondov, who'll share her journey from post-college life in Washington, D.C., to an outdoorswoman's life in Hamilton, Montana; and Wendy Willard, a graphic designer and stay-at-home mom from Bel Air, Maryland, who'll show you how a little hymn-singing can lead to a big attitude adjustment, even if you're up to your elbows in dishwater.

For more than thirty years, millions of readers have found strength, refreshment and renewal in the pages of *Daily Guideposts*. And they've found a family—readers, writers and all of us here at Guideposts—brought together by faith, prayer and the shared experience of God's daily blessings. Whether you're picking up *Daily Guideposts* for the first time or the thirty-first, we hope that these words of faith and hope in Scripture, prayer, and true, first-person stories will lift your heart and lighten your step as you walk with God through all the days of the year.

—ANDREW ATTAWAY
EDITOR, *Daily Guideposts*

January

The joy of the Lord is your strength.

—*Nehemiah 8:10*

MON
I

BUT IN EVERY THING BY PRAYER AND SUPPLICATION WITH THANKSGIVING LET YOUR REQUESTS BE MADE KNOWN UNTO GOD. —Philippians 4:6

I MADE MY FIRST New Year's resolutions as 1983 turned into 1984, alone in my bedroom with some favorite books, my cat, and a radio playing "Auld Lang Syne." I'd been a widow for five months.

"Father," I wrote, "I want to be a wife again. I trust Your selection. I must know that I'm in Your perfect will, and I trust You to give me that unmistakable knowledge. I'm not going to be anxious or eager as I wait for Your choice for me. Believing that You answer specific prayers, I submit these specifications to You:

1. Jesus is number one in his life; I'll be number two.
2. I can help in any ministry he has.
3. He's called of God in a specific way.
4. He possesses a keen sense of humor. We laugh a lot.
5. He needs me.
6. There's intense romance.
7. He hears You clearly and obeys.
8. He encourages me.
9. We communicate.
10. We have deep admiration/respect for each other."

I presented those same resolutions to the Lord as 1985 and 1986 came to a close. On April 8, 1987, I received a phone call from a stranger in Oklahoma. The professor-minister had read something that I'd written about losing a spouse. He knew that pain also. Gene Acuff and I were married in August 1987.

Oh, Father, a brand-new year! What a time to make my deepest, even secret, requests known to You. —MARION BOND WEST

LESSONS FROM THE JOURNEY

OVER THE YEARS, Elizabeth Sherrill has traveled around the world in search of stories to share with Guideposts readers. In the course of her travels, she's learned some things about journeys, and at the beginning of each month this year, she will share some tips that can help all of us on our own spiritual journeys. —THE EDITORS

KEEP A TRAVEL DIARY

TUE

2

"WRITE IN A BOOK ALL THE WORDS THAT I HAVE SPOKEN TO YOU." —Jeremiah 30:2 (RSV)

MY HUSBAND JOHN thought we'd seen the whales off the coast of California; I was sure we'd seen them from Maui. He said we'd gone to Canada before the year we spent in Bolivia; I thought it was after we got back. And that shoebox full of photos! Was this slate-roofed house in Austria or Switzerland? And what were the names of this couple who'd been so kind to us when our car broke down?

After years of such unsolvable mysteries, I'd finally begun to keep a travel diary, a separate notebook for each trip, small pages so it wouldn't become a chore. It was still an effort some nights, after a day on the move, to get the notebook out and record the highlights.

But the rewards! I have forty years of trip logs now, and opening any one of them at random brings back people, places, small crises, discoveries and surprise encounters—most of which I'd forgotten.

Shortly after I began taking notes on trips, I started a spiritual diary. I jotted down quotes, poems, insights, questions, prayers, confessions, words I believed I was hearing from God—always with date, place and shorthand summary of the situation.

And like the external events in the travel diaries that would otherwise be forgotten, these inner episodes come as revelations when I read them now. I had no idea how many prayers had been answered until I read entry after entry and marveled at outcomes I could never have foreseen. I had no idea how truly a journey this Christian walk is until I could trace mine over time. Not, alas, ever upward and onward. Like any journey, this one is beset with detours and setbacks and disappointments. But full, too, of sudden glorious vistas, and always with fresh glimpses of Him Who is both the goal and the way.

Lord of the journey, what notes will I make today on the trip whose destination only You can see? —ELIZABETH SHERRILL

EDITOR'S NOTE: As you read *Daily Guideposts* this year, why not take time to keep your own spiritual travel diary? Jot down your notes in "My Walk with God," the journal pages at the end of every month.

WED
3

"YOU ARE MY LAMP O LORD; THE LORD TURNS MY DARKNESS INTO LIGHT." —II Samuel 22:29 (NIV)

LAST YEAR I WORKED HARD to rid myself of a bad habit—gossip. I decided that I'd try to measure my speech by the old rule of "Is it true? Is it necessary? Is it kind?" Although it took a lot of prayer to keep my lips clamped together, I discovered a certain peace in my relationships that wasn't there before.

Then one cold winter morning I felt a chill in the office that had nothing to do with the weather. *Maybe I'm imagining it,* I thought. I ignored it for a week, but by the eighth day I knew that I had to approach my co-worker Mary. *God,* I prayed, *give me the guts to talk with her directly.* "Is something wrong?" I ventured. "I noticed you've been chilly toward me."

"I heard that you said that I wouldn't be a good manager because I had no brains," she said.

"What?" I couldn't believe that such an ugly rumor had gone around, especially since I'd been so good about not gossiping. "I never said anything of the sort—" and then I stopped, remembering. "I said promoting you to management would be a no-brainer!"

Mary and I both had a good laugh over that one, and I realized that eight days of coldness, hurt feelings and worry could have been avoided with one straightforward discussion. But at least I had my new personal resolution for the new year cut out for me: Don't let things fester. If something seems wrong, speak up!

God, with Your help, let me courageously face whatever I'm afraid of.
—LINDA NEUKRUG

THU
4

"FORGET THE FORMER THINGS; DO NOT DWELL ON THE PAST. SEE, I AM DOING A NEW THING! . . ."
—Isaiah 43:18–19 (NIV)

WHEN THE SCHOOL I worked for in France told me about the all-expenses-paid ski trip to the French Alps, I should have been ecstatic. I wasn't. My last ski trip had ended with a vow never to ski again.

Years ago I'd accompanied a friend who insisted I try snowboarding. "You're athletic," she assured me, "you'll pick it up fast!"

After a few runs on the bunny slope, I felt ready to hit the mountain. Once at the top, I slid down about three feet, then slammed onto the icy ground. That was pretty much the pattern the whole way down. "You go ahead," I insisted, frustrated and embarrassed, "I'll figure it out." Stubborn as I was, I went up three more times—each run as painful and exasperating as the first.

Fed up, I finally decided to trade in the snowboard for skis. I had skied twice as a teenager and thought I'd do better with those. Of course, I left my gloves on the counter and didn't realize it until I was on the lift up the mountain. I fell just as many times, except now my hands were frozen and bleeding. I took off my skis and walked down the slope, only to discover that my friend had broken her ankle. Needless to say, I was through with skiing!

I shared my story with one of the other teachers, and she encouraged me to give it another chance. "Don't let one bad incident deprive you of what might be a wonderful experience."

She was right. The view was breathtaking, the snow was powder-soft, and the ski instructors were patient and effective. By the end of the week, I was flying down the Alps with a freedom and exhilaration that I'd never known—and that I'd come close to never knowing at all.

Dear Lord, free me from the memories that keep me from facing the future with confidence. —KAREN VALENTIN

FRI
5

AFTER THE EARTHQUAKE CAME A FIRE, BUT THE LORD WAS NOT IN THE FIRE. AND AFTER THE FIRE CAME A GENTLE WHISPER. —*I Kings 19:12 (NIV)*

THE NEW YEAR HAD BEGUN, so I was writing my usual list of resolutions. At a weekly get-together with friends over coffee, we each read our goals. I ticked off mine as if I were reading a grocery list.

"Lose five pounds. No more sweets. Get up an hour earlier every morning for prayer time. Write in my journal daily. Exercise every evening for thirty minutes. Turn in my school assignments early. Wash my car every week. Go to bed by 10:00 PM. Read one book a month." I snapped my notebook shut, proud of my goals.

Jesse, new to the group, had a different idea. "My goal is to get up ten minutes earlier every morning for prayer." There was a bewildered silence.

"Is that it?" I asked.

She smiled. "I learned a long time ago that keeping one realistic commitment is far better than a litany of promises that are too overwhelming for me to ever accomplish."

On Sunday the pastor offered a suggestion for those writing New Year's resolutions. He told the story of Elijah, who was looking for God in the big things—a powerful wind, an earthquake, a fire. "But the Lord was not in the big things," he said. "After the fire came a gentle whisper. There Elijah found the Lord."

The pastor paused, looking across the pews. "The Lord was in the gentle whisper," he said softly. "Mother Teresa believed in doing small things with great love. Maybe our resolutions should reflect the same."

I left church knowing what I needed to do. I would rewrite my resolutions, not with an attitude of impractical zealousness but with a sense of humility that tells me grandiose goals don't count if they don't get done.

Like Elijah, Lord, may Your whispers guide me to higher mountains than I ever thought possible. —MELODY BONNETTE

SAT
6

THEY PRESENTED UNTO HIM GIFTS. . . .
—*Matthew 2:11*

I WAS TRAVELING THROUGH southern Arabia in the sultanate of Oman when we stopped in front of a lonely tree in the desert sands. It was no more than six feet high, practically leafless, and with a gnarled and tortured bark. "Go ahead, tap it," said my guide. "Make an incision." I did, and out came a yellowish-brown, milklike sap. "Taste it," he said. It was slightly bitter. "Does your nose detect a fragrant odor?" I nodded. "That's frankincense."

Frankincense. I realized that I knew nothing about it, except that the wise men brought the Christ Child three precious gifts: gold, frankincense and myrrh. Gold I knew about, but the two others were mysteries. Since I've been home, I've discovered lots about them.

Myrrh is similar to frankincense, and the dried pellets of both were priceless for four thousand years. Native to Arabia and Somalia, they were coveted by the peoples of the Middle East (and later throughout the world) for medicines, fumigants (think of all those unwashed bodies in poorly ventilated structures), tributes of honor (like bringing out your best china), but mostly for incense on religious occasions.

At last it came to me. The censers I've seen in churches follow an ancient custom. The burning incense pays honor to the Lord, yes, and also wafts its perfume to me, connecting me all over again to the holy night on which the wise men appeared.

Even slow learners like me, Father, profit from travel. —VAN VARNER

SUN 7

AND BE KIND TO ONE ANOTHER, TENDERHEARTED,
FORGIVING ONE ANOTHER, AS GOD IN CHRIST
FORGAVE YOU. —*Ephesians 4:32 (RSV)*

A FEW SUMMERS AGO my wife and I left our church. I thought we had good reasons for leaving. I was wrong.

My dad died that December. During his lifetime he made very few notes in his Bible. Next to Ephesians 4:32, however, he wrote three words: "How to live." My younger brother found those three short words in Dad's Bible after his death. He shared his discovery with us during our father's funeral in Ohio.

Many condolence cards awaited my wife Dianne and me when we returned to Durango, Colorado. Most of those precious cards and the handwritten, loving letters enclosed in them were from people who belonged to the church we had left. Oh, how we longed to see our friends again!

We returned to our church in January. I was afraid we wouldn't be welcomed and that returning would be difficult. I was wrong again.

I'm still trying to learn from my father what our friends have already learned from our heavenly Father. I want to be tenderhearted when someone I love leaves my life or my church. I want to be forgiving if that someone finds the courage to return. I want to be the worthy son of a man who knew how to live.

Dear God, thank You for wise fathers and for friends who are kind to one another. —TIM WILLIAMS

MON 8

IT IS A GOOD THING TO GIVE THANKS UNTO THE
LORD.... —*Psalm 92:1*

FOR MY FIFTIETH BIRTHDAY I had an outrageous plan: a concert where I'd sing my favorite songs for my family and friends, and some of them would sing too. The highlight would be my fourteen-year-old son Timothy playing his guitar and singing The Beatles' "When I'm Sixty-Four." It would bring down the house. Only one downside—his older brother, seventeen-year-old William, wouldn't be there. He couldn't get away from school.

"I've got to study for finals, Dad," William explained.

"I know, I know," I said, thinking, *But I'm only going to be fifty once.*

I rented the hall, sent out the invitations, picked just the right hors d'oeuvres. Of course, I loved every minute of it: all those great people in one place; all that music that has meant so much to me over the years, one song after another. "And now," I announced, "from the next generation, I present the budding rock star, Timothy Hamlin!"

He strummed the opening chords, but his voice was hesitant. He seemed distracted. And then from the doorway I heard a second voice on the refrain. Timothy looked up and smiled. We all turned. There was William, singing in his strong baritone (and wearing *my* suit). Both their faces said, "Surprise, Dad!" It brought down the house. If I had ever doubted it for a moment, I knew then how blessed I am.

"That was the best song all night," I said. "You'd better do it again when I'm sixty-four!"

I rejoice, Lord, in all the blessings of life. —RICK HAMLIN

TUE
9

AND THIS I PRAY, THAT YOUR LOVE MAY ABOUND YET MORE AND MORE IN KNOWLEDGE AND IN ALL JUDGMENT. —*Philippians 1:9*

LAST NIGHT STEPHEN toddled out to the living room holding a little chair from the kids' dollhouse. He placed it on the floor and looked at me. "Chair," he said. Then he tried to sit on it. Fortunately it was a pretty solid thing.

Giggling, I remembered this stage with my other children. Elizabeth once dropped a toy down the half-inch crack between the elevator and the floor, and for six months afterward was afraid she'd plummet down the shaft. John regularly bumped his head as he tumbled off five-inch trucks he tried to ride. As adults who know better, we find the misperceptions kids have amusing. It only takes a little experience to figure out that when the toilet flushes we're not likely to go down the drain too.

On the other hand, even as a grown-up I sometimes lack proper perspective. When someone says something that pricks my pride, it's amazing how out of proportion my reaction can be. A little insult, an unfortunate choice of words or a bad-humored comment can be as distressing to me as that crack by the elevator was to my daughter.

What makes it seem huge, however, isn't lack of experience but lack of humility.

It won't be long before Stephen grows up enough to discover that dollhouse furniture is designed for dolls, not people. I'd like to think that eventually I'll be able to distinguish between what's truly distressing and what's merely wounded pride.

Lord, help me to see that small offenses are, in fact, small.

—JULIA ATTAWAY

WED
10

AND I THANK CHRIST JESUS OUR LORD, WHO HATH ENABLED ME, FOR THAT HE COUNTED ME FAITHFUL, PUTTING ME INTO THE MINISTRY. —I Timothy 1:12

MORE THAN TWENTY YEARS AGO I completed my first manuscript. Written with pencil on a stack of yellow legal pads, my story, I was sure, would never be published. Finally I gained courage to have the manuscript typed and I sent it to a friend to read. He liked what I had written and forwarded my work to an editor he knew, Mr. Floyd Thatcher. Within a month I received a letter from Mr. Thatcher offering to publish my book. Later, he invited me to write for Guideposts.

Over the years, Floyd and I became friends, and he served as a mentor and confidant. Several days ago he died at the age of eighty-eight. His wife Harriett asked me to deliver the homily at his funeral.

As I prepared the homily, I looked through a small notebook that Floyd kept in his desk drawer, listing the writers with whom he had worked over the long course of his life. I was amazed at the hundreds of men and women whom he had helped to share their stories, express their thoughts and communicate their faith.

Floyd was "a friend at the door," a man who opened opportunities for the mute to speak and the deaf to hear. He was a man who helped others express their deepest thoughts and hopes and dreams. He was an encourager.

I want to live my life this way too—open locked doors for others to pass through. Like Floyd Thatcher, I yearn to be "a friend at the door."

Father, help me to unlatch a door that a friend cannot open. Amen.

—SCOTT WALKER

THU
11
BLESS THE LORD, O MY SOUL, AND FORGET NOT ALL HIS BENEFITS. —Psalm 103:2

THERE ARE TWO BEAUTIFUL swimming pools across the street from my home in Florida. I'm in the pool usually twice a day, often swimming laps. The problem with laps is keeping track. My mind wanders. I'll watch a dolphin jumping out of the Intracoastal Waterway or a heron swooping by when I'm doing the backstroke, and I lose count of my laps.

The solution came one winter day when I was feeling especially joyful about being in that pool under a robin's-egg-blue sky on a glorious eighty-degree day. I started thanking God for all my blessings, using the number of the lap I was on.

ONE: One God Who gave me one life.

TWO: Two daughters. Two sons.

THREE: Three part-time freelance jobs, instead of one monumental stressful one.

FOUR: Four sister-cousins in my hometown in Illinois who keep an eye on my folks and help keep their lives active.

FIVE: The tasty five-bean salad I made yesterday and the five friends who ate it.

SIX: The six days of the week when I really try to get some work done.

SEVEN: The seven seas where I've swum.

EIGHT: Eight grandchildren, tied tightly to my heartstrings.

NINE: The nine lives that cats have. I take care of Bubba and Boomer when my friends Wally and Shirley are on vacation.

TEN: This is the examine-my-conscience lap. I run through the Ten Commandments trying to decide if I've blown it and whether I need to apologize to anyone for anything.

Every day I get out of that pool a new person—blessings counted, life evaluated, attitude adjusted and exercise completed. Jump in! The water's perfect!

Lord, thank You for water, swimming pools and blessings to count.
—PATRICIA LORENZ

FRI
12

THROUGH LOVE SERVE ONE ANOTHER.
—*Galatians 5:13 (NAS)*

MY HUSBAND LEO answered the phone. "Hello? Oh yes, Frances, I'm feeling much better, thanks. My beauty queen took real good care of me!"

Beauty queen? Huh?

His words jolted me right out of the fever-induced stupor brought on by a bad case of the flu. The previous week, Leo had been the one burrowed under the covers, shivering and sweating from alternate bouts of chills and fever. The same vicious bug had then bitten me.

Blowing and coughing and wheezing, I had managed to crawl out of bed just long enough to shuffle back and forth to the bathroom. Even in my weakened condition passing the mirror had been a shock to my system—red nose, sunken eyes, hollow cheeks, tattered sweater over baggy flannel pajamas, the bottoms tucked into big woolen socks. My hair was sticking out in all directions and my whole being was enveloped in the strong fumes of a decongestant.

Some "beauty queen"!

As more of Leo's conversation with Frances filtered into my brain, it became clear that he wasn't referring to my physical appearance. (After fifty years of marriage, we both know I'm no beauty queen!) His perception of beauty was being conveyed in phrases like "hot soup . . . tucking me in . . . calling the doctor . . . doling out pills . . . stroking my brow," the many little things one does to nurse a loved one back to health—the many little things Leo was now doing for me.

Help me, Lord, to look beyond the physical and see as You do the beauty that is soul-deep in others. —ALMA BARKMAN

SAT
13

THAT OUR DAUGHTERS MAY BE AS CORNER STONES, POLISHED AFTER THE SIMILITUDE OF A PALACE.
—*Psalm 144:12*

SEASONAL AFFECTIVE DISORDER: SAD. Every year I think I'll escape it, yet every autumn it ambushes me. My energy level drops as the days shorten. After work I slink home to flop on the couch, snooze and nibble snacks I don't need until the trees bud once again.

Last year I felt more discouraged than ever, facing SAD along with an empty nest—my first autumn alone in thirty-three years. By January I had moved out of the woods to a town twenty times larger, with dozens of opportunities to motivate me. But the first week in my quaint but drafty and echoing one-hundred-year-old apartment, the temperature plunged to twenty-five degrees below zero. With no rugs or drapes to insulate against the cold, gasping radiators made little difference. Alone, cold and new to town, I spent my first few evenings in my new home wrapped in a blanket, weeping. It was only January. How could I last until spring?

My daughter Tess noticed that I needed a lift and arrived with five-year-old Hannah for a weekend. Tess rearranged the living room furniture and added brick-red pillows and a small bright rug to match. After cooking grilled cheese and soup, she popped in a silly Muppets video as all three of us snuggled under a blanket on the sofa. Once Hannah was asleep, Tess and I shared tea and confidences. That night I slept soundly and woke cheerfully, knowing that I had precious company in my chilly new home.

Later, as Tess and I hugged good-bye, I thanked her for taking care of me. "Mom," she assured me, "you know I always will." Winter would last another three months, but my daughter's love would last forever.

Thank You, Lord, for the blessing of children.
—GAIL THORELL SCHILLING

SUN

14

FATHERS, DO NOT EXASPERATE YOUR CHILDREN; INSTEAD, BRING THEM UP IN THE TRAINING AND INSTRUCTION OF THE LORD. —*Ephesians 6:4 (NIV)*

COACH PANNELL'S NINTH-GRADE Bible class fell silent. David asked again, "Is it okay that sometimes my parents have to make me go to church?" I heard the echoing footsteps of kids running outside in the hallway, but no one in our classroom turned a page. David had asked the question the rest of us were afraid to ask: Does God count it as church if we fight going each week? We sat riveted for the answer.

Coach Pannell cleared his throat, stroked his cheek and smiled. "David," he said, making eye contact with each of us in the room, "do you ever not want to eat your vegetables or take the garbage out, even though you know you're supposed to?"

"Of course," David replied.

"How about going to the doctor or dentist, even though you know you don't want to?"

David laughed. "I do that all the time!"

"That's just it," Coach Pannell said. "Sometimes parents know better about what's good for you, whether it's eating right, staying healthy or furthering your relationship with God. Right now church might not be as important to you as the other things on your schedule, but someday, thanks to your parents, you'll understand."

Over the years I've thought a lot about Coach Pannell's words. On a Sunday morning when the alarm goes off, I want to push the snooze button and go back to sleep. But by the closing strains of the final hymn, I don't regret being in church for a moment, the grumbles replaced by heartfelt praise. It's a habit that began on the Sundays of my childhood with my father's footsteps and my mother's voice.

God, thank You for giving me Sundays as a reminder that I spend every day in Your arms. —ASHLEY JOHNSON

READER'S ROOM

WHEN MY DAUGHTER was home from college this winter, she decided to take me to a movie she had seen. As we parked the car, she explained that *Ocean's Twelve* would be a movie I would love as much as she did. She warned me, "Mom, there will be many times you don't understand what's happening, how it all fits into the story, but just know that it will all make sense in the end." The movie was great, and true to her prediction, I was confused at many points along the way. I accepted the "mystery" of WHY things were happening, and I trusted that I would understand in the end. And in the end, I was delighted! On the way home, God said to me, "So, Terrie, if you can let go and trust the filmmakers when you don't understand where they are taking you, can you try trusting ME when My mysteries are bewildering? Can you believe that I have a delightful ending in store?" When will I get it?

—*Terrie Becan, San Antonio, Texas*

MON

15

THERE IS NEITHER JEW NOR GREEK, THERE IS NEITHER BOND NOR FREE, THERE IS NEITHER MALE NOR FEMALE: FOR YE ARE ALL ONE IN CHRIST JESUS.
—*Galatians 3:28*

I WAS HAVING DINNER with Peter, an African American friend, and as we discussed a criminal case with racial overtones that was causing a ruckus in the New York City media, my mind flashed back to the late 1950s and an incident from my childhood.

My parents had taken me along on a business trip to Roanoke, Virginia. One night when they had a function to attend, they left me in the care of an African American babysitter at our hotel. I had my heart—and stomach—set on a real Southern-fried chicken dinner, and I wanted to be served at a swanky table by a tuxedoed waiter rather than order room service.

The babysitter took me down to the hotel restaurant, where I was addressed as "sir" and ceremoniously ushered to a table draped in white linen by a window. Alone.

I glanced behind me: My sitter was standing with the mâitre d', pointing to something on the menu and then at me. He nodded. Then she went outside and kept an eye on me through the window while I ate my Southern-fried feast in solitude.

I was puzzled, to say the least, by why she couldn't sit with me, and later I asked my mom about it. "Sometimes we don't treat each other the way God wants," she said. "But things are getting better."

I looked across the table at my friend Peter as he scanned the menu. Things *have* gotten better. They aren't perfect, but they are not as bad as they used to be. Mom was right. Little by little, I believe we are learning to treat each other the way God wants.

Father of us all, teach me to reach out rather than pull back, to include rather than exclude, to trust rather than fear. —EDWARD GRINNAN

GOD-FINDS

IN *Daily Guideposts, 1999,* Roberta Messner told us about reader Michelle Grebel's innovative approach to life. Each day, this Valley City, North Dakota, resident asks God to help her discover a God-find, a special person who has blessed her or reminded her that God is working in her life. Since meeting Michelle, Roberta has adopted the same spiritual discipline, and each month this year she'll share some of her own treasured God-finds with us. —THE EDITORS

FINDING BEAUTY

TUE
16

ONE THING I HAVE ASKED FROM THE LORD, THAT I SHALL SEEK . . . TO BEHOLD THE BEAUTY OF THE LORD. . . . —Psalm 27:4 (NAS)

PAINT-BY-NUMBER KITS are making a comeback these days, and every time I spot one of my patients working on one, I remember Shattuck Hartwell. Dr. Hartwell was my first surgeon at the Cleveland Clinic and a God-find of the highest order. I met him when I was fifteen and had just learned that I had the incurable disorder neurofibromatosis.

In those days patients often stayed in the hospital while completing a workup. I was scheduled for some preoperative tests the morning Dr. Hartwell, followed by an entourage of residents and fellows in impeccably starched white lab coats, entered my room. They had all come to see "the unusual tumor that was causing this young lady's eye to bulge."

I was mortified to be found working on the paint-by-number horse that the activities volunteer had distributed to the patients on the pediatrics ward. I tried to cover my feeble attempt at art with the bedspread, but Dr. Hartwell would have none of it. "Excellent, Roberta!" he exclaimed. "Always make room in your life for art."

My beloved Dr. Hartwell, who sculpted my disfigured face into one the kids would no longer gawk at, knew the benefit of seeking out God's beauty every single day. And today, whether I take up rug hooking, quilting, collage or painting-by-numbers, I never fail to find God in it all.

Your world never ceases to amaze me with its beauty, Lord. Thank You for every lovely thing. —ROBERTA MESSNER

WED

17

"I WILL BE GRACIOUS TO WHOM I WILL BE GRACIOUS, AND WILL SHOW MERCY ON WHOM I WILL SHOW MERCY." —Exodus 33:19 (RSV)

THERE ARE TWO KINDS of people in the world: those who love New York City and those who don't. I don't. But my husband Charlie does, and so a few times a year, with a shameful amount of grumbling and grousing, I accompany him into the city. To me everyone there seems rushed, irritated, suspicious. To Charlie everyone is busy, committed, successful.

On our last trip we ate lunch in a fast-food shop near Lincoln Center. The place was mobbed, every table taken. Next to our table-for-two were three very large, very hip-looking young men. Between attacks on heaped plates of pizza, pasta, ribs and roast chicken, they worked their cell phones as if their lives depended on it. We overheard enough to learn that they were rap artists trying to schedule a West Coast meeting. In the midst of their intense business lunch, an elderly woman clutching her tray wandered over, eyeing the empty fourth seat at their table. She hesitated. The table went silent. Finally, she asked, "Can I sit here? I won't bother you."

The three exchanged somewhat panicked glances. Two of the men ducked their heads, but then the one who'd been doing most of the talking looked up at her and said, "Sit right down, Mommy. We got love for you."

When Charlie and I left, they were discussing music and telling her about the best places to hear it. I took Charlie's hand and squeezed it.

He looked down at me, surprised to see just a glint of understanding in my newly opened eyes. Hey, New York, we got love for you!

Father, remove my blinders so that I can see Your goodness everywhere.
—MARCI ALBORGHETTI

THU
18

FOR I WILL RESTORE HEALTH UNTO THEE. . . .
—*Jeremiah 30:17*

LAST YEAR MY AGENCY began a staff wellness program. Each participant agreed to do three things: (1) increase the daily number of footsteps walked by five hundred to one thousand; (2) eat four to six fruits and vegetables per day; and (3) meet one personal health goal. My personal goal was to take forty-five thousand footsteps per week.

I ate a healthy diet and walked on my treadmill nearly every day. So I was shocked (and embarrassed) when I reviewed my first two weeks on the program: I hadn't met my steps goal. And one day the *only* vegetable I ate was French fries.

Fortunately, our wellness coordinator Pilar helped me spot the problem: travel habits. At home I was fine, but when I traveled I ate mainly fast food and walked less than a third of my target amount. Pilar shared three tips that helped me establish and maintain good health habits at home and on the road:

1. *Give the program thirty days of real effort.* According to experts, that's the minimum time required to change eating and exercise patterns.
2. *Write it down.* Writing down what I ate and the number of steps according to my pedometer provided argument-proof data—and an incentive to walk into a restaurant and eat a salad instead of gobbling a burger while I drove.
3. *Keep on keeping on.* I still travel a lot, and there are days when I don't meet my goals. But I've learned to forgive myself and get right back on the program.

At year's end I'd met my goals more than ninety percent of the time. My physical and mental health improved. This year I've set a higher goal: ten thousand steps per day, the surgeon general's recommendation for healthy men and women. I'm applying these wellness principles to my spiritual life, too, and I'm beginning to feel the difference.

Divine Teacher and Healer, guide me as I seek wholeness and wellness in every area of my life. —PENNEY SCHWAB

FRI
19
"MY FATHER, IF IT IS POSSIBLE, MAY THIS CUP BE TAKEN FROM ME. YET NOT AS I WILL, BUT AS YOU WILL." —*Matthew 26:39 (NIV)*

AFTER MAKING A MIRACULOUS recovery from a major stroke and two brain surgeries a couple of years ago, my husband Lynn was recently diagnosed with a malignant brain tumor. Again the doctors performed surgery, removing most of the tumor. Over the next several weeks, a whole bunch of new words started to define our lives: *grade-three brain cancer, pathology reports, chemotherapy, radiation, MRI results, life expectancy statistics.* We are still reeling from all these new realities.

"How are you?" people keep asking me. I'm not sure how to answer the question. I know I should sound deeply spiritual, totally trusting God's will for our circumstances, regardless of the outcome. But here's the reality: In spite of my faith and trust in God's promises—that the ultimate outcome will be good—I feel afraid of the pain that might be experienced between today and that outcome.

Then I remember that Jesus probably experienced similar fears. In the Garden of Gethsemane the night before He died, He honestly expressed both His fear and His faith to God in prayer. Fear in the moment, but faith in God's plan for the ultimate outcome. His fear must have been about the pain He knew He would experience between that moment in the garden and God's good outcome. Expressing that fear seemed to strengthen His faith.

So when others ask, "How are you?" I sometimes tell them about my fears. But more importantly, I regularly tell God.

Lord, You know my fears. Please strengthen my faith.
—CAROL KUYKENDALL

SAT
20

AS WE HAVE THEREFORE OPPORTUNITY, LET US DO GOOD UNTO ALL MEN. . . . —*Galatians 6:10*

I WAS LAUGHING SO HARD that my stomach hurt. My family was gathered at my parents' house for a belated birthday party for my brother-in-law Ben. My son Harrison and little niece Abby were entertaining us, making pig noises while crinkling up their noses, when the phone rang. I picked it up. "Brock, it's Mary Jane Scott."

I froze, and the room went silent. "Hello, Ms. Scott," I said. My father is a minister, so we all knew what was coming next. Ms. Scott, an elderly member of our church, needed us for something.

"I hate to be calling," she said, "but I ran out of gas about twenty minutes from your house."

I bit my lip. "Okay, Ms. Scott, we'll figure something out and call you back." There was a glum silence. One of us would go and the party would be over. I hated to feel so selfish, but we hadn't been together like this for weeks.

"I'll go," said Dad.

"We'll go," said my sister.

"Wait a minute," Mom said. "Rita is at church tonight, not far from where Ms. Scott is stranded. Let's give her a call."

Rita is the church sexton. "Hillsboro Presbyterian Church," she answered cheerfully when we called.

"Rita, I hate to bother you, but Ms. Scott just ran out of gas and I was wondering . . ."

"Don't be silly, Brock. What's her cell phone number?"

I read off the number and thanked Rita profusely before hanging up. With my hand still on the phone, I tried to digest what had just transpired. Our family got a call for help from a member of our church family, and it all worked out because of the willingness of another church family member to help.

Father, let me know when it's my time to serve. —BROCK KIDD

THE BEAUTY AT THE BOTTOM OF THE WORLD

EVER SINCE her childhood, Isabel Wolseley has been fascinated by the explorers who found Antarctica so enthralling that they risked— and sometimes even gave— their lives to be there. But why should Isabel decide to visit this eternally cold continent during her admittedly senior-citizen stage of life? Find out this week as she takes you on a voyage of discovery to the mysterious land at the bottom of the world. —THE EDITORS

DAY ONE: THE SEVENTH CONTINENT

SUN
21

IT IS GOD WHO SITS ABOVE THE CIRCLE OF THE EARTH. . . . —Isaiah 40:22 (NLT)

BACK WHEN I WAS a first-grader and the Sunday school teacher read the verse above, I looked at the globe that she had on her desk and asked, "If God sits way up there, can He see the *bottom* of the circle too?" After a startled pause, she answered, "Yes, God can see everything."

I wanted to see the bottom too. But when I was growing up, explorers —not tourists—went to Antarctica. Eventually I traveled the other six continents, but I stayed curious about the only one I still hadn't seen: this windiest, fifth-largest land mass God had created, the one with ninety percent of the world's ice and seventy percent of its water; the one with the highest average elevation, largest earthquake-free area, driest desert; the only continent where, except for marine life, penguins and native birds, no one lives.

Besides all that, it's the only continent owned by no one but governed by the most successful international treaty ever negotiated—the Antarctic Treaty, whose members represent eighty percent of the world's population.

I can't imagine a continent that doesn't have war, where the environment is fully protected, where research has priority. This land I must see, and getting there is now possible!

This trip will involve nearly thirteen hours of flying nonstop from New York City to Buenos Aires, Argentina, another four-hour flight to the southern tip of South America and a two-day, seven-hundred-mile trek around Cape Horn and across treacherous waters to Antarctica. But I'm eager to go!

Father, the hymn writer Edward Hopper's words come to mind:

> *Jesus, Savior, pilot me*
> *Over life's tempestuous sea;*
> *Unknown waves before me roll,*
> *Hiding rock and treacherous shoal.*
> *Chart and compass came from Thee;*
> *Jesus, Savior, pilot me.*
> —ISABEL WOLSELEY

DAY TWO: FLYING SOUTH

MON

THE ONE WHO WATCHES OVER YOU WILL NOT SLEEP. INDEED, HE WHO WATCHES OVER ISRAEL NEVER TIRES AND NEVER SLEEPS. —Psalm 121:3–4 (NLT)

WE LEAVE JFK International Airport on a snow-covered, mid-December night as our plane's low whine turns into a scream. Runway lights flash in quick succession, then become a blur as a slick, licorice-ribbon of tarmac whizzes beneath. Our wheels lift and enter their bays with a dull clunk.

Blankets and pillows are distributed, and the cabin darkens for the long flight. Suddenly I'm gripped by fear: Outside the window looms an inky, freezing vault of unheeding night sky; below is the blackness of the Atlantic Ocean. Yesterday's excitement dims as I ask, "God, what am I doing here?" But He reminds me, *I never tire and never sleep,* and in seeming confirmation, red lights blip consoling signals from the plane's wingtips. I relax.

Eighteen hours later, after a stop in Buenos Aires, we land in

Ushuaia, Argentina. This city—the world's southernmost—is hemmed in by concentric circles of jutting, snow-capped mountains. Little houses dot their slopes; regal multihued lupines bloom, thicker than dandelions. In this somewhat-summer setting, it's incongruous hearing "Jingle Bells" and seeing department-store penguins dressed like Santa Claus to promote sales.

In shirtsleeve weather, I find it difficult to grasp that a mere seven hundred miles south of us is a continent composed of ice and snow. Even so, I'm excited and eager to be on my way to the bottom of the earth. And when our white ship pulls into the pristine blue harbor, I rush to be among the first to board.

Thank You, Lord, for traveling with me wherever I go.
—ISABEL WOLSELEY

DAY THREE: DRAKE'S PASSAGE

TUE
23

AND THERE AROSE A GREAT STORM OF WIND, AND THE WAVES BEAT INTO THE SHIP, SO THAT IT WAS NOW FULL. . . . AND HE AROSE, AND REBUKED THE WIND, AND SAID UNTO THE SEA, PEACE, BE STILL. . . .
—*Mark 4:37, 39*

LAST EVENING OUR SHIP left South America's southernmost tip, and in spite of my being in an undulating bunk—or maybe because of its rocking-chair motion—I dropped off to sleep instantly. But suddenly, I'm awake, the cabin so light-filled that I'm sure I've overslept. My watch says three o'clock. All is quiet, except for a heartbeatlike throb from the vessel's engines far below. I quickly slide a pair of insulated slacks over my nightwear, snap on a lined parka and dash to the nearest exit. It seems that no one else is up.

As soon as I open the deck door, a wickedly cold wind threatens to blow away my hood. It's not merely the wind I have to contend with, mostly it's the warring waves.

This turbulent spot, Drake's Passage, is where the Atlantic, Pacific, Indian and Antarctic oceans circle clockwise around the land to squeeze through the comparatively narrow seven-hundred-mile opening between

South America and Antarctica. It's next to impossible for me to walk on the deck.

In spite of the gale, a still-sleepy sun peers through the long, narrow slit dividing sea from sky, then pries the slit a bit wider and spills orange-red across the water. Leaning into the wind and clutching the rails, I wish one leg were either six inches shorter or six inches longer to match the rhythm and motion of the waves as I return to my cabin.

Lord, like Your disciples of old, I'm uneasy on life's choppy seas. Calm me as You did them. —ISABEL WOLSELEY

DAY FOUR: NATURE'S BOUNTY

WED
24

AND GOD SAID, "LET THE WATERS SWARM WITH FISH AND OTHER LIFE. LET THE SKIES BE FILLED WITH BIRDS OF EVERY KIND." —*Genesis 1:20 (NLT)*

BREAKFAST IS ANNOUNCED over the intercom, and I totter to the dining room where the chains that normally dangle beneath each table and chair now have their loose ends fastened to the floor. Those of us who are not overcome by seasickness have ample choice of seats.

It's mandatory that all visitors attend at least one ecological orientation meeting before we disembark in Antarctica. We're told to wash and sanitize our boots each time we leave the ship. We cannot pick up pebbles or feathers as souvenirs. If even a tissue blows away, it has to be retrieved. The landscape is to remain "as is."

An announcement interrupts our meal. "Killer whales at eleven o'clock, three hundred meters [about a thousand feet] off the prow!" We diners dash to portholes or to decks to see five dark bodies with sharp, jutting fins cutting through a slick atop the churning waves. The slick means a kill, signaling free food for all types of wildlife, including thousands of birds and countless fish, each willing to brave the roiling waves to fight for whatever shredded remnants float on top of and just below the ocean's surface. Overhead, a wandering albatross with a wingspread of eleven and a half feet, the largest of any flying bird, soars and watches the melee.

What a marvelous world You have made, Father! —ISABEL WOLSELEY

DAY FIVE: PENGUIN ISLAND

THU 25

THE BOAT WAS . . . BUFFETED BY THE WAVES BECAUSE THE WIND WAS AGAINST IT. . . . BUT WHEN HE [PETER] SAW THE WIND, HE WAS AFRAID AND . . . CRIED OUT, "LORD, SAVE ME!"
—*Matthew 14:24, 30 (NIV)*

THIS AFTERNOON WE'RE TAKING a jaunt to an island in the South Shetland chain off Antarctica's coast. Zodiacs—inflated rubber boats propelled by outboards, each large enough for a dozen passengers—will take us, as the landing site is too shallow for our ship.

"Dress warmly," we're instructed. I don three pairs of socks, two pairs of long johns, a turtleneck sweater, a fleece-lined jacket, two pairs of gloves (the outer ones rubber), a two-piece wet suit and knee-high rubber boots. *I look like a child in a snowsuit. Or like the Michelin man! Or a penguin! I certainly waddle like one.*

Climbing down the gangplank-ladder and into a Zodiac in heaving seas is akin to boarding an elevator gone wild. I don't know whether to step up or down. Like the apostle Peter, I silently call, "Help, Lord!" A crew member, sensing my alarm, assures me, "Don't worry. It won't sink." *So said they about the Titanic,* I tell myself, casting a wary eye at the water, which looks to be moving in for the kill. The wind continues, as do the cold and the elevator-like action of the waves, slam-dunking our Zodiac to their valley bottoms, then throwing us up again.

Finally, a welcoming party of emperor penguins—upright, fat, funny, waddling, wing-waving, yellow-beaked and completely unafraid—paddles toward us across the ice-carpeted terrain.

However small the boat, Lord, and however tall the waves, You can calm the waters and bring me through. —ISABEL WOLSELEY

DAY SIX: PARADISE BAY

FRI

26

"Be silent before the Lord, all humanity, for he is springing into action from his holy dwelling." —*Zechariah 2:13 (NLT)*

THIS IS OUR SIXTH DAY of sailing from the southernmost tip of South America to Antarctica, but the first filled with spirit-lifting sunshine. Today I'll step onto Antarctica itself, fulfilling the dream I've had since childhood!

Zodiacs line up at the bottom of the ladder-gangplank. A dozen of us clamber in, and we roar off in a blast of diesel odor, leaving V-like wave troughs in our wake. As we approach our destination, centered in a sea of icebergs, we drift slowly toward an ice pancake, its top claimed by a pair of fat, whiskered seals, one asleep, the other slithering over the edge.

The noise of the outboard is replaced by the strange nothingness of total silence, broken only by faint ripples and the occasional *plip* of an iceberg shifting position in its sea berth. We normally noisy passengers become speechless, overwhelmed by the immeasurable vastness that threads around, through, behind, and beyond ice floes and white floating islands so high that they seem to hold up the sky.

The steep cliffs have no visible tops, only clouds. Fingers of fog, wispy as gossamer, caress and cling to rock walls. The air is pure and clear and as cold as an ice mask, chilling but comforting.

Will I ever again experience anything this awe-inspiring? On earth, no. In heaven, maybe. No wonder this spot is called "Paradise Bay."

Eventually our outboard cracks the silence and the spell. We wend our way back to our ship, which sits in the distance amid the ice, glinting in a sun whose rays turn some of the ice floes into crystal, some into pieces of sky.

"When I in awesome wonder, consider all the worlds Thy hands have made," I, like the hymn writer Carl G. Boberg, can only conclude, Father, *"how great Thou art!"* —ISABEL WOLSELEY

DAY SEVEN: THE WORK OF GOD'S HANDS

SAT 27

"WHO IS THE MOTHER OF THE ICE? WHO GIVES BIRTH TO THE FROST FROM THE HEAVENS? FOR THE WATER TURNS TO ICE AS HARD AS ROCK, AND THE SURFACE OF THE WATER FREEZES." —Job 38:29–30 (NLT)

ANTARCTICA'S ISLANDS AND ICEBERGS remind me of a spilled sack of beans: kidney bean islands, some ice-frosted; white navy bean icebergs, from ice-cube size to larger than houses. There are odd geometric shapes—some jagged, some smooth. And the colors: muted browns, ethereal blues, crystal clear as Steuben glass.

Most days the wind continues, as do the cold and the elevator-like action of the water. Those of us brave enough to venture out are clothed to our eyeballs in padded waterproof gear during each Zodiac outing. I cling to the rubber side of the boat with one hand and with the other, clench my camera gear encased in plastic to protect it from the salt spray, drenching buckets of saltwater and shredded ice being slung at us by every wave.

Daily we see whales surfacing, penguins waddling across ice floes, seabirds swirling. The scene almost becomes commonplace . . . almost, but not quite. It's summer in December, and sunset is 12:05 AM, with sunrise at 2:30 AM, yet the weather turns colder. Our ice-breaker vessel jolts and bucks as the sea becomes a nearly solid sheet of thick ice. The captain keeps turning the huge ship, concerned it will freeze fast.

Finally, after much maneuvering, he gets us into open waters. Again we head into the turbulent Drake Passage—dubbed "Drake's Shakes"— recrossing it to disembark at Ushuaia, Argentina, from where we'll fly home.

My original purpose in journeying to Antarctica was a selfish one: I wanted to be able to say that I'd seen all seven continents. I didn't expect to see the glory of God displayed in sheer white beauty.

Thank You, Lord, for this astonishing work of Your hands and for the people who work to preserve it. —ISABEL WOLSELEY

SUN

28

AS THE FATHER HATH LOVED ME, SO HAVE I LOVED YOU: CONTINUE YE IN MY LOVE. —John 15:9

THE SUNDAY SCHOOL lesson today was about how God sometimes disciplines His children. Like a parent, the text said, God's love may include correction and chastisement if circumstances warrant. The writer of the lesson used John 15 as his biblical text, pointing to Christ's words as He and His disciples passed through a vineyard on their way to the Garden of Gethsemane. "I am the true vine, and my Father is the gardener," Jesus said. "He cuts off every branch in me that bears no fruit, while every branch that does bear fruit he prunes so that it will be even more fruitful" (John 15:1–2, NIV).

That led to several comments from the class and this question: "Which is more helpful to a seeker of spiritual truth? Emphasis on the threat of God's punishment or the reality of His measureless love?"

The discussion reminded me of something the late Bill Bright, founder of Campus Crusade for Christ, once told me. When he wrote *The Four Spiritual Laws,* Bill began with a negative: People are sinful and separated from God. The part about God's love came later. One night Bill's sleep was interrupted; he realized he had things in the wrong order. The next day he changed the sequence of the laws. Now, number one is "God loves you and has a wonderful plan for your life."

My mother always told me that a spoonful of honey is worth a gallon of gall. When it comes to telling others about God's unconditional love and matchless grace, I'll begin—every time—with my awe and wonder at His goodness.

Thank You, God, for Your watchful protection,
For daily forgiveness with no threat of rejection.
—FRED BAUER

MON

29

"AND WE HAVE HEARD HIS VOICE FROM THE FIRE. . . ."
—Deuteronomy 5:24 (NIV)

MY SISTER SUSAN and I stood at the checkout counter at a discount store in a neighboring town behind two carts overflowing with lamps, pillows and other household necessities. It was hard to believe that Susan's home had burned down just days before, and that she had frantically pushed Dad in his wheelchair out of the burning house in the middle of the night right before the roof caved in.

I stared at the things in the cart. It was hard to see God's hand at work in the face of such a sudden and terrible loss.

When Susan mentioned to the cashier that her house had burned down, a white-haired lady in line behind us asked, "Are you Bob Brown's daughter?"

Susan nodded and the lady went on. "I'm a volunteer over at the hospital where your dad used to help out." The woman pulled an envelope out of her purse and handed it to Susan. It had Dad's name and address on it, and had already been stamped.

When we got home, Dad opened the envelope and found a card of encouragement with a hundred-dollar bill folded inside. Suddenly I was overcome with a feeling of God's continuing presence. Though the card had been intended for the mailbox, God had decided that it would mean much more sent special delivery through a chance meeting at a checkout counter. And the wonder of it all helped remind me that God was indeed at work, even in the midst of overwhelming loss.

God, thank You for seeking me out with Your comforting presence.
—KAREN BARBER

TUE
30

WE ARE NOT TRYING TO PLEASE MEN BUT GOD, WHO TESTS OUR HEARTS. —*I Thessalonians 2:4 (NIV)*

MY FRIEND MARGARET ANN is an intelligent, no-nonsense, self-sufficient lawyer. One of the things I admire about her is her self-assurance.

The subject line on her e-mail read, "No One Clapped for Me!" At first, I thought it was some profound spiritual message. Then I laughed; it was just as likely one of the humorous, wisecracking e-mails she sometimes sends me.

But my empathy was stirred when I began to read. Margaret Ann had given a presentation in a religion class she was taking. The class had clapped and cheered for the other presenters, but not for her.

I called her, and we groaned and laughed together on the phone. So she wouldn't feel alone, I shared my own need for approval with her. Performance appraisals are the things I miss least about working a regular job. An average rating at work felt like failure; a bad review felt like a punch in the gut. And when I was a student, I was tempted to look at other people's papers to see their grades. I, too, craved applause, trumpets and gold stars, as though good grades and applause would make me better.

Margaret Ann and I chuckled over the telltale knots in our stomachs that diagnosed our condition. Then we discussed the reasons why she might not have gotten applause: Perhaps they were stunned by the brilliance of her talk or were too excited or needed a bathroom break. Maybe they just forgot.

The good news is that our addiction to praise isn't deadly, and it's very manageable. I know from personal experience. Being able to admit and laugh about it is a good sign that it's under control.

God, help me to remember that Yours is the only performance review that counts. —SHARON FOSTER

WED
31

FOR THE SON OF GOD, JESUS CHRIST . . . WAS NOT "YES" AND "NO," BUT IN HIM IT HAS ALWAYS BEEN "YES." —*II Corinthians 1:19 (NIV)*

LET'S BE HONEST, sometimes you need little things in your pockets and on your desk that recharge your heart like tiny batteries. I have lots of them.

I have yellowing envelopes filled with what happened when my children got their first haircuts. I have some of their baby teeth, which my wife thinks is nuts, but whenever I touch those infinitesimal mountains I remember that I saw miracles emerge wet and mewling and miraculous from my wife. I have a note in my wallet sent to me by a Muslim woman in Australia after September 11, in which she said she was praying for the murdered and for the murderers, too, and that note is a university to me. I have a stone from the beach where my mother's people lived for a thousand years before coming to America. I have my wife's father's watch, which he wore until he died, which was long before I met him. I wear the ring my wife gave me when she said *yes*, a yes that made me speechless, and still does.

It seems to me that all these things are ways of saying *yes* on the days when you are worn down by the ocean of *no*. But you know and I know that *yes* is the road to light.

Dear Lord, may I ask for the daily strength to say yes even when I am really tired and sad and there's hardly any hope? Because You are the Yes, and the fact is that I need Your Yes as food for my hungry soul.
—BRIAN DOYLE

MY WALK WITH GOD

I _____

2 _____

3 _____

4 _____

5 _____

6 _____

7 _____

8 _____

9 _____

IO _____

II _____

I2 _____

I3 _____

14 _____

15 _____

16 _____

17 _____

18 _____

19 _____

20 _____

21 _____

22 _____

23 _____

24 _____

25 _____

26 _____

27 _____

28 _____

29 _____

30 _____

31 _____

February

Let the words of my mouth, and the meditation of my heart, be acceptable in thy sight, O Lord, my strength, and my redeemer. —*Psalm 19:14*

LESSONS FROM THE JOURNEY
TRAVEL LIGHT

THU
1

"A MAN'S LIFE DOES NOT CONSIST IN THE ABUNDANCE OF HIS POSSESSIONS." —Luke 12:15 (RSV)

WHEN I'VE FINISHED PACKING for a trip, I open the suitcase and take out about a third of the stuff. It's a lesson learned after years of lugging overloaded bags up flights of stairs and sitting on trains with that extra suitcase wedged between the window and my ribs.

Over time my husband John and I have gotten smarter, limiting ourselves to one smallish suitcase each. The more stops on our itinerary, the fewer clothes we take, changing locales instead of outfits. We consult each other as we pack: John's going to be looking at this green sweater and striped blouse day in, day out!

Traveling light . . . it's a good rule for the inner journey too. John and I met a couple in England who'd created time and space for their spirits the way I lighten a suitcase—by simply paring down *things* in their lives. The writer Malcolm Muggeridge and his wife Kitty gave away three-fourths of their possessions and exchanged their mansion for a cottage. Simpler meals required fewer pots and dishes to wash. Ignoring the caprices of fashion meant time saved that once went into clothes shopping. Their clutter-free house "takes no time to clean," Kitty told me.

I'm trying to apply their wisdom to our own home and finding it hard! John and I have lived in the same house for forty-seven years; things accumulate. My last foray into the attic turned up some badly warped wooden skis and our fifty-six-year-old son's seventh-grade math papers.

I'm making progress, though, and identifying other things I'd like to get rid of along the way: resentments and jealousies and fears and covetousness. All this is baggage, too, spiritual burdens that slow the journey to joy.

Lord of the journey, help me lay down any object, any attitude, any habit that obstructs the pathway to You.—ELIZABETH SHERRILL

FRI
2
EVERY GOOD GIFT AND EVERY PERFECT GIFT IS FROM ABOVE. . . . —James 1:17

HATS ARE DIFFICULT TO MAKE; it's hard to get the size just right. But I decided to knit one for Daisy. Maybe if it fit me, it would fit her. After all, she's one of my dearest friends, and our lives have fit together honestly and affectionately over the years. Perhaps the hat would do the same.

The yarn was soft and pretty, but hard to knit with. On my first try the hat got so big that I had to start over. Would I have enough yarn? *This is a "thought hat,"* I reminded myself. *It can be less than perfect and still get the job done.*

Thought hats are important to me. I make very few of them. I don't work on them while watching television or chatting with my husband. I work on them alone and in quiet. Every stitch in Daisy's hat is a thought about the times we've shared: the amazing voyage in the Fiji Islands, the walk along the sandy beach in South Carolina, learning to kayak in Narragansett Bay. The changes we've looked at together: passing sixty (she got there first); being grandmothers (I'm there, and she's waiting and wondering); hard times (the deaths of her parents, my struggles with depression).

I've found that thought hats often work in two directions. Maybe Daisy's warm ears will bring back some memories for her too. We don't get to see each other very often these days. That's another reason why she's getting a thought hat for her birthday this year. It's white with colored flecks. I think it will suit her.

Lord, thank You for friendship, Your good gift, a blessing beyond words.
—BRIGITTE WEEKS

SAT
3
MINE AGE IS AS NOTHING BEFORE THEE. . . .
—Psalm 39:5

A WHILE BACK I bumped into a friend whom I hadn't seen in a while. We were discussing our children when he said, "Our kids grow up and we grow old. Growing up is fun, but growing old sure isn't."

His remark gnawed at me. It forced me to admit that I, too, was coming along in years. Not that I was a senior citizen, but I could see white hair edging out the gray.

I began to feel sorry for myself, and to snap out of it, I decided to dive into some work. The basement needed cleaning, so I started by tossing away empty bottles and broken tools. Then I tackled a box of discarded books. Among the dusty college textbooks and now-forgotten best sellers was a Boy Scout Handbook from some forty years ago. On the cover, three boys sat around a campfire under the stars. I remembered camping out with my own troop; I could smell the wood smoke, feel the bite of the night air—too many years ago.

Thumbing through the book, I discovered a wealth of interesting things. Many of them I still remembered, like how to start a fire or pitch a tent. But others were brand-new. *Wouldn't first aid be a good thing to learn, even now? And what about knot-making?* When I was a kid, those complicated patterns had seemed silly, but now they fascinated me. Sure, I wasn't a youngster anymore, but for just that reason I could enjoy these things in a way no child ever could.

Since then I've learned to tie a rolling hitch and to navigate by the stars. And I've learned that while growing up is fun, so is growing old.

I give thanks, Lord, for every precious day of my life.
— PHILIP ZALESKI

SUN
4

"THERE IS A GOD IN HEAVEN WHO REVEALS MYSTERIES. . . ." —*Daniel 2:28 (NIV)*

I'VE NEVER BEEN A sports fan. Monday mornings at school, I was always part of the small group of kids who didn't know what had happened in the weekend's games and didn't care either. Though I could sometimes manage to enjoy playing in games myself, watching them was another matter.

Football was the biggest mystery of all. How was it that just about every one of my schoolmates—the males at least—could get so worked up about a bunch of people running around on a field chasing a ball? I just didn't get it.

Then, about ten years ago, I started going to the gym regularly. Each day at lunch or after work, I'd spend half an hour on a treadmill, staring up at the banks of overhead TVs. Inevitably, a couple of the screens showed sports. One show in particular always seemed to be on. It featured highlights from great football games of the past. Jogging along, I'd find myself looking at the high points of all those games from the early 1970s that had bored me so at the time they took place.

And after a while, something funny started happening. Watching shot after grainy shot of those long-ago passes spiraling through the air and miraculously landing in the arms of the receivers in the end zone, I'd find myself picking up my pace without even meaning to. There was a strange sort of poetry to those passes when you saw one after another of them—a poetry I'd missed when they'd been buried in the long hours of the actual game itself. Soon I made a point of showing up at the gym at the hour when I knew one of those shows would be on. Football was really kind of inspirational. Who'd have guessed?

Lord, thank You for reminding me that inspiration is hiding all over, often in the last place I'd think to look. —PTOLEMY TOMPKINS

MON
5
AND MOSES WAS AN HUNDRED AND TWENTY YEARS OLD WHEN HE DIED: HIS EYE WAS NOT DIM, NOR HIS NATURAL FORCE ABATED. —*Deuteronomy 34:7*

HER OLD, ELEGANT HANDS reach for the grand piano's polished keys. Fingers find familiar patterns. Love songs to God, love notes for her husband—gone these fifteen years—ripple and eddy around her petite body. Lustrous white hair forms a feathery halo in the lamplight.

Deep-set eyes—blue behind closed lids—are submerged in reverie. She is in conversation with her music, communing with her past. There is her "precious Bill," the handsome tennis player she still can't believe fell in love with her; her mother Nanny, who saved her minister-husband's meager wedding and funeral earnings to give her oldest daughter a start at college; her friends in China, with whom she weathered perilous World War II years on the mission field; her three accomplished children—and maybe, too, the infant daughter she buried on foreign soil.

"I don't feel old when I play my piano," she tells me. "It's like I have a friend who talks to me and I talk back." She needs this friend who won't leave her, who keeps her secrets, harbors her sorrows and releases her joys.

She is my aunt, Elizabeth Blackstone. And she is one hundred years and two months old. As I watch her fingers swirl across the piano keys, I know why I traveled 2,500 miles to Monte Vista Grove in Pasadena, California, to be her caregiver.

Her hands grow tired and the music slows. Her eyes open. "The Lord's been good to me," she says, rising gracefully from the piano seat.

Silently, I thank her real Caregiver for inviting me to join Him.

As I grow older, Lord, may I continue to pound life's keys with passion.
—CAROL KNAPP

 TUE
6

LET ME DWELL IN THY TENT FOREVER. . . .
—*Psalm 61:4 (NAS)*

WHEN KEITH AND I FIRST discussed moving out of Los Angeles after he retired, I had mixed feelings. I was not so wedded to the city, but I loved our home. We'd remodeled it so that it was exactly what we wanted, and it was really the only house I'd ever lived in where I was altogether happy. The idea of selling it made me uneasy. "I think of our home as a place of safety, a place that surrounds me with its walls and holds me gently," I said. "I'm afraid to go away from it."

Keith smiled, the way he does when I get frantic over something and he has to point to the terra-cotta plaque on our wall that reads: "Be still, and know that I am God." Keith said, "It's not the house that shelters you."

And I knew that he was right. It was God Who held me safely when I was at home—and also when I went away from it. And God would continue to shelter me, whether I lived in Los Angeles or anywhere else.

Thank You, God, for the loving shelter in which You are letting me live my life. —RHODA BLECKER

WED
7

WHEN TIMES ARE GOOD, BE HAPPY; BUT WHEN TIMES ARE BAD, CONSIDER: GOD HAS MADE THE ONE AS WELL AS THE OTHER. . . . —*Ecclesiastes 7:14 (NIV)*

THE PHONE AWAKENED my wife Rosie and me at about 11:20 PM on a Wednesday. The voice on the other end of the line told us that our son Reggie had been killed in a car accident. Two months later, our phone awakened us again at about 11:20 PM. The voice on the other end of the line told us that our grandson Little Reggie had been born.

What a miracle! One phone call brought words of death and then exactly two months later at the same time, the other brought words of life.

Today, more than a year later, we've had the privilege of keeping Little Reggie almost every weekend since he was born. Rosie has a great relationship with Michelle, Little Reggie's mom, and, of course, I have a great relationship with Little Reggie.

Through all of this, Ecclesiastes 7:14 has had a greater meaning for us. Yes, we lost Reggie and our hearts are broken, but we are so happy that God has provided us with Little Reggie, a real joy in our lives.

Lord, help me to lean on You even when I understand neither the good times nor the bad times. You understand them all and I put my trust in You. —DOLPHUS WEARY

THU
8

THIS WOMAN WAS ABOUNDING WITH DEEDS OF KINDNESS AND CHARITY WHICH SHE CONTINUALLY DID. —*Acts 9:36 (NAS)*

"SOMEONE LEFT THIS on my desk," my husband David said as he walked through the kitchen and tossed a gold box on the counter. My name was written on the tag, but I couldn't identify the handwriting. I untied the ribbon; inside was a colorful array of candy-coated almonds.

Smiling to myself, I popped one into my mouth and thought, *Someone is having a "Deanna Day."*

Candy-coated almonds have been my favorite treat since childhood.

I don't remember how our friend Deanna discovered my preference, but candy-coated almonds began appearing on my birthday, Christmas, Easter. Always packaged in some clever way, the candy told me I was special, cared about, loved.

After Deanna died in a terrible car wreck, our church family began sharing stories of her thoughtfulness. Deanna had regularly put envelopes of clipped cartoons and jokes on David's desk to help with his sermons. For Gloria, it was licorice. There were well-timed phone calls to shut-ins and holiday open houses for the lonely. Deanna's kindness was endless, and her passing left a gaping hole that I thought would never be filled.

Then I received the letter: "Dear Pam, I want you to know that God speaks to us through your photographs. . . . Today is my Deanna Day. Remembering how Deanna used to write thoughtful notes to people and how she always had a way of making others feel good about themselves made some of us decide to take one day a month to do something Deanna would have done. The fifth day of every month is my Deanna Day and that's why I'm writing this note to you. Love, Mary Ev."

My almonds had come midmonth, so they weren't from Mary Ev. There was really no way to know whom they were from, because the ripples of Deanna's kindness were spreading through our entire church congregation and beyond.

Father, the world is waiting for me to act on Your teachings. Let me make today my Deanna Day. —PAM KIDD

FRI
9

AS COLD WATERS TO A THIRSTY SOUL, SO IS GOOD NEWS FROM A FAR COUNTRY. —*Proverbs 25:25*

BECAUSE I'M AT WORK most days, I come home eager to be told what the children have been up to. Getting news out of the older children is often an arduous process; they specialize in one-word answers to almost any question. "Fine" or "Good" or "Okay" seem to do for all activities, whether classes or play dates or ballet rehearsals or trips to the museum. Thankfully, their mother can usually fill me in on the details. But I never have a problem with two-year-old Stephen.

As soon as I come through the door, even before I've hung my coat in the hall closet, Stevie is there, ready to tell me all about his day.

"I saw a video today, Daddy. Big Bird was in it. Miss Finch sends him to the Dodos, but he wants to go back to Sesame Street. He wants to see his friend Snuffy. Two men paint him blue and he cries. I was scared. Elmo and Cookie Monster and Bert and Ernie and some people go to help him and take him home.

"After the video, my friend Adam came to play with me. I shared my toys with him. We played cars and trains. Maggie played with us too. Then his mother came to take him home. I cried. I wanted him to stay."

"I'm sure you'll see him again soon," I say as I pick up my little guy and head to the table for supper.

Lord, give me just a little of Stevie's eagerness to share Your good news with those around me. —ANDREW ATTAWAY

SAT
10

AND OF HIS FULNESS HAVE ALL WE RECEIVED, AND GRACE FOR GRACE. —*John 1:16*

I PLAY GUITAR—and I'm using the word *play* here in its broadest sense. When I start to strum, my kids scatter, dogs howl at noises only they can hear, car alarms go off and neighbors hurriedly shut their windows. By the time I get to "Positively 4th Street," Bob Dylan is positively turning over in his grave—and he's not even dead.

I'm not good at guitar.

Mr. Joe, my incredibly patient guitar instructor, never complains about my aggressively tone-deaf version of "Let It Be." He says, "Okay, you did some good things there." He seems to enjoy our time together. Not me. To paraphrase Harry Chapin, I don't know how well I play because I only hear the flaws.

But last week when we played together—Mr. Joe on rhythm, me on lead—something clicked. We found a shared riff and hitched a ride. For about fifteen seconds, we sounded great. When we finished, we both laughed for the sheer joy of it.

I've had those moments before. This is what grace must be like: unexpected, unexplained, undeserved, like manna from heaven. Being human, we want to figure out what happened, so we can repeat it over and over. But grace doesn't work that way. Grace is a perfect snowflake, an unsolicited compliment from a perfect stranger, a perfect sunset. And here's my perfect prayer:

Lord, help me to be able to accept those grace-filled moments for what they are, and offer my humble, off-key song in absolute, absolute, absolute praise. —MARK COLLINS

SUN 11

THE LORD SHALL GUIDE THEE CONTINUALLY. . . .
—Isaiah 58:11

EACH TIME NEW ENGLAND enters a deep freeze, my thoughts race back to February 1934, the coldest month ever recorded in my hometown of Williamstown, Massachusetts. The temperature plunged to twenty-seven degrees below zero, then crept up to ten below, where it remained for days. Another force gripped our village then, the Great Depression. We constantly worried about money, jobs and the future, which squeezed the joy from our lives and discolored our outlook.

But there was a bright spot. Each Sunday evening I walked against the punishing wind and the biting cold to St. John's Church on Park Street. No matter how warmly I was dressed, I reached St. John's with chattering teeth and icy fingers. Once there I hurried downstairs, and as I opened the kitchen door, the warmth rushed out to greet me. This barren room contained a stove, a sink, a long table and folding chairs. Gathered at the table were our pastor, his wife, a nurse from the Williams College infirmary, a college professor and several students.

We were attending the Young People's Fellowship. As we sipped cocoa, the professor talked about his struggle to acquire an education. The nurse spoke of her joy when a patient was on the road to recovery. Students from the college shared their dreams. We left the kitchen feeling warmed and lifted. Outside, the wind seemed less troubling and the Great Depression less oppressive. We had each other and we had faith. That faith has guided and strengthened me all my life.

Blessed Jesus, the glow from that barren room glows in my life today.
—OSCAR GREENE

MON
12

I HOPE TO SEE YOU SOON AND THEN WE WILL HAVE MUCH TO TALK ABOUT TOGETHER. —*III John 14 (TLB)*

CHARLIE AND HIS WIFE CAROL have been my next-door neighbors since I moved here several years ago. We got along well, and their two sons used to mow my grass in the summer.

Then one day Charlie and I had a dispute over something I can't even remember. We stopped speaking. Carol and I waved when we drove past each other on the road, but Charlie looked the other way. It was an uncomfortable situation, but I didn't know what to do about it. God did.

The couple who had bought the farm across the street from me, Bob and Rosemary, were expecting a baby, their first, and all the neighbors were excited because we hadn't had a new baby on our street for a long time. When Rosemary called me from the hospital to tell me she and Bob had a son, I was thrilled—until she asked me to call a few neighbors to tell them the good news.

"Don't forget Charlie and Carol," she said, not knowing we weren't on speaking terms. "They've been on pins and needles."

I called everyone on our street, except Charlie and Carol. Finally, I couldn't put it off any longer; I had given my word to Rosemary.

I dialed the number and held my breath. Charlie answered in the pleasant, friendly way I remembered. I hurried to tell him about the new baby before he could hang up on me. He didn't. "Gee, that's wonderful," he said. "It was nice of you to call."

"Actually, Rosemary asked me," I said, "but it's nice to talk to you."

"Same here," Charlie said, and we went on to talk about all kinds of things that had happened in our lives. Our years of silence were over. God had found a way to make us neighbors again.

Heavenly Father, when I put distance between myself and others, please take our hands and bring us back together again. Amen.

—PHYLLIS HOBE

TUE
13

"I AM A LITTLE CHILD; I DO NOT KNOW HOW TO GO OUT OR COME IN." —I Kings 3:7 (NKJV)

ONE CORNER OF MY CLASSROOM is filled with oversized items, including a wooden chair as big as a refrigerator.

On the chair are giant dominoes, huge coins and big pencils, and under the chair is a large mousetrap with a stuffed mouse sitting on it.

The collection started when Stan Richardson, one of my students, heard me lecturing in Child Growth class. "Children live in a land of giants," I was explaining, "because they are only half our size. Wouldn't it be neat if we had a room full of supersized furniture, so that we grown-ups would know what it feels like to be children again?" Stan made the chair and that started the collection.

It's no wonder children get so tired. Every day they climb an Everest of stairs. They jump to reach light switches, climb to get a cookie. They take two steps for every one of ours. They are living in a world that is designed for grown-ups.

Like Solomon, I often feel like a child. Complicated technology makes me feel like I'm back in the first grade, learning how to write, and I remember the tears that formed on my cheeks. I still find them on my cheeks when I can't figure out what happened to my files. Sometimes the playground of life is too big for me. The swings go too high and the slide is too steep. The merry-go-round is spinning too fast and I want off. More and more I find myself saying, "Can someone please help me?"

The good part? People do help. I guess it's okay to feel like a child, as long as I'm willing to be assisted. And I thank God for all the people who take me by the hand and say, "You can do this. I'll show you how."

I'm in my second childhood, Lord, and I need just as much help this time around. —Daniel Schantz

WED
14

He turned to the woman and said to Simon. . . . "She has kissed my feet again and again . . . her sins—and there are many—are forgiven, for she loved me much. . . ." —Luke 7:44–45, 47 (TLB)

Recently i received a letter with SWALK written across the flap on the back of the envelope. It had been ages since I'd seen the once popular slogan. Sure enough, it was from a friend I have known since the 1950s, who reminded me that her note was "Sealed with a Loving Kiss."

The X we use to denote a kiss comes from the Middle Ages, when the cross of Saint Andrew (the white cross on a blue background that is now the Scottish part of the Union Jack) was used for a signature on important documents by those who couldn't write. This was a sign of binding honesty, and after writing the X, it was kissed to further guarantee faithful performance of the obligation. Hence X became associated with a kiss.

How I treasure the love letters from the man I was to marry, always signed with many X's, some wandering around the borders of each page. I have kept them bundled with blue ribbon. Over our forty-five years of marriage, I frequently untied them and wiggled against my husband in our oversized armchair and read them out loud. "Good heavens," John would tease, making a wry face, "did I write all that mush?" We'd cuddle and kiss and reaffirm our love.

Now that he is dead, I sit alone in the big armchair and fill the empty space with a chunky cushion. I once again read his letters. They give me the strength that only love can give. They ease my hurting heart. As I tie them back up, I kiss them. The X seal reminds me that love is eternal.

Jesus, Your never-ending love strengthens and sustains me. Thank You for those You have given us to love. —FAY ANGUS

GOD-FINDS
FINDING OUR HEAVENLY FATHER

THU
15

THEREFORE ENCOURAGE ONE ANOTHER, AND BUILD UP ONE ANOTHER, JUST AS YOU ALSO ARE DOING.
—*I Thessalonians 5:11 (NAS)*

IT WAS DINNERTIME, and I had just whizzed into the drive-through to pick up a cup of coffee and a cheeseburger on my way home from work. But something told me that the homeless man rolling a dolly loaded with suitcases and blankets around the parking lot needed the sandwich much more than I did.

I slid into a parking spot, then tiptoed toward the man, who was now kicking a restaurant-sized peanut can. I barely breathed as I listened for the rattle that would mean another meal for him. Nothing.

As I handed him the bag containing the cheeseburger, I was filled with a sense of self-satisfaction that I instantly abhorred. "This is for you," I announced, glancing into his bloodshot gray eyes. "God bless you." As soon as the words rolled off my tongue, I hated the way they seemed to distance us even more. Instead of meeting the man's gaze, I focused my eyes on the collar of his tattered jacket, raised high against the cold.

Ever so gently, he held my hand until at long last our eyes met. Then he brushed his hand against mine and, as if granting me the key to the universe, responded: "God bless *you*."

In that moment, one of God's eternal truths took up residence in my heart: Every one of God's children—rich or poor, young or old, educated or common—has equal access to the heavenly Father and can freely offer His blessings to another.

Thank You, Father, for those who unknowingly point me to You.
—ROBERTA MESSNER

READER'S ROOM

I HAVE BEEN A *Daily Guideposts* reader for so many years that it has become a standard gift given to me on Christmas by my son. I wrote notes in them throughout the years as I communicated daily with God; that is, until I became a stroke survivor in February 2003 and lost the use of my entire right side. I have always loved to keep journals and enjoyed reading over what I had written in past years. God gave me these words of wisdom about five years ago that I would now like to share with my fellow *Daily Guideposts* readers:

> Do the part of it you love to do.
> Don't force it to be what you want it to be,
> It will become what it was meant to be.
> Love it; let it flow through you; Nurture it.
> Enjoy the journey.

These words have helped me readjust to the things that I can no longer do and have led me to a richer more meaningful appreciation of the things that I can.
—*Cecelia McLeod, Glen Burnie, Maryland*

FRI
16

*AND THIS COMMANDMENT HAVE WE FROM HIM, THAT
HE WHO LOVETH GOD LOVE HIS BROTHER ALSO.*
—I John 4:21

WE'D HAD A PLEASANT DRIVE through the West Virginia hills, an area with few jobs and much poverty, but a land with a great tradition, history and people. This journey through the mountains had begun several months earlier, when I received a call from World Vision, which distributes thousands of Guideposts Knit for Kids sweaters to needy children. "Would you and the outreach staff be interested in bringing sweaters to the small mountain town of Philippi in West Virginia?"

I gratefully accepted this opportunity to experience firsthand the joy of giving the sweaters knitted by our readers, but I wasn't sure what to expect from the kids. Would they sit quietly and listen to me? How would they feel when they got their sweaters?

The children sat on the floor, excited and eager. I stood next to a long table displaying the sweaters. The boys and girls sat and gazed at the array of colors. The collage of sweaters looked like a rainbow.

While I was talking, Christopher, a little boy who sat in the front row, raised his hand. His big smile and the sparkle in his eyes got my attention. "Can I take a sweater home for my baby sister Katie?" he asked.

"We'll find something for her," I told him.

When it was Christopher's turn, I got on my knees and helped him into the sweater he'd chosen. He popped his head through the neck hole, beaming with joy. Then he jumped and gave me a bear hug that toppled us both to the ground. His smile spoke volumes as he clutched the stuffed animal we'd found for Katie.

We'd gone to Philippi to spread God's love. But it was already there, in the heart of Christopher.

Lord, bless all of the Knit for Kids knitters and all the children for whom they knit with so much love. —PABLO DIAZ

EDITOR'S NOTE: For a free copy of our sweater pattern, go to www.dailyguideposts.com/help/sweater.asp or send a self-addressed stamped envelope to Guideposts Knit for Kids, 39 Seminary Hill Road, Carmel, New York 10512.

SAT
17
I WILL NOT LEAVE YOU COMFORTLESS: I WILL COME TO YOU. —*John 14:18*

FORTY YEARS AGO, when I was baptized, I welcomed Christ into my life. Since then I've claimed a line of an old gospel song by Herbert Buffum: "The Comforter abides with me."

Ten months ago I welcomed a cat into my life. Since Kitty arrived— from the home of my sister Alice—she's never ventured outside my house. I walk in the front door; Kitty greets me with an ankle nudge. I awake in the morning; she races me down the stairs. I take a phone call; she jumps on my lap. In short, she abides with me as a quiet, comforting companion; she is so present that I'm nearly always aware of her whereabouts, upstairs or down.

But Saturday afternoon Kitty wasn't perched on an upstairs windowsill or asleep on my bed. Downstairs, she wasn't in sight, and there aren't many places to hide. The front door was latched. *I know she's here somewhere.* I looked behind the couch, under the bed, in two closets. I called her. I hunted the house a second and third time, increasingly agitated. I called Alice. "I can't find her!"

"You *know* she's there. Keep looking," Alice advised ever so reasonably.

One more search, room by room. Sure enough, I discovered Kitty— nose poking out from between boxes in a closet.

Today I sing that old song with new appreciation for *both* of my abiding comforters: one small creature who is, admittedly, mortal; one immortal Spirit Who is, unquestionably, faithful.

Jesus, You sent Your Spirit, the Comforter, to abide with me. Help me lay claim to this truth with my mind and my heart. —EVELYN BENCE

SUN
18
THE SPIRIT HELPS US IN OUR WEAKNESS. . . .
—*Romans 8:26* (NIV)

I HAVE THE PRIVILEGE of writing and directing the plays we put on at our church. One of the greatest joys of the job is that I get to work with talented people who work hard to get everything just right.

One Sunday, Paul, our most accomplished actor, was playing a CEO who suddenly finds himself exposing his deepest hurts to a midlevel manager. The entire scene grows in intensity and hits a boiling point when a deep, dark secret is revealed. At least, that was my intention.

But in this particular performance, Paul "went up" on his lines, which is theater talk for totally forgetting where he was and jumping way ahead in the script. A blank stare came over Paul's face and he skipped over all the dialogue that made the ending make sense.

The actor playing the manager picked up on where they were and the play ended nicely, but I was disappointed that so much of the pertinent information had been omitted. Would anybody catch the message of the play?

Paul came offstage. "Sorry, man," he said. "I did my best."

Apparently that was all he needed to do. Our pastor told us later that after the service, a man who'd never been to our church before came up to him in tears and said that he'd recognized himself in Paul's character and had come to see his own need for God.

Lord Jesus, when I do my best in Your name, I can leave the results to You. —DAVE FRANCO

MON
19

BLESSED IS THE NATION WHOSE GOD IS THE LORD. . . .
—*Psalm 33:12 (NIV)*

ABRAHAM LINCOLN AND I have a lot in common. He grew up in Indiana; I grew up in Indiana. He loved his mother very much; I loved my mother very much. He worked as a store clerk; I worked as a store clerk. He had a cat named Bob and a turkey named Jack; I had . . . a dog named Ginger. He was president of the United States; I was . . . well, president of my senior class. Okay, maybe we aren't so very much alike. But I'd like to think that we share one important characteristic: Lincoln was a man of prayer. He prayed alone; he prayed for guidance; he prayed in gratitude. I try to begin every day this very same way.

"I have been driven many times upon my knees by the overwhelming conviction that I had nowhere else to go," said Lincoln. "My own wisdom and that of all about me seemed insufficient for that day."

This gives me one more way I can try to be like Lincoln: to be humble.

You, O Lord, have been our help and salvation throughout all generations. Thank You for godly leaders who challenge and inspire us.
—MARY LOU CARNEY

TUE
20

THEN SHALL BE BROUGHT TO PASS THE SAYING THAT IS WRITTEN, DEATH IS SWALLOWED UP IN VICTORY.
—*I Corinthians 15:54*

MY WIFE JULEE and her mom Wilma Cruise were extraordinarily close. No matter where Julee was in the world—and it could be anywhere—she called her mom in Creston, Iowa, every day without fail. Even after Wilma's capacity for speech was pretty much wiped out by a stroke, Julee was the one person who managed to carry on conversations with her. The nursing home would call Julee when they couldn't figure out what Wilma wanted; somehow Julee always knew.

Wilma died this year, very peacefully. I did everything I could for Julee as she sank deeper into mourning. I tried to get her to eat, to exercise, to make it to her doctor's appointments. I told her that God was with her no matter how alone she felt, that He was really there, closer than ever. I sat up with her late into the night, sometimes without even talking. But still she grieved.

Finally, in frustration and despair, I told a friend there was nothing more I could do. "I feel so inadequate," I said.

My friend looked at me for a long time, then said simply, "It's death. We're supposed to feel inadequate."

We humans can overcome just about anything, but we can't overcome death. And the deeper we love, the harder we grieve. Finally we come through the other side, as I know Julee will, when our love becomes acceptance—perhaps of our own inability to let go of people all at once. We don't want to let go, so we let go in stages—imperfect, painful, not always pretty. And each and every step of the way God takes hold of what we have let go.

Only You, eternal Lord, can turn death into eternal life.
—EDWARD GRINNAN

WED
21

"WHAT ELSE WILL DISTINGUISH ME AND YOUR PEOPLE FROM ALL THE OTHER PEOPLE ON THE FACE OF THE EARTH?" —Exodus 33:16 (NIV)

GROWING UP, I ALWAYS WENT to Ash Wednesday Mass with my family early in the morning before school. Then I'd spend the rest of the day with that black smudgy cross on my forehead, hearing kids say, "You have dirt on your face." Some really didn't know what it was, others were teasing. But I didn't care. I liked having that mark to set me apart, a physical sign that helped me say, "I am a child of God."

So now it's another Ash Wednesday, and once again I'll display the cross made of ashes on my forehead and wash it off a few hours later. Tomorrow, what will remain to show the world that I am still God's child? Will my eyes reflect the peace of the Lord in my heart? Will my hands reach out in compassion to someone in need? Will my smile share the joy of Jesus?

In the Lenten tradition I knew as a child, I can give up something in these next forty days—give up a part of myself to someone else as a tangible way of showing God's grace. I might look that store clerk in the eyes when I ask, "How are you?" and wait for the answer, even if it takes a little extra time. Or turn the other cheek the next time someone speaks harshly to me, instead of getting in the last word. The ashes may disappear, but I'll be showing an unmistakable sign that I belong to the Lord.

Dear God, inspire me to carry Your Spirit throughout this season, as I await Your glorious Resurrection. —GINA BRIDGEMAN

THU
22

"MY GRACE IS SUFFICIENT FOR YOU, FOR MY POWER IS MADE PERFECT IN WEAKNESS." . . .
—II Corinthians 12:9 (NIV)

"IT'S LIKE TYPING WITH a hand and a half," I grumbled as I backspaced to correct yet another error.

For months, pain in my left wrist had made typing difficult, hampering my writing. Assuming it was a flare-up of arthritis, I took my prescribed medication but didn't see the doctor. Then last week, during a sudden movement, the pain became nearly unbearable.

At the doctor's office, my physician probed a tender spot just below my thumb, sending pain darting up my arm. "It's tendonitis," he said. "You evidently injured your wrist, and a tendon has become inflamed." He prescribed heat treatments and a different medication, and said I could wear a brace to immobilize the thumb.

Recovery is agonizingly slow. I can barely use my left hand—except for typing. The brace leaves the fingers free, and I don't use my left thumb in typing anyway. My hand feels clumsy on the keyboard, but I'm still able to write.

Then yesterday I read an article about the author of the book *Seabiscuit*. It said the author, Laura Hillenbrand, suffers from chronic fatigue syndrome, causing exhaustion, vertigo, headaches and sensitivity to light. In fact, she often has to spend days in bed. It took her four years to research and write her book about the famous racehorse, which became a best seller and a hit movie.

Her determination and dedication in the face of daunting pain and fatigue really put my tendonitis into perspective. Today I'm typing with renewed vigor. This handicap may slow me down, but it won't stop me.

Father, thank You for the inspiration You give me through people like Laura. Help me to finish my work in Your strength.

—HAROLD HOSTETLER

FRI
23

SHEW ME NOW THY WAY . . . THAT I MAY FIND GRACE IN THY SIGHT. . . . —Exodus 33:13

WE HAVE MANY PONDEROSA PINES in our yard, most of them planted by nature on our mountainside lot. Sadly, ponderosas are susceptible to many diseases, so we've had to have several of them cut down. We've replaced them with long-lived blue spruces like those Grandfather Banta planted so many years ago. Young trees are rather fragile, so my husband Robert waters them frequently, even in winter, and they are growing healthily.

Just as young trees need steady care, so do our souls. We all need to love the fragile parts of ourselves, the parts that need the loving care that only we can give.

Loving oneself has always sounded self-centered to me. But I've learned that my soul needs my love, especially in its weak places, in order to grow. Only then can it form welcoming branches for the benefit of the whole tree, and for those who look to it for inspiration.

I can nurture my soul by regularly practicing prayer and contemplation, by keeping a prayer journal, and by asking for guidance. At the beginning of each day, I try to remember to ask God, "Do You have a soul-task for me today?" Then I listen.

This morning, as I gaze at the tall, majestic trees Grandfather planted, I am deeply inspired. With good care, our young spruces will stand tall someday, inviting our grandchildren to look skyward in praise to God.

Oh, God, do You have a special soul-task for me today?

—Marilyn Morgan King

SAT
24

Do everything without complaining or arguing. —*Philippians 2:14 (NIV)*

Yesterday I asked my daughters Caeli and Corinna to hang up their jackets.

"Sure," said three-year-old Caeli, who hung her jacket on its hook.

"Ugh!" said five-year-old Corinna, throwing herself onto the couch. "It's the same every day! Why do I have to hang it up every time I come home?"

Later that same day, I sat reading to the girls while they colored: Caeli drawing circles with whatever colors were in front of her and Corinna complaining that she didn't have the colors for a true full rainbow. Eventually, I put the children's storybook down to continue my Bible study. The girls enjoy being read to regardless of the story, so I began reading aloud from chapter two of Paul's letter to the Philippians: "Do everything without complaining or arguing."

Suddenly Corinna stopped coloring, looked up and asked, "Are you sure that's in the Bible?"

Laughing, I repeated the verse, assuring her that I wasn't making it up. She decided that if it was really in the Bible, she needed to learn it. So we wrote the verse on a piece of paper and started memorizing it. Not only did Corinna recite the verse at dinner, but she also called her grandparents to recite it for them.

Corinna's behavior hasn't changed overnight, but she's moving along the right path. Now she understands that these are God's rules, not just

Mommy's. When she complains, we repeat the verse and try to think of the positive aspects of the situation. What a great daily reminder for me too!

Heavenly Father, help me to have such faith that just hearing one of Your commandments will cause me to stop, listen and learn.
— WENDY WILLARD

SUN
25

AS THE LORD HAS FORGIVEN YOU, SO YOU ALSO MUST FORGIVE. —*Colossians 3:13 (RSV)*

ONE SATURDAY EVENING, as I sat in my living room, sorting materials for my Sunday school class the next morning, I came across the sign-up sheet for the volunteers who take turns doing the children's sermon each Sunday. It was my task to coordinate those volunteers. Dismay shot through me when I saw that the sign-up line for the next day was empty. How could I have overlooked that?

A vague memory that there might have been a more recent sign-up sheet crossed my mind, but when I went through the stacks of scribbled papers in my memo box, I didn't find it.

I called Patty and asked if she would do the children's sermon the next day. She agreed.

The next morning, I announced that Patty would be giving the sermon and thanked her for filling in at the last minute since we'd had no volunteer for that day. I sat down and watched as Patty called the children forward. The woman next to me tapped me on the shoulder and whispered, "Did you forget that Carol volunteered for this Sunday? I happen to know she worked hard all weekend to get ready."

Stricken with remorse, I turned and saw Carol staring at me from across the church, her face drawn with disappointment and hurt.

As soon as church was over, I rushed to her and apologized. She accepted my apology, but I saw by the look in her eyes that she still felt hurt.

Later, I called my friend Paula and told her about the terrible mistake I'd made.

"We all make mistakes," she said, "but have you learned anything from this one?"

"I've decided I need to find a better way to organize."

"Sometimes I think our mistakes serve another purpose too," she said. "They give us another reason to reach out and touch God."

Father, please help me forgive others who make mistakes, as I hope they'll forgive me. —MADGE HARRAH

MON
26

BUT THE LORD SAID TO SAMUEL, "DO NOT CONSIDER HIS APPEARANCE OR HIS HEIGHT, FOR I HAVE REJECTED HIM. THE LORD DOES NOT LOOK AT THE THINGS MAN LOOKS AT. MAN LOOKS AT THE OUTWARD APPEARANCE, BUT THE LORD LOOKS AT THE HEART."
—*I Samuel 16:7 (NIV)*

IN OUR HOUSEHOLD I'm the go-to guy on laundry day. And, truth be told, I'm pretty much a wiz. Grass stains? Can do. Mud, lasagna—does anyone know how a teenager gets lasagna on the back of a T-shirt?—no problem. There's only one thing about the laundry that week-in, week-out would send me around the bend: clothes coming out of the dryer inside out.

No big deal, you say? For whatever reason, it was to me. Until I went back to school.

Not laundry school but third grade. A teacher-friend of mine had invited me to visit her classroom whenever I wanted and, Curious George that I am, I dropped in unannounced one day. Frankly, the room looked like every third-grade classroom you've ever seen, with one notable exception: All the children, absolutely every one of them, had their clothes on inside out. Shirts, pants, caps—I didn't ask about their underwear! But I did ask what was going on.

Here's what one of those third-grade students told me: Occasionally, they wear their clothes inside out to remind themselves that with people it's what's on the inside that counts the most.

You won't find me at work today with my clothes reversed, but every time I do the laundry now and clothes come out of the dryer inside out, I don't grumble. I remember it's what's on the inside that counts most.

Lord, whatever my outward circumstances may be today, let Your love shine from my heart. —JEFF JAPINGA

TUE
27

"He calls his own sheep by name and leads them. . . ." —*John 10:3 (NIV)*

WAYNE AND I CHOSE a family name for the middle names of each of our four children. Jody Rose, our oldest daughter, was named for my mother; Jenny Adele was named for Wayne's mother. Later, as Jody grew, it became apparent that she resembled Wayne's side of the family far more than mine. My blonde, blue-eyed daughter was all Macomber. Jenny, on the other hand, with her dark hair and eyes, resembled the Adler side of the family. It seemed to us that we'd picked the wrong names for the girls.

The thought was even stronger when Jody entered her teens and often clashed with my mom. As Jody matured, however, her relationship with my mother mellowed and the two grew especially close.

Shortly after my father died, we moved Mom to an assisted-living complex in Port Orchard, Washington, where we live. It was Jody who stopped by the complex two or three times a week to visit Mom; it was Jody who took her to her doctor's appointments if I was out of town; and it was Jody who sat with Mom and me after Mom suffered a stroke and slipped into a coma. During Mom's final minutes on earth, it was Jody who sat by my side and prayed with me as God's angels ushered Mom into glory.

At the funeral, as my daughter offered the eulogy, I sat with tears in my eyes. Wayne and I had given our daughter the right name after all. God knew all along that she was meant to be Jody Rose.

Father God, how grateful I am that You know us all better than we know ourselves. —DEBBIE MACOMBER

WED
28

When I am afraid, I will trust in you.
—*Psalm 56:3 (NIV)*

I WAS UP AGAINST two of the best disabled ski racers in the world. Both were World Cup champions, one from the United States and the other from Australia. And then there was me, a young amateur who had never won a single race. Any sports psychologist will tell you that confidence is the most important factor in determining your performance in competition. I knew this, but try as I might,

I couldn't calm my fears or anxious nerves. *There's no way I can win this! These guys are too good,* I thought.

As the clock signaled the final five seconds before the race began, I decided that I would ski as fast as I could even though I would probably lose. Suddenly, the race began and my adrenaline kicked into high gear as we carved around slalom gates on three identical courses. I immediately fell behind the Australian and spent most of the race in second place. But on the final steep section before the finish line, I caught a burst of speed and pulled ahead.

In the months since that race, I've felt the same kind of fears and doubts when I've wanted to talk to a friend about my faith or needed the courage to stand up for what is right. In those times God reminds me that He just needs me to be willing, not necessarily confident. The rest is up to Him.

Lord, Yours is the best sports psychology I've ever heard. Thank You for calming my anxious heart. —JOSHUA SUNDQUIST

MY WALK WITH GOD

1 _____

2 _____

3 _____

4 _____

5 _____

6 _____

7 _____

8 _____

9 _____

10 _____

11 _____

12 _____

13 _____

14 _____

15 _____

16 _____

17 _____

18 _____

19 _____

20 _____

21 _____

22 _____

23 _____

24 _____

25 _____

26 _____

27 _____

28 _____

March

God is our refuge and strength, a very present help in trouble. —*Psalm 46:1*

LESSONS FROM THE JOURNEY
END LIGHTER

THU

1

IT IS MORE BLESSED TO GIVE THAN TO RECEIVE.

—Acts 20:35

OUR TRUSTED SLOGAN "TRAVEL LIGHT" was unexpectedly challenged when we set out on a trip with our friend Brother Andrew. This was in the 1960s, when it was "impossible" for Christians from the West to meet with Christians behind the Iron Curtain. For years, however, Andrew had been doing just that.

This was to be a short trip, just into East Germany for a few days to watch him in action, so my husband John and I brought only a single small bag for both of us. Andrew was packing when we arrived at his house. Into a large suitcase on his bed he was putting shirts, sweaters, jackets—most with the store tags still attached.

"Why so many clothes for four days?" John asked.

"Oh, I won't be bringing any of this back," Andrew said.

The people we'd be visiting, he explained, like all believers behind the Iron Curtain, paid a tremendous price for their faith, forgoing good education, good jobs, good housing. "They have so little that even a pair of socks can make a difference." All he brought back from trips, he said, was a satchel with his soiled clothes, "so the customs inspector doesn't get curious."

I looked at the faded sweater Andrew was wearing. "You look like you could use a few new clothes yourself," I said.

Sure, he agreed; he'd buy a new sweater one of these days. "But you know what? I won't enjoy it half as much as I do buying a sweater for someone else. It won't be mine the same way. The only things you have forever are the ones you give away."

It's wisdom as we travel through life, too, I thought. Our talents, our experience, our time, our things—they don't mean much until they're shared.

Lord of the journey, what am I clinging to that You want me to give away? —ELIZABETH SHERRILL

FRI
2

My sorrow is beyond healing, my heart is faint within me! . . . Is there no balm in Gilead? Is there no physician there? . . .
—*Jeremiah 8:18, 22 (NAS)*

DRIVING TO WORK YESTERDAY, I stopped at a red light. As I absently looked at my hand on the steering wheel, I noticed the long scar on my wrist. Suddenly I drifted back in memory thirty-six years to the summer following my high-school graduation. I was living in my hometown of Fort Valley, Georgia, and working on the assembly line at the Blue Bird school bus factory. Eighteen years old, I was making school buses in order to save money for college.

Bus-body assembly lines are dangerous places. Amidst powerful machinery, hydraulic presses, hot metal and a vast assortment of high-powered tools, it's easy to be injured. One day, as I cut through a steel beam with a blow torch, my wrist grazed the sharp, molten edge of the beam. Suddenly I was cut to the bone with a wound that would scar my wrist for life.

For a while the scar was prominent and jagged. Sometimes it would swell, becoming inflamed and painful. But I noticed yesterday that now the jagged scar is smooth, faded, almost unnoticeable. Time has worked its healing wonder.

Sometimes events in our lives wound us so deeply that an emotional scar is left for a lifetime. The death of my father when I was fourteen years old cut much more deeply than that steel beam. Yet, over time, I have learned that God has a way of making emotional scars grow smaller too. A grief that we feared would consume us; a disappointment so intense that it maimed us; a shameful mistake that seared our self-image—all of these things can be healed by time and the loving grace of God.

Father, I am thankful that in You I have found a balm in Gilead that can make the wounded whole. Amen. —SCOTT WALKER

SAT

3

"I WILL SURELY SHOW YOU KINDNESS. . . . AND
YOU WILL ALWAYS EAT AT MY TABLE."
—II Samuel 9:7 (NIV)

WE HADN'T KNOWN Erin and Peter very long when they invited us to their house for dinner. We were surprised to discover that they lived in one of Nashville's grand old homes. Every room was impressive, but when Erin ushered us into the dining room, I was astonished by the dazzling chandelier that set the entire room ablaze.

"Oh my goodness!" I gasped. "That's the most gorgeous thing I've ever seen!"

Erin looked at me, surprised. "You like the chandelier?"

"I love it!"

"Do you want it?"

I was struck mute.

"It's just not our style," Erin continued. "We've already bought a replacement. We have an electrician coming next week to install it."

"Oh no," I answered, "I couldn't take it."

"I'd like to give it to you," she said. "Why don't you just think about it?"

As we drove home, I talked it over with David.

"Why don't you take it?" he said. "Erin is showing great kindness in offering you such a lavish gift. Are you being a little prideful?"

He had a point. Why did I feel embarrassed when Erin offered me the chandelier? Was it because it was something we could never afford? How would I feel if I offered someone a gift, no matter how big or small, and she refused to take it?

Finally, I found myself dialing Erin's number. Peter answered. I swallowed hard. "Peter, Erin offered me your chandelier. I would love to have it . . . if . . . you're sure . . ."

"Great!" Peter answered. "Erin will be so happy. We'll both be happy, Pam."

These days, one of my favorite things is to get up early, grab a cup of coffee and sit in my blue chair in the living room. From there I have a full view of the dining room and the most beautiful chandelier I have ever laid eyes on.

Father, let me remember the great kindness not only of giving but of receiving. —PAM KIDD

SUN
4

ONE OF HIS DISCIPLES SAID UNTO HIM, LORD, TEACH US TO PRAY, AS JOHN ALSO TAUGHT HIS DISCIPLES.
—*Luke 11:1*

RECENTLY I HEARD someone quote Frank Laubach, the father of the "each one teach one" literacy movement that's helped countless people learn to read. In addition to writing language primers translated into more than 150 languages, he also authored many books about discipleship.

In one, *Prayers of a Modern Mystic*, he describes his method for being attuned to God throughout the day. His experiments in "flashing" prayers at people who seemed to be troubled or stressed convinced him that prayer could be done anytime, anywhere. Brother Lawrence, the monk who did his praying over pots and pans in a monastery, discovered the same truth centuries earlier.

Norman Rockwell's painting "Saying Grace" shows a grandmother and her grandson praying before their meal in a train station. Rockwell observed the scene in Philadelphia, was touched by it and back in his Stockbridge, Massachusetts, studio painted what would become the all-time favorite *Saturday Evening Post* cover.

Parents who encourage their children to pray in family gatherings are setting an important precedent, even though the kids may need some practice. You may have heard about the mother who invited some friends in for dinner and asked her six-year-old daughter to say the blessing.

"I wouldn't know what to say," the little girl answered.

"Just say what you hear Mommy say," the woman prompted.

Whereupon her daughter bowed her head and prayed, "Lord, why on earth did I invite all these people to dinner?"

Remind us, Lord, it doesn't take a special time or place,
To thank You for Your daily gifts and daily grace.
—FRED BAUER

MON **5** *"So do not worry, saying, 'What shall we eat?' or 'What shall we drink?' or 'What shall we wear?' For the pagans run after all these things, and your heavenly Father knows that you need them." —Matthew 6:31–32 (NIV)*

LIKE OTHER SINGLE PARENTS, I've had many years of worrying about feeding my children, clothing them and providing shelter. I worried that I'd fail. I worried that I'd die and my children would become orphans. Surrounded by endless cares, it was easy to feel alone.

When my daughter Lanea was about nine, I decided to transfer her to a private school. We lived in Richmond, Virginia, but I worked twenty miles south of there. My son Chase was in daycare where I worked, but I worried about Lanea in Richmond. Though it put a strain on our budget, the new school was much closer to where I worked.

Lanea has fond memories of musicals and school celebrations. But she still groans about her memory verses. Braids and beads jiggling, she would sigh as she obediently recited the lines: "Do not store up for yourselves treasures on earth, where moth and rust destroy, and where thieves break in and steal. But store up for yourselves treasures in heaven" (Matthew 6:19–20, NIV).

The words were a duty to her, but they were encouragement to me. "So do not worry, saying, 'What shall we eat?' or 'What shall we drink?' or 'What shall we wear?'" She would look around the room as she shifted foot to foot and continued, " . . . your heavenly Father knows that you need them" (Matthew 6:31–32, NIV).

What Lanea thought were tears of pride sliding down my face were really tears of joy and relief. She didn't know that I was worrying and that I felt alone. But her drills reminded me that God knew and that He cared. When I worry today, the memory of Lanea's voice reminds me that He still does.

God, today and every day You are with me and You care for me. Help me to hear Your reassurance, even in the voice of a child.

—SHARON FOSTER

TUE
6

BLESSED ARE THEY THAT MOURN: FOR THEY SHALL BE COMFORTED. —*Matthew 5:4*

MY DOG SHEP IS DEAD. She knew she was ill but couldn't tell me. An X-ray found the tumor on her heart; it was bleeding. She died with her head in my hands.

It's happened all over again: Cricket, Clay and now Shep. These were the dogs that I liked to say were mine, whom I fed, walked, protected, and who in return made me feel exalted, like a man buoyed by their steady, uncomplicated devotion. Many of you know how I felt. It was different from the death of a person, yet it seemed the same, except that no person had been my responsibility as these completely loyal animals had been.

Two days after her death, I was returning in despair to my apartment. I dreaded it. There would be no frantic rush when I opened the door, no Shep turning in circles, no unspoken words of "Welcome! Welcome! I thought you'd never come back." Then I saw it: a bowl of flowers, all white with green ferns, white roses, white lilies, white hydrangeas; it was uncommonly beautiful. The attached card read:

Thinking of you with love,
Your Guideposts family.

I took in the flowers, set them on a table and sat down. Yes, Guideposts has been my family for more than fifty years; the caring on both of our sides has not stopped. The more I smelled the flowers' fragrance, the more the meaning of Guideposts returned: the positive approach to living, the sureness of victory over death. Shep's closeness, day and night, her unending cheerfulness, were things to be honored, not bemoaned, in the days ahead.

Father, I am a Guideposter. Thank You. —VAN VARNER

EDITOR'S NOTE: We invite you to join us a month from today, on April 6, as we pray for all the needs of our Guideposts family at the 37th annual Guideposts Good Friday Day of Prayer. Send your prayer requests to Good Friday Day of Prayer, 66 East Main Street, Pawling, New York 12564.

WED

7

THERE CAME UNTO HIM A WOMAN HAVING AN ALABASTER BOX OF VERY PRECIOUS OINTMENT, AND POURED IT ON HIS HEAD. . . . —Matthew 26:7

WHEN OUR AUNT HENRIETTA DIED at seventy-nine, my sister Amanda and I cleared out her apartment. To our surprise and dismay, we found a closet filled with boxes that contained almost every gift she'd received for at least five years.

"We gave these blue-striped towels last Christmas," Amanda said, peeking into an oblong box. "The ones she was using were thin and worn."

I spotted a familiar-looking gift bag. Sure enough, it contained the lavender-scented lotion I'd found at a specialty shop—unopened and unused, although Aunt Henrietta had written a gracious thank-you. So it was with box after box. Rose-bordered tea towels, exquisite writing paper, carved picture frames—lovingly selected gifts were saved, apparently for a special time that never came.

How sad! I thought. Poor Aunt Henrietta never benefited from gifts that would have made her life more comfortable. Even worse, she missed out on the joy of remembering the giver every time she used the gift.

Then I thought of someone on the way to becoming as "poor" as my aunt: me. Didn't I insist that my family use the old towels and save the new ones for company? Hadn't I often set the table with chipped dishes while two "company sets" languished in the cabinet?

My basic nature is still a lot like Aunt Henrietta's. But I learned something important from her overflowing closet: The best way to honor the giver is to make full and joyful use of the gift. And it's the same whether the gift is a matchstick cross lovingly glued together by nine-year-old Mark or the wondrous gift of salvation given by Jesus.

Lord, You received the gift of precious ointment with love, and You gave Your life with love. Help me to honor all Your gifts. Amen.

—PENNEY SCHWAB

THU

8

"FREELY YOU HAVE RECEIVED, FREELY GIVE."
—Matthew 10:8 (NIV)

I'D BEEN IN A QUANDARY for days. I was scheduled to be lay leader in our worship service on Sunday—a time to ask for and bless the offering—and I couldn't come up with an idea about what to say. Other lay leaders usually used personal stories or examples of stewardship.

I was still stewing over this challenge when my daughter-in-law and two granddaughters stopped by our house on Thursday.

"Oma, can I please have a cookie?" three-year-old Gabriella asked me. The question is a predictable part of our first few moments together.

As I handed her a chocolate chip cookie, her mom asked, "What do you say, Gabriella?"

"Thank you," she grinned, twirling around with her treat in hand.

This exchange was so automatic that I hardly noticed; a parent teaching a child to say *thank you*. I did the same with my children, just as my own mother did with me, hoping not only to teach good manners and gratitude, but also to teach our children to become generous givers because they have been receivers.

The "thank-you habit": a good idea that is also God's idea. So as Gabriella twirled around the kitchen, I knew I had my Sunday stewardship story.

Lord, You are the "giver of all good things" and we say thank You by giving back out of what we've received. —CAROL KUYKENDALL

FRI
9

THEN OUR MOUTH WAS FILLED WITH LAUGHTER, AND OUR TONGUE WITH JOYFUL SHOUTING. . . .
—*Psalm 126:2 (NAS)*

NERVOUSLY, I KNOCKED AT Mary Dell's door for the first time that day in 1994. Our sons were good buddies, and I knew I needed to introduce myself to her.

I remember waiting for someone to answer the doorbell and being too aware of myself that day—what I wore, what I might say. I was depressed, but help was about to reach me in a marvelous way.

As soon as she opened the door, I felt relieved. Mary Dell was refreshingly real—she came to the door wearing big fuzzy slippers, her hair in a messy ponytail, no makeup, wearing one of her husband's raggedy T-shirts and sweatpants covered in bleach stains.

Mary Dell's whimsical bay window was covered with bright markings drawn right on the glass—happy pictures, family jokes and silly sayings. Their ancient dog Belle traipsed by me and made her way out the door leaving muddy tracks. Mary Dell didn't wipe them up.

"Want to go to the park?" She pulled on her tennis shoes, still wearing the same odd outfit.

"Sure," I said, trying to sound casual. *What will we talk about?*

We walked laps as our sons rode their bikes. I began to feel comfortable talking to Mary Dell. Really talking. She made me laugh about almost everything—even the unknown, the things I couldn't control. And she knew how to laugh at herself—something I'd never learned to do.

Now, when we walk, I smile. And I finally have the freedom to dress in clothes as mismatched as Mary Dell's.

Lord, how I thank You for Mary Dell and her gift of laughter. Surely it came from You. —JULIE GARMON

SAT
10

LOVE YOUR ENEMIES, DO GOOD TO THEM WHICH HATE YOU, BLESS THEM THAT CURSE YOU, AND PRAY FOR THEM WHICH DESPITEFULLY USE YOU.
—*Luke 6:27–28*

JOHN FLEW OUT OF HIS ballet rehearsal looking as if he was two seconds from exploding. "I don't like that girl!" he sputtered. I handed him his snack, dreading what would come next.

"Do you need to talk?" I asked as blandly as possible.

"No!" he shouted and tore up the stairs to sit by the doorway, alone.

After a few minutes I ventured up to ask, "Can you control your feelings for another twenty minutes, until the end of rehearsal?" John scowled but nodded. I wasn't sure if I should believe him. He'd been feeling frustrated even before this. The music for *Suites from Cinderella* was hard, he was one of the youngest dancers, and he was being asked to perform steps he'd never been taught. I sighed, sent up a prayer and went back to the waiting area. Soon John returned to the rehearsal studio.

I had a pretty good hunch about what was going on. I'd noticed earlier that a young but talented dancer was looking at John's struggles with disdain. Since I don't deal well with people who sneer at me, I was glad that John hadn't sought my advice.

Much to my astonishment, John came out of rehearsal beaming. "You look happy!" I commented, baffled.

"Yup. I figured out what to do," John replied. I was intrigued. How had he found a way out of his feelings of rejection and anger?

"I figured the best thing to do was to make friends with her. So I did."

As my jaw dropped, my son called cheerfully to the formerly troublesome girl. She smiled and waved back, and John bounded happily off to the dressing room.

Wow, Lord, could You teach me some more ways to love my enemies?
—JULIA ATTAWAY

SUN

11

THERE ARE DIFFERENT KINDS OF SERVICE, BUT THE SAME LORD. —I Corinthians 12:5 (NIV)

OF COURSE, I WOULDN'T have admitted it to anyone, but I felt very proud and important that morning as I taught our adult Sunday school class, eagerly outlining some of my new and profound thoughts on prayer. Just as I reached the conclusion of the lesson, my husband Gordon quietly slipped out of a chair in the back of the classroom to go out in the drizzling rain to help direct traffic in the parking lot.

Afterward, when I'd finished accepting compliments from class members, I went to the lobby to meet Gordon for church. I was surprised to see him in his orange traffic vest sitting on a bench with his hand pressed against a bloody handkerchief on an elderly gentleman's forehead. The man was wrapped in a blanket and a first-aid kit was open on the floor. Two doctors from the church were kneeling on the floor and someone else was calling EMS. I sank down on a nearby bench, feeling useless.

After EMS had declared the man shaken but otherwise fine, Gordon told me what had happened. "I was near him in the parking lot when I heard him fall. He must have slipped on the wet pavement. I remembered my Boy Scout first aid and pressed my handkerchief against his head and tried to determine whether it was safe to move him."

I noticed a bit of blood on Gordon's hand and felt humbled. How often had I secretly and silently ranked the jobs in our church, putting Sunday school teacher on a higher plane than parking-lot attendant?

"Thank God you were there," I said. And as we walked into the sanctuary together, I thought, *Lesson learned.*

Dear God, thank You that every way we serve is important to Your kingdom. —KAREN BARBER

MON
12

FOR TO THIS END WE TOIL AND STRIVE, BECAUSE WE
HAVE OUR HOPE SET ON THE LIVING GOD. . . .
—*I Timothy 4:10* (RSV)

"I CAN'T PEDAL ANYMORE," I panted. "Go on ahead, I'll catch up."

"We're almost to the top. You can do it," Travis replied, pedaling his bicycle next to mine. The scenery around me had slowed to a jerky crawl. I dismounted and began pushing my bike up the hill.

I can't count how many times this scene has played out since I started cycling with Travis. He and I are hardly a matched pair: I'm stocky, stiff and slow, while Travis has thousands of miles of cycling experience. He does his best to find easy but interesting rides for us, but on every route, it seems, I encounter a hill I can't climb and I walk my bike to the crest.

One afternoon we came across what looked like a short hill. *I'll make it this time,* I promised myself; however, every turn in the road revealed not the crest but another climb. The scenery, though lovely, slowed to that familiar, agonizing crawl as I pedaled in my lowest gear. My legs were burning, I was out of breath and the same old feeling of failure had just set in when I heard Travis call out, "We're almost to the top! You can do it!"

I had been ready to announce, "I can't pedal anymore!" but realized, quite suddenly, that I *could* keep going.

I didn't waste my breath on a reply; I pedaled. A few long minutes later I rounded the last bend in the road and saw Travis waiting for me at the crest, cheering me on. Another minute ticked by and I passed him, legs pumping for all I was worth. As I started to coast down into the valley, I heard him call after me, "Go on ahead, I'll catch up!"

Loving Father, when You strengthen me, I can do more than I believed was possible. Amen. —KJERSTIN WILLIAMS

TUE
13

LET'S SEE IF THE WHOLE COLLECTION OF YOUR IDOLS CAN HELP YOU WHEN YOU CRY TO THEM TO SAVE YOU! THEY ARE SO WEAK THAT THE WIND CAN CARRY THEM OFF! . . . BUT HE WHO TRUSTS IN ME SHALL POSSESS THE LAND. . . . —Isaiah 57:13 (TLB)

I LIVED IN A six-bedroom brick house in Oak Creek, Wisconsin, for twenty-four years. I raised my four children there, mostly as a single parent. But six years after my empty nest began, I decided to downsize and move to Florida, where the winters are more to my liking.

Imagine the stuff you collect over the years when you have a two-car garage, a big shed out back and all those bedrooms! I only wanted to take about one-third of what I owned to Florida, so I gave prized possessions to my kids, begged them to take much of the other stuff, had two huge garage sales and donated the rest. After I had settled into my small condo in Florida and rearranged my furniture and knickknacks at least a dozen times, I discovered that I didn't miss any of my old stuff.

Not long after that, I saw thirteen women on TV who had purchased a beautiful diamond necklace to share among themselves. Each woman gets the necklace for four weeks a year. The joy on their faces as they talked about how they share the necklace was inspiring. One woman said, "You aren't what you own, you're what you do."

Giving away my things now feels like a wonderful cleansing of sorts. And I have lots of "doing" down here. I entertain my children when they come for visits. I swim every day with my friend Jack. I ride my bike. I volunteer. I am what I do, not what I own. Amen to that!

Lord, help me always to be a doer, not a collector. —PATRICIA LORENZ

GOD-FINDS
FINDING OUT ABOUT TEAMWORK

WED
14

THERE IS ONE BODY AND ONE SPIRIT. . . .
—Ephesians 4:4 (NAS)

IT HAD BEEN A challenging morning in my work as an infection control practitioner, and I'd never felt more alone.

As I sat at my desk and tried to complete a report with accompanying charts, the required computer skills eluded me. Elsewhere in the medical center, two other members of a committee I chair were working on other parts of the report as a deadline loomed. There we were, three of us, all going it alone as we analyzed data on a new quality improvement initiative we'd implemented.

When I broke for lunch, Robin, the checkout clerk in the cafeteria, was furiously scribbling something on three-by-five cards in between ringing up customers. "We just got a new girl," she explained a little sheepishly, "and she's frantic about not knowing what to do. I'm making her cue cards." There on Robin's lap were cards showing how much to charge for a vegetable plate, a hot dessert, the caregiver's special.

Later, as I walked back to my office, I had my cue. The secret in getting the job done was in working together and helping one another, not going it alone. I telephoned my committee members right away to see if we could meet that afternoon. Thanks to Robin and some good old-fashioned teamwork, the three of us cranked out that report in no time.

Show me how to work with others to get the job done, Lord.
—ROBERTA MESSNER

READER'S ROOM

AS I PULLED INTO my driveway that gloomy March evening after a particularly bad day at work, it came to mind that I hadn't seen my first robin of spring. Seeing that first robin each year was a ritual when I was growing up. My mother always pointed them out. I also remember the day I went into the hospital to have my daughter on February 27 (twenty-one years ago!). I was feeling anxious until I saw one lonely little robin picking at the ground outside the hospital door. It filled me with hope and calmed my fear.

So on that cold, dank evening, all I could think about was retreating to an early bedtime. The next morning, I glanced out onto the front lawn after lifting the blinds. I saw not one but a whole flock of robins! Spring had sprung, and hope was in the air once more!

—*Susan Morton, Riegelsville, Pennsylvania*

THU
15

"WHY THEN DID YOU NOT OBEY THE VOICE OF THE LORD? . . ." —I Samuel 15:19 (NKJV)

WHEN I VISITED MY PARENTS, I noticed that my step-father was doing something unusual. While my mother and I had coffee, I asked, "Joe, is that plain hot water you're drinking?"

He grinned. "Caught me." He explained that he was putting steaming hot water into a dark brown ceramic mug to fool himself into thinking he was drinking his usual coffee. It turns out that when Joe went to the doctor, he was told that he needed to watch his cholesterol. The doctor told him to follow certain rules—more vegetables, less fat and no coffee—and sent him home, explaining that if that didn't work, he'd have to go on medication.

But what happened about a month later was a surprise. The doctor checked and rechecked him, then excused himself from the room. Joe was quite nervous by this point. "What's going on, Doc?" he asked.

After a few long moments the doctor returned, "Your numbers were so much better this time that I thought the nurse or I might have made a mistake with them. What on earth have you been doing to lower those numbers?"

Perplexed, Joe shrugged. "You know, more vegetables, less fat . . ." His voice trailed off. "Doc, I only did exactly what you told me to do."

And, eyes wide, the doctor replied, "But I tell that to everyone. You're the first person who actually listened!"

After they had a good laugh, the doctor clapped him on the back, and Joe and my mother went out for a cup of hot water to celebrate.

God, let me be a faithful follower of Your instructions today . . . and the instructions of Your earthly helpers. —LINDA NEUKRUG

FRI
16

IT IS ENOUGH. . . . —Mark 14:41

WHEN I HEARD my friends and our pastor discussing *The Passion of the Christ*, I was overjoyed that the film had been made. There was just one problem: I couldn't bear to see it.

"Mom, when are you going to see the movie?" my daughter Julie asked.

"Oh, Julie, I can't see it. I wish I could."

"You have to," Julie said. "Please! I'll go with you."

"I'm a coward," I explained.

My determined daughter bought me the video. Nearly a year later I hadn't even unwrapped it. Then one night, she phoned. "Why don't you watch *The Passion of the Christ* tonight, Mother?"

"Maybe," I answered, knowing that I had no plans to see it.

The next night Julie phoned again. "I'm coming over to watch that movie with you. You'll be glad you saw it. See you at seven."

I was slowly unwrapping the video when she came in. I put it in the VCR and we sat down to watch.

Julie watched steadfastly, riveted to the screen; I looked away. When it was nearly over, she said softly, "Don't you see? It's enough, more than enough, for any of our prayers to be answered. It's all about victory—for us, for our prodigal children."

Dear sweet Jesus, it is enough! Much more than enough for any need, any problem, any pain. —MARION BOND WEST

SAT
17

AFTER THIS MANNER THEREFORE PRAY YE: OUR FATHER WHICH ART IN HEAVEN, HALLOWED BE THY NAME. —*Matthew 6:9*

MY GRANDFATHER WAS a quiet, skinny man who smiled a lot. He liked to sit on the front steps of our house with us grandkids and, as he said, watch the parade of the world wander by. He taught us much, sitting on the steps. One day he taught me a prayer that he said would be food for the long voyage ahead. Being Irish, he taught me the prayer in Irish Gaelic.

"*Ar nathair,*" he said, "which is Our Father, *ata ar neamh,* Who is in heaven, though, of course, He is in us and everywhere and that's a stone fact. *Go naomhaitear d'ainm,* hallowed be Thy name, *go dtaga do riocht,* Thy kingdom come, which it is already, as we see by just paying attention to the miracle of what is. *Go ndeantar do thoil,* Thy will be done, *ar an talamh mar a dheantar ar neamh,* on earth as it is in heaven. *Tabhair duinn inniu,* give to us, *ar n'aran laethuil,* our daily bread, and *agus maith duinn ar bhfiacha*, forgive us our debts, *mar a mhaithimidne dar bhfeichiuna fein*, as we forgive our own debtors, which it would be hilarious if anyone ever owed *us* money, the very idea, eh? Well, boy, the prayer as usually said then goes on to say *agus na lig sinn i gcathu*, and lead us not into temptation, but Himself would never lead His children astray—we are all too good at going astray on our own. *Ach saor sin o olc*, deliver us from evil, and we finish with *aimein*, which let us say together as men do."

So *aimein!* we said together, sitting and smiling and watching the parade of the world wander by. And forty years later I'm still watching, with my grandfather's prayer humming in my heart.

Dear Lord, thank You, from the bottom of my heart, for grandfathers and prayers and parades and hummings in hearts. Aimein!
—BRIAN DOYLE

SUN
18

WHERE IS THE WAY WHERE LIGHT DWELLETH? AND AS FOR DARKNESS, WHERE IS THE PLACE THEREOF?
—*Job 38:19*

FOR YEARS MY FATHER was an alcoholic. It was not until I was eighteen years old that he finally discovered a way to loosen the grip of the addiction that controlled him.

Things had gotten so bad that my mother had him committed to a mental hospital in Goldsboro, North Carolina. While he was there, he and all the others in the alcoholic unit were bused to town once a week to attend Alcoholics Anonymous at a local church.

Daddy had no interest in AA. He was biding his time until he could find a way to escape the hospital and make his way back home to Richlands. There, our family, church and friends were all praying for him.

Later, Daddy told us his story: "I remember stepping off the bus at the church in downtown Goldsboro and looking into the darkness around me. It was a powerful darkness. Blacker than the shades of any night that had ever enveloped me. I hesitated for a moment, strangely drawn to the only light that kept the terrible darkness at bay—the soft glow at the door of the church. Suddenly, the very voice of the universe seemed to speak, giving notice that this was my final chance. At that critical moment, before the door closed leaving me forever in the darkness, I made my decision. I followed my fellow inmates through the bright opening and into the light of the church."

That night marked the first day of thirty years of sobriety for Daddy, and his decision changed the lives of our entire family.

Today, when I have a tough decision to make, I think of the light that led Daddy and I know that it will do the same for me.

Father, how thankful I am for Your holy light that dispels all the darkness around me. —LIBBIE ADAMS

MON
19

BUT IN FACT GOD HAS ARRANGED THE PARTS IN THE BODY, EVERY ONE OF THEM, JUST AS HE WANTED THEM TO BE. —*I Corinthians 12:18* (NIV)

I READ RECENTLY that by the time you reach age seventy-five, you might easily have slept the equivalent of twenty-five years of your life. I think I've already spent at least that much time watching. Last week I watched my son Ross play trombone in a jazz band concert, my daughter Maria dance in a recital and my husband Paul's barbershop quartet in concert. Soon, I'll begin the springtime rite of sitting on hard metal bleachers watching countless hours of high school baseball.

I was telling my mom that maybe I should be doing more and watching less when she laid the truth on me in her reliably sensible way. "We all can't be stars," she said. "Somebody has to watch, or it would take all the fun out of performing." Then I remembered how our daughter rushed up to us after last year's school musical. "Did you see my dance?" she wanted to know. The fact that Mom and Dad had seen her seemed as important as the dance itself.

My mom also pointed out that there's more to my role than simply watching: Somebody has to drive to rehearsals, get the piano tuned and volunteer to bring the post-game snack. None of that may be glamorous, but I've learned that the performance—or whatever form that "starring role" takes—couldn't happen without the supporting players. We watchers play an important role in the lives of others, who need to know that someone is cheering especially for them.

Lord, whether watcher or doer, help me find my place in Your great creation, knowing that it's the exact place You have planned for me.
—GINA BRIDGEMAN

TUE
20

THEN HE SAID TO ANOTHER, "FOLLOW ME." . . .
—*Luke 9:59 (NKJV)*

FOR YEARS MY WIFE Kathy and I had talked about taking dance lessons. When I pastored in southeastern Pennsylvania, we had attended many wedding receptions where we had watched the dancing, wishing we knew how. And Kathy remembered standing on her father's shoes as a little girl, feeling the thrill of gliding on the dance floor. So as a surprise, I arranged for us to take a lesson.

We arrived early and watched the instructors and their clients finishing the class before us. It looked simple enough—slow, slow, quick, quick, slow. Years of music lessons and marching band had helped me with counting, coordination and rhythm. *I should be able to do this,* I thought.

By the end of our first lesson, we understood the elementary steps of the fox-trot, the swing and the rumba. We left the studio, smiling, and with a commitment for ten more lessons.

Now you need to know something about the world of ballroom dancing: A gentleman must lead with a strong right hand. I am strongly left-handed. Once we had learned more than one step, Kathy couldn't know which step to dance unless I led. By the end of our ten lessons, I felt ready for Remedial Dance 101.

"This is no fun. I can't do this," I said.

"Ted, you have to lead. And you have to practice until it becomes part of your subconscious. Then dancing becomes satisfying. Don't give up," encouraged our instructor.

How many times had I said similar words to those who have asked me about prayer? "Pray. Pray until it becomes part of your subconscious. Don't give up."

Well, I took my own advice: I'm not giving up. I may still be awk-ward, but I'm beginning to enjoy myself. In dancing, as in prayer, prac-tice makes perfect.

Father, as You lead, I will follow. —TED NACE

WED
21

> WHY ART THOU CAST DOWN, O MY SOUL? AND WHY
> ART THOU DISQUIETED IN ME? . . . —*Psalm 42:5*

I WAS FEELING SORRY for myself. Lethargic and blue, I trudged along. The weather had been rainy and cold for days. The spring that all New Englanders yearn for seemed perpetually out of reach, and Lent seemed to be dragging on forever. Everything was gray and tedious and miserable as I wrestled with the umbrella that had become a seemingly permanent part of my walking garb.

Suddenly a flatbed truck came careering around the corner. Just as it passed me, the tractor it carried came loose and flew toward the side-walk. My guardian angel must have been with me, because I somehow managed to drop my umbrella and roll onto the soft wet grass, barely out of the path of the crashing tractor.

The truck came to a screeching halt, and the driver came running back, all apologies. I was fine, but trembling violently. No one had been hurt, and the young man couldn't reload his equipment and get out of there fast enough.

After he left, I sat in the wet grass and looked around. Everything was different. The grass was the soft, luminescent green of early spring. As I looked hard at the grass, I could see some tiny crocuses poking up. The magnolia across the street appeared to have tight, tiny buds. And the sky definitely looked ready to clear. Easter was still a couple of weeks away, but I'd already gotten a chance at a new life, and I wasn't about to waste it.

Father, help me to remember each day what a magnificent gift You've given me. —MARCI ALBORGHETTI

THU

22

FOR I KNOW THE THOUGHTS THAT I THINK TOWARD YOU, SAYS THE LORD . . . TO GIVE YOU A FUTURE AND A HOPE. —Jeremiah 29:11 (NKJV)

THE WINDSHIELD WIPERS SCRAPED aside the morning sleet. Miles of red glowing taillights lined Route 50 leading into Washington, D.C. This was part of my daily routine: Each day I woke up, inched through traffic, worked eight hours, sat in more traffic, walked my German shepherd Kai and went to bed. I was single and twenty-two years old. The year before, I'd dropped out of college. *God, I prayed, isn't there more to life than this?*

I'd grown up in a small Minnesota town. But I'd fled the miles of cornfields by transferring to a college in the D.C. area. After a year in the city, I didn't know what to do with my life or where to live.

That weekend Kai and I walked along a leaf-littered trail. The breeze caressed my cheeks and the sun warmed my back. Kai bounded ahead and splashed into the creek. All he wanted was to be with me, playing outdoors. I ached for my life to be that simple. I sat on a boulder and Kai paddled over with a gift, a rock. I tossed it into the water. He dove after it, expecting adventure. *Adventure—that's what I need,* I thought. *So why am I living here?*

My dream had always been to work outside, preferably on horseback. I thought of my brother Chuck, who lived in Montana. Peace overwhelmed me when I remembered horses grazing under ponderosa pines on Rocky Mountain slopes. It was almost as if God's still, small voice was urging me to plunge into a new adventure.

That evening I phoned Chuck. "I'll be moving to Montana April first," I told him. "Can I crash on your floor until I get a job?"

Lord, teach me to listen to Your still, small voice. —REBECCA ONDOV

FRI

23

I COME SEEKING FRUIT ON THIS FIG TREE, AND FIND NONE: CUT IT DOWN. . . . —Luke 13:7

IT'S TOO COLD AND GRAY in New Hampshire for me to raise figs, yet I'm disturbed by the image of the poor plant in the parable being threatened with destruction because it doesn't bear fruit. It's worn out and needs help.

The wise gardener in this Scripture pleads for time, a year "to dig about it and dung it." "Digging about," or cultivating, will break up compacted soil, and let both water and nutrients reach the plant's roots. Though the plants need water only two or three times a season, the soil needs to be loose to let it through. Thus nourished, the plant has a fighting chance of producing fruit. Once the soil is loosened, the fig tree can be propagated from a branch bent into the soil. More plants mean more fruit.

And why is this parable about figs rather than dates, which are so common in the Holy Land? Perhaps because dates contain only one large seed and the fig contains hundreds. Each tiny fig seed produces yet more fruit, a hefty return from simply breaking up the hard soil and letting in life-giving water.

So I ponder the fig. How many times do I harden myself by complacency or pride or anger, and not produce fruit? How can I replenish myself? Like the fig, sometimes I need help from others—and a little time.

Lord of creation, thank You for the quiet wisdom of flowering things.
—GAIL THORELL SCHILLING

SAT
24

FOR WE WRESTLE NOT AGAINST FLESH AND BLOOD, BUT AGAINST PRINCIPALITIES, AGAINST POWERS, AGAINST THE RULERS OF THE DARKNESS OF THIS WORLD. . . . —Ephesians 6:12

LAST WEEK, OUR SMALL TOWN experienced a loss of staggering proportions. Ed Deuberry died—Coach Deuberry, a father (and grandfather) not only to his own large household, but to thousands of boys in our community. Ed was a wrestling coach, but he was much more than that. He was a man of extraordinary compassion, a coach who defined the best of that breed: He loved the sport, and he loved his boys even more. I know, because for eleven years he coached my son Brett.

We met Coach Deuberry through a YMCA wrestling program. At countless Saturday meets, Coach was there on the mat, encouraging Brett, convincing him that, "You can pin this guy!" But Brett learned more than wrestling moves from Coach Deuberry. He learned about the value of hard work, about fair play, about being a man of his word.

Ed Deuberry is at rest now. He has rolled up his last wrestling mat and posted his last score. And while I'm not sure what heaven is like, I can't help but wonder if Coach isn't up there showing Jesus a few new moves.

Thank You, God, for those who've come alongside us to mentor and inspire our children. May we cherish their legacies and remember to continue that work on our own every day. —MARY LOU CARNEY

SUN
25

FATHER, FORGIVE THEM; FOR THEY KNOW NOT WHAT THEY DO. . . . —Luke 23:24

MY SUNDAY SCHOOL CLASS of fifth- and sixth-graders was studying the Last Supper and Christ's betrayal. I wanted them to think about the disciple Judas and what his motives might have been. I wanted them to look more closely at what had happened those last few days of Christ's life. Maybe a bit of role-playing would help.

"Here's the assignment," I said. "Each of you should imagine you're Judas. You're standing before God in heaven after the Crucifixion. What can you say for yourself? How can you justify the terrible thing you've done?"

"Who's going to play God?" one student asked.

"Me," I said, "at least for this exercise."

They came up with some interesting and rather sophisticated arguments. The Crucifixion wasn't really Judas' fault, said one boy. Judas only betrayed Christ at Jesus' urging, claimed another. After all, it was Jesus Who said, "Do what you must do." One girl went so far as to say that if Judas hadn't done what he'd done, there might not have been a Resurrection at all.

Still, none of the arguments moved me. Then one of the youngest boys in the class looked up a little sheepishly at me. "I'm really sorry," he said.

"What for?" I asked.

"That's what Judas should say. 'I'm really sorry. I had no idea what I was doing. Please forgive me. I would never have done it if I'd really understood Who He was.'"

I'm not God. I don't know how His conversation with Judas went. But as a Sunday school teacher I learned a lot that day. Arguments are compelling, but nothing is quite as powerful as asking for forgiveness.

I am sorry, Lord, and I repent for all the wrongs I've committed.
—RICK HAMLIN

MON
26

YOUR ATTITUDE SHOULD BE THE SAME AS THAT OF CHRIST JESUS: WHO, BEING IN VERY NATURE GOD . . . MADE HIMSELF NOTHING, TAKING THE VERY NATURE OF A SERVANT, BEING MADE IN HUMAN LIKENESS.
—*Philippians 2:5–7 (NIV)*

IN CHARLES DICKENS'S NOVEL *Bleak House,* a hypocritical character whose acts of charity benefit only faraway causes and never people at hand is known for her "telescopic philanthropy."

I know something about this. Tsunami or hurricane devastation? I write a check and think, *Oh, if only I could go there and help,* all the while knowing that I'm glad to be insulated from meeting a real need in any hands-on way.

This penchant came to the fore last week when I received an e-mail from the Colonel, a World War II veteran I know from church. Since the accident that had totaled his car, he'd lost his license. His wife was debilitated. Now a request: Could I possibly drive them to Walter Reed Army Medical Center for an appointment on Monday?

Why, that's clear across town! Before bed that night, I explained my excuses to God: *There's construction on Nebraska Avenue. The parking's impossible. It will take most of a day.* But when I glanced up, the moon shining from far beyond the oaks in my yard sent me a silent message: Go for an attitude of generous servanthood. Not telescopic, but near and neighborly.

Monday morning, I cheerfully picked up the Colonel and his missus. We three went clear across town and back, after ice cream at a favorite café.

Jesus, teach me more about Your servant heart. —EVELYN BENCE

TUE
27

THE BEASTS OF THE FIELD SHALL BE AT PEACE WITH THEE. —Job 5:23

TAKING DOWN THE PLASTER WALLS of our house was like peeling back time: first a layer of paneling, then sheets of floral wallpaper, and then the plaster and lathe. Behind the lathe the south side of the house was one large mouse's and squirrel's nest tucked with newspaper and cloth and even a teddy bear.

Most of the squirrels had been frightened away by our banging, but one headstrong little red squirrel was unwilling to give up its home. While we worked, it stood outside the house, stamping its feet, batting its tail and chattering incessantly. When we left, it would find a way back inside and make a new nest—usually with scraps it stole from my husband's newspaper.

As autumn neared, black walnuts from the tree in the front yard appeared on the now-visible rafters, evidence of our little squirrel's hard work. As I took them down, I thought about the squirrel carrying one nut at a time, running over the ground, up the side of the house and then back again. We had a lot in common: Each of us was trying to get our house ready for winter.

By then, my husband and I had moved in and the little squirrel had disappeared. On frigid nights when the wind whipped against the house, I prayed that the little creature was safe and warm. Closing my eyes, I imagined scraps of my husband's half-finished crossword puzzle tucked beneath the squirrel in a neighbor's attic.

I had almost forgotten about the squirrel when I spotted it early that spring in a nearby apple tree. It was thinner and its expression had changed from anger to surprise. I imagine it saw the same expression on my face—surprise, mingled with relief that each of us had survived the winter.

Lord, thank You for hard work and a warm house and a no-longer-angry new friend. —SABRA CIANCANELLI

WED
28

RESTORE US TO THYSELF, O LORD, THAT WE MAY BE RESTORED! RENEW OUR DAYS AS OF OLD!
—*Lamentations 5:21 (RSV)*

OUR YOUNGEST SON GLEN restores antique pianos. While visiting him one year, I fell in love with a beautiful burled walnut piano he had on display in his showroom. The grain of the wood, the detail of the carvings, the contour of the cabinet all impressed me.

"Oh, but, Mom! You should have seen it when it came into the shop from that old farmhouse. The finish was peeling off from water damage. I had to strip it down and start from square one with the innards, but considering it was built in 1890, the outcome made all my work worthwhile."

That piano came to mind today when I was brought face-to-face with a similar piece of work. The legs were a little unsteady, the finish patched up, the joints wobbly, screws coming loose with age. Remembering how it looked several decades ago, I sighed. This wasn't just any old piece of furniture I was looking at, this was me.

I remembered what a friend said about the ravages of time. "Yes, my body is aging," he conceded, "but my spirit stays as young as ever, because God 'restoreth my soul.'"

No, my mirror doesn't lie. But realizing that God offers the opportunity each day to "start from square one with the innards," there might be some real improvements to my soul.

Considering I date back to 1939, Lord, may the final outcome make all Your hard work worthwhile. —ALMA BARKMAN

THU
29

Now THE LORD GOD HAD PLANTED A GARDEN IN THE EAST, IN EDEN. . . . —*Genesis 2:8 (NIV)*

IT WAS A BEAUTIFUL spring morning as I walked out to get the paper from the driveway. Mary, my next-door neighbor, was already working in her garden; flats of bright yellow marigolds lay nearby ready to be planted.

A twinge of longing ran through me. *Oh, how I wish I was planting flowers!* I thought. But I had decided against it. My husband and I, newly married, were planning to buy a home. In the meantime we were renting a small duplex that was landscaped with a few evergreen shrubs.

"Your flowers are beautiful!" I called out as I walked over to get a closer look.

"Thanks," she said as she picked up another flat of marigolds. "I bought these over at the high school. The horticulture students are selling them. You might want to pick some up. You can't beat the price."

"Thanks," I said, "but we'll be moving at some point, so it would really be a waste of time. But I've been planning the flower gardens I'll have when we buy our own home—camellias, wisteria, azaleas and lots of zinnias—so I can have fresh-cut flowers inside."

"Sounds wonderful," Mary said as she dug a hole for the next flower. "It's great to have plans for the future, but don't forget about today. What a waste it would be to miss it."

Mary was right. I was so busy planning tomorrow that I wasn't fully living today. Later, while running errands, I stopped by the high school and bought a flat of marigolds. It was time for me—and a few spring flowers—to bloom where we were planted.

Keep me present, Lord, to appreciate and participate in Your daily gifts.
—MELODY BONNETTE

FRI
30

"WHOEVER DOES GOD'S WILL IS MY BROTHER AND SISTER AND MOTHER." —*Mark 3:35 (NIV)*

"ARE YOU KIDDING?" I shouted into the phone. "I'd love to go!"

A friend who was away at college had just asked if I wanted to go to the Bahamas for spring break. She and a few of her schoolmates were renting a villa on the beach, she said; I wouldn't have to pay much for my stay. I needed little convincing. I made my airline reservations that week, and before I knew it I was flying over the turquoise tropical ocean.

Once I got there, however, paradise quickly soured. Although the picture-perfect landscape surpassed my expectations, everything else was a disappointment. The villa was inexpensive because "a *few* schoolmates" turned out to be twelve people occupying a small two-bedroom house. And in the company of her schoolmates, my friend was distant and unwilling to spend much time with me.

I felt betrayed and alone, yet I tried not to let my circumstances get in the way of experiencing the Bahamas. Every morning I'd wake up and explore the downtown markets, the rainforest and the beaches with sand that felt like baby powder under my feet.

After a few days I searched the phonebook to find a church and attended a Friday-night service. The congregation was warm and friendly, and one family quickly invited me to a delicious home-cooked meal in their home. I was fussed over like a daughter as they refilled my plate. "Do you need anything?" they asked. "Are you okay with money?" In the presence of these wonderful people, I no longer felt alone. On the contrary, I discovered how large my family truly is.

Lord, thank You for the brothers and sisters who await me wherever I go.
—KAREN VALENTIN

LOOKING TO THE LORD

THERE IS no better source of strength for our journey than the One Who poured out His life for us on a dusty hillside almost two thousand years ago. This Holy Week, join Roberta Rogers as she follows Jesus through the streets of first-century Jerusalem in search of faith and hope for all our twenty-first century lives. —THE EDITORS

SATURDAY BEFORE PALM SUNDAY

SAT
31

For now we see through a glass, darkly; but then face to face: now I know in part; but then shall I know even as also I am known.
—*I Corinthians 13:12*

OUR TV HAS PIP: "picture in a picture." In a corner of the main screen, I can open a small window that allows me to watch the progress of the Red Sox at the same time I keep an eye on my son Tom at the Talladega NASCAR race. Since his lifelong friend Todd oversees the disbursement of two hundred thousand seats and twenty-eight thousand camping slots there, I'm hopeful of a sighting of the guys in the stands, but at the same time I've got to know how those Sox are faring. With a tap of the remote, I can make the smaller window the larger and vice-versa.

It's like that with me—and others I've met—during Holy Week. Starting tomorrow, for the next week, I'll live life in two windows. Most of the time I'll function as wife, mother, grandmother, friend, neighbor in the very present world around me, but at the same time in the "small" window of my mind, the events of Holy Week will unfold. With the tap of my remote, a quiet moment, the events in Jerusalem two thousand years ago will become the larger while my day-to-day life in the twenty-first century goes on in smaller, muted form.

Holy Week is a familiar yet new adventure each year, as if somewhere it is all happening again and I am living it, too, this time from a different angle. It's a hard week, but, oh, what lies at the end of it!

Lord, lead me through this coming week with new insights, new honesty, new hope in Your love. —ROBERTA ROGERS

MY WALK WITH GOD

1 _____
2 _____
3 _____
4 _____
5 _____

6 _____

7 _____

8 _____

9 _____

10 _____

11 _____

12 _____

13 _____

14 _____

15 _____

16 _____

17 _____

18 _____

19 _____

20 _____

21 _____

22 _____

23 _____

24 _____

25 _____

26 _____

27 _____

28 _____

29 _____

30 _____

31 _____

April

Worthy is the Lamb that was slain to receive power, and riches, and wisdom, and strength, and honour, and glory, and blessing. —*Revelation 5:12*

LOOKING TO THE LORD
PALM SUNDAY

SUN
I

REJOICE GREATLY, O DAUGHTER OF ZION! SHOUT, DAUGHTER OF JERUSALEM! SEE, YOUR KING COMES TO YOU. . . . —Zechariah 9:9 (NIV)

MY HUSBAND BILL AND I love to go to the New Market Rebels' games. College players from all over the East and Midwest come to the Shenandoah Valley every June and July and play baseball. But Bill and I don't like crowds. We usually head for the picnic pavilion past third base and watch from the benches there. We hang back and observe, and when cheering is justified we cheer.

So that's how I know that today, as Jesus rides into Jerusalem on that donkey's foal, I'm not shouting and pushing my way to the front. I'm standing on the outskirts of the crowd. I'm not sure about this triumphal sort of procession, this man.

I've seen this Jesus in other places, most recently in Jericho and Bethany. I've seen Him perform incredible miracles. And He's never done it like a magician, to wow the crowd, to be applauded. I feel a little uncomfortable, but when I look at Him, He's not uncomfortable at all. He sits erect and confident, even as the donkey's slow steps sway Him from side to side. Suddenly, His eyes look over the crowd and meet mine. He smiles.

And just as suddenly I catch a glimpse. This is a king, moving among us as one of us. He has no trumpets blaring fanfare, but rather human voices caroling praise. I'd like to think that at that moment I would have begun to shout the loudest "Hosanna!" I could and push my way forward. But would I? I honestly don't know.

Lord, forgive my reluctance and pride, my holding back. Please help me commit myself to You in whatever way You show Yourself.

—ROBERTA ROGERS

MONDAY IN HOLY WEEK

MON
2

FOR THOSE WHO ARE SELF-SEEKING AND WHO REJECT THE TRUTH AND FOLLOW EVIL, THERE WILL BE WRATH AND ANGER. —*Romans 2:8 (NIV)*

HERE WE ARE BACK in Jerusalem from Bethany. We're entering the Temple area. It's crowded and noisy. There are religious leaders, folks in from all around the country for the Passover week, the smells of sweat and animals, the clink of coins, endless voices mingling. I'm digging out the money that I need for my sacrifice when I become aware of the crowd drawing back, a space forming, vendors rising from their tables. As I turn, there is the sound of wood smashing onto stone and objects clattering and thumping to the ground. Coins roll; children scamper to recover them. What I see amazes me—Jesus, described in my childhood hymns as "meek and mild," His strong carpenter's hands grasping and turning yet another vendor's table. Two already lie broken on the pavement.

The crowd gasps, the Pharisees glower, rage shows in the vendors' eyes, and there is an instant of silence where I hear Jesus say, "My house is meant to be a house of prayer. You have made it a den of robbers!"

When He finishes overturning the tables, He blocks the way of those who are about to carry merchandise through the Temple court. His head shakes slowly, His eyes flash. No one continues.

Jesus, Who said to turn the other cheek, has turned the tables. This is a side of Him I have never seen before. And one, pray God, I never will again.

Lord, sometimes, knowing Your love, I forget that You get angry too. Oh, thank You for keeping me "from the wrath to come" (I Thessalonians 1:10).
—ROBERTA ROGERS

TUESDAY IN HOLY WEEK

TUE
3

"WHEREVER THE GOSPEL IS PREACHED THROUGHOUT THE WORLD, WHAT SHE HAS DONE WILL ALSO BE TOLD, IN MEMORY OF HER." —*Mark 14:9 (NIV)*

THERE ARE SO MANY PEOPLE in here! I stand to one side and am aware of the rumble of male voices, some laughing, some arguing.

"So who do you think gets to sit by Him?"

"Did you hear what happened to those money changers!"

"What did He say about 'the end of the age'?"

"What does He mean by 'the Son of Man'?"

Then a woman enters. I press into the wall behind me; I know what she's going to do, and I always have a problem with my reaction to Jesus' reaction. She edges through the mostly male crowd, carrying that alabaster jar. She upends the jar and the scent of the dreadfully expensive pure nard fills the room. Everyone stops talking. The nard drips from the top of Jesus' head, dribbles down His chin, soaks into His clothes, some even drops to His feet, dampening His sandals. Everyone, including me, gasps, indignant that this woman has interrupted us in such an embarrassing way. I can hear her sobbing quietly between her hands, which now cup and hide her face.

"Oh, for goodness' sake! Why would you do that, woman?"

"That stuff is so expensive—why not give that wasted money to the poor?"

I hear the sudden outburst and nod in agreement. But not Jesus.

He reaches out to touch her bowed head gently. She knows something we don't, and He knows she knows. His hand lingers a moment to comfort and thank her. She nods between sobs, and then, head still lowered, passes among us and out of Simon the Leper's house.

Lord, there are many things that You did and taught that I don't understand. Some of them still make me uncomfortable. But strengthen me to live from Your perspective, not mine. —ROBERTA ROGERS

WEDNESDAY IN HOLY WEEK

WED

THEN JUDAS ISCARIOT, ONE OF THE TWELVE DISCIPLES, WENT TO THE LEADING PRIESTS AND ASKED, "HOW MUCH WILL YOU PAY ME TO BETRAY JESUS TO YOU?" —*Matthew 26:14–15 (NLT)*

IT'S WEDNESDAY. It's one of the two "silent" days this week for me, days when I don't have a feel for where Jesus is or what is going on. The only thing Scripture tells me about today is that I have to face Judas Iscariot, and I don't want to.

There he goes, head down, glancing from side to side, clutching his tunic. I follow. He seeks and gains admittance to the highest authorities. He makes arrangements to turn over Jesus. But it's the thoughts swarming in his head that I really have to face: *If He's so wise, how come He doesn't know about me, about what I'm doing? . . . How can He be the Messiah? . . . Isn't He really just a nice, kind madman? . . . I don't need a lot of money, but I sure could use just a bit more. . . .*

I can guess at Judas' thoughts; I've had them all in one form or another. I hate facing him because I have to face the Judas in me. And now here he comes, back into the narrow street, clutching a goatskin bag of silver pieces. *Too late for you, Judas!* The taunting voice in his head becomes louder. In a few days, it will kill him and those coins will buy his burial place. He goes past me, shoulders hunched, mumbling. This time I don't follow him.

Lord God, thank You for forgiving the Judas moments in me. When the doubter whispers in my ear, keep me faithful, Lord, keep me faithful.

—ROBERTA ROGERS

MAUNDY THURSDAY

THU
5

"FATHER, IF IT IS YOUR WILL, TAKE THIS CUP AWAY FROM ME; NEVERTHELESS, NOT MY WILL, BUT YOURS, BE DONE." —Luke 22:42 (NKJV)

EARLIER TONIGHT I WATCHED the Passover from a dark alcove just off the room above a Jerusalem shop. I saw Jesus kneel to wash His disciples' feet. I heard the murmurs just before Judas left suddenly. I watched as tiny pieces of the broken matzo crumbled to the seder plate as I heard Jesus say, "This is my body. . . ." I saw the wine poured.

Now it is late, and I have followed him with Peter, James and John into Gethsemane. Like the disciples, I'm sleepy, full of food, tired after a long week and anxious to avoid facing something I don't want to see. I slump down, the ground hard beneath me and a gnarled olive tree rough at my back. I begin to nod off.

Then I hear it: the anguish of a very mortal man crying out to God to keep Him from the dreadful pain and suffering that He knows is coming. Three times I hear Jesus beg His heavenly Father to take "this cup" from Him, and three times I hear the one word that will change all of history for all of us for all of time, the word that I find hard to say today in my comparatively smaller trials: *"Nevertheless . . ."*

All of history swings on that word; it pulls me forward into the rest of His prayer, "Not my will but Yours. . . ."

Lord Jesus, how thankful I am for that word that gave us all the opportunity for eternal life. —ROBERTA ROGERS

GOOD FRIDAY

FRI

MY GOD, MY GOD, WHY HAVE YOU FORSAKEN ME? . . . FUTURE GENERATIONS WILL BE TOLD ABOUT THE LORD. THEY WILL PROCLAIM HIS RIGHTEOUSNESS TO A PEOPLE YET UNBORN—FOR HE HAS DONE IT.
—*Psalm 22:1, 30–31 (NIV)*

WHEN THE MOVIE *The Passion of the Christ* came out, my husband Bill and our pastor friend Don Shull went to see it. "Nope. You won't be able to handle it," Bill said when I asked if I'd like it.

I knew that was true even before he spoke. Good Friday is never "good" for me except as viewed from the twenty-first century. I can't look full-face at the Cross with Jesus hanging on it. Instead, I see only His bloody feet. Out of the corner of my eye, I see Mary, ashen, beyond tears and pain, a mother like me, with a son in agony. And I hear the incredible concern in His voice for her as He gives her into the care of the disciple John. How can He be so cogent, so kind, in the midst of such pain?

I hear His human "I thirst!" and His acceptance of the wine and vinegar lifted up to Him. I am aware of darkening skies and ominous earthly rumbling. I go on staring at those mangled bloody feet as Jesus cries out in the words of the Psalm, "Why have You forsaken me?" And then finally I hear the long sigh and "It is finished." I stare dumbly as He is hauled down and carted off. I am numb, beyond tears.

What is going on here? From the twenty-first century I know an answer lies in the verses between Psalm 22:1, 31, but it's still beyond my comprehension.

Father God, how amazing that instead of ending our world on Good Friday, You made it the pivot point of history. —ROBERTA ROGERS

EDITOR'S NOTE: Pray with us today as we observe our annual Good Friday Day of Prayer. Today and every day, Guideposts Prayer Ministry prays for each prayer request by name and need. Join us at www.dailyguideposts.com and learn how you can request prayer, volunteer to pray for others or contribute to support our ministry.

HOLY SATURDAY

SAT

THEN THEY WENT HOME AND PREPARED SPICES AND OINTMENTS TO EMBALM HIM. BUT BY THE TIME THEY WERE FINISHED IT WAS THE SABBATH, SO THEY RESTED ALL THAT DAY AS REQUIRED BY THE LAW.
—*Luke 23:56 (NLT)*

FOR JESUS' FOLLOWERS AND FRIENDS, Saturday was a day of rest. It was their Sabbath. There were long hours to sit and think, remember, cry, and maybe, from time to time, hope. "He *did* say something about 'rising on the third day,' didn't He?"

This Saturday I concentrate on cleaning the house and planning tomorrow's Easter dinner. It's what I call "the day in between." It's a "normal" day, like thousands of others.

But deep inside the tomb, deep inside the Father's heart, resurrection life is stirring. Is this the day Jesus "descended into hell" to lead forth those who would come with Him? Is He there now as I dump clothes into the washer? Are the angels on edge with anticipation? I wonder as I spread out a clean tablecloth and set a glass vase of my daffodils in the center. At what moment will the power of God's love overrule death and leave those grave cloths empty in Joseph's tomb? Has it already? I remove the brownies from the oven.

I can't follow Jesus on this day; no one but He and the Father know exactly what happened when.

Lord God, Lord Jesus, thank You that the ultimate joy of tomorrow still lies ahead for all of us, no matter how horrible or humdrum today is.
—ROBERTA ROGERS

EASTER

SUN
8

He said, The things which are impossible with men are possible with God. —Luke 18:27

ALMOST EVERY EASTER our youth group made a pilgrimage to Goodwin Park in Hartford, Connecticut, to stamp cold feet on the dew-damp grass and watch the sun rise red over the hills. Then we went back to the church and had pancakes. Although we sang a hymn or two, I recall mostly a sweet silence as the light of day filled up the world around us. But the original Easter morning was not quiet. . . .

Sometime in the predawn, as the Roman soldiers try not to doze by the stone-blocked tomb entrance, there is a dreadful rumble, a violent earthquake. An angel appears, so massive in power that the soldiers shake and faint. The stone rolls back. Then, right after sunrise, the rushing and running begins.

First come the women, moving as quickly as they can, carrying cloths and embalming herbs. Then, jars forgotten, there is the thumping of their feet running out of the garden. Soon there are the pounding feet of Peter and John, who have the wisdom to believe what Mary Magdalene told them: The stone has been rolled aside, the grave cloths are lying untouched, the tomb is empty! Jesus is alive! He has broken out of death and lives!

"He said he would rise on the third day! He did! He has!" the men cry as they race back to the others. "Death didn't hold Him! Death didn't win!"

All day there is bewildered joy, a dawning realization, the rush of new faith and energy, and at the end of it—appearing among them suddenly—Jesus.

Lord, You live! And through You, we will live too—the ultimate impossibility becomes possible. —ROBERTA ROGERS

LESSONS FROM THE JOURNEY
EXPECT DELAYS

MON

9

My times are in thy hand. . . . —Psalm 31:15

THOUGH I DEARLY LOVED my mother-in-law, I dreaded the times when she traveled to visit us. She took the arrival time printed on an airline ticket as a guarantee and fretted if a flight was even a few minutes late.

When she planned to visit us in Uganda in the early 1960s, John and I wrote to warn her that East Africa was often in turmoil and flights were erratic. As the day of her arrival approached, we made the eighteen-hour drive to Nairobi, Kenya, and were parked by the landing field at her plane's scheduled arrival time.

Of course, we brought along food and lots of bottled water and games and schoolbooks to keep the children occupied. To our delight, instead of the ten- or twelve-hour wait we were prepared for, Mother Sherrill's plane touched down only four and a half hours later. As the steps were rolled up to the aircraft, we stood at the barrier to watch the passengers deplane.

The door opened and Mother burst onto the gangway; she must have been literally pressing against the door. Our welcome was drowned out in a volley of tearful apologies. It took a good part of the drive back to Uganda to convince her that no, we hadn't been worried; no, the late arrival hadn't spoiled our plans.

And as I tried to reassure Mother, I seemed to hear a silent voice speaking to me too. Living in developing countries had taught John and me that trip schedules were not in our control. But what about my schedule for the spiritual journey? What about the timetable I set up for prayers to be answered? What about my impatience over someone's slowness to see the truth I saw? Like Mother pushing on an airplane door, didn't I often strain at delays as though the timing of spiritual growth—mine and others'—was in my hands?

Lord of the journey, help me to rest in Your perfect time.

— ELIZABETH SHERRILL

TUE
10
Cease from anger, and forsake wrath. . . .
                                                    —*Psalm 37:8*

"CAN I OPEN IT?" my daughter asked. She was holding up a large cardboard box, red with yellow flowers, that she had found in the storage locker we were clearing out. I shook my head. "Oh please, Mom. I want to see what it's like."

In the box, unopened for thirty-seven years, was my wedding dress. My mother had made the dress, far away in the English village where I was born. It was beautiful—white silk trimmed with lace and a long veil. She could sew better than anyone I've ever known. But my mother was not at my wedding to see me walk down the aisle in the dress she had made.

My parents had disapproved of my husband-to-be without even meeting him. He was American, of a different religious denomination and, worst of all, he was of German heritage. My parents had lived through two horrific world wars.

Finally I said, "Okay, sweetheart. Open it if you like."

There it lay, slightly yellowed, but otherwise just as it had been all those years ago. I touched the skirt. The silk was smooth and gentle. As I looked down at my fingers, I realized that even after my husband was accepted and the family happy again, I had never stopped caring, never stopped being hurt and angry that my parents weren't there on the day that changed the rest of my life.

As my daughter held up the dress, saying, "Oh, Mom, it's beautiful!" I looked my hurt and anger in the eye and let it go forever.

Lord, let me remember that forgiveness is a divine gift to the forgiver as well as to the forgiven. —BRIGITTE WEEKS

WED
11
But we all, with open face beholding as in a glass the glory of the Lord, are changed into the same image from glory to glory, even as by the Spirit of the Lord. —*II Corinthians 3:18*

I REACH FOR THE KALEIDOSCOPE on my desk. I put it to my eyes and twist the spiral bottom. "Ah!" I cry out. "What beauty!" I see bits of colored glass dancing before me, assuming various shapes and patterns. They change as I twist again. No pattern remains the same. That is the way with a kaleidoscope, which draws its name from the Greek words *kalos,* which means "beautiful," *eidos,* which stands for "form," and *scopos,* which means "to look at."

I remember how enthusiastic Jane Canfield was after she came out of the hospital. "Your kaleidoscope was enchanting. It doesn't wilt like flowers!" And my nieces—their imaginations were revved up by the fanciful scenes they saw. To this day, I have some of their paintings that the kaleidoscope inspired.

The kaleidoscope I hold in my hands is, like life, forever changing. I recognize that, but I tenaciously hold on to the past even though, I tell myself, the past was formed by change. My kaleidoscope urges me to look at the future as something different, exciting, maybe not dazzling, but by God's guardianship, agreeable.

After all these years, Father, I still look forward in faith. —VAN VARNER

THU
12

EVERYONE WHO HAS THIS HOPE IN HIM PURIFIES HIMSELF, JUST AS HE IS PURE. —*I John 3:3 (NIV)*

DURING MY LAST YEAR at college, I spent days in front of my computer, working on my senior thesis. Outlines turned into drafts, drafts transformed into revisions, revisions into new revisions and, before I knew it, November had turned into April. Somehow in the midst of all that work I found myself slipping away from having time with God. Sure, I still went to Bible study, but I kept thinking of all the other things I needed to do before I could get back in God's good graces: catch up on my Bible reading, update my prayer list, clean my room so I'd be more focused in prayer.

I spoke with a friend from home. "I have to go," she said only a few minutes into the conversation. "The housekeeper is coming tomorrow, and I have to get this place straightened up." I hung up, laughing to myself. *Who would clean house before allowing a housekeeper inside?*

As crazy as that sounds, that is just what I was doing with God. He wants to talk, even if I haven't called in a while or if the pages of my Bible have become a little dusty. All I have to do is take the first step. He'll cover the rest.

Lord, turn my feet toward Your path and help me remember that I don't need a perfect heart to talk to You, only a willing one.
—ASHLEY JOHNSON

FRI
13

GRANDCHILDREN ARE THE CROWN OF THE AGED. . . .
—Proverbs 17:6 (RSV)

EVEN THOUGH I'M RETIRED, I still look forward to Friday evenings as the end of the workweek, a time just to stay home and relax. So when my wife Carol and our daughter Laurel had plans to do something together on a Friday night recently, I was unprepared for what Carol asked.

"Why don't you and Kaila do something special while we're gone?" she suggested. She mentioned the name of a local "family fun" park where my eight-year-old granddaughter once had a birthday party.

"*Mmm*, yeah, maybe," I replied, trying to think of some way to stay in my recliner. But Carol persisted.

That night Kaila and I played miniature golf at the fun park. "Isn't this great, Papa?" she asked after a couple of holes.

"*Mmm*, yeah," I said, trying to work up some enthusiasm. Truth was, my back hurt when I bent down to tee up or retrieve my ball.

"I'll get the ball for you, Papa," Kaila offered when I groaned.

By the tenth hole, where Kaila and I each got a hole-in-one, I was actually beginning to enjoy myself. When the game was over, Kaila began skipping and said, "Let's go play some games."

I bought a handful of tokens and followed her around to various video and arcade games. There she racked up points and received tickets redeemable for prizes. It didn't matter that they were only inexpensive trinkets; she was having a great time.

And when the evening was over, my time had been redeemed too. The smiles on Kaila's face were my prizes.

Father, thank You for our children and grandchildren. May we be as much a blessing to them as they are to us. —HAROLD HOSTETLER

SAT
14

AT OUR GATES ARE ALL MANNER OF PLEASANT FRUITS, NEW AND OLD, WHICH I HAVE LAID UP FOR THEE, O MY BELOVED. —Song of Solomon 7:13

EVERY FAMILY HAS its own way of celebrating special occasions like birthdays, anniversaries and holidays. Some families sing together, others play touch football. At my house, we bake *pastizzi*.

Pastizzi is the traditional pastry of the tiny Mediterranean island of Malta, land of my maternal ancestors. Malta is a tiny country (about one-fifth the size of Rhode Island), but its inhabitants have huge hearts, and much of their love and energy goes into pastizzi. The dish consists of a filling *(hashu)*, made from ricotta cheese, sometimes mixed with peas, baked within a pastry shell to a rich golden-brown. The shell is the key to great pastizzi, and to make it is a labor of love, for it takes hours to roll out the dough into paper-thin sheets and press each one with the fingertips until it reaches the required consistency.

As my wife and I have grown older, preparing the dough has become more tedious, so much so that at one family gathering we decided to skip the pastizzi altogether. This resulted in howls of protest from three generations of pastizzi-lovers, so next time around we tried using store-bought flaky pie crust in place of the traditional finger-pressed dough. The results left us a bit unsettled: The pastizzi was delicious but had an unfamiliar texture.

Everyone liked it, though, so nowadays, while we prefer the old recipe, sometimes we use the newer method. We've come to see it as a way of exploring new territory while remaining faithful to the past. Like our ancestors, who retained their ancient customs when leaving the Old World for America's distant shores, we've discovered that combining the best of the old with the best of the new is sometimes the best way to make a successful journey—and a successful pastizzi.

Help me, Lord, to see what is good in the old and the new.
—PHILIP ZALESKI

SUN
15

FOR, LO, THE WINTER IS PAST, THE RAIN IS OVER AND GONE. —Song of Solomon 2:11

I SPOTTED MY BUS turning the corner a couple of blocks away and I raced to catch it, darting through pedestrians, crossing the street against a flashing DON'T WALK sign, nearly running into a car. I could have gotten hit, I suppose, but all I was thinking was *I have to get that bus!* On Sunday afternoon buses don't come that often. And what would I do if I had to wait fifteen minutes for another one?

Despite my athletic prowess I still missed it. Now there was nothing to do but walk. In a huff I began my hike through the park, taking big strides on the path that wound under the pine trees.

It was early spring, the sky gray but the grass lime green, daffodils pushing up under the trees. A Little League team had gathered in a pine grove to practice. The wobbly tosses and swings proved it was early in the season. A kid raced past me on his bicycle, and a golden retriever scurried after a squirrel. I slowed my step. The smell of the damp earth, the sight of the buds, the sound of the whacked ball gave me a feeling of gladness. Winter was done. Spring was here. And to think, if I hadn't missed my bus, I would have missed it.

God, I love spring! —RICK HAMLIN

READER'S ROOM

MY YOUNGEST SON was 21 and graduated from college on May 7, 2005, and was commissioned in the Air Force on the same day. He had a chance to go into pilot training. On April 3 he came home from college and said he would be stationed in Albuquerque, New Mexico, for three months to a year. That afternoon as I was reading my *Daily Guideposts,* I couldn't believe the Scripture Rick Hamlin used with his devotion.

"Be strong and of good courage; be not frightened, neither be dismayed; for the Lord your God is with you wherever you go" (Joshua 1:9, RSV).

A few days later I had to share the devotional for that day over the phone with a friend, and as I read the last sentence at the bottom of the page, it came to life for me as if I had not read it before. It stated, "God, we give You our children. They have been Yours all along." I had to cry as I read it. —*Ann Johnson, Tifton, Georgia*

MON
16

Commit your way to the Lord; trust in him, and he will act. —Psalm 37:5 (rsv)

SLOWLY, I DROVE DOWN Higgins Avenue past the brick buildings, checking off "places to apply." I'd just moved to Missoula, Montana, from Washington, D.C. Over the last week every business said, "Try back in June, when the college kids leave for the summer." I sighed. My German shepherd Kai nuzzled my ear. I patted him. Although my brother had been gracious enough to let me stay with him, I wanted my own place and I needed an income. I'd done everything possible to find a job.

As businesses gave way to residences, I passed a church and felt my face flush. I'd done everything . . . except ask God for help. *God, I'm sorry. Here I am, taking the reins again. I know that You want me to have a job. Lead me, give me a sign. And, please, make it obvious.*

Kai whined. "Okay, boy, it's time for a walk." I wheeled down an industrial road on the way to Blue Mountain, his favorite place to romp. On my right was a small sign hanging off a dilapidated building, SADDLE SHOP. That little sign almost seemed to glow. I knew I had to stop.

As I opened the door, a cowbell clanked and the smell of leather greeted me. A tall wiry cowboy wearing a battered gray hat smoothed his salt-and-pepper beard. "Hi," he said. "I'm Snuffy. What can I do for you?"

"I'm looking for a job."

"Can you cook?"

Snuffy told me he needed a cook at his ranch. In exchange, I could live in the apartment off his barn, rent-free. Then he gave me a lead to the job I got the next day, training nineteen wild mules.

Lord, remind me to hand You the reins, because You know the way.
—REBECCA ONDOV

GOD-FINDS
FINDING FOREVER

TUE
17

IN MY FATHER'S HOUSE ARE MANY MANSIONS. . . .
—*John 14:2*

MY DEAR FRIEND and co-worker Sylvia Gardner retired from the V.A. Medical Center in Huntington, West Virginia, this past year, and her leaving reminded me of a time when she was my treasured God-find. It was a chilly day in April, the day we buried my mother.

What made the day even more difficult was the fact that my dad was in the hospital and unable to attend Mother's service because of the stroke he had suffered the day Mother died. As we five siblings and five grandchildren huddled around the casket at the gravesite, I imagined Dad in his hospital room grieving all alone. *Why didn't you think to have someone stay with him?* I berated myself. But it was too late to change things.

What I hadn't counted on was Sylvia, a Yankee nurse practitioner who had relocated to the hills of Appalachia in the 1970s and quickly claimed the mountain people as her own. Instead of attending Mother's service, Sylvia had gone to the sixth floor of St. Mary's Hospital. Along with a hospital chaplain she'd met on the elevator, she headed to Dad's room in hopes of conducting a makeshift funeral service. Once there, Sylvia, always a nurse with a hearing heart, gave Dad the greatest gift of all by simply listening. Dad, nearly blind, his speech slurred from his stroke, recited words he had long ago committed to memory for such a time as this:

"Let not your heart be troubled: ye believe in God, believe also in me. In my Father's house are many mansions: if it were not so, I would have told you. I go to prepare a place for you. And if I go and prepare a place for you, I will come again, and receive you unto myself; that where I am, there ye may be also" (John 14:1–3).

Thank You, Lord, for Your promise of life eternal. —ROBERTA MESSNER

WED
18

At Gibeon the Lord appeared to Solomon during the night in a dream, and God said, "Ask for whatever you want me to give you."
—*I Kings 3:5 (NIV)*

RECENTLY, I WAS in the middle of a particularly busy stretch at work—too many tasks, too few hours in the day. As the week dragged on and I got further and further behind on my to-do list, I grew increasingly short with my colleagues. "Nothing," I answered the first time someone asked what was wrong . . . and the second time and the third.

The fourth time I said something. "I think it's obvious I could use some help here, but I don't beg."

My colleague smiled. "Someone once told me that a Christian is a beggar telling another beggar where to find bread. We owe our lives to the generosity of someone else. Now how can I help you?"

There are certain things I know to be true about myself. I'm studious and cautious; conservative; I don't embrace change very easily. And I'm shy; I don't say a lot and certainly don't demand a lot from others.

I never thought that I would change—until that horribly busy week at work. That's when I learned I could be a little less self-reliant and a little more God-reliant, and even ask for help.

Like Solomon, God, I rely on You for all that I am. May I never be too busy or too proud to ask for Your help. —JEFF JAPINGA

THU
19

Underneath are the everlasting arms. . . .
—*Deuteronomy 33:27*

AFTER MY FATHER DIED, when I was very young, I had only one fear—that something might happen to my mother. Most of the time I was able to cope with it, but occasionally something would happen that would set loose my fears.

Many of my mother's clothes came from her sister in New York. They were gently used, but quietly elegant and perfect for her job at the local bank. Whenever a carefully wrapped box arrived from her sister, I adored watching Mother try on the clothes. But one day a package arrived without my knowing about it.

I was in the living room when Mother walked in, modeling some of her new clothes. Mother beamed. "Do you like this cape, Mannie?" she asked.

I gazed in silent horror. I had no idea what a cape was; I had never seen one before. The scary red and gray thing with fringes hung from my mother's shoulders. *Why is she still smiling? Where are her arms and hands?* Tears rolled down my face onto my green overalls.

"What's wrong, Mannie?" Mother asked.

"Where are your arms, Mama?" I wailed.

She knelt down on the floor beside me, and out from under the cape came my mother's wonderful arms—hands and all—as she embraced me in a long, tight hug. Then she threw the cape on the floor and somehow made me laugh.

Later in life, when fear stalked me once again, I discovered another set of faithful arms. All these years later, they continue to comfort me.

Father, the old hymn is true! "Leaning, leaning, safe and secure from all alarms, leaning, leaning, leaning, leaning on the everlasting arms" (Elisha A. Hoffman, 1887). —MARION BOND WEST

FRI

20

THOU SHALT BE CALLED BY A NEW NAME, WHICH THE MOUTH OF THE LORD SHALL NAME. —*Isaiah 62:2*

PTOLEMY. IT'S NOT THE easiest name to go through the world with. Once in my elementary school days, tired of the endless questions, confusions and not-infrequent teasing it brought on, I asked my father if I could change it.

"Why on earth would you want to do that?" he asked, genuinely surprised. He'd given me the name because he'd been reading about an Egyptian philosopher named Ptolemy the night my mother reached over and told him that she was going into labor. To him, that bit of serendipity had sealed the issue once and for all.

"Why don't you wait a bit before changing it," he suggested. "Who knows? Someday you might be glad you're a Ptolemy."

When I came to Guideposts a little over six years ago, I figured the name would burden me as never before. But in fact just the opposite happened. I received all kinds of wonderful letters from people about it. My favorite came just this year, from an *Angels on Earth* reader named

Susan. Spotting my name on the masthead, she was reminded of a mouse that her grade-school class kept as a pet. There had been a contest to name it, and she (like my father, she had been in an Egyptian phase at the time) had won. When summer vacation arrived, Susan took Ptolemy the mouse home with her. "This was the first time I had ever won anything, and the first creature I had ever cared for. I loved that mouse. So thank you, Ptolemy, for helping me remember."

Am I glad I'm a Ptolemy now, as my father predicted I would be? Some days yes, some days no. But I have to admit, there are a lot more yes-days than there used to be.

Lord, help me to remember that You know us all by name, no matter how unusual it may be. —PTOLEMY TOMPKINS

SAT
21

I AM PURPOSED. . . . —*Psalm 17:3*

"HEY, PAM, WHY ISN'T your water heater insulated?"

The question came from Emma, my eleven-year-old neighbor. I was standing inside our garage, stuffing our recycle bin with papers, as she walked by with her dog Foxy.

"Why, Emma, I hadn't noticed that our water heater isn't insulated. I'll tell David to get right on that."

She was right, of course. Our local power board says that the cost of insulating a water heater will be paid back in energy savings in just a few months. Apart from being one smart cookie, Emma is very in tune with environmental issues. If she brings up a particular subject, I can pretty well rely on the information she offers. The problem is, sometimes it's information I just don't want to hear! But I had no idea what an impact this child was making on me until my washer died.

They were having a great sale at the appliance store, where David spotted a washer that would serve us well. It was actually less than we had budgeted for this unexpected expense.

"What's this funny-looking machine over here?" I made the mistake of asking the salesman. This one opened from the front and had a sort of indented glass window.

"Oh, those are the new front-loaders. They come from Europe, where folks have to save on energy."

"How's that?"

"Well, the machine you're buying uses about forty gallons per wash," he answered. "This one uses about nine gallons. Uses less soap, too, and because of the way they spin, they cut the drying time by at least twenty-five percent. Saves on electricity."

Well, Emma wasn't anywhere in sight. She'd never know about the washer. But even though it cost almost twice as much, David and I tightened our belts and bought the energy saver.

Funny how an eleven-year-old with a purpose could wield such influence.

Dear God, help me to work like Emma to make this world a better place.
— PAM KIDD

SUN
22

THINKING HE WAS THE GARDENER, SHE SAID. . . .
—*John 20:15 (NIV)*

SEVERAL MONTHS AFTER my sister Susan's house burned down, we took a short trip to the coast of South Carolina to escape some of the stress. On Saturday afternoon we visited a small town where we were drawn to a little cypress-wood church overlooking a tidal marsh. We roamed the grounds, hoping to find a sign telling when Sunday services were held. But all we saw was a casually dressed man with graying hair pulling weeds in a flowerbed. "He's probably with a lawn company and doesn't know anything about services," I told Susan doubtfully.

Nevertheless, we approached the man, and he told us that there'd be a service featuring a praise band on Sunday morning.

On Sunday, as we settled into a pew, Susan nodded toward the minister sitting up front in spotless white robes. "That's the man who was pulling weeds yesterday afternoon," she whispered.

The bulletin listed a Saturday-evening service, and I realized that the minister must have been on his way to prepare for it when he had taken a moment to tidy up the flower bed.

I smiled, wondering if perhaps the Holy Spirit had caused the minister's eyes to notice those weeds so that he would linger a moment in the churchyard—precisely where we could find him to learn about the service.

The rafters of the church rang as Susan added beautiful harmonies to the praise songs. The service filled both of us with renewed joy. And I left with a new sense of how the humble acts that we sometimes unconsciously pause to do can turn into divine appointments that we could never orchestrate ourselves.

Father, help me to see the small signs of humble service that invite, "Wait here for your next heavenly appointment." —KAREN BARBER

MON
23

BE PREPARED IN SEASON AND OUT OF SEASON. . . .
—II Timothy 4:2 (NIV)

WHEN I WAS IN the Army, part of basic training was instruction in the proper handling and firing of a rifle. The phrase "going off half-cocked" took on new meaning when explained by a firing-range sergeant who had a long preparatory checklist for novice weapons handlers. And that's the phrase that came to mind when I heard the story of the naval officer who sailed off in his ship without full preparation.

It was the first time the officer had been in charge of getting a ship underway, through the harbor and out into the open sea, and he was understandably nervous. With meticulous care, he ran through his checklist before he ordered his crew to weigh anchor and set sail. All went smoothly, and the young lieutenant was feeling very proud of himself until, several miles at sea, he received a message from shore. "Nice job. You accomplished your assignment perfectly, with one exception. You forgot to make sure that I was on board." It was signed, THE CAPTAIN.

Unfortunately, all of us sometimes begin endeavors, major and minor, half-cocked. We forget to make sure our Captain is on board, the One Whose guidance and counsel are available any time, day or night. Not surprisingly, those who start the day with prayer and quiet time for meditation and listening are much better equipped to handle life's setbacks and difficulties—those problems that can be as big as camels or as small as gnats.

Help us remember, God, that with You in charge,
We can scale mountains impossibly large.
—FRED BAUER

TUE
24

A BOOK OF REMEMBRANCE WAS WRITTEN BEFORE HIM FOR THEM THAT FEARED THE LORD, AND THAT THOUGHT UPON HIS NAME. —*Malachi 3:16*

IT'S LATE AT NIGHT, and I finally head to bed. As I get in my pajamas, I see two books on my pillow. Elizabeth's is off-white with a delicate beige pattern. Mary's has a photo of snowy woods in winter. These books show up in my room almost every night. Writing in the books is the last thing—except for praying—that I do each day.

I don't write for long. I abide by only one rule: Everything that goes into the books must be encouraging. The idea is to take time to stop, reflect and find something positive to say to each child about the day. Sometimes that's easy, as in "What a generous heart you had when you shared your treat with Stephen!" Other days I have to scratch around for a while. There are times when "I noticed it took you less time to calm down today when you were upset" is the best I can do.

I'm not a born optimist, so this exercise is as important for me as it is for my kids. I have to teach myself to find the bright side in upsetting incidents, personality flaws and stressful situations. I have to look carefully for what God wants me to see in each day. The challenge is to find it—and pass the insight on to my kids.

When I'm done writing, I slip into the children's room. I listen to their quiet breathing and slip each book halfway under the appropriate pillow. In the morning the girls will awaken and read what I've written. And they'll have a record of how much they are loved, in all situations.

Lord, let me be an encourager today in thought, word and deed.

—JULIA ATTAWAY

WED
25

AM I THEREFORE BECOME YOUR ENEMY, BECAUSE I TELL YOU THE TRUTH? —*Galatians 4:16*

THE HOT DOG VENDOR near my office is a friend of mine. He dispenses kielbasa and unsolicited advice in equal measures. I was walking near his stand recently; ahead of me was a woman with an extremely short haircut.

"Hey," the vendor said, "nice hairstyle."

She shot him a withering look, then picked up her pace.

The vendor looked at me, arms out. "I was serious," he pleaded.

For some reason, I felt compelled to make things right. I caught up with the woman. "Look," I said, "he's a good guy. He meant it as a compliment."

She said nothing for a moment, and I figured I had just compounded the problem.

"It's not a 'style,'" she said. "It's chemotherapy, and it's not 'nice.'"

Now it was my turn to say nothing. A thousand thoughts went through my head, and I'm embarrassed to say that the first one was *How did I get myself into this?* But it wasn't about me. I decided to speak the truth, because this woman had no doubt exhausted her patience with lies—little ones, big ones, the whole lie family.

"I think it looks nice too," I said. "Seriously. I can't explain why—it just does."

More silence. We were used to silence by now.

"Thanks," she said finally. "I don't see how it's possible, but thanks." And we parted without another word.

I won't—I can't—pretend to know what that woman had gone through, is going through. She assumed that the loss of her once-longer locks was symptomatic of a more massive loss. But you can't fool hot dog vendors. They know the real you. A thousand people a day parade past, but they know the truth about you: *My goodness, you're good-looking. My goodness, you've got style.*

Lord, thank You that even our suffering can't completely destroy the beauty You've given us. —MARK COLLINS

THU
26

HIS COMPASSIONS FAIL NOT. THEY ARE NEW EVERY MORNING. . . . —*Lamentations 3:22–23*

MY AUNT, AT one hundred years old, doesn't string her present moments together as she used to. She says her memory's getting "thin." That's hard for her to accept when her reasoning still works fine.

Each experience is a first-of-its-kind for Aunt Betty, a "fresh first." Whether it's a tree she's seen dozens of times, a neighbor she's greeted often or a gift she was given weeks ago, she extends her full delight as if it's entirely new. Watching her is like riding a Ferris wheel and rediscovering the same exhilarating sights every time it goes around.

One of my favorite "fresh firsts" is the pie that her daughter Margy gives her. Every morning Aunt Betty is surprised to find pie on her kitchen counter. "Where'd this come from?" she asks. When she learns it's from Margy, she gets another surprise. "How dear of her," she responds.

Why do I allow my daily life to become dull with familiarity? Why can't I catch a ride on the Ferris wheel and see the same things with new enthusiasm? How long since I've felt stirred by God's gifts of sight and sound and movement, of sun and rain and sky, of friends and faith and purpose?

Aunt Betty's wheel of "fresh firsts" is a sweet spin of gratitude and joy, eagerness and surprise. It's the best ride going, whether you're one or one hundred.

Creator God, lead me in circles of recurring wonder for things that seem commonplace. —CAROL KNAPP

FRI
27

AND YET SHOW I UNTO YOU A MORE EXCELLENT WAY.
—*I Corinthians 12:31*

CHANGE CAN BE FRIGHTENING. Years ago I was laid off from my job as a first-class machine operator. This wasn't just a temporary layoff, it was permanent. Getting a new job would mean relocating to another city or taking work on the evening shift.

I was about to accept the evening shift when my wife Ruby said, "You're thirty-nine years old, Oscar. Don't you feel it's time you used your college education? The night job is okay, but it's a dead end. Do you want to work nights for the rest of your life? Don't you want to grow? Pray about it."

Her words startled me because moving up would mean having to take an exam. *What if I fail? How will I study?* I hadn't been in the classroom for sixteen years. I prayed, took the exam . . . and was offered a new job as a mechanical tester in engineering.

At the interview, though, the supervisor said, "You have no experience. You'll have to start as a trainee." *A trainee?* That would mean an initial fifty percent reduction in pay! *How will we manage? Have I made the right decision? What if things don't work out all right?*

"Trust God," Ruby insisted.

As it turned out, I loved my new job. Within months I was given a raise, then along came a project with unlimited overtime. Soon I was making as much as I had before, and over the years that new pathway led me to technical writing, then management. I will always thank Ruby for her suggestions. All I needed to do was take a risk and work hard. The rest was in God's hands.

Lord, You pointed the way. Then You stepped away and waited for me to follow. —OSCAR GREENE

SAT
28

"BE GLAD AND REJOICE FOREVER IN WHAT I CREATE. . . ." —Isaiah 65:18 (NAS)

EARLY ONE SPRING MORNING, the sun not even up yet, I was heading back to one of my favorite places in the world: the Caney Fork River. About an hour from my house in Nashville, it's one of the best places for trout fly-fishing in our state. The week at work, with talk of war, budget deficits, low consumer confidence and their effects on the economy, had worn me down. *At least I'm headed to a place where life is more predictable,* I told myself. *At least I'll have more control over my destiny.*

I pulled up to my favorite stretch of the river, slipped on my chest waders and assembled my four-piece fly rod. "Here I come, fish," I said. "You're in trouble now." I knew exactly where to go and where to stand. My feet crunched across the beach, the pebbles sinking into the sand. The fog over the river made it hard to see very far, but I wasn't worried. I knew everything about this bend in the river.

Full of anticipation, I began wading upstream to my favorite hole. The sun's rays were stretching out above me. Just a couple more strides and I'd be in the perfect position to strike some rainbows and browns.

All of a sudden, the ground gave way and I began to sink. Water poured into my waders. The cold stunned me. It took me a second to realize that I had stepped in the hole that I supposedly knew so well.

Back on the bank, I dumped gallons of water out of my waders and began to see the humor in it all. With chattering teeth, I laughed out loud. Nothing, not even the Caney—especially not the Caney—is predictable. After all, what would life be without a few surprises?

Father, I rejoice in Your creation. It might not be predictable, but it's mighty good. —BROCK KIDD

SUN
29

"Haven't you read," he replied, "that at the beginning the Creator 'made them male and female,' and said, 'For this reason a man will leave his father and mother and be united to his wife, and the two will become one flesh'? So they are no longer two, but one. . . ."
—*Matthew 19:4–6 (NIV)*

THERE ARE NO TWO WAYS about it: My husband Wayne and I are about as different as any two people can be. He's introspective and quiet; I thrive on being around people. When we met, it was just he and his mother, whereas I came from a large extended family with lots of cousins. He's a night owl, and I'm a morning person.

For the last thirty-seven years, for the most part, we've managed to love and accept each other's strengths and weaknesses. There are times, however, when I can't help being frustrated with him.

Last week, I wanted to go to a movie, but he didn't. We stayed home. I wanted to invite friends over for dinner; the two of us ended up watching television. An exhibit on 9/11 had come to Tacoma: I wanted to go; Wayne didn't. Frustrated, I went without him, grumbling the entire way.

I wasn't quite done being upset when I was dressing for church the following morning. After the singing—I sang, Wayne didn't—the pastor began his sermon.

I don't remember the topic; in fact, I don't think I can even tell you on which Bible passage he was preaching. But at one point he said, "The grass isn't greener on the other side of the fence. It's greener where it's watered."

Wayne looked at me and I looked at him. He smiled and so did I. I offered my husband my hand, and we scooted just a bit closer to each other. We'd both heard something we needed to hear.

Lord, thank You for my husband, for his quiet strength and his love.
—DEBBIE MACOMBER

MON
30

Yea, the sparrow hath found an house, and the swallow a nest for herself, where she may lay her young. . . . —*Psalm 84:3*

I'VE BEEN SITTING front row center for a miracle this month—a robin built a nest in my second-story office window. There, two Wedgwood-blue eggs nestled safe from the rain. The mother sat on them for days, her tail feathers pushed up against my screen. She got used to the *tat-a-tat* of my keyboard, the *brring-ring-ring* of my phone.

When the babies hatched, they were the size of my thumbnail, with pinkish skin, tiny wisps of white down and huge eyes. Almost at once the mother began to feed them, flying down into the front yard and procuring a range of delicacies: worms and bugs and silky-winged insects.

Now, after a few short weeks, the birds are dark and fully-feathered. Their chests are the pale red of diluted cranberry juice. They flutter their wings and stretch their legs. I become concerned that they might not fly. What if they fail and crash onto my concrete porch below?

I came into my office yesterday and the nest was empty. (Yes, I did check the front porch.) Looking out from my desk, I saw one tiny bird still perched on the window ledge. I needed to open the window, but I was afraid I'd frighten the little thing, throwing off its first attempt to fly. Cautiously, I opened the window a crack. The bird looked at me with a familiar eye. Then I lifted the window to its full height. With a single screech, the reluctant robin threw itself off the ledge and soared to the top of a pine tree fifty yards away.

You care for all Your creatures, Lord. Sustain me with Your love and truth. And nudge me when I linger too long on the window ledges of life!
—Mary Lou Carney

MY WALK WITH GOD

I _____

2 _____

3 _____

4 _____

5 _____

6 _____

7 _____
8 _____
9 _____
10 _____
11 _____
12 _____
13 _____
14 _____
15 _____
16 _____
17 _____
18 _____
19 _____
20 _____
21 _____
22 _____
23 _____
24 _____
25 _____
26 _____
27 _____
28 _____
29 _____
30 _____

May

If any man thirst, let him come unto me, and drink. —*John 7:37*

LESSONS FROM THE JOURNEY
USE DELAYS

TUE

I

I DELIGHT TO DO THY WILL, O MY GOD. . . .
—*Psalm 40:8*

LAST MONTH I WROTE about traveling in Africa, how the frequent delays there were teaching me to relax in God's timing. But there are delays on any trip and they're teaching me something else: God may allow delays because there's something He wants us to do with the "wasted" time.

I hate the long wait to get through airport security. My friend Sandra says she handles waiting by finding something to do, like praying for those waiting with her. I've been trying this too. I inch forward, shove my suitcase ahead of me and ask God to bless that kid with the heavy backpack. I find I can maintain this altruistic attitude about fifteen minutes, before those I'm interceding for become again simply the people ahead of me in line.

But for those fifteen minutes waiting has another dimension, and I've begun to look for ways to make all airport delays useful. Once when a flight was delayed, I entertained a wiggly two-year-old while his tired mother went for a cup of coffee. Another time I scribbled down loudspeaker messages for a deaf lady. Recently I listened for half an hour to a man who was on his way to his wife's side in a hospital; he thanked me for my excellent advice, when I hadn't spoken more than five words.

Whenever I remember to listen for God's assignment, I come away from the experience certain that in His economy there are no unusable minutes. The plus in delays—anywhere, at home or away—is that they wrench us from our schedule, that road we were barreling down with tunnel vision. When our agenda is put on hold, we just may get a glimpse of His.

Lord of the journey, help me to know that there are no delays in Your schedule, only plans You didn't tell me about in advance.

—ELIZABETH SHERRILL

EDITOR'S NOTE: Please take a few moments to look back at what you've written so far in the journal pages "My Walk with God," and let us know what your spiritual journey has been like this year. Send your letter to *Daily Guideposts* Reader's Room, Guideposts Books, 16 East 34th Street, New York, New York 10016. We'll share some of what you tell us in a future edition of *Daily Guideposts*.

—❦—

WED
2

"THE LORD YOUR GOD WILL BE WITH YOU WHEREVER YOU GO." —Joshua 1:9 (NIV)

DURING MY JUNIOR YEAR of college, my parents called to tell me that they'd found a new house for us and during summer break we'd be moving. At first I was excited, but as we continued to discuss the move I started to worry. Would I have enough space in my new bedroom? How much storage room was there? What was the new neighborhood like?

After hanging up, I sat down at the kitchen table and stared at the walls of my small apartment. My worries began to snowball. *Where will I live next year at college? Can I get an apartment near friends? Will it be like the place I have now? And what about after graduation? What kind of job will I get and where will I live? I could end up halfway across the country!*

I became so worried about moving that I began a mental checklist of my possessions, trying to decide what I needed to keep and what I could do without. This absurdity went on for days until one morning when I read the story of Joseph in the book of Genesis. When he's sold into slavery, a certain phrase is used. It pops up again when Joseph is falsely accused of a crime and sent to prison: "The Lord was with him."

Those words reminded me that no matter where I ended up geographically in the coming months and years, I could rest assured that God would be there too. The only thing I'd have to worry about is meeting the new neighbors.

Lord, I'm so grateful that there isn't a place on earth I can go without You.
—JOSHUA SUNDQUIST

THU
3

FOR THE MOUNTAINS SHALL DEPART, AND THE HILLS BE REMOVED; BUT MY KINDNESS SHALL NOT DEPART FROM THEE. . . . —Isaiah 54:10

ON MAY 3, 2003, the Old Man of the Mountain, New Hampshire's beloved landmark, tumbled from Cannon Mountain into the valley below. The five ledges of granite that had formed the distinctive profile viewed by millions of tourists now lay in a broken heap of rubble. Natural weathering, especially cycles of freezing and melting in the small fissures in the stone, had taken its toll. Even cables screwed into the stone decades earlier and routinely tightened by turnbuckles could not hold the face together any longer. The entire state mourned the loss.

Only my family and I mourned when my dad's equally precious but less well-known stone walls were bulldozed by the people who bought the house where he and Mom lived for thirty-five years. He had painstakingly crafted the retaining wall from flat rocks, often lugging stones home from work in the hopes they would fill an oddly shaped chink. Dad died before his walls and the Old Man met their ends.

Sometimes I wonder what Dad would think of these changes that leave us feeling bereft. I think that he'd shrug, shake his head, call it "a doggone shame," then go build a wall somewhere else. Dad knew that security doesn't come from stones.

Lord, You are, indeed, my rock and my salvation.
—GAIL THORELL SCHILLING

FRI
4

"GO AND LOOK TOWARD THE SEA," HE TOLD HIS SERVANT. AND HE WENT UP AND LOOKED. "THERE IS NOTHING THERE," HE SAID. SEVEN TIMES ELIJAH SAID, "GO BACK." THE SEVENTH TIME THE SERVANT REPORTED, "A CLOUD AS SMALL AS A MAN'S HAND IS RISING FROM THE SEA." —I Kings 18:43–44 (NIV)

"MY SISTER'S COMING HOME next week!" The excitement in my cousin LaJuana's voice kicks her east Texas twang into high gear.

My daughter Lanea, LaJuana and I pray by phone together just about every night. We begin by sharing what the Lord has done for each of us that day, things for which we're grateful. It might be an unexpected blessing or an answer to prayer.

"We talked about the Lord. And you won't believe it, but she's been encouraging people and telling them that they have to have faith!"

Some of the things we pray for are easy to believe, but of all the prayers we have prayed, the one for LaJuana's sister has been about the most difficult. The fifty-something grandmother had no desire for any kind of spiritual connection; she was serving time in jail for drug abuse and theft, and there was a history of family strife between the sisters. I prayed year after year for her, with no answer, no obvious sign, no miracles in sight. I prayed without much hope. I think I was afraid to hope.

"We talked and laughed for hours and hours!" I can hear the smile in LaJuana's voice.

I'm speechless, something that never happens when I talk to my cousin. As I listen, I'm overjoyed. There's new hope rising in me, and I begin mentally to scan my list of "lost cause" prayers, eager for signs of God's faithful answers.

God, even when the answer seems to be impossible or a long way off, give me the courage to keep praying. —SHARON FOSTER

SAT
5

FOR GOD IS NOT UNRIGHTEOUS TO FORGET YOUR WORK AND LABOUR OF LOVE. . . . —*Hebrews 6:10*

MY NEPHEW GORDY had a surprise for me. He has been retired for a couple of years but retired only from a business career. He spends his time in his workshop or he's off to volunteer at Habitat for Humanity. "You should have been a carpenter," I said.

"But I am," Gordy replied as he led me down to the basement and directed me to a small table he had made. "It's yours," he said.

The table was wonderfully fashioned in natural wood so that the veins were exposed. The top and the four tapering legs were smoothly polished. "It's handsome," I said.

"Look farther."

I bent down for a closer look. Here and there on the table's surface I could see odd streaks of green. I was impressed by their quality, almost phantomlike in the patina, yet they were clearly meant to be there as though their color were part of the plan.

"I got it from a bit of lumber I bought when they tore down the stables at Faraway Farm."

I knew immediately what he was telling me. The stables had been the home, from birth to death, of War Admiral. Many of you know my love for that great racehorse. Gordy certainly did. He made this table, making sure that the green paint remained, an essential part of it. I stood there speechless. Such a gift—the perfect gift—one that I didn't know I wanted but would never part with, one that was for me and nobody else, one that through his thought and labor showed the depth of his love in an unusual display of affection. It was heaven-sent.

I am blessed, Father, by having such a loving nephew. —VAN VARNER

SUN

6

IN HOPE OF ETERNAL LIFE WHICH GOD, WHO NEVER LIES, PROMISED AGES AGO. —*Titus 1:2 (RSV)*

MY DAUGHTER MARIA AND I were watching the dogs play at the park. We used to bring our bichon frise Cookie here to watch her play with all the other dogs, but that seemed long ago. At twelve, Cookie is long past rambling in the park. Her sight almost gone, she can barely amble from her bed to our backyard, her legs stiff and tired. Watching the dogs scamper around, I wondered how the time had gone so fast since Cookie's playful puppy days. I wasn't as quick and limber as I had been twelve years ago, either, nor was I so carefree. Age seemed to bring with it more worries, more concerns.

Just then a little white puppy ran past, snapping me out of my reverie. She dashed right up to a small brown dog, then took off at full speed, pink tongue flapping, little legs running all-out with the joy of being a puppy at the park on a warm, sunny spring day. Suddenly I saw a flash of Cookie's sweet old face. Tears sprang to my eyes, but then another thought came just as quickly. *That's what Cookie will be like in dog heaven.* Her old legs fast and young, she'll be able to see and run after a ball as in the old days.

In that moment I understood God's great promise. One day—a never-ending sunny spring day—we'll all be young pups again, pain gone, fear forgotten. The infirmities burdening this life will disappear. We'll be perfect, yet best of all we'll spend eternity with the Perfect One.

Lord Jesus, spending the day with You is the very definition of heaven. Thank You for Your promise of eternity. —GINA BRIDGEMAN

A WORRIED MAN

LIKE SO MANY OF US, Edward Grinnan often finds it hard to shake off the worries and stresses of the workaday world. Over the next five days, he'll show you how facing our worries can lead us to a deeper trust in God.
—THE EDITORS

DAY ONE: WHY WORRY?

MON
7

IN THEE, O LORD, DO I PUT MY TRUST; LET ME NEVER BE ASHAMED. . . . —Psalm 31:1

I WAS DRESSING in the locker room at the gym one Monday morning, half taking in the usual banter but mostly focusing anxiously on the week ahead. Next to me, an older gentleman stretched his arms to the ceiling and announced to no one in particular, "If I knew life was going to turn out this good, I never would have worried so much!"

I hate to admit it, but I'm a worrier. And Monday morning is the time of the week when the worry engine gets revved up. Certainly some of the things I worry about are reasonable—how to get everything done that I need to get done, for instance. But my worry has a way of becoming the animating force of my day, even my whole week.

Back to that gentleman. I happened to know that his life was not without difficulty. He'd had some serious business setbacks, his wife had had a health scare not so long ago, and his kids sometimes gave him fits. But here he was, sending out this message at just the moment I needed to hear it: All that worrying had been for nothing.

Worry consumes a tremendous amount of energy that could be put to use in more positive ways. I have a friend who says worry is an absence of faith. That's a little tough. I think it's more like a gap in my faith, a moment when I refuse to trust in God alone. In the coming week I'm determined to fill, or at least lessen, some of those gaps.

Lord, this week help me to rely more on You and less on myself.
—EDWARD GRINNAN

DAY TWO: A WORRIED MOM

TUE
8

I WILL BE GLAD AND REJOICE IN YOUR LOVE, FOR YOU SAW MY AFFLICTION AND KNEW THE ANGUISH OF MY SOUL. —Psalm 31:7 (NIV)

MY MOM WAS A world-class worrier. All moms worry; that's their job. But no one worried more fervently than Estelle Rossister Grinnan. If I was late coming home, she didn't just worry about where I was or what might have delayed me; she was already fretting over funeral arrangements. "I didn't know if we should bury you back in Philadelphia, where the family plot is, or out here in Detroit, where you grew up."

"Mom!"

"The Lord only knows where you've been."

"Mom, that's crazy."

"What, I'm not allowed to worry about you?"

As I got older and developed a more mature appreciation for the strength of my mother's faith, it puzzled me that a woman who believed so deeply could still worry so much. Didn't her faith protect her from such anguish? One day I asked her.

"Oh no," she said. "I believe God worries, too, about us, even with us. Jesus worried. He wept. When I worry, I feel closer to Him, like we're working on the problem together. And you know, I can't worry without praying. It's the same thing sometimes. If I couldn't worry, I'd go crazy! How can you love and not worry?"

Mom handled her worry by making it a spiritual exercise, a way to grow closer to the God she knew protected her. Worry was not just a form of prayer but a form of love.

Dear God, if I can't be spared from a worry or two, especially for the people I love, please let my worries draw me closer to You.
—EDWARD GRINNAN

DAY THREE: CORRECTING THE FOCUS

WED

9

CAST ALL YOUR ANXIETY ON HIM BECAUSE HE CARES FOR YOU. —*I Peter 5:7 (NIV)*

WE SAT AT A TABLE by the window of a busy coffee shop, an old New York City coffee shop where the coffee is weak and scalding hot and comes with as many refills as you can stomach. I'd been meeting my wise old friend at this place for years, and today I told him that I'd been thinking a lot about the problem of worry.

"Worry is usually a very self-centered activity," he said, buttering his English muffin.

"No," I argued, "I worry about more than just myself. I worry about friends and family, my co-workers, about my dog, about the economy, world peace, the melting ice caps—"

He interrupted. "Those are the *subjects* of worry. Worry itself relates very much to what we're feeling. It's a kind of negative focus on self. Think about it," he said. "When you worry, you become fixated on your own anxiety. Worry blocks the positive thoughts you could be having about all these things. And it blocks out God, Who's really in control of all the stuff you think you're in control of. Worry is mostly self-centered fear."

Self-centered fear. I stared out the window, watching the people being swept along the avenue to work and school and who knows what. If anything, I'd always thought of worry as being at least partly noble, a concern for others. But maybe my friend was right. Maybe it's more about control and self-centeredness. And maybe that's why worry makes me so uncomfortable.

"We all do it," he chuckled. "At least you're asking the right questions. And here's something you don't need to worry about." He snatched the check from the waiter's hand. "I've got it."

Dear God, help me turn all my worry over to You, and make sure that I hand over the controls too. —EDWARD GRINNAN

DAY FOUR: A WORRIED DOG

THU
10

WHEN ANXIETY WAS GREAT WITHIN ME, YOUR CONSOLATION BROUGHT JOY TO MY SOUL.
—*Psalm 94:19 (NIV)*

ONE THING THAT BREAKS my heart is to see Sally, my fifteen-year-old cocker spaniel, worry. I've begged God to tell me what goes through her head when she paces or whines or simply taps me on my leg with her paw and gives me a plaintive look that isn't about food.

Sometimes I can figure it out. When Marty, the dog we lost a few years back, was staying overnight at the vet's, I knew Sally's whimpering was her worry about him. When he was young and used to swim way off into the lake in pursuit of something Daddy had thrown much too far, she would pace up and down, squinting out over the water and yelping, and occasionally giving me a dirty look for being so reckless. And when my wife Julee leaves town on a concert tour, Sally will spend the first several nights sleeping pressed up against the front door.

The worst, though, is when she worries about me. If I'm late coming home, she'll go to Julee and nudge her, as if to say, "Where is he? Do something!" A treat helps distract her, but soon she's pacing and crying a little. Finally she'll get up on her hind legs and stand vigil at the window, sore hips and all, watching for my car in the driveway.

One time I was pulled over on the Taconic Parkway for speeding. I promised to slow down and explained to the trooper that I was driving a little too fast because I didn't want my cocker spaniel to worry about me. I admit that it's a pretty poor excuse for breaking the law, but it was the only time I ever got out of a speeding ticket.

Lord, I don't always know what my dog is thinking, but You do. Please comfort her and let her know that I'm on my way. —EDWARD GRINNAN

DAY FIVE: THE PERFECT ANTIDOTE

FRI
11

NEVER FLAG IN ZEAL, BE AGLOW WITH THE SPIRIT, SERVE THE LORD. —Romans 12:11 (RSV)

IT'S FRIDAY, AND I'M at a work luncheon. Over dessert someone asks, "What keeps you up at night?"

We go around the table. One editor says that he tosses and turns over newsstand sales and circulation. Another is concerned about staff cutbacks. The woman next to me says, "I worry that we aren't connecting with younger readers."

My turn comes and I try to joke that as the editor of a magazine like *Guideposts*, nothing should keep me awake at night. I get a few chuckles, then admit that I have many of the same problems my colleagues have.

Then a young editor speaks up. "Maybe I haven't been in this business long enough," she says, "but what keeps me awake at night is the good stuff—that great idea I had while I was brushing my teeth or something I heard on the evening news that would make a good article. I can hardly keep my eyes closed I'm so wound up. It's like I worry about the good stuff."

She smiles at the rest of us almost sheepishly, and I want to tell her that she should never be embarrassed by enthusiasm. Enthusiasm is one of the greatest blessings we can receive—and, I'm beginning to think, the perfect antidote to worry.

Walking back to my office, I think about the rest of the day: not what I should be worried about, but what I should be excited about. Yes, there are worries, but every worry is a new and exciting opportunity to trust in a power greater than ourselves to see us through.

Father, I ask a lot of You. Here's one more thing: Help me to worry about the good stuff. —EDWARD GRINNAN

SAT

12

"FLOWERS APPEAR ON THE EARTH. . . ."
—*Song of Solomon 2:12 (NIV)*

FLOWERS DON'T JUST APPEAR on the desert earth where I live. If the earth receives enough winter snow, and if March stays cool and overcast, and if we get some rain in April, then flowers will appear. But when all the "ifs" aren't in place, stubborn flowers like the sego lily and the many hues of desert paintbrush still grace the baked earth for a few colorful weeks.

Not even sagebrush can grow on the south-facing hillsides that steam and dry in the winter sun while shaded valleys still hide under several feet of snow. These eroded slopes remain barren for eleven months, from June to May, and then no matter how dry and hot the weather, a lone white primrose appears. The next day it looks as though a crazed florist has flung baskets of white, yellow and pink primroses across the rocky earth.

I always call the first primrose I see the "Dargie primrose." Dargie lived in one of the poorest homes in the neighborhood of poor homes where I grew up. Both her father and mother were alcoholics. One of the surest signs of spring that I remember is Dargie emerging from her house on a Saturday morning with a plate full of cookies, coaxing even the roughest young bullies on the block into her backyard to listen to some Bible stories. I shyly watched boys who had beaten me up the previous week listen to a young woman explain that God loved each one of them. I watched the belief in their hardened eyes, a belief born from the kindness of the messenger. I don't know how many unloved young boys bloomed under her care or for how long they continued to bloom. I do know that for at least a single spring morning, beauty reigned in a barren place.

Dear God, help me to be a "Dargie primrose" today. —TIM WILLIAMS

SUN

13

DO NOT FORSAKE YOUR MOTHER'S TEACHING.
—*Proverbs 6:20 (NIV)*

IT SEEMS TO ME more and more, as I shuffle toward half-time in my life, that pretty much all the tools and wisdom and food I needed to try to be a man were given to me, and still are, by my mother. She is eighty-four now and getting fragile and papery, but she's still smarter than I am, and getting pithier too. Recently, when I was swimming in the ocean of distress, I called her up and said, "Mum, what shall I do?"

Her answer was a prayer, a signpost, a handful of holiness. "Be tender," she said.

"Is that it?" I asked. "Is that all?"

"What else is there?" she said.

I hate to admit when she's right, because when I admit it to her she grins that wry grin, but she's right, and I told her so recently when we were walking slowly through the woods.

The woods were all wet and shining, and my children were running ahead. My mother doesn't walk so well these years, and there came a point where she teetered and she took my hand, and we walked that way for a while through the smiling wet woods, and I realized that I hadn't walked hand in hand with my mother for forty years, since she was walking me to school and church and across roads filled with growling huge things that could flatten me. Her hand was so pale you could almost see through it, and we walked slowly because her wheels don't move as they used to, but both of us were so happy we were humming.

I keep thinking that while I'm still crossing roads where growling things are gunning for me, I have the most powerful potent prayers on my side: my mother's love, grinning its wry grin, and her wise, wild words, "Be tender."

Dear Lord, thanks for mamas and prayers and rain and tenderness and telephones in which you can hear your mum's voice grinning from very far away, but not far at all. —BRIAN DOYLE

MON
14

ACCORDING TO THE KINDNESS THAT I HAVE DONE UNTO THEE, THOU SHALT DO UNTO ME. . . .
—*Genesis 21:23*

WHEN I GOT THE LETTER from the "no-account loser," I hardly knew what to think. At least that's what he called himself, "a no-account loser living in a patched-up trailer." He was writing me to ask how he might improve his life.

In the midst of what my husband David was fondly calling "Pam's kindness kick," I knew I couldn't simply ignore the letter and lay it aside. Kindness demanded a response. First, I took some time to ask God to help me with my reply, and then I sat down and began to write: "Dear Robert, in your letter you write, 'There must be some way I can be a more worthwhile person.' I've been thinking about that and finally I realize there is only one answer: You already are."

I encouraged him to talk to God about the person he would like to become. I reminded him that God delights in his efforts and can't wait to see what he might do next.

One letter followed another, and soon Robert was sharing his life story with me, offering me a window into worlds I hadn't imagined. He sent thoughtful scientific and philosophical articles for David and me to read. We began exchanging favorite books. And the nature of our correspondence was beginning to change. In the beginning I was Robert's cheerleader. Now he was cheering me on too. When I felt blue, Robert was the first to point me to the bright side, and when David and I traveled to Africa, it was good to know that Robert was praying for us twice a day.

In the beginning I reached out to Robert out of a commitment to being kind. In the end I gained a friend.

Father, thanks so much for being You . . . and for returning what I offer others tenfold back to me. —PAM KIDD

READER'S ROOM

OUR CAT RUBY was partial to people food. One evening, when supper was ready, I called Charlie, who was busy in the basement, and told him it was time to eat. He said he would be up in about five minutes. I decided to start putting the food on the table. I thought it would be all right to start feeding Ruby, so I put the food on her plate, but Ruby just sat there looking at the food and not touching it. Charlie finally came and we sat down at the table. Charlie said the prayer and when he said "Amen," Ruby began to eat her food. She was hungry and really seemed to like what we were serving. Charlie and I looked at each other in surprise. Could it be possible that our Ruby had been waiting for us to pray?
—*Elizabeth Rolph, Monticello, Wisconsin*

GOD-FINDS
FINDING DAD

TUE
15

AND HE SHALL TURN THE HEART OF THE FATHERS TO THE CHILDREN, AND THE HEART OF THE CHILDREN TO THEIR FATHERS. . . . —Malachi 4:6

IT WAS THE THIRD ANNIVERSARY of my father's death, and by the accounts of the grief experts I should have been over it and getting on with my life. Instead, I found myself rehashing snippets of the final two and a half years of Dad's life, the sharp decline he'd taken physically and mentally after my mother passed away. Gone was Dad's quick wit, his ability to spin a hilarious tale, the way he challenged the contestants on *Jeopardy!*

I also yearned for one of Dad's hugs. For try as I might, I couldn't recall a time in those last years when I knew for certain that he loved me. *Dementia stole Daddy from me, God.*

I dined alone that night at a restaurant and lamented the secret place in my heart that only a father's love could fill. Just then, I spotted a man and his little girl sitting shoulder-to-shoulder in a red vinyl booth, coloring a picture on a placemat. The girl, maybe three, reached for one of her daddy's French fries. The man tugged on the girl's blonde pigtails. *I used to have pigtails like that, God. Happy, bouncing ones with pretty grosgrain ribbons. Back when I was Daddy's girl.*

Suddenly a warmth started at the top of my head and traveled to the tips of my toes—the warmth of a father's love. *Dementia, you're the great deceiver. My daddy never stopped loving me.*

Thanks to a daddy and his little girl, my God-finds for today, I found my father again.

Daddy's living with You now, Lord. Would You please tell him how much I love him? —ROBERTA MESSNER

WED
16

"LET THE CHILDREN ALONE, AND DO NOT HINDER THEM FROM COMING TO ME; FOR THE KINGDOM OF HEAVEN BELONGS TO SUCH AS THESE."
—*Matthew 19:14 (NAS)*

TODAY HAS BEEN FILLED with committee meetings and counseling. Late this afternoon, as I walked down a hall toward our midweek church family dinner, I felt emotionally drained, fatigued from listening to complex stories of grief, disappointment, failure, sickness and loss.

Lost in thought, I suddenly glimpsed a six-year-old girl around the corner in front of me. Seeing me, she stopped, broke into a wide smile and ran toward me. "Dr. Walker!" she squealed and jumped into my arms, giving me the tightest hug her little arms could muster.

As I looked over her tiny shoulder, I saw her mother and little brother following behind her, also with smiles on their faces. Her mother looked at me and said, "I think somebody loves you, Scott," and I felt my eyes brim with tears. This little girl had put joy back into my life.

Sometimes the most precious gift I can give to another isn't wisdom or answers to problems; it's a genuine smile, a gleam in the eye that says, "I love you. I care for you."

Dear God, unfreeze my smile, release my muted laughter and place words of affirmation upon my lips so that I may share the joy of the kingdom of heaven with others. Amen. —SCOTT WALKER

THU

HE RETURNED TO HEAVEN AFTER GIVING HIS CHOSEN APOSTLES FURTHER INSTRUCTIONS FROM THE HOLY SPIRIT. —*Acts 1:2 (TLB)*

THE SHERIFF'S REPORT is my favorite part of the county newspaper. Although serious crimes occur in our rural area, most arrests are for minor offenses. The bulk of the report details deer vs. motorist accidents, stubble-field fires, transports to the hospital and funeral escorts. Occasionally there are items such as this one: "Officer responded to a report of an erratic go-cart driver near the Plains Grade School. Subject located and given a do-better talk."

I thought of the "do-better talk" when I saw Ascension Day listed in our church calendar. Isn't that what Jesus did for His disciples during the forty days between His Resurrection and His ascension into heaven? Give them "do-better talks"? He could have chastised them for deserting and denying Him, or for failing to believe He had risen from the dead. Instead, He asked Mary, "Why are you crying?" He explained the Scriptures to travelers on the road to Emmaus. He allowed Thomas to feel the nail prints in His hands, the spear wound in His side. He even prepared a seaside breakfast for the apostles and gave Peter both forgiveness and a special mandate: "Feed my sheep."

Do better, Jesus said to them. And through the power of the Holy Spirit, they spread the Gospel throughout their world, telling everyone they met about the Christ. *Do better,* He says to you and to me. By the awesome power of the Holy Spirit, we can be powerful witnesses to His Resurrection, ascension and presence in our lives today.

Risen Lord, thank You for always giving us the opportunity to "do better" for You. —PENNEY SCHWAB

FRI
18

I AM THE ROSE OF SHARON, AND THE LILY OF THE VALLEYS. —*Song of Solomon 2:1*

MAGGIE APPEARED in the doorway, ready for a trip to the park. She was dressed in the height of four-year-old fashion: fancy velvet dress over an old striped turtleneck, flowered tights and black boots. "Look, Mom," she said, gesturing toward the sparkly red headband in her blond curls. Tucked beneath it was a toothpick. "I'm a rose. This," she said, pointing, "is my thorn."

I laughed, shook my head and herded my creative one out the door. I know plenty of little girls who layer plaids over stripes. (My sister had a button for her daughter that said, "I dressed myself today!") I know other girls who remove one glittery ballerina outfit only to don another. At some point each of my children has pretended to be a tree or a plant or a flower. But Maggie's imagination is something else entirely. It amazes me that she dressed up in splendor and then stopped and went in search of a toothpick so she could *truly* be a rose. Who else would think of it?

At this point in my musing I stopped short, amazed by a different thought. It wasn't Maggie whose idea was unusual, but mine! Foolish creature that I am, I'd somehow gotten stuck on the idea that the essence of a rose is its flower. But when God created the rose, He made the whole plant. The thorns weren't an unfortunate afterthought, something to be ignored. To truly be a rose requires looking at roses from God's perspective. Or Maggie's.

Father, teach me to see things Your way. —JULIA ATTAWAY

SAT
19

THOU SHALT NOT BE AFRAID FOR THE TERROR BY NIGHT; NOR FOR THE ARROW THAT FLIETH BY DAY.
—*Psalm 91:5*

LAST SUMMER I WAS privileged to participate at a ceremony at Fort Drum in upstate New York in support of the partnership between Guideposts and the 10th Mountain Division, which was preparing to deploy to Iraq and Afghanistan. We were providing packets with inspirational materials for the troops and their spouses.

After the ceremony, Installation Chaplain Nichols escorted us to the reception hall for a military buffet-style lunch. The room was filled with chaplains, soldiers, spouses and guests.

I ate my lunch of Sloppy Joes, salad and brownies across from a major and his wife. "Are you being deployed to Iraq?" I asked.

"Yes, sir," he said proudly. "This is my second tour."

"It must be hard for you to leave your family behind, especially the second time around."

"I have the easy job," his wife quickly interjected. "He's the one with the tough assignment." The major's eyes gleamed with pride as he smiled at her.

During my trip home, I thought about the extraordinary courage of the spouses on the home front and our troops on the front lines. I once read that having courage doesn't mean that we aren't afraid, but that in spite of our fears we go forward with the confidence that God is with us. That's the kind of courage I found in the hearts of these unsung heroes.

Thank You, Lord, for all those who face their fears and go forward when their country calls. —PABLO DIAZ

SUN
20

THE LORD DOES NOT LET THE RIGHTEOUS GO HUNGRY. . . . —Proverbs 10:3 (NIV)

I WAS INVITED to speak at the community-wide home-coming at a rural church one Sunday morning. This is a big event for many churches in Mississippi, when every family attends services at the church, followed by a celebration in their homes. My wife Rosie and our grandson Little Reggie went with me for the occasion.

Afterward we were invited to the home of a family with ten children —seven girls and three boys—some of them older than Rosie and I, others younger. Their mother moved around in a motorized wheelchair. They had prepared a reunion feast, and we had the opportunity to share pig's feet and ham hocks with them. We talked about the difficult times, about not having much but the joy of having each other. It was a great time of fellowship and food.

As we drove away, Rosie and I blessed this matriarch, nearly ninety years old, surrounded by all her children and grandchildren. We were overwhelmingly blessed as we saw a grateful family gathered at the home of their mother. Over the years they'd gone through ups and downs, but truly the Lord had not let the righteous go hungry. And on this day there was plenty of physical food—and no hunger for love either.

Lord, help me to know that You are shaping me to be a part of Your greater family, now and in glory. —DOLPHUS WEARY

MON
21

CALL UPON ME, AND I WILL ANSWER. . . .
—Psalm 91:15 (NIV)

MY MIND WAS ON my daughter Amy Jo and her four-week-old baby. Brock was golden-haired and healthy and constantly hungry. Every hour he needed to eat. Plus, he cried a lot! So I prayed for little Brock. I prayed that he would sleep that night, that he would rest and be at peace, that his little stomach would stay full beyond those sixty short minutes. Amy Jo's husband was away on business and she was exhausted beyond words. As I prayed, I visualized an angel—

complete with giant wings and flowing robe—standing beside Brock's crib, comforting him and singing him back to sleep.

Later, as I climbed into bed, Amy Jo called. "Can you come over? I just need someone else to hold the baby and let me get a few minutes sleep." Gladly, I went.

After Amy Jo nursed Brock, she handed him to me and shuffled off to bed. "Wake me up when he starts crying," she said over her shoulder.

So I began rocking Brock. After a while, I laid him in his crib and patted his stomach. The minutes slipped by and turned into hours. For three hours Brock slept—and so did Amy Jo. Every time he stirred, I prayed and hummed hymns until he was quiet. "That's the most sleep I've gotten in the last month!" Amy Jo said happily when I put Brock into her arms.

As I drove home, the blackness of night giving way to the first hint of dawn, I realized just how miraculously my prayer had been answered. Brock was attended to by an angel that night . . . an angel named *Nana*.

How doubly generous, God, to let me be part of Your answer to my prayers! —MARY LOU CARNEY

TUE
22

BUT THE FRUIT OF THE SPIRIT IS LOVE, JOY, PEACE, LONGSUFFERING, GENTLENESS, GOODNESS, FAITH, MEEKNESS, TEMPERANCE: AGAINST SUCH THERE IS NO LAW. —Galatians 5:22–23

RUDENESS IS THE SUBJECT of the book I'm reading at the moment, and the author suggests that we have an epidemic of it in this country. I agree. My only caveat is that it isn't limited to us. As someone who has done some traveling in other lands, I can report that rudeness is not just an American phenomenon.

On a trip out of the country a couple of years ago, I noticed that people had a total disregard for standing in line. With impunity, both men and women crowded ahead of one another. Of course, there are many other examples of the problem that take place in cars, at our places of work and on the phone. Loud cell phone conversation in public areas is one of my pet peeves.

What does the Bible say about rudeness? I'd point to the fruits of the spirit listed in Galatians 5:22–23, such as peace, patience, kindness, gentleness and self-control. All are the antithesis of being rude.

Instead of crowding ahead, Lord, teach us après vous,
The beautiful French phrase for "after you."
—FRED BAUER

WED
23
I WILL STRENGTHEN YOU AND HELP YOU; I WILL
UPHOLD YOU WITH MY RIGHTEOUS RIGHT HAND.
—Isaiah 41:10 (NIV)

WHEN MY HUSBAND LYNN spent his first night in ICU following surgery to remove most of a malignant brain tumor, he couldn't sleep. In spite of some strong medication, he appeared agitated, especially as he tried to absorb the meaning of the news that he had brain cancer. I kept talking to him, gently trying to calm him, but in listening and responding, his blood pressure kept rising.

"Why don't you go home and get some sleep," a nurse kindly suggested at about 11:00 PM. "Then he might fall asleep too." Reluctantly I left.

The next morning Lynn seemed much better. "I couldn't fall asleep after you left," he told me. "I had too many frightening thoughts running through my mind. Finally, a nurse came in."

"What did she say to you?" I asked.

"I don't remember that she said much. She just held my hand."

Over the next several days I learned about the holiness of that simple gesture. Sometimes, in our adjustments to difficult realities, we get all tangled up in words, trying to fix each other's pain. Sometimes, in those hard moments, the most profound way we can comfort each other is by simply, silently, holding hands.

Father, You express Your love and mercy by holding us in Your hands.
Help us to communicate love and mercy as we hold each other's hands.
—CAROL KUYKENDALL

THU

24

"GRACE HAS BEEN SHOWN. . . ." —*Ezra 9:8* (NAS)

DURING MY FRESHMAN YEAR of college, I lived for my English literature class. I always arrived early, sat in the front row and never missed a session. One glorious September morning, our professor Dr. Walker told us to write an essay. After class I had a free period, so I hurried to my dorm room and started writing, copying my work several times to make sure it was neat.

I held my breath when Dr. Walker laid the folded essay on my desk. I so wanted to do well; I so wanted him to encourage me. I opened the essay . . . an *A*! "You have thirteen misspelled words," he'd written. "You can write. Learn to spell." I didn't know whether to laugh or cry.

Our final exam that May consisted of two discussion questions. I adored exams like that; they allowed for creativity and gave me a chance to cram in everything I'd learned. When Dr. Walker returned my paper, I had another A and another note: "You forgot to answer the second question, however, I'm confident that you know the answer. Just be more careful. Have a happy summer."

Many years later, our Bible study group was studying grace. The definition I liked best was "undeserved merit." And I couldn't think of a better example of it than what Dr. Walker had extended to me.

Father God, help me to extend Your grace to someone today.
—MARION BOND WEST

FRI

25

"AND WHY WORRY ABOUT A SPECK IN THE EYE OF A BROTHER WHEN YOU HAVE A BOARD IN YOUR OWN?"
—*Matthew 7:3* (TLB)

IN 2004, AFTER BEING single for nearly twenty years, raising my four children, then living alone for six years in an empty nest, I sold my house and my little red car and moved from Wisconsin to Florida. I met Jack, whose wife of forty-three years had died a few months earlier.

We became friends, but after a year I began to have second thoughts. We'd been together nearly every day that year, because we live only fifty-seven steps from each other on the same floor of the same building.

I began to think: *This is too much togetherness, especially since I've gotten used to being alone most of the time. He's overweight, he won't exercise with me, he watches too many sports on TV.*

One night on the phone, I blubbered to my close friend Melanie. She reminded me that no relationship provides all we need in life. "Jack doesn't have to be everything for you or be the perfect man. You're not perfect either, you know. Invite him to exercise with you. Let Jack enjoy his sports on TV. That just gives you more time for your own work, hobbies and activities."

My relationship with Jack changed at that moment. I took responsibility for my own happiness and encouraged him to develop his own interests. He became president of our condo association, joined my water aerobics class, and encouraged me to spend time with new friends and new activities. Know what happened when we each stepped back a bit? We became even closer, and our friendship continues to grow.

Lord, don't let me depend on others to make me happy. Let me depend on You by developing the talents and interests You put inside me when You gave me life. —PATRICIA LORENZ

SAT
26

"YOU SHALL BE A SPECIAL TREASURE TO ME. . . ."
—*Exodus 19:5 (NKJV)*

NO ONE COULD MAKE Sunday dinner like my mother-in-law Ruth Dale. Her Swiss steak was the richest and juiciest I've ever eaten. My wife Sharon tried to duplicate her recipe in vain. She watched her mother cook it, thinking maybe she was doing something she wasn't aware of, but she wasn't. Sharon even bought her meat at the same store, but it didn't help.

When Sharon's mother died, her secret died with her. We cleaned out her little house, keeping some things and giving the rest to our daughters.

One evening my wife made Swiss steak for supper, complete with whole potatoes and carrots, the way her mother made it. I braced myself for the usual carving challenge, but I was pleasantly surprised.

"Why, this steak is delicious! It's just like your mother's!"

She smiled and pointed at the stove. "It was the pan she used."

I looked at the pan that Sharon had salvaged from her mother's kitchen. It was a heavy-duty aluminum pan, the kind my father used to sell door-to-door when I was a boy. It held the juices perfectly.

I was glad to know that Ruth Dale's secret was not lost, but I was also sad. It was *her* secret, *her* special talent. I know, "imitation is the sincerest form of flattery," but I'm beginning to think that the most flattering thing I can do for someone is not to copy them but to let them be that special, unique person they are.

There was no one quite like Ruth Dale, and there is no one exactly like you or me. Somehow I think that's how God meant it to be.

Help me to be happy, Lord, being me, instead of imitating others.
—DANIEL SCHANTZ

SUN 27

AND I WILL PRAY THE FATHER, AND HE SHALL GIVE YOU ANOTHER COMFORTER, THAT HE MAY ABIDE WITH YOU FOR EVER; EVEN THE SPIRIT OF TRUTH; WHOM THE WORLD CANNOT RECEIVE BECAUSE IT SEETH HIM NOT, NEITHER KNOWETH HIM: BUT YE KNOW HIM; FOR HE DWELLETH WITH YOU, AND SHALL BE IN YOU.
—*John 14:16–17*

ALTHOUGH I'M NOW in remission, there was a time when I suffered greatly from rheumatoid arthritis. One day when the tissue surrounding most of my joints was inflamed and throbbing with pain, my husband Larry gently put his arms around me and said, "I think you need a little comfort."

As I leaned my forehead against his shoulder, I felt renewed strength flow into me from the love and sympathy of his embrace.

We don't all have a loving companion to comfort us during the hard times, but we do have another source of comfort available any time of the day or night if we could only know it. That comforter is God's Holy Spirit, not visible, but always with us, just as Jesus promised.

Father, on this day of Pentecost I will share with others the good news of the Holy Spirit, the "Comforter" who brings hope to us all. Amen.
—MADGE HARRAH

MON
28

These stones shall be for a memorial unto the children of Israel for ever. —*Joshua 4:7*

WHEN PUBLICATIONS RUN pictures of Memorial Day, they usually show cemeteries like Arlington with its thousands of pristine markers in unbroken waves or the American cemetery at Normandy with its countless crosses and stars of David. But the memory I have of the day is of quaint Mountain View Cemetery in the foothills of Pasadena, California, where my grandfather, a staunch member of the American Legion, made sure every veteran's grave was marked with a small American flag.

My grandfather, for reasons that were never clear to me, used to call us kids "you stick-in-the-muds." And I always thought of that expression on Memorial Day when we kids scattered through the cemetery in the day's waning light to collect the flags before sunset, digging them out of the mud. You could find them at the feet of the most ornate marble angel or next to a simple granite stone. Some of these graves had pretty rosebushes around them or fresh flowers in a vase nearby. Others were neglected and overgrown, as though no one had visited in years— not until our young feet scampered by. Most of the flags were for people I'd never known, some of whom, from the dates on their stones, died all too young. But all of them were, like my grandfather and father, veterans of war.

By sunset the flags were put away in boxes and bags in the back of Grampie's car, ready for next Memorial Day. We dashed home. But we all learned that remembering the dead wasn't passive. It was an action, something my grandfather organized year after year. And I suspect he asked us "stick-in-the-muds" to help him so that someday we would realize that thanks are owed to generation after generation, in graves fancy and plain, known and unknown, with more flags than fit in the back of a Buick. It's something you couldn't forget.

Lord, I give thanks for those who serve. —RICK HAMLIN

TUE
29

A HAPPY HEART MAKES THE FACE CHEERFUL....
—*Proverbs 15:13 (NIV)*

MY WIFE JULIA had taken John and Mary to their ballet lesson, and she had left me instructions to take four-year-old Maggie and two-year-old Stephen to the playground. Eleven-year-old Elizabeth needed time to herself, and she'd been complaining lately about Maggie. "Whenever we're home together, she pesters me. She keeps asking to play with me. Why can't she leave me alone?"

At ten o'clock Elizabeth had a chess lesson, and when it was over I asked the kids if they were ready to go to the playground.

"Will the ice cream truck be there today? Can I buy an ice cream?" Maggie asked. She'd just received a few weeks' back allowance, and the money seemed to be burning a hole in her pocket.

"Yes and yes," I answered. I helped Maggie find her shoes and socks, and got Stevie into his stroller. I'd assumed that Elizabeth would be staying home to read, but to my surprise she wanted to come with us.

The ice cream truck was nowhere in sight when we got to the playground. At four, Maggie is finding it hard to deal with disappointment, and I was prepared for a major fuss. But the attraction of playing with her big sister was irresistible, and Maggie and Elizabeth ran off to climb the slide while I took Stevie to the kiddie swings.

When the ice cream truck finally arrived, Maggie bought treats for Elizabeth, Stevie and herself, and the three of them sat on a bench and ate. Then we all ran back to the swings, and Elizabeth pushed Maggie while I pushed Stevie.

Later, as we walked home, Elizabeth held Maggie's hand while I wheeled Stevie in the stroller. Gazing up at her big sister, eyes wide with admiration, Maggie said, "Elizabeth, this was my best-ever day."

Lord, today, help me to put aside my own concerns and to give someone a "best-ever day." —ANDREW ATTAWAY

WED

30

AND IT SHALL COME TO PASS, THAT BEFORE THEY CALL, I WILL ANSWER; AND WHILE THEY ARE YET SPEAKING, I WILL HEAR. —*Isaiah 65:24*

IF YOU HAD BEEN looking for me fifty years ago on any Wednesday evening, you would have found me beside the black rotary-dial phone, waiting for it to ring. And it always did.

Those were courtship days, and Leo and I allowed ourselves just one five-minute long-distance call per week. Back then, even the thirty cents it cost was viewed as an extravagance, especially by those who were not yet in a close relationship.

After we married, Leo continued to call me every day during his lunch break. We quickly shared the developments of the day, whether good or bad. As the children came along, a request I frequently heard while they ate their lunch was "When Dad calls, tell him ..." or "When Dad calls, ask him ...." It was their moment to share some personal achievement or to ask him for some advice, neither of which could possibly wait until he got home.

Sometimes Leo would dial our number and I'd pick up the receiver before the phone even rang. Such instant connections were always a bit of a surprise, considering the split-second timing involved—and yet not really. Over the years I've found that caring and consistency are the basis of all good communication—including prayer.

Lord, make me as receptive to Your voice as You are to my calling.
—ALMA BARKMAN

THU

31

So I COMMEND THE ENJOYMENT OF LIFE, BECAUSE NOTHING IS BETTER FOR A MAN UNDER THE SUN. ...
—*Ecclesiastes 8:15 (NIV)*

I RUSHED HOME from work to babysit Indy and Noah, my two grandsons. I hadn't seen them much lately. I was juggling my job, school, housework and gardening. There was no time for anything else.

I was still in my business suit and heels when they arrived. Four-year-old Indy grabbed my hand, ready to run to the pond to feed the ducks.

"Grandma," he said excitedly, "go get your play clothes on!"

"Oh, Indy," I laughed, "I don't have any play clothes."

He looked at me wide-eyed. "What do you wear when you play?"

It was the third time that week the issue of play had come up. When a delivery man hustled to my door with a package, I joked that he was as busy as I was. He smiled and said that the key to life is to remember to find time to play too. I responded with a blank stare.

It came up again two days later at a seminar. When asked to create a personal schedule that included time for me to do something just for fun, I came up empty-handed.

The following Saturday afternoon when the boys came over, I wore my newly labeled play clothes—jogging pants, tie-dyed T-shirt and tennis shoes. I took their little hands in mine and we ran to the backyard, not to weed the garden, not to rake the leaves and not to do homework at the patio table, but simply to play. Now that's an accomplishment!

Father, Indy, Noah and I are lying here on the grass and watching the sun set across the pond. We just wanted to say thanks for a really fun day and a beautiful pink sky tonight. —MELODY BONNETTE

MY WALK WITH GOD

1 _____

2 _____

3 _____

4 _____

5 _____

6 _____

7 _____

8 _____

9 _____

10 _____

11 _____

12 _____

13 _____

14 _____

15 _____

16 _____

17 _____

18 _____

19 _____

20 _____

21 _____

22 _____

23 _____

24 _____

25 _____

26 _____

27 _____

28 _____

29 _____

30 _____

31 _____

June

The Lord is my strength and song, and
he is become my salvation. . . .

—*Exodus 15:2*

LESSONS FROM THE JOURNEY
BRING ALONG A SONG

FRI

I

"The Lord is my strength and my song. . . ."
—*Exodus 15:2 (RSV)*

JOHN AND I STUMBLED on the power of singing during months-long car trips when our three children were small. When they travel today, *their* children plug their earphones into CD players and disappear into their own musical worlds, but we were dependent on our voices. John's is a sonorous bass, mine a wobbly, off-key alto, but in a closed car with the kids' treble voices joining in, we drowned out the missed notes.

Not being believers then, we didn't know any hymns; "Home on the Range" and "Old MacDonald Had a Farm" sped us through the miles. As the children grew older, we added show tunes, blues, country and western.

Then, belatedly, I came upon the riches between the covers of a hymnal. Worship, petition, penitence, rejoicing—whatever the circumstances there was a hymn to fit. Like the immediacy of a Bible verse, hymns, more than other songs, were always new.

There was the night I was groping my way alone through the unlit streets of a town in Communist Hungary with no idea where we'd parked the car, softly singing "Lead kindly Light. . . . The night is dark and I am far from home." I'd sung it through six times when I came to a building I remembered and found the car parked behind it.

Or when boarding an unreliable-looking small plane in the Amazon, how glad I was for "Eternal Father, Strong to Save"!

> O Wind of heaven, by thy might
> save all who dare the eagle's flight,
> and keep them by thy watchful care
> from every peril in the air.

I almost believe that song kept that rickety old machine up!

Hymns are designed for ease of memory; I know dozens of them by now without ever setting out to learn them. John and I still sing Frank

Sinatra and Stephen Foster. But for the journey, over the miles or through the years, hymns make the best music.

Lord of the journey, give me a song for today. —ELIZABETH SHERRILL

SAT
2

HAGGAI, THE MESSENGER OF THE LORD, SPOKE TO THE PEOPLE WITH THE LORD'S MESSAGE, "I AM WITH YOU, SAYS THE LORD." —*Haggai 1:13 (RSV)*

WHEN WE BOUGHT our old farmhouse, I imagined it taking us six months or perhaps a year to renovate it. Yet nearly two years later, there was still wiring and plumbing to be done. My husband and I often talked about our meager finances and slow progress. Usually our conversations ended with one of us saying, "We'll be okay"—three words of reassurance that had become a prayer as much as anything else.

One afternoon, I sat on the newly finished floor, going through some things left behind by the previous owners. Inside a box I found a local paper from 1910, a magazine from 1942, and hundreds of letters and Christmas cards. I was reading a letter when my husband came in. He had just gotten an estimate on the front porch, another ten thousand dollars we didn't have. "We'll be okay," I said halfheartedly and went back to the pile.

Among the scraps a hand-painted Christmas card stood out. It was from the 1920s, a dreamy night scene with a white church covered in snow. It was exquisite but for the tiny holes that pierced the picture. *Such a shame,* I thought. *So many precious things have been damaged by mice during all the years the house was vacant.*

Before tossing the card on the throw-out pile, I held it up to the window. In the sunlight, the holes became stars that shone down on the church—pinpricks carefully punched by the giver to create a special message. It was showing me how a slight shift in perspective can make all the difference.

I knew we truly would be okay.

Thank You, Lord, for the special messages You send to encourage me.
—SABRA CIANCANELLI

SUN
3

WHY ART THOU CAST DOWN, O MY SOUL? AND WHY ART THOU DISQUIETED WITHIN ME? HOPE IN GOD: FOR I SHALL YET PRAISE HIM, WHO IS THE HEALTH OF MY COUNTENANCE, AND MY GOD. —*Psalm 43:5*

MY HUSBAND NORMAN and I both knew a man who often felt discouraged and weak from the blows of life. One bleak, rainy morning, he entered a diner for breakfast. Several others were there, but no one spoke to anyone else. Our friend sat down on a stool and tried to decide what to order for breakfast. Even that was a difficult chore.

At the other end of the diner, he noticed a young mother with her little girl. Suddenly, the child broke the silence by asking her mother, "Don't we say grace here, Mommy?"

Behind the counter, the cook looked at the little girl and said, "Sure we do, honey. Will you say it for us?"

The little girl bowed her head, clasped her hands and said in a loud voice, "God is great and God is good, and we thank Him for our food. By His hand we all are fed. Give us, Lord, our daily bread." All of a sudden, the atmosphere in the diner changed and people began talking to one another.

Our usually gloomy friend later told us how that experience was pivotal for him. He saw the little girl's faith and he, too, started to believe in God, to believe in other people and to believe in himself. He began to pray regularly, no matter how much rain was coming down outside. He experienced the power of prayer in the midst of adversity and that made all the difference!

There's no sense in worrying or despairing over past failures, present situations or potential mishaps. As long as we truly do our best as praying, positive-thinking people, God will see us through.

In good times and in bad, Lord, let me hope and trust in You.

—RUTH STAFFORD PEALE

MON

THEY WERE ON THEIR WAY TO THE TOMB AND THEY ASKED EACH OTHER, "WHO WILL ROLL THE STONE AWAY FROM THE ENTRANCE OF THE TOMB?"
—*Mark 16:2–3 (NIV)*

WHEN OUR SUNDAY SCHOOL TEACHER asked us, "What does it mean to have mountain-moving faith?" I wanted to answer, "I don't know, but I desperately need it right now!"

We'd just received word that our son Chris was on his way to Afghanistan with the Army, and I wondered where I could possibly get the kind of faith that could move my mountain of fear for his safety and well-being.

That week I was in Orangeburg, South Carolina, rummaging through an antique store, and I found an old-fashioned radio cabinet that was perfect for a spot in a small entryway. Unfortunately, the old radio and its gigantic speaker were still in the cabinet, and there were no men working in the shop to help me get it into my car. The woman in charge managed to help me get the radio cabinet onto a dolly and wheel it out to my car. Just as I opened the trunk, wondering what to do next, a man in worn-out clothes and a scruffy beard rode down the alleyway on a bicycle. The woman beckoned the passerby, and without a moment's hesitation the man came over and hoisted the radio cabinet into the trunk.

I suddenly understood that mountain-moving faith wasn't about my making the mountain move but rather about my moving *toward* the mountain as if it wasn't insurmountable. So as my son Chris settled into a base surrounded by rugged mountains in Afghanistan, I prayed:

Father, help me to continue on this difficult journey, knowing that the mountain I see ahead is no obstacle to Your strength to move it or carry me over it. —KAREN BARBER

TUE

5

AND THE LORD'S SERVANT MUST NOT QUARREL; INSTEAD, HE MUST BE KIND TO EVERYONE. . . .
—*II Timothy 2:24 (NIV)*

AFTER DAVID AND I were married, we went as missionaries to a small coal mining community in Appalachia. Soon after our arrival, we met Father Killian Mooney, the priest of a nearby parish, and his friendship became very important to us.

As time went by, we got to know several nuns and priests who had come to the area to serve. It only made sense to introduce the people of our little Presbyterian church to our Catholic friends, so we announced an ice-cream social to follow our Wednesday night service. Not one member of our congregation attended the social.

Over the next few days, I hatched a plan. Some of the ladies in our congregation had told us that they wanted to learn to knit. Sensing an opportunity, I called Father Mooney. As luck would have it, Sister Gloria, one of the nuns, was an expert knitter.

The next Sunday I posted a notice: "Free knitting classes at the manse every Tuesday night. Refreshments served. Needles and yarn supplied."

At the first gathering I introduced Gloria as a friend. After a few lessons, the women were learning fast and every one of them had taken to Gloria. I was serving brownies, warm from the oven, when I casually said, "Did I ever tell you that Gloria's Catholic? In fact, she's a nun. Sister Gloria, actually."

Not a single lady choked on a brownie or dropped a stitch. But still I was worried. What if no one showed up for the next class?

The next Tuesday, I was nervous as could be until the ladies began filing in, happily showing Gloria the work they had done that week. And the next time we had an ice-cream social, everyone came!

Father, Your way is kindness, not quarreling. Help me remember.

—PAM KIDD

WED
6

THOU THEREFORE ENDURE HARDNESS, AS A GOOD SOLDIER OF JESUS CHRIST. —II Timothy 2:3

WITH MY TWENTY-FIRST BIRTHDAY a day away, I wangled a three-day pass, the first of my Army career. My pal Wally did likewise, but when they came, his pass was marked eight hours earlier than mine. "I can get just a few hours at home in Michigan," he said. Home was the first thing a guy thought about in those days. "Join me if you can," he said.

He headed from Augusta, Georgia's Daniel Field to Atlanta by morning train, the pokey Central of Georgia Railway that took eight hours to get there. I got free earlier than I expected and hitchhiked the two-way roads over sun-baked Georgia. Eight rides later, I arrived; his train had left the station. And then, to my amazement, there was Wally. "I was nuts," he said about his attempt to get home. "Anyway, we have to celebrate your birthday."

It was late when we returned to our luckily found room in the Henry Grady Hotel. And it was late the next day when we drowsily got up and found our way down to food. "It's odd," I said. "There's something different about today."

"Your birthday, my conceited friend."

"No. I feel it. It's in the air."

It was about four o'clock when I saw the blazing headline in the Atlanta *Constitution*: D-Day had arrived! Word had come in while we were celebrating my birthday. I was somehow ashamed, but not as much as when I received a letter from Mother. "I dropped everything and set out to find the nearest church," she wrote. "I prayed for all our soldiers, as I am sure you do."

Things have not changed, Father. I pray for all our soldiers today.
—Van Varner

THU
7

And Noah walked with God. —Genesis 6:9

I GOT A LAUGH today while waiting with my aunt in a restaurant. A tall athletic man who'd learned Aunt Betty was one hundred years old wanted to know her secret for long life. Ninety-two pounds of spunk looked up at him and said, "Well, I guess I just kept on breathing!"

There's a little more to it than that. My aunt's quick wit is hard to beat, and she's also independent and adventurous. She drove her mother and five siblings cross-country in a seven-passenger car when she was barely sixteen! And she worked her way through college in the 1920s peeling potatoes at 4:00 AM.

She's a lively student and teacher. The other night she sat leaning forward, arms wrapped around her legs like a teenager, listening intently to her daughter Jeanne read aloud from her doctoral dissertation. If she caught a grammatical error, she said so.

The most inspiring thing I've seen Aunt Betty do happened in a medical lab: She helped hold open a heavy door for a woman pushing a patient in a wheelchair. Wobbly herself, steadying her steps with a cane, yet trying to ease the passage for someone else—this is her way.

It's a combination of things that gets a person to the century mark. Fundamental for my aunt is prayer. She's a great believer in "going to my knees." Maybe that's how she's stayed so limber in body and spirit. Her knees don't meet the floor these days, but her heart bows to the Lord she loves.

I wish I could find that man from the restaurant. I'd like to tell him the whole story of how my aunt made it to one hundred.

The roads we travel are different distances, Lord. Please walk mine with me, whatever its length or terrain. —CAROL KNAPP

FRI
8

IN HIM WE WERE ALSO CHOSEN, HAVING BEEN PREDESTINED ACCORDING TO THE PLAN OF HIM WHO WORKS OUT EVERYTHING IN CONFORMITY WITH THE PURPOSE OF HIS WILL. —*Ephesians 1:11 (NIV)*

I'M A PLANNER, my mother is a planner, and her mother is one too. We all like to know in advance what's going to happen when. So I struggled when we put our house on the market and it still hadn't sold several months later. School was ending, and we wanted to be settled into our new house before the new school year began.

My mind raced as I thought about our situation: *What if we don't sell our house in time? We can't afford two mortgages. Should I start packing the house, so we're ready to go as soon as it sells? Or will I look like a fool if I've packed everything up and we end up staying?*

Finally I decided to talk things over with a very wise and much more laid-back friend. "Try taking things a day at a time," she suggested. "Ask God each morning what He wants you to accomplish that day. That way, you'll only be planning according to His will for your life, one day at a time."

That sounded like the best kind of planning I could do. And wouldn't you know it? We got a contract on our house just two weeks after school ended, leaving us the perfect amount of time to find a house and get settled before the schol year started again.

Oh, Lord, remind my planning brain not to get ahead of the plans that You place in my heart each day. —WENDY WILLARD

SAT
9

AND YE SHALL KNOW THE TRUTH, AND THE TRUTH SHALL MAKE YOU FREE. —*John 8:32*

A DEAR FRIEND of ours visited us for her fortieth birthday. It had been three years since we had seen her, and she looked remarkably beautiful. All the people we introduced her to said something about her beauty, and I noticed men looking at her whenever we walked into a restaurant or a store. She had always been quite stunning, but now she seemed to be even more so. The years had not just been kind to her, they seemed to be working in her favor.

But during a long conversation, she told us that now that she was entering middle age, she couldn't believe that she was attractive anymore. Her days of feeling good about herself were over, she said, and she longed for her youth.

My first reaction was to tell her that the opposite was true. But then I realized that I could tell her that all day and I'd never truly get to the heart of the matter. What was bothering her was something much deeper than that.

And that's when it occurred to me that I was no different. I'd always felt that I had the word *failure* written on my forehead because of business difficulties and that it was all anybody saw when they looked at me. But if a beautiful woman like my friend could believe she was unattractive when everyone around her saw the opposite, maybe there was something wrong with my self-image too.

My friend helped me see that most of my negative thinking was based on problems that exist in only one place in the world: in my head.

Lord, help me to see the positives in everyone, including myself.
—DAVE FRANCO

SUN

10

A FALSE BALANCE IS NOT GOOD. —*Proverbs 20:23*

SPRINKLES OF SUNLIGHT played across the ranch yard as I quickly heaved the packsaddle onto the tall, red mule named Johnston. She switched her tail and gave me the evil eye. I glared back.

In less than thirty days, my boss wanted all nineteen mules ready to go down the trail, loaded with packs. The only problem was that I didn't know how to pack a mule. The trainer couldn't come for another week, and I couldn't bear the thought that they might not be ready, so I asked Snuffy to teach me.

I ducked back and forth under Johnston's neck, buckling the leather straps. Johnston stomped her foot and pinned her long ears to her neck. "Don't be mouthy," I said. "Snuffy will be here in a couple of minutes. Today it's work, work, work."

As I tightened the cinch, Johnston inhaled a deep breath, puffing out her belly. I tightened some more and then felt Johnston hump up. Her lightning-fast hind foot smacked me in the thigh and sent me sprawling. Behind me I heard Snuffy roar with laughter. I brushed myself off, then felt my leg.

"That was a warning. If she had been serious, your leg would be broke." Snuffy patted Johnston. He loosened the cinch. "It's not the cinch that holds the whole load. The two sides have to be balanced so when the mule walks, the loads rock evenly from side to side. It's all about balance." Johnston affectionately nuzzled Snuffy. What a change in attitude!

Balance, not the cinch. Maybe I should balance my work, too, and make it fun, instead of just work, work, work.

Over the next few days I spent time petting and scratching the mules in their favorite places. Instead of taking longer to finish, I got done on time and had fun doing it.

Lord, help me to lead a balanced life, with You at the center.

—REBECCA ONDOV

MON

11

"I TELL YOU THE TRUTH, ANYONE WHO WILL NOT RECEIVE THE KINGDOM OF GOD LIKE A LITTLE CHILD WILL NEVER ENTER IT." —Mark 10:15 (NIV)

STEPHEN AND I went out together this morning to do a couple of errands. We walked in that slow-as-molasses, stop-and-look way that's mandatory with a two-year-old. We went down to the corner, crossed the street and arrived at the short block of stores where everyone in the neighborhood shops.

First stop: the bank, to pick up two rolls of quarters. I let Stephen carry one. "It's heavy!" he said with a grin. New Yorkers rarely have washing machines in their apartments, so we all hoard change. I supplement ours by getting quarters from the bank.

Next stop: the grocery store. Our local store is large by city standards; it has seven aisles. Since we shop there almost every day (we only buy as much as we can cart or carry home), we know most of the cashiers. Today we picked up laundry detergent and toilet paper, both on sale.

Final stop: the bakery, to buy a loaf of seven-grain bread and a large rye. The ladies behind the counter were happy to see us and asked after the other kids. They gave Stephen a little bag of cookies to share with his siblings. He smiled proudly as he carried the goodies out the door.

We waved to Mr. Ahn, the greengrocer, and crossed the street. With the unerring radar of a two-year-old, Stephen spotted a backhoe at work at the corner. He munched a cookie as we watched it dig for a while. Then we turned toward home and giggled our way back up the block, trying to step on each other's shadows.

Lord, it's pretty amazing that You put so much joy in quarters and cookies and backhoes and shadows. Thanks. —JULIA ATTAWAY

TUE

12

BE OF GOOD COURAGE, AND HE SHALL STRENGTHEN YOUR HEART, ALL YE THAT HOPE IN THE LORD.
—Psalm 31:24

IT WAS ABSURD that I had to wear a hat every time I went out my back door, down the pathway to the garage. A tiny hummingbird was dive-bombing me! The audacity of that little creature exhibited the courage of David to Goliath.

Her nest, the size of a walnut, was perched in a low-slung branch of the avocado tree outside my bedroom window. Her eggs had hatched, and two tiny beaks, like needles poking out of a minuscule pincushion, were barely visible. Within a few weeks the nest was empty.

Wrapped snug in a robe, sipping coffee in my favorite chair on the patio, I was treated to an aerial show like none other. The shimmering green and metallic red throats of a family of hummingbirds soared skyward, then dipped down to hover blossom-to-blossom through the clumps of bird of paradise and hibiscus. This four-inch bird can not only soar, dip and dive, but hover in place and fly backward at will!

I called upon that strength this morning. I'd found my energy diminishing. It seemed to take me twice as long to do half as much. Emotionally I was wobbly and apprehensive about fulfilling my commitments. I wondered where God was leading me and feared the future. A little hummingbird adjusted my perspective.

I will put my hope in the Lord and trust the One Who has wondrously empowered small wings to strengthen my heart. I will soar in prayer to the highest heaven. I will hover in place as I wait for new direction. For affirming reassurance, I will fly backward and remember God's never-failing goodness and mercy.

Your perfect will for me . . . let it be, dear Lord, let it be. —FAY ANGUS

GOD-FINDS
FINDING A SUPPORT SYSTEM

WED
13

I HAVE NOT SEEN THE RIGHTEOUS FORSAKEN, OR HIS DESCENDANTS BEGGING BREAD. —Psalm 37:25 (NAS)

WHEN I DIVORCED, my greatest fear was *Who will now accompany me on my many trips to see my doctors?* Despite the differences we had, my husband had been an incredible support when it came to my neurofibromatosis, and I didn't know how I would manage without him.

"What if I have to have another big surgery?" I agonized to God. All of my family had demanding jobs, and there seemed to be no solution. Then the dreaded event happened: I was scheduled for an operation to remove a large tumor inside my head.

On hearing the news, my friend and co-worker Cathy telephoned me. "I'm in 'use or lose' status with my leave," she said. "Please let me take a week off and go with you to the Cleveland Clinic."

Another friend, who had lost one partner to death and another to divorce, mobilized my neighborhood to bring meals that I could reheat in the microwave. "You help everyone else," Pat said. "Now it's time to return the favor."

Then there was Sue. A group of God-finds gathered around her dining room table the Sunday afternoon before my surgery, all praying for a miracle and reminding me that God hadn't forsaken me.

And that's how it was when I discovered a whole community of caring God-finds, one that today still celebrates the success—the miracle, even—of that surgery. Since then, I've had no new tumor growth and the best three years of my life.

All along I'd been limiting God to supplying my needs through those who share my name. But God-finds are everywhere, I've learned, standing at the ready to be called into His service.

Thank You, Lord, for taking care of Your own . . . always.
—ROBERTA MESSNER

THU
14

LIFT YE UP A BANNER UPON THE HIGH MOUNTAIN, EXALT THE VOICE UNTO THEM. . . . —Isaiah 13:2

NOT LONG AGO, I had the opportunity to talk with a Vietnam veteran named Dean Parrett, who had just returned from a ceremony at Arlington National Cemetery. He and his wife Dianne had made the trip to attend the funeral of twelve of Dean's comrades, who were killed in May 1968 at a remote outpost along the Laos-Vietnam border. Dean, himself seriously wounded, had been evacuated to a hospital ship and afterward had lost contact with his company.

Thirty-seven years later, Dean was notified that the remains of his fellow Marines had been recovered and brought home for burial. He was invited to attend their memorial service and a reunion of survivors from the 2nd Battalion, 13th Marines.

The reunion was the high point of Dean's life. By his own admission he had never expected to see such a day. Overcome with emotion, he later showed me an item that had been given to him by one of his fellow Marines—a small American flag lapel pin. To Dean, that tiny symbol summed up the great weight of events and emotions that he'll forever be unable to verbalize.

The reverence and appreciation vested in that small symbol by a veteran who gave so much for his country has renewed my own awareness and respect for our national emblem and for this special day that has been set aside to honor it.

Father, when I cast my gaze upon the flag today, may I see not only the beauty in its rich colors but recognize the depth of its meaning to our country. —LIBBIE ADAMS

READER'S ROOM

THE FATHER IS INDEED working in my life! I've started a Christian coffee shop three doors down from my place. The coffee shop is free, with just voluntary donations, and we are running it as God provides.

Also, I've been keeping a correspondence with a prisoner, and he writes beautiful, loving letters. In his last letter he said, "You mean so much to me," and I know that he meant it. I look upon him as my blood brother.

Oh! And I've found inner peace, which I never want to lose in Jesus' name. We're all born with inner peace, but as we grow older, at some point we might lose it. But with Jesus, the Gospel and prayer we can regain that peace.

I wanted to tell you one more thing but I forgot what it was. We must pray about everything?

—Sylvie Busser, Lee, Massachusetts

FRI
15

*"THE GOOD MAN BRINGS GOOD THINGS OUT OF THE
GOOD STORED UP IN HIS HEART. . . ."*
                                    —Luke 6:45 (NIV)

"LET ME TELL YOU a story," she said.

I just rolled my eyes (after turning my face away). I should have known not to complain to Edith. It's bad enough to think I don't have power or influence, but seeing the cuts in my budget made me believe it. And when someone wants to tell you it isn't true, it's even worse.

Edith was undeterred. "Last week I approached a man who was breaking into my friend's car and asked, 'Do you have change for a dollar?' For just a moment he froze, then nonchalantly started walking away for a quarter block and then took off running." She smiled and sat back.

"People who make a difference don't let others define a situation. They see truth by how they live and what they do. Maybe it's time you quit letting others define the situation." She smiled again.

Edith's quirky stories are legend. Some make no sense; this one, remarkably, did. Because of her encouragement, I looked harder at my situation and discovered that the money left over after ending one part of my work was enough for a fresh start in a new direction. A whole new opportunity was there—one that I hadn't seen by focusing on what I didn't like and despite what someone else said was most important.

I've got Edith to thank for that.

Thank You, God, for the people who enter my life and help me find new ways to faithfulness. —JEFF JAPINGA

SAT
16

*THEN JESUS REBUKED THE UNCLEAN SPIRIT, HEALED
THE CHILD, AND GAVE HIM BACK TO HIS FATHER.*
                                    —Luke 9:42 (NKJV)

RYAN'S CALL CAME while we were attending a ballroom dance weekend in the Catskill Mountains. His newborn son, our first grandchild, Austin Theodore, was struggling to breathe and needed to be transported to a neonatal intensive-care nursery two hours away. So, less than forty-eight hours after we had marveled and beheld this ten-pound, twenty-three-inch miracle, we were meeting our family at the hospital to pray over him before he was to be tucked inside the traveling respirator.

It was Father's Day. We thought we were going to be celebrating this day with an incredible gift: Austin's homecoming. Instead, I held my wife Kathy as we cried together over the news, then called our son Kyle to join us at the hospital. I hesitated to call our son Joel and his wife Alyssa, who were vacationing in St. Thomas, but I knew they'd wish to know, so they could pray too. I called.

Immediately I was transported back more than thirty years, when I had called our parents to tell them that their first grandchild, our newly born Ryan, was struggling for his life.

During the hour-long car ride to the hospital, Kathy and I verbalized again the truths we had learned when Ryan had been born critically ill.

1. Birth is a miracle. It's a blessing to have children, a gift for however many minutes, days, months, years we'll be allowed to have them.
2. We're not being punished for any sins of the past. The New Testament's good news has promised this.
3. The children are not ours. They are God's. But they are ours to love and raise as long as we have the privilege.
4. God will carry us through whatever is ahead.

Thank You, heavenly Father, for the miracle of life. And thank You for saying yes, for healing Austin. —TED NACE

SUN
17

MY SOUL IS CRUSHED WITH LONGING. . . .
—*Psalm 119:20 (NAS)*

GROWING UP IN Elberton, Georgia, my childhood was happy, except for one particular holiday. I dreaded it, pretended it didn't exist, tried to ignore it. But no matter what I did, a secret longing remained in my heart: *You can't celebrate Father's Day. Your father's dead. You don't even have a real memory of him.*

As an adult I still couldn't come to terms with that longing. I still wanted to celebrate Father's Day with my own daddy.

Then, a few years ago, the *Atlanta Journal-Constitution* invited readers to submit memories of their father's shoes and what the shoes had meant to them as children. My memory was as real as if it had happened yesterday. I was about eight and accidentally discovered a pair of my father's shoes hidden way back in my mother's closet. My paper dolls suddenly forgotten, I touched the dusty shoes tenderly, examined them thoroughly in the sunlight, laced and unlaced them, and finally cradled one in each arm.

I mailed my memory to the newspaper because it satisfied something in me that I didn't fully understand. Lo and behold, the newspaper sent a photographer to my house. He took pictures of me holding an eight-by-ten photograph of the father I'd never known.

That Father's Day, I crept out before sunrise and found our newspaper in the driveway. There, in living color, was a picture of me with my father. And, for the first time, I genuinely celebrated Father's Day.

Father, Your unexpected ways of healing are as remarkable as Your indescribable love. —MARION BOND WEST

MON
18

AND SEEING THE MULTITUDES, HE WENT UP INTO A MOUNTAIN: AND WHEN HE WAS SET, HIS DISCIPLES CAME UNTO HIM: AND HE OPENED HIS MOUTH, AND TAUGHT THEM. . . . —*Matthew 5:1–2*

RECENTLY, MY WIFE SHIRLEY and I and nine other members of our family visited China. Whenever I go to another country, I'm always intrigued to learn more about its religious beliefs and practices. Since the seventh century, China has been strongly influenced by the teachings of the Buddha. Not surprisingly, there are many shrines and temples that feature statues of the Buddha, but what did surprise me were the various expressions on the faces of the statues, happy and sad and prayerful and angry.

One temple visit reminded me of a huge Buddha I saw many years ago in Japan, the famed Kamakura Buddha, south of Tokyo. That statue was fashioned from bronze in 1252 and was once housed in a temple that was destroyed by a tsunami more than five hundred years ago. Now the enormous image is in the open. The memorable thing about that Buddha is that visitors can go inside the statue and get a bird's-eye view of the world. I remember thinking at the time, what an experience it would be if we could see things from God's perspective.

Then it came to me: That is exactly the reason God sent Jesus—to share with humankind His love, His very nature, His wishes, hopes and dreams for His creation. Nothing, it seems to me, captures a God's-eye view of life better than the Beatitudes, which advise all who would follow Him to be humble, seek righteousness, be merciful and makers of peace.

> *Help us God, to see the needs of others first,*
> *Your will to seek with deep hunger and thirst.*
> —FRED BAUER

PAIN AND GRACE

WE'VE ALL experienced pain, sometimes physical, sometimes emotional, sometimes both at the same time. Marilyn Morgan King recently endured severe pain for five months before she underwent back surgery. Over the next week, she'll share what she discovered in the week before her surgery about the sometimes  surprising ways in which pain can bring us closer to God and to our innermost selves. —THE EDITORS

DAY ONE: AMAZING GRACE

TUE
19

WHEN I AM WEAK, THEN AM I STRONG.
—*II Corinthians 12:10*

AFTER FIVE MONTHS of excruciating lower back pain that has become steadily worse, extending into my left hip and leg, my doctor has sent me to a spinal surgeon, who tells me, "I'll have to fuse three vertebrae together, and soon, because your left leg and foot are already showing nerve loss. My earliest opening is in a week."

"Oh, I couldn't possibly have surgery then!" My voice is shrill. "We'll be in Nebraska. It's a family tradition!" Every year in June, I have one big birthday party for my three children, my ten grandchildren and six great-grandchildren in Kearney, where our family started. "I've already chosen a date and made all the arrangements. They're all counting on it, and so are we!"

As Dr. Kurica shows my X-rays and explains my MRI results to my husband Robert and me, we can see the urgent need for surgery. And the pain is really too intense for us to make the eight-hundred-mile drive to Nebraska and back. So we agree to my doctor's date for surgery. *What a disappointment!*

I pass the news to my children, then sit down with my journals and look back at what I've written during the previous months of agonizing pain. Strangely, I realize that I've been experiencing life more fully, more deeply since I've had this limiting physical problem. *What a rich inner life my pain has brought!*

Thank You, Holy One, for enfolding grace within pain. May I always find it there. —MARILYN MORGAN KING

DAY TWO: WHAT ABOUT DEATH?

WED
20

AND HE WAS TRANSFIGURED BEFORE THEM.
—*Mark 9:2*

4:30 AM: I wake from a dream in which I'm lost in a strange city. As I look for my car in a parking lot, I notice that all the cars are slowly sinking into the sand. (I've had several dreams like this in recent days.) Since a car often symbolizes the physical body, or the "vehicle" in which we move through life, could the dream-cars sinking into the sand represent my fear of death?

Well, what are my feelings about dying? I'm sure there's some fear and dread in me. Will I survive the surgery? If so, will it be successful? Or is this the beginning of the end? I am, after all, in my seventies. And if I die in surgery, what's next?

At this point, I have a flashback to a dream I had at age seventeen—a dream that was so real and so vivid and so filled with love, I absolutely *knew* in the depth of my soul that there is another reality beyond this one. Everything I saw was made of light: the poplar trees at the end of our driveway, the house next door and, oh, the Being of light Who is, even now, walking toward me. I knew without a doubt that I was being given a glimpse of a radiant reality beyond my human understanding.

I still can't explain it. I can't believe it was "just a dream," because the truth of that moment came in an instant and has never left me.

Dear God, I will see You again someday, where eternal light dwells.
—MARILYN MORGAN KING

DAY THREE: RELEASE FROM FEAR

THU
21

FEAR NOT, FOR I AM WITH THEE. . . . —Isaiah 43:5

CLOCK TICKING. Time dwindling. I guess I do have some fear of not making it through surgery. As I write this, there's that old familiar falling sensation in the chest that I often ignore or push down. I want someone to hold me and tell me that they'll stay with me and keep me safe. I imagine my mother, who has been gone for almost thirty years, sitting by my hospital bed, even though I can't see her.

"Don't worry," she seems to say, "I'm here and I'll never abandon you. It won't hurt, because you'll be asleep. Afterward, if it hurts, your father will give you some medicine to make you feel better."

My father has been gone for twenty-five years, but I sense his presence too. A very good and trusted doctor, he always kept me safe and I know I can trust him now.

How thankful I am that I grew up with a mother and a father I could always trust—a big, protective, but very strong and sure source of safety and confidence! Largely because of them, I am able to trust my heavenly Father to care for me, His child. Like the parents I can't see, I know God is with me here, now, my sure source of safety.

Heavenly Father, as I face my fear, it's You I need the most.
—MARILYN MORGAN KING

DAY FOUR: PAIN AND PURPOSE

FRI
22

SO WE, BEING MANY, ARE ONE BODY IN CHRIST, AND EVERY ONE MEMBERS ONE OF ANOTHER.
—*Romans 12:5*

YESTERDAY I prayed for the courage to live. Today I awake with great gratitude for my life and deep awareness of my many reasons for living. Of course, my husband, children and grandchildren are the first to come to mind. How very blessed I am by their love for me and mine for them. And I'm always grateful for the all-encompassing Holy One, Who is love.

I guess I expected that the desire to live would center around what I might accomplish to make my life valid, what I might do to earn my right to continue living. No, the courage to live came by way of love, from connecting deeply with my own soul and with the Holy Spirit, as well as from the gift of being able to look past personality barriers to see the beautiful soul of every person.

I need to let my husband and children know of the marvelous beauty I see in their souls. When my son Paul was a teenager, he had the usual rebellious attitude, but one day I saw through that front and realized what a beautiful spirit he was. I need to tell him that again.

Once more, I am in touch with the mystery, with a reality beyond (and within) this extraordinary everyday reality. I want to be a traveler in this stunning web of interconnections that brings answers to the soul's hunger and thirst. So I'm grateful for the gift of my body and its ability to speak its messages, even though one of its languages is pain.

Spirit of God, help me to know, always, that You are love unbounded.
—MARILYN MORGAN KING

DAY FIVE: HOLY MOMENTS

SAT
23

"SHE HAS DONE A BEAUTIFUL THING. . . ."
—*Mark 14:6 (RSV)*

MY DEAR FRIEND Mona and I are in the habit of spending Saturday afternoons together. When we meet at my house, she brings a carry-out lunch, and vice versa. After we eat, we talk about what's going on in our lives. We share what we're reading, pages from our journals, including our dreams, and discuss matters of the spirit. The day I tell her about my upcoming surgery is her day to come to my house. She brings me a lovely bouquet of peonies from her garden and a special treat, lemon pie.

After eating, we do our usual sharing. She encourages me to talk about my feelings about my back surgery, only a few days away. We talk about life and death and God and healing and our families, our hopes and dreams, fears and sorrows. It seems to clear out the fear I'd been feeling.

After Mona has left, I sit at the dining room table eating my lemon pie, savoring its sweet tanginess, its rich yellow color, the frothy feel of meringue on my tongue. As I breathe in the lovely scent of peonies and enjoy the pale pink beauty of the petals and the quiet solitude, I know that this is a holy moment. Perhaps such moments are reason enough for living. Without a body and senses, I could never have known the sacredness of this moment. Could it be that's all life asks of me? Could it be that holy moments fully lived can transform the world?

Creator God, help me to remain alive to Your magnificent creation and to pass that joy to others. —MARILYN MORGAN KING

DAY SIX: PAIN AND JOY

SUN
24

*AND GLADNESS SHALL BE FOUND THEREIN,
THANKSGIVING, AND THE VOICE OF MELODY.*
—*Isaiah 51:3*

ONLY TWO MORE DAYS until surgery. All through winter's end and spring's return, I've been in so much pain, I haven't been able to shop for birthday presents for my husband, children, grandchildren and great-grandchildren. So I've had to fall back on gift certificates, as impersonal as that feels to me. Of course, I know that my loved ones will understand. It isn't the unwrapping of gifts that matters; it's being together. And yet this year our family's together time will have to be postponed. My son John and his family, who live in Virginia, won't be coming now. I was especially eager to see them. How long it's been since I've seen them!

Now fear reasserts itself. *What if I die during surgery and never see my family again?* As these words on the journal page start to blur, I stop writing, unable to bear the emotional pain of that thought.

When I close my journal, the phone rings. Robert answers and says, "Sure, just a minute," and brings the phone to me. I roll my eyes, not wanting to talk to anyone. Oh, it's John! I *always* want to talk to him!

"Hi, Mom. I'm just calling to tell you I've made a flight reservation. I'll be there tomorrow night."

"But, honey, you'll miss work."

"I've got permission, Mom, and I've made up my mind. Karen and Saralisa will be there too." As we complete our call, delight ripples through me like water radiating outward when a stone is tossed in, completely swallowing up my fear.

O Great Comforter, thank You for hearing my fear and transforming it into joy! —MARILYN MORGAN KING

DAY SEVEN: THE GRACES OF PAIN

MON

25

The Lord will give grace and glory....
— *Psalm 84:11*

DR. KURICA walks by the gurney as the nurse wheels me out of surgery and surprises me by asking, "How's the pain down your leg?"

I draw in a shocked breath. "It's gone!" It is the first time I have noticed my freedom from pain. My doctor gives me a smiling thumbs-up.

In deep gratitude to God for the graces pain has brought me, I vow:

- to feed my soul every day by prayer, spiritual reading and contemplation;
- to live from that place in me where God is love;
- to appreciate that life is precious, not because I have some great world-transforming purpose, but because I have this body and these senses for such a short time, and because they are openings to holy moments;
- to fully experience each moment, for as St. Irenaeus said, "The glory of God is a man fully alive"—may I be that fully alive person!
- to be aware that God is always waiting for an open heart and that the opening comes only when the ego gets out of the way;
- to recognize that living takes great courage and that on some level we make a life-or-death choice each day;
- to keep choosing life.

Thank You, God, for the gift of pain, which teaches me compassion and so much more; and for relief from pain, a grace beyond measure.
— MARILYN MORGAN KING

TUE

26

"I will punish every one who leaps over the threshold...." — *Zephaniah 1:9 (RSV)*

"KEEP THE DOGS OFF the grass for at least three weeks," the landscaper said after he finished putting a new lawn behind our house. Easy for him to say. For twenty years, our three dogs had used the fenced backyard for both play and business. We would have to put them on leashes, arm ourselves with plastic bags and maneuver them down our narrow, rosebush-lined walkway to the front lawn, where the neighborhood was in full view and alive with action.

We braced ourselves and stepped out the front door, the dogs pulling against their leashes to sniff at the thick bushes and dig in the dirt. We held tight and navigated the thorny walkway until we reached the relative safety of the front lawn. For two weeks our vigilance paid off. The dogs seemed to get used to the routine, even Hobo, who was resistant to change.

Then one day we stepped out the front door, and before I could close it behind us, Hobo yanked his leash out of my husband Keith's hand and plunged headfirst into the roses after a nearby cat. The cat tore down the street to safety; the thorny bushes had stopped Hobo in his tracks. He whimpered piteously while we carefully removed the thorns from his head and ears, and treated the cuts with antiseptic.

We thought he might be afraid to go out front again, but the next day our Hobo was just as eager . . . except that he waited until he was clear of the roses before he bounded to the end of his leash in pursuit of the cat. Some things never change.

Help me, too, Lord, to temper my impatience with prudence.
—RHODA BLECKER

WED
27

HE THAT HUMBLETH HIMSELF SHALL BE EXALTED.
—*Luke 18:14*

WHEN I WAS A CHILD, my parents' home was established as a resort for African Americans. We entertained paying guests throughout the summer. In June we received a request for accommodations for the first two weeks of August. The letter was signed "Joseph H. Mitchell, Jr." Something about the letter attracted Father's eye. It was clear, simple and direct, with no conditions attached.

When a friend came to call later that day, Father told him about Mr. Mitchell's letter. "Do you know who he is?" our visitor asked. "He's a famous lawyer! He serves on the Governor's Council at the Boston State House!" That afternoon we began a special housecleaning.

Mr. Mitchell arrived by train, and Father picked him up at the station. We were expecting a forceful man, self-important and a little overbearing. Instead he was quiet, almost shy. During the two weeks he stayed with us, I served Mr. Mitchell his meals and was impressed by how considerate he was. After eating, he would tiptoe to the kitchen door and thank Mother warmly. She beamed with delight. Whenever he left for a walk, he told us where he was going and when we could expect him back. Mr. Mitchell relaxed in a corner wicker chair on our front porch. He was always neatly dressed in a suit, white shirt and tie.

That summer I changed my mind about what made people distinguished and important. Yes, of course, it was partly from the work they did, but more than that it was their attitude toward others. This humble man seemed to prove the words of St. Augustine, "A man is what he chooses." Mr. Mitchell had chosen to be gracious.

Lord, thank You for the gift of graciousness You bestow on those we meet.
—OSCAR GREENE

THU
28
"OUT OF ALL THE GIFTS TO YOU, YOU SHALL PRESENT EVERY OFFERING DUE TO THE LORD, FROM ALL THE BEST OF THEM. . . ." —*Numbers 18:29 (RSV)*

ON OUR TWENTIETH wedding anniversary, my husband walked in the door with a dozen red roses. I went to the living room cabinet for a vase and saw several of our wedding gifts sitting on the shelf—china, crystal, silver—as though they were museum pieces. "We'll save them for a special occasion," I'd told Paul. But in twenty years we'd hardly used them. Most of the time they sat waiting on that shelf. *Well, if this isn't a special occasion,* I thought, *I don't know what is.*

Reaching for a vase, I thought of other gifts I might have stored away, waiting for just the right moment. Like my gift for music. I hadn't sung in the church choir for years; I always said I was too busy. But just like those wedding gifts, weren't God's gifts meant to be used and enjoyed?

That night we set the table with our best tablecloth, our silver flatware and a cut-crystal vase filled with red roses. The kids especially enjoyed drinking sparkling juice from etched crystal goblets that they'd never seen on our dinner table. We laughed as the four of us clinked our glasses together. "Let's do this more often," my daughter said.

"We will," I replied, as I made a mental note to go to choir practice that week. After all, if every day is a gift from God, then all of life is a special occasion.

Give me one more gift, Lord: the courage to use all You've given me for Your glory. —GINA BRIDGEMAN

FRI
29

FOR IF YE FORGIVE MEN THEIR TRESPASSES, YOUR HEAVENLY FATHER WILL ALSO FORGIVE YOU.
—*Matthew 6:14*

SO I WENT TO a new place to get my hair cut. (I have exacting standards for my barbers: Are they cheap? Are they close by?) The stylist greeted me with clipboard in hand. She had a few questions, among them: "Do you blow-dry your hair?" (*Not recently—maybe in 1975?*) "Do you use oil or gel?" (*Oil. Quaker State. 10W-30. Oh, you mean on my scalp?*) And the kicker: "Do you dye your hair?"

I looked at her. My hair is nearly all white. Do I *dye* my hair? Yes. Yes, I do. I *chose* this color. I go to the drugstore and look through all the possible variations, and I pick the box labeled "Premature Gray." What was she thinking?

I'm very good at recognizing dumb things people say because I'm very good at saying dumb things. Ironically, I'm not so good at forgiving others their imperfect moments.

That's why Peter is my favorite apostle. This guy was thick with a capital *TH*. When Moses and Elijah appear out of nowhere beside Jesus, Peter suggests that they build a nice little house for each visitor, "for he did not know what to say" (Mark 9:6, RSV).

Apparently not. His boss is transfigured before him, and Peter pipes up with the first thing on his mind: real estate. It would, of course, be better if he simply enjoyed the moment, but Peter is too human for that.

You've got to love the guy. Luckily, Someone did. Someone saw something in the fisherman that no one else saw, and a church began. The premise was simple and simply outrageous: You're forgiven for the dumb things you say, as long as you forgive your neighbor.

Even the gray-haired one, Lord, who's so quick to judge, who's so slow to forgive, who needs much more than dye to hide his many, many human imperfections? —MARK COLLINS

SAT
30

FOR THE FRUIT OF THE SPIRIT IS IN ALL GOODNESS AND RIGHTEOUSNESS AND TRUTH. —*Ephesians 5:9*

WHAT DO I GET from my garden? A few leaves of mint, some basil, a couple of cherry tomatoes, about five peony blossoms, one rosebud and some parsley. An exceedingly modest summer crop, you may think. But my garden gives me an excuse to dig in the damp soil, to pull weeds with my bare hands, to clip a hedge and to smell the crushed grass, to shake off the petals from a flower, to feel the earth under my nails. To warm myself in the afternoon sun, to look for the rainbow in a spray of water, to catch a ladybug on my finger and let it fly away—not without making a wish. To know that there's always another season ahead in case this season feels too warm or too cold. The winter's frost will fade into spring's rains to be followed by summer heat and then autumn leaves. My garden takes me away from my checkbook and my unanswered e-mail. I'm reminded that there are things more permanent—and fleeting—in life, like dandelions, bees, and green blades of grass that you can hold between your fingers and blow on so that they sound like an oboe.

What does my garden give me? Patience, peace, perspective and a chance to talk to my Maker. What better harvest?

I thank You, Lord, for this good earth and all its bounty.

—RICK HAMLIN

MY WALK WITH GOD

1 _____

2 _____

3 _____

4 _____

5 _____

6 _____

7 _____

8 _____

9 _____

10 _____

11 _____

12 _____

13 _____

14 _____

15 _____

16 _____

17 _____

18 _____

19 _____

20 _____

21 _____

22 _____

23 _____

24 _____

25 _____

26 _____

27 _____

28 _____

29 _____

30 _____

July

The Lord will give strength unto his people; the Lord will bless his people with peace. —*Psalm 29:11*

LESSONS FROM THE JOURNEY
CHOOSE YOUR COMPANIONS

SUN

1

BLESSED IS THE MAN THAT WALKETH NOT IN THE COUNSEL OF THE UNGODLY . . . NOR SITTETH IN THE SEAT OF THE SCORNFUL. —Psalm 1:1

SOME PEOPLE ARE no fun to travel with, like the British couple at our hotel in Naples, yearning aloud for a proper cup of tea, a decent tub bath and the London *Times*. There are ultraplanners, like the aunt I traveled with, who knew in such detail what we were to see and when, that she had no eyes for anything else. And overambitious travelers with so many sights to see that there's no time to savor any.

But, oh, how other companions enhance travel! I had the privilege of going to Israel with an elderly woman on her first trip abroad. Her delight at how different everything was, even things as simple as doorknobs and road signs, made them new for me too. And companions who share their knowledge, like Cecily, whose love of Wales as she drove us around that land let us see vanished knights and Celtic bards in what could have been merely scenery. And those who see every trip as an adventure, like my travel partner for fifty-nine years, John, who never makes reservations because "Who knows where we'll want to stop?"

I've had companions on the spiritual journey too. Some made the way seem daunting, like the fervent Canadian preacher with a program of salvation as rigid as my aunt's travel plans: Only these precise steps in this fixed order would do. Or the believer so eager for me to get where she was that she rushed me through all the stages of discovery, conversion and commitment with no pause for joy and awe.

But then there are those God-given companions who've lighted the road! Like Jean, whose joy was so contagious I asked how she'd found it. And Joe, who'd traveled long and far, but offered only what my first steps could use.

Lord of the journey, give me travel companions who let me see and love You better. —ELIZABETH SHERRILL

MON
2

HOLD THOU ME UP, AND I SHALL BE SAFE. . . .
—*Psalm 119:117*

THE SUMMER OF MY final year of college I worked in New York City, a real woman of the world, commuting by bus from my parents' house in New Jersey.

One evening on the way home from work, the bus came to a stop inside the Lincoln Tunnel. Traffic was at a complete standstill. Word got around: The entire region was in a blackout. "Better get comfortable," the driver said. "We aren't going anywhere for a good long while." At least my parents would know what was keeping me.

Finally we inched forward. After endless stops and starts, we emerged from the tunnel and slowly made our way to my neighborhood. With street lamps and traffic lights out, I strained my eyes to see as we approached my stop. The candy store on the corner was in darkness, and I dreaded the walk home alone.

I signaled the driver to stop. "Good night," he said. "You be careful." I stepped out into the pitch black, feeling more like a frightened child than a woman of the world. The bus pulled away. What was that light in the doorway of the candy store? A flashlight. *Someone's there.* "Dad!" He reached out and put his arms around me. I started to cry. "How did you know when I'd get here?" I asked.

"I didn't," Dad said. "But I would have waited all night." Then he took my hand, and with his flashlight to guide us, we walked home together.

My father let me know I was safe that night, Father, the way I know I'm always safe with You. —PHYLLIS HOBE

TUE
3

"GOD IS MY STRENGTH AND POWER, AND HE MAKES MY WAY PERFECT." —*II Samuel 22:33 (NKJV)*

FOR THREE DECADES the Nace family has been visiting Yellowstone National Park. Once we found ourselves enjoying a multinight stay in a rustic cabin nestled within Yellowstone's boundaries.

One morning we rose early and drove out to a lovely picnic area located along the Yellowstone River. After spotting a quiet lagoon, unloading our picnic supplies and starting the grill, we ventured around the bend to see the rushing river.

Across the river was a huge herd of buffalo, intent on crossing toward us. The mama bisons nosed, prodded and pushed their babies into the rushing waters. We worried as each of the bawling babies was quickly swept off its spindly legs. Calmly, each mother stepped into the water and swam upriver of her young one, snorting encouragement. Meanwhile the males bellowed support, not stepping into the river to cross until every mother and baby were onshore. The entire crossing lasted nearly an hour, as the dripping creatures ambled ashore slightly downriver of us.

We wondered why the female bison didn't swim downriver of their young to brace the babies upright against their bodies. Later we learned that the mothers had provided their young with the most protection by swimming upriver and breaking the crushing current of the stream.

Father, when I'm facing turbulence in my life, I know that You're beside me, breaking the current. —TED NACE

WED

4

HIS BANNER OVER ME IS LOVE.
—*Song of Solomon 2:4 (NIV)*

I'M A TRADITIONALIST WHEN it comes to congregational worship styles. I'm a little nervous that some people at my church are talking about change.

I'm also a traditionalist when it comes to a local holiday salute. For years I'd gather a few friends and go downtown to the National Symphony Orchestra holiday concerts on the west lawn of the U.S. Capitol. Spreading out a picnic, we'd enjoy the music and the view down the mall toward the Washington Monument.

This was back when holiday concerts were just local events. Back when the crowd might demand—and get—a favorite Sousa-march encore by chanting, "Stars and Stripes! Stars and Stripes! Stars and Stripes!" Back when the first chords of the program's first song, "The Star-Spangled Banner," prompted the crowd to stand and turn its back to the musicians and toward the American flag flying on the Capitol itself.

But it's never been quite the same since the network TV crews descended, scaffolding the view, scripting the talk, choreographing the minutes. And they added color-guard flags down by the orchestra, which meant that some of the crowd paid respects to the color guard while others held to our tradition of facing the beflagged Capitol.

Old and new traditions, side by side. It may not have made for a clean televised photo, but we were all standing in respect to the same colors.

I guess there is room at my church for both traditionalists and innovators. After all, we're all worshiping the same Savior, Whose banner is the color of love.

Lord, on this Independence Day I pray that we as citizens and as Your children will be unified in spirit, even when we value differing traditions.
—EVELYN BENCE

THU
5

"I AM THE LORD YOUR GOD, WHO BROUGHT YOU OUT OF THE LAND OF EGYPT, OUT OF THE HOUSE OF SLAVERY." —*Exodus 20:2 (NAS)*

IT WAS A GORGEOUS DAY, but my feelings didn't match the weather. I'd slammed down the phone after another heated discussion with Jamie, our twenty-three-year-old daughter. As I trudged to the mailbox, the chirping birds and the dancing butterflies irritated me. *Stop being so happy,* I thought.

Jamie seemed determined to forget the truth she'd learned as a child. It was as if she had to prove she could make it without God. And I couldn't change her.

I opened the mailbox. There, on top of a stack of bills, was a small, delicately decorated envelope. Instantly, I knew who'd sent it—Robin, my best friend since high school. She'd drawn a vine of colorful flowers along the edges. In her lovely handwriting she'd written a Scripture that circled the envelope: "Faith is being sure of what we hope for and certain of what we do not see" (Hebrews 11:1, NIV). It was addressed, "To my favorite friend, Julie Garmon."

Robin was walking the same path I was walking with one of her children. As I looked at the envelope, I felt a sweet softness, a moment of understanding, and I remembered my own rebellion. I'd so wanted Jamie to see things my way that I'd stopped trusting God and had closed my heart.

A week later, Jamie and I patched things up. And yesterday, we had another conversation on the phone. "Mom, you know what?" she said. "Everything you need to know in life, you learn in elementary school. Don't take drugs. Eat your fruits and vegetables. Go to church. Make your bed. Things are easier if you live God's way."

"I know," I said. "I've been learning the same thing!"

Father, my rebellion is like Jamie's; I so want things my way. Forgive me.
—JULIE GARMON

FRI

6

"TEST ME IN THIS," SAYS THE LORD ALMIGHTY, "AND SEE IF I WILL NOT THROW OPEN THE FLOODGATES OF HEAVEN AND POUR OUT SO MUCH BLESSING THAT YOU WILL NOT HAVE ROOM ENOUGH FOR IT."
—*Malachi 3:10 (NIV)*

AFTER GRADUATING FROM COLLEGE, I began working freelance from home, and though I loved my work, the words on the screen started to look flat to my critical eye. Days passed, and my endurance for facing that same computer screen wore down.

I began looking for a morning job, something to distract my mind from the work that wasn't getting done, and I found Ella, a five-month-old girl in need of a nanny. She was just cutting her teeth and learning to scoot backward across the floor. We spent our mornings stacking blocks, reading books and taking walks around her neighborhood. One day I placed the brightest and newest toys in front of her and sat back to watch.

Along came Rigi, Ella's ten-year-old husky. Ella's eyes lit up and she reached to grab Rigi's scratchy fur. She beckoned with baby talk and petted her dog's pointed ears. When Rigi's patience wore thin, Ella was left with a handful of dog hair. She batted it between her tiny fingers, examining each gray strand, then extended her hand to me to share her prize.

Ella grew out of most of her clothes that summer but never out of her intense curiosity. Each day, each season, each moment was new to her. She savored the brisk morning, the feel of the stroller straps, the light coming through the trees, the flowers along the sidewalk. I pointed out things to her on our walks, only to begin noticing them myself.

Ella's viewpoint poured into my own life, giving me more energy and focus for my work. Things that had once seemed everyday or ordinary started to seem brand-new—just as they were for Ella.

Lord, thank You for flooding my world with reminders of the extraordinary details of life. —ASHLEY JOHNSON

SAT
7

BE STRONG AND OF A GOOD COURAGE. . . .
—*Deuteronomy 31:6*

ON JULY 7, 2004, we were about to board a plane in Scotland, on our way to England to continue our summer vacation, when my wife Carol and I noticed a small knot of people gathered around the airport television. We soon learned that terrorist bombs had exploded in central London. Memories of 9/11 filled our minds, but we decided to continue our trip, trusting in the British security system.

A few days later, we arrived in London. The police, world-famous for being unarmed, patrolled the streets with machine guns slung across their chests. Electronic signs warned us to be vigilant about abandoned luggage and odd behavior. Sandbag barricades surrounded every government building. Many public places were closed entirely or accessible only through metal detectors.

Our first tourist stop was the Cabinet War Rooms. Watching grainy newsreel footage of World War II, I saw sandbag fortifications surrounding key buildings and armed men patrolling the streets. The film had been made in 1942, but it could just as easily have been filmed now. Other exhibits showed how the British had handled this earlier crisis with fortitude and faith, exemplified by the intrepid, bulldog face and ever-present cigar of Winston Churchill, declaring in his gravelly voice that this was Britain's "finest hour" and that if the population kept up their courage, they "would not flag nor fail."

We continued our travels, a bit more cautious perhaps, but with our hearts lifted even higher by the knowledge that the need for fortitude and faith is eternal, and every moment can be a "finest hour."

Give me the faith and courage, Lord, to face whatever may come my way.
—PHILIP ZALESKI

SUN
8

WE WHO BELIEVE ARE CAREFULLY JOINED TOGETHER WITH CHRIST AS PARTS OF A BEAUTIFUL, CONSTANTLY GROWING TEMPLE FOR GOD. *—Ephesians 2:21 (TLB)*

MY CHURCH HOSTED OUR first-ever interparish softball game on a sweltering Sunday evening in July. Because it was still one hundred degrees at game time, refreshments were served first—thick sandwiches, chocolate cake and three kinds of homemade ice cream. The church basement was delightfully cool; there was some sentiment for skipping the ball game in favor of another round of ice cream, but finally the bats and gloves were lugged to the field.

Before the umpire could call "Batter up," the game hit its first hitch: One of the teams didn't have enough players. Interchurch rivalry was immediately scrapped in favor of choosing sides. One of the "choosers" was a teenager from our church, and the other was a boy from another denomination who showed up and wanted to play. Players ranged in age from thirteen to seventy-plus, and everyone got in the game.

The three cheerleaders—Katelyn, MaKayla and Danielle—cheered for both teams. They also ran bases for players who had eaten too much ice cream. I'm not sure who won and who lost because no one kept score. When the game was over, the first baseman (a woman) took pictures of the players, cheerleaders and onlookers, then everyone went home tired but happy.

I think the softball game will be an annual event. It was a good way to have fun. More important, it was a great example of how to *be* the church—the welcoming, caring and lively Body of Christ.

"I am the church! You are the church! We are the church together! All who follow Jesus, all around the world! Yes, we're the church together!"
—PENNEY SCHWAB

MON

9

The Lord is my chosen portion and my cup. . . .
—*Psalm 16:5 (RSV)*

"DON'T FORGET THE WEDGWOOD," Aunt Kate said shortly before her death. "It's out in the storage room in a big wooden crate. You can just throw away those old dishes in the kitchen. I've been saving the good china for you."

That was one hundred percent Aunt Kate. She paid careful attention to every game the Cincinnati Reds played, but she was also always thinking of me and worrying over what she might pass on to me and to our children Brock and Keri. But the material things weren't really important. I just wanted her to stay with us. I wanted to hear her stories and enjoy her unique approach to life.

But finally I knew it was time to let her go—because she told me so. She slipped away quietly, and then it was time to clean out her apartment. In her kitchen cabinets I found only one plate and one cup and saucer. The bowl of the once-white cup was brown with coffee stains. It was chipped in two places, and the saucer had a tiny hairline crack that wrapped across its rim. As Aunt Kate had said, these dishes weren't worth keeping. But before I realized what I was doing, I found myself carefully wrapping and packing that old cup and saucer.

Now when I need to feel close to Aunt Kate, I go to the china cabinet and pull out that old cup and saucer. Every crack speaks to me of unselfishness. Every chip reminds me of the joy that comes when you consider someone else's pleasure more than you think of your own.

Aunt Kate left us many things, but the least valuable of all her possessions, a simple cup of kindness, is the greatest heirloom of all.

Father, how can I look past myself and give someone a cup of kindness today? —PAM KIDD

TUE
10

WHICH OF YOU BY TAKING THOUGHT CAN ADD ONE CUBIT UNTO HIS STATURE? —*Matthew 6:27*

THE NEWS FROM my doctor was bad.

"Five-seven," he said, studying the height scale during my annual physical.

"And a half," I lobbied.

"All right, I'll give it to you."

Still, it was an inch shorter than the last time my height was checked way back in my twenties. My weight I tracked scrupulously, but I had never bothered with height. I knew I was five feet eight and a half inches tall (and that half inch meant a lot). Why would that ever change? "Our spines compress," my doctor said breezily as I dressed. "It's a natural part of aging. You're fortunate. Count your blessings." He sent me on my way. I called my wife immediately and told her the grim news.

"Don't scare me like that!" Julee barked. "I thought for a second something was really wrong." Then she pretty much hung up on me.

Could I blame her? I was being totally silly. And vain. That's what this was about—vanity. And I disliked catching myself being vain, disliked it even more than my shrinkage.

Hustling down the sunny street toward the subway, I took a second and looked around me. The street was full of people, all sorts of people, all sorts of colors and sizes and styles and ages. No two of them were alike. And it was wonderful. It was beautiful. It was an incredible thing to realize that I fit in nicely as I was, as God made me. *Yep,* I thought, *very fortunate.*

Lord, I need to count my blessings from time to time, all five feet seven and a half of them. And don't forget the half. —EDWARD GRINNAN

WED
II

ALTHOUGH THE FIG TREE SHALL NOT BLOSSOM. . . .
—*Habakkuk 3:17*

MY SON JON, our beloved prodigal, happened by our house unexpectedly one summer day. Smiling and walking confidently as if his life were totally okay, he put down a brown paper bag in the kitchen. "It's you, Mom, isn't it, who loves figs so much? Aren't they beautiful?" He held one in his huge, square hand.

"Yes, Jon." I touched it softly, our hands touching.

"Taste it," he urged.

"Okay," I said and then asked, "Do you remember the Scripture from Habakkuk about the fig tree without blossoms?"

"Sure, I know it." No matter where Jon's unwise choices take him in life, his love for Scripture remains. He picked up a paring knife and carefully sliced the fig into perfect halves, offering one to me.

I pointed to the pretty bits of pastel scrunched up inside. "Those are the blossoms, Jon."

"No way, Mom! Sounds like something you made up."

"It's true. I discovered it accidentally at the library." We both stared at the open fig in his hand. "Do you know what it means?" I asked.

He smiled and nodded. I knew that look; he understood fully. Even so, I said, "God's at work . . ."

Jon finished the thought: ". . . even when we can't see a thing happening."

Nothing else was said; nothing else was needed.

Lord, I don't understand what happened when Jon and I ate that fig, but I believe it was a powerful promise from You. —MARION BOND WEST

THU
I2

HE WAKENS ME MORNING BY MORNING, WAKENS MY EAR TO LISTEN LIKE ONE BEING TAUGHT.
—*Isaiah 50:4 (NIV)*

A FEW YEARS AGO, I took a long-awaited trip to Italy, spending a week in the Tuscany area. As we neared the end of our time there, our tour guide arranged for a "Meet the Locals" night. Five people from the town of Cortona came to give us a slice of what their lives were really like.

We met an artisan who worked in gold and his new wife, who had given up country life to live in town. There was an aged pastry maker. And a batik artist and her daughter, who sold handmade sweaters. We asked them questions about their genealogy, education, real estate prices and opportunities for young people there. Then someone asked, "What do you think of tourists like us?"

The batik artist shook her head as soon as the question was translated. "Not the word! Not the word for you. A *tourist* is someone who comes to eat lunch. A *traveler* is someone who comes to make a discovery." Her gesture took in our entire group. "Ah, travelers!"

Today I am far from the quaint streets of Cortona, with its ancient doors and geranium-filled windows. But while I cannot choose to stroll in the plaza or visit the Etruscan museum, I can choose how I will spend this day—as a *tourist* who goes routinely from activity to activity or as a *traveler*, intent on discovery. And that decision, rightly made, can transform every day into a vacation from the ordinary!

Thank You, Father, that You have given each of us a sense of wonder and curiosity. Help me to exercise mine today. —MARY LOU CARNEY

FRI
13

HAPPY SHALT THOU BE, AND IT SHALL BE WELL WITH THEE. —Psalm 128:2

MY STEPMOTHER HAD a house on Long Island where I spent many childhood vacations. Just down the road from us was a family with a dog—a collie mix—with a name like Shep or Chuck. Whatever his real name was, when he came over to our house, he became Doggie. I liked to walk on the nearby beach, and when I did, Doggie inevitably showed up out of nowhere to walk along with me.

Most dogs have to be persuaded to go for a swim, but not Doggie. Warm weather or cold, he'd wade in and out of the waves, seemingly relishing the rush and pull of the water against his legs. When we got back to my driveway, Doggie would either come in for a while or saunter home, his tail wagging in the slow and easy way it always did, letting me know that all was well with the world.

Twenty years later, my wife and I have two dogs of our own. They're both a blessing and a joy, but also—from three-times-daily walks to vet visits—very much a responsibility, one of many that have come along in the years since I took those walks along the beach with a dog whose real name I didn't even know. Fortunately, the memory and the spirit of those walks stay with me. On days when worries and responsibilities threaten to overwhelm me, I think of that slow and steady wag of Doggie's tail, and remember that though times and responsibilities have changed, all is well with the world.

Lord, thank You for those in my life—human and otherwise—who have embodied the simple joy of living. —PTOLEMY TOMPKINS

SAT
14

HE GENTLY LEADS THOSE THAT HAVE YOUNG.
—Isaiah 40:11 (NIV)

I RECENTLY SPENT an afternoon helping my very pregnant daughter-in-law Alexandra prepare for the birth of her second child. I organized toys while she measured spaces for storage containers that would separate one child's stuff from another's. She penciled some numbers down on paper, made decisions about where to put the tiny new diapers and how to make a single bedroom work for two children.

As we worked, Alex confessed that she was concerned about having enough time to be enough "mom" for a second child. "How will I do everything?" she asked. I admitted that I'd had the same concerns a generation earlier.

Meanwhile, three-year-old Gabriella played nearby, naturally mimicking many of her mommy's actions.

"You weigh thirty-seven, Oma," she told me matter-of-factly as she measured my arm with the tape measure. She then sat down at her little table and began doodling on a piece of paper. "I'm making a meeting," she announced. A short time later, she put her purse over her arm, picked up her baby, stuffed a pacifier in the doll's mouth and headed for the back door. "We need some fresh air," she informed us.

People say she looks just like her daddy, but I can tell you, she walks just like her mommy. As I sat there that day, surrounded by the piles of clothes and toys and the normal happenings in this home, I realized—again—the power of a mother's influence, communicated by simply being Mom. It's one of God's great provisions to moms, a gift that makes us enough to meet the needs of all our children.

Lord, help mothers to trust in You, to know that You are enough to make us enough. —CAROL KUYKENDALL

SUN
15

WHY ART THOU CAST DOWN, O MY SOUL? . . . HOPE THOU IN GOD. . . . —*Psalm 42:11*

MY BIRTHDAY THAT SUNDAY was not lining up to be much of a celebration. I hadn't received any phone calls or cards, and my gift was one of those practical ones for which husbands are famous and that wives don't appreciate. My hints about going out to eat had fallen on deaf ears. A birthday cake was nowhere in sight.

The one highlight of the day would be at church. Our pastor asks the congregation to sing "Happy Birthday" to anyone whose birthday falls on a Sunday. And so I waited expectantly through the announcements, waited through the opening hymn, waited while the pastor mentioned another birthday coming up the following day.

And then he began his sermon.

How could he be so forgetful? I felt slighted, overlooked, disappointed. *Why do people take me for granted, Lord? Especially today of all days!*

A few minutes later, an old hymn, "Be Thou My Vision," redirected my focus. Two lines in particular spoke directly to my soul: "Riches I need not, nor man's empty praise, Thou mine inheritance, now and always."

But, of course! How could I be so forgetful as to overlook God's blessings during the past year, let alone a lifetime? Even as I closed the hymnbook and placed it back in the rack, I could feel my heart beginning to celebrate a happy birthday.

Thank You, Lord, that the up side of down times is that You use them to put things into their proper perspective. —ALMA BARKMAN

READER'S ROOM

I HAVE HAD THREE heart attacks since 1998, and I now have a nurse part of the time and am on a good diet. I am now ninety-seven years of age and sing in the choir at church. Since I am the only man in the choir, I feel that I am needed. I also work in my garden. I used to teach earth science to eighth graders and have collected thousands of rocks and minerals, so now I am giving collections to schools and to children. I know it is by the grace of God that I am able to do this, so I thank God for the gift of each day, and I am trying to make the best use of each day.
—*Edward Freas, Walnut Cove, North Carolina*

GOD-FINDS
FINDING MY VOICE

MON

16

LET YOUR SPEECH ALWAYS BE WITH GRACE, SEASONED, AS IT WERE, WITH SALT, SO THAT YOU MAY KNOW HOW YOU SHOULD RESPOND TO EACH PERSON.
—*Colossians 4:6 (NAS)*

I WAS CONDUCTING a telephone interview with a renowned interior designer. I had asked him if he might offer some tips on achieving a French country look for the readership of a home-decorating magazine where I work part-time. *"Temps?"* he articulated. "Or did you mean *Tenth?* I can't make out a word you are saying, ma'am."

Close to tears, I fought to say my words more deliberately. But I was tired from working all day at the hospital and the words weren't coming out as clearly as I wanted. Because of my neurofibromatosis, tumors inside my mouth can cause my words to come out mushy. Folks sometimes have difficulty understanding me, especially if I'm trying to talk when I'm rushed or fatigued.

In the months that followed, that dreadful interview was never far from my thoughts, especially when I had to teach a class or interview someone I'd never before met. Then I addressed a women's group on living the faith-filled life. In my talk I mentioned some of my illness-related struggles, not broaching the topic of my garbled speech.

Several days later, I had an e-mail from Shelly, who had attended my talk and was writing to tell me how much my words had touched her life. *My words?* "It was the way you *said* them," she told me. "You have the sweetest Southern drawl. And when you talked about God, you said it all with such care, I could just feel the love you have for Him."

Slowly. Deliberately. While I was covering up a defect, Shelly had simply seen the Savior—and pointed me back to Him.

May the words of my mouth be acceptable in Thy sight, dear Lord.
—ROBERTA MESSNER

TUE

17

IF YOUR ENEMY IS HUNGRY, GIVE HIM FOOD TO EAT. . . .
IN DOING THIS, YOU WILL HEAP BURNING COALS ON HIS
HEAD, AND THE LORD WILL REWARD YOU.
—*Proverbs 25:21–22 (NIV)*

WE ADOPTED OUR youngest son Ted when he was eight years old. His few possessions fit into one grocery sack, but we were repeatedly warned by Social Services that his psychological baggage could fill an entire grocery store.

In one of these mental suitcases was our son's ability to see the good in people whose goodness I couldn't see at all. For instance, Ted's keen eyesight saw the good in the neighbors who rented a mobile home east of our property. They owned guns and dogs and not much else. We chased their dogs away from our home many times. Finally two of their dogs tore apart our son's rabbit cage and killed one of Ted's treasured 4-H rabbits. Ted was heartbroken but not angry. He opened yet another suitcase from his past and out spilled coals of kindness. He carried these coals to our neighbors' house.

"They feel real bad," Ted told us. "As soon as they get some money they are going to pay me for my rabbit."

Our neighbors abruptly moved away the next month. "Don't worry," our son said. "I gave them my address before they left."

"People who spend all their money on cigarettes, beer and guns don't set aside money to honor a debt," I said angrily. Ted looked at me. I knew he was looking for good in what I said and he wasn't seeing it.

Several months later a letter arrived. A letter and forty dollars, sent by someone who needed to douse the fire on his head.

Dear God, help me to see everyone through Ted's eyes.
—TIM WILLIAMS

WED
18

THOU WILT SHEW ME THE PATH OF LIFE: IN THY PRESENCE IS FULNESS OF JOY; AT THY RIGHT HAND THERE ARE PLEASURES FOR EVERMORE. —*Psalm 16:11*

THERE IS A GREAT flurry of activity in our house this morning surrounding a wooden puzzle piece shaped like a chick. Its name, I'm told, is Parachute Licorice. The kids call her Paralic for short. All five children have other animals from Stephen's wooden animal puzzle, and a rollicking story is evolving between them and Paralic. At the moment the pig has scarlet fever.

I am in mother heaven: My offspring, from ages two to eleven, are happily playing together. On top of that, because they're all occupied, I'm miraculously free to do what I want. It makes me giddy. *Ah, how I wish life could always be like this! Wouldn't that be grand?*

As these words pass through my brain, an inner alarm goes off somewhere. I retrace my thoughts and notice that they've undergone a subtle shift. I've moved from appreciating the gift of a peace-filled morning into hoping for more mornings like it. In short, I'm being greedy.

I sigh, and reluctantly admit it's probably a good thing that mountaintop experiences like this are few and far between. As a former backpacker, I know the main joy of hiking isn't reaching the peaks; it's the quiet and constant focus on the trail. The pleasure lies in the immediate challenges, in the beautiful things that God places along the path and in the rhythm of the hike. Peaks are where we look out to get the big picture. Then it's back to the trail.

The kids laugh loudly in the other room. Paralic has apparently healed the pig. I smile and store this peak experience in my heart.

Dear Lord, when I'm tempted to judge the journey by the peaks, remind me of the good things on the path. —JULIA ATTAWAY

THU
19

THE MERCIFUL MAN DOETH GOOD TO HIS OWN SOUL. . . . —*Proverbs 11:17*

THE STOCK MARKET was picking up, and as an investment adviser I was busier than ever. I had several appointments lined up, driving from one part of town to the other. I sped through a yellow light and noticed the traffic ahead slow to a standstill. "Now what?" I muttered to myself. "An ambulance? A police car?" No, it was a funeral procession.

Usually this is something I really love about the South: Everyone stops for a funeral procession, every car showing respect for the grieving. But not that day; not when I was in such a hurry.

Up ahead I could see a green funeral flag flapping on the lead motorcycle as the police escort approached. I parked on the shoulder, becoming more frustrated by the second. Then I looked at the guy behind me. He'd stepped out of his car and was standing at attention.

All of a sudden I was twelve years old, trying to understand why my grandfather was gone. I remember riding in the long black funeral limo, holding my mom's hand. She was pointing out the window, showing me how the world had stopped out of respect for my grandfather's life. I remembered how the cars were pulled over and how the people looked at us as we passed. They told a little heartbroken boy that his grandfather mattered.

My appointments could wait. I got out of the car and stood in silence as the hearse passed. Next came a black Lincoln, with an elderly lady alone in the backseat. Our eyes met. I nodded gently at her. She gave me a slight wave of her hand and I could read "thank you" on her lips. Then she was gone.

The entire incident took only six minutes out of my day. Sure, I could have used those minutes in other ways. But that was the best six-minute investment I'd made in a long time.

Father, fill me with Your mercy. —BROCK KIDD

FRI
20

"SUBMIT TO GOD AND BE AT PEACE WITH HIM. . . ."
—*Job 22:21 (NIV)*

THE RAIN LEAKED THROUGH my slicker. Thick black clouds hovered over the Rocky Mountain peaks. I limped through the muck in the corral, leading an old black mule. I'd taken a job training nineteen wild mules, even though I didn't know the first thing about them. Every day they kicked, bit and stomped me into the mud. *God,* I prayed, *why did You lead me to this job? I should quit!*

I tied the mule to the only stout thing around, the post of the barbed-wire fence. When I turned away, the mule transformed herself into a cyclone. She reared up, spun around, and landed backward and upside down on that fence. The wire stretched so tight it sang. She rolled over, her legs poking between the strands of barbed wire. Then she flailed. I wanted to cover my eyes, but I just stood there gawking. Suddenly she grunted and quit.

I ran over. She looked up longingly. Her big brown eyes seemed to say, "I trust you to get me out of here."

She calmly watched as I clipped the wire. When I finished, I tugged on her halter and she stood as if nothing had happened. From that day on, that mule would do anything for me.

Over dinner I told Snuffy, my cowboy-mentor, what had happened. He stroked his salt-and-pepper beard. "Most folks think mules are stubborn, but they're not. If a mule thinks it's going to get hurt, it'll quit. That mule knew she couldn't get out, so she surrendered instead of tearing herself up."

I had been the stubborn one. I'd been training the mules *my way.* From that day on, I learned to train them like mules and hardly ever got kicked or bit anymore. And I decided to keep the job God gave me.

Lord, when I do things my way, I'm fighting You. Help me to surrender, so I can be at peace with You. —REBECCA ONDOV

SAT
21
Trust in the Lord instead. Be kind and good to others; then you will live safely here in the land and prosper, feeding in safety.
—*Psalm 37:3* (TLB)

ALTHOUGH I ENJOY SWIMMING, biking and kayaking, my favorite outdoor activity is snorkeling. I snorkeled for the first time when I was celebrating my fiftieth birthday with two of my children in Hawaii. By the time I turned sixty, I'd had the fun of snorkeling off nine different islands in the Caribbean.

The absolute peace I feel down in the ocean is incredible. Fish and coral are Technicolor-magnificent: stunning yellow, orange, electric blue, wild red, fluorescent green. Thousands of fish in a tight school swim past your face in the same direction, looking for food.

It's also scary down there. My heart raced when a four-foot-long barracuda darted past me just inches away and when a long black eel slithered alongside me before disappearing into a large rock cave. Thousands of cantaloupe-sized sea urchins that look like pin cushions with six-inch-long, razor-sharp needles projecting from their bellies are nestled on every rock and coral reef. Even the hard, sharp-edged coral, which you're not supposed to touch because it's an endangered living thing, is dangerous to soft flesh.

I've learned that life is a lot like the ocean: scary and rough in spots, but mostly beautiful and exciting. Over the years I've navigated through two marriages, single parenting four children, having them in college for seventeen years in a row, and finally uprooting myself and moving to Florida, arriving thirty hours before a major hurricane. But like snorkeling, life can be managed beautifully if you keep your eyes open, use the proper equipment, rely on your faith and always swim with a friend.

Heavenly Father, keep an eye on me whether I'm down in the ocean enjoying Your splendor or working through another struggle that keeps me strong and invigorated. —PATRICIA LORENZ

SUN
22
WEEPING MAY ENDURE FOR A NIGHT, BUT JOY COMETH IN THE MORNING. —Psalm 30:5

WHEN I WAS ELEVEN and twelve, I went to Camp Tonda for Boys in the foothills of the Adirondacks. The very mention of Tonda makes me feel the itch that the woolen T-shirt and short pants gave me. (Yes, a woolen uniform for special events.)

There are a host of other memories—of horses to ride, crafts to master (I still have the little three-legged stool I made), swimming, hiking. Several times we would go down a twisty road to the girls' camp and have punch and fumble our way at conversing and dancing (no cheek-to-cheek allowed). "Goodnight, Sweetheart" was the tune that always ended it. On the way back, I remember how we kidded a counselor about his swooning for a certain "counselorette." On Parents Day, my mother would appear and, once, my father did. They were divorced. But Dad, who lived in Kentucky, was present by letters, and he often sent an entire box of candy bars.

But most of all I remember my daring deed: I requested permission to lead our homegrown Sunday service. I chose the hymn "When Morning Gilds the Skies" and spoke, nervously but from the heart, on a Bible verse, Psalm 30:5. I remember clearly saying hopefully that homesickness would vanish with morning's light. I also said that my cabinmate Lute Thompson would defeat his slump with a home run in our baseball games. I don't know if he did. There must have been other things I said, but those are locked in memory.

*As are You, Father, locked tightly. —*VAN VARNER

MON
23
BUT THERE WAS FOUND IN IT A POOR WISE MAN, AND HE BY HIS WISDOM DELIVERED THE CITY. YET NO ONE REMEMBERED THAT POOR MAN.
—Ecclesiastes 9:15 (RSV)

THERE ARE ABOUT one hundred apartments in our building. Many of the residents are older and need help getting around, their mail brought to them and little things around their apartments fixed. In addition, we have a large pool with a deck and seating area that requires maintenance, not to mention the rigorous opening and closing processes in May and October. Our plumbing and heating systems are always in need of some kind of care, and someone has to maintain the laundry machines and empty the coin changers regularly. The air-conditioning and ventilation systems are from the Stone Age and need constant watching. These are just a few of the tasks necessary to keep a big community like ours going.

You can't imagine what we pay our manager.

Nothing.

Arnold is in his seventies, a former railroad man (as they say), and devoted to making everything run smoothly. From changing light fixtures in the lobby to pouring nasty stuff down the shower drains to keep them clear, he does all the grunt work. Heavy boxes addressed to us appear outside our door long before my husband has a chance to get home from work and fetch them from the mailroom. When Arnold isn't helping all of us, he's caring for an elderly friend who is bedridden.

Sometimes I think Arnold doesn't get nearly enough credit for all the things he does. But that doesn't seem to bother him. One afternoon this summer, I watched him replacing planks in the pool deck. He labored meticulously, contentedly in the sun, wearing pads to protect his bony knees. For Arnold, a job well done is reward enough.

Father, help me remember that good work, well done, is Your work.
—MARCI ALBORGHETTI

TUE
24

HE THAT RECEIVED SEED INTO THE GOOD GROUND IS HE THAT HEARETH THE WORD, AND UNDERSTANDETH IT; WHICH ALSO BEARETH FRUIT, AND BRINGETH FORTH. . . . —*Matthew 13:23*

ON OUR VISIT TO CHINA, our tour guide to the Badaling section of the Great Wall, northwest of Beijing, was a young woman whom I'll call Sarah. She spoke nearly flawless English, and she was well-trained in the history of this 2,500-mile-long structure.

After the others in our party left to scale a distant part of the wall, my wife Shirley and I stayed behind with Sarah in one of the lower watch-towers. There we talked about all sorts of things, including religion. Her parents were practicing Buddhists, she told us, but "like most young people, I am not a believer." Then Sarah asked a question I wasn't expecting: "Are you Christians? And if so, why?"

I took a deep breath, knowing that our party would be returning soon. How do you answer such a question in five minutes? I began by saying that I grew up in a community of believers, so it was easy for me to accept Jesus as my personal Savior, sent by God to proclaim His Word, which is recorded in the Bible. I went on to tell her that Christians believe in a personal God, one Who guides them, one Who hears and answers prayers, one Who is all knowing, all powerful, always present, one Who loves unconditionally, one Whose mercy and grace are limitless.

"It must be very comforting," Sarah replied. I nodded. By now our group was returning and that was the end of our conversation. I wonder if our little talk planted any seeds.

> *Remind us, Lord, that Your words fell on hard ground—*
>   *and soft,*
> *Those with eyes who saw and those who blindly scoffed.*
>   —FRED BAUER

WED **THE LORD WORKS OUT EVERYTHING FOR HIS OWN**
25 **ENDS. . . . —*Proverbs 16:4 (NIV)***

MY RESIDENT ARTISTS—my husband Paul and eleven-year-old daughter Maria—have created a drawing game they both enjoy. Maria draws a line on a piece of paper—straight, curved, zigzag, whatever she wants. Then Paul must draw another line—again, any kind—connected to the first line. Then Maria adds another, and they keep adding lines until they eventually create a picture. Most of the time neither one knows exactly where the picture is going until they're almost done. The fun is in accepting the challenge and continuing to be creative until the drawing is complete.

Not being an artist, I don't understand how you start with a squiggle and end up with a lion or a house or a dog. It makes me think about what some people do with life's zigzags. Like the couple in our church, who, unable to have children, have opened their home to foster children over the last several years. They've turned a disappointment into something hopeful. It makes me wonder if I can be that flexible and imaginative with disappointments.

When I asked Maria the secret to her drawing game, she gave me the perfect answer for dealing with unanticipated zigzags. "You don't look at the line on the paper and see only what it is," she said. "You see all the things it can be."

The possibilities are unlimited.

Heavenly Father, open my eyes to the beauty, and the possibility, in the zigzags. —GINA BRIDGEMAN

THU
26

LET ALL BITTERNESS AND WRATH AND ANGER AND CLAMOR AND SLANDER BE PUT AWAY FROM YOU. . . .
—*Ephesians 4:31* (NAS)

I'M SITTING IN AN airport terminal and I am fuming. I'm trying to decide how angry I will allow myself to become. My departure flight was an hour late this morning because of bad weather and dangerous flying conditions. As a result, all of my connecting flights have been thrown off schedule. Now I'm enduring a five-hour layover in an airport instead of attending an important meeting.

Who is to blame? No one. But I'm still angry at the situation, and a tension headache is pounding my temples. Above all I'm irritated that I've allowed myself to become so upset.

I have a choice—a conscious decision—as to how far I'll permit my emotions to escalate. I have a choice of either allowing my frustration to ruin my entire day and transform me into an unpleasant grouch, or letting go of my anger.

So here I am, sitting at a restaurant table with my laptop computer. And I've determined to make this time productive and enjoyable. Already my headache is fading and my spirits are lifting. I've made the decision to not let anger control me.

Dear God, give me the strength not to be ruled by frustration and anger, but to choose a better, more constructive way. Amen. —SCOTT WALKER

FRI
27

For it is by grace you have been saved, through faith—and this not from yourselves, it is the gift of God. —Ephesians 2:8 (NIV)

IT WAS THE FINAL DAY of a summer missions trip with my high school youth group, and we had some free time to explore the Mexican town where we were staying. That afternoon in the central plaza, my friend Steve took out his guitar and started playing, and the rest of us sang fragments of any song we could remember. Our repertoire included "The Star-Spangled Banner," "Amazing Grace" and a couple of rock songs. Our cacophony drew many curious glances from the townspeople, and to our delight a few passing tourists threw money into Steve's open guitar case.

By the end of the concert, a group of raggedly dressed children had gathered around, staring in wide-eyed amazement at the pile of pesos in the guitar case. Hoping to make them smile, we took the money to a corner store where we purchased nine cans of soda. Eight of the children jumped for joy when we handed them the drinks, but one little girl wouldn't take it until I spoke to her father. Thinking that the free soda must come with strings attached, he asked me in Spanish who had given it to her. I replied with the first words I could think of: It was *"un regalo de Jesus Cristo"*—a gift from Jesus Christ. He nodded slowly at the little girl, and she drank excitedly.

Two months later I began my freshman year of college, quickly involving myself in a long list of activities. As I reached the brink of burnout, I remembered that man on the plaza and saw how much of my life had become an attempt at proving I was worthy of God's love. I took a deep breath and reminded myself that His love is *un regalo,* no strings attached.

*Lord, thank You for loving me unconditionally. —*JOSHUA SUNDQUIST

SAT
28

There is no fear in love; but perfect love casteth out fear: because fear hath torment. He that feareth is not made perfect in love.
—I John 4:18

EVERY NIGHT OF MY LIFE, from my early childhood until my early thirties, I had nightmares. I would awaken, sweating, breathless and paralyzed by fear. I tried to avoid things like horror movies that I thought might trigger the dreams.

Recently, I was in Maryland at a family gathering. With bags of fresh, hot popcorn and cups of soda, cousins, in-laws and children of varying ages settled in for the evening's entertainment—the latest, scariest horror flick! I groaned inwardly, but not wanting to ruin everyone else's fun, I sat quietly and said nothing.

When the movie was over, I went to bed and quickly fell asleep. In the middle of the night, drifting somewhere between sleep and waking, I became aware of a small presence at the foot of my bed.

It was seven-year-old Cortez, one of my cousins. "I'm scared. I'm having bad dreams," he said. "Can I sleep with you?"

"Yes," I answered.

"I keep thinking about the movie," he said as he climbed in.

"Think of something else," I told him as he snuggled beside me. "Think of your favorite cartoon." In my fog I began to sing the theme song from *SpongeBob SquarePants* to him. His shock that I knew the words probably jolted him out of his fear. "Perfect love casts out fear," I said. "So say to yourself, 'God loves me, my grandmother loves me. . . .'" That's the last thing I remember until I woke up.

It wasn't until morning that I realized I'd forgotten to be afraid.

Lord, surround me and fill me with Your perfect love. —SHARON FOSTER

SUN
29
THE LOT IS CAST INTO THE LAP, BUT ITS EVERY DECISION IS FROM THE LORD. —*Proverbs 16:33 (NIV)*

MY GREAT-AUNT LILLIAN was a faithful reader of *Daily Guideposts*. Her bookcase held years and years of them, shelved in order among the Franklin Mint Civil War figurines and her other beloved books. She often quoted from the devotionals and wrote her favorite prayers on index cards that she put on her refrigerator beneath shiny fruit magnets and read every night until she knew them by heart.

When she died two years ago, I decided to try my hand at writing for the book she had loved so much. A few months later, I was thrilled to learn the devotionals I had written would be included in the next edition. What seemed most fitting was that one of the devotionals was about Aunt Lillian, about coping with her death and realizing how the legacy of her life, her stories and the light she brought to a room would always be with me.

"Wouldn't Aunt Lillian be thrilled?" I asked my sister Maria. "It's a shame she doesn't know."

"She knows," Maria said.

Months later, the book came in the mail. Excitedly, I looked through it for my devotionals. Each fit within the context of the seasons, but otherwise they seemed randomly placed throughout the book. I found the first two and was searching for the one about Aunt Lillian. I turned the page and there it was—July 29, my birthday. The date wasn't random at all.

Lord, thank You for helping me to see, with Aunt Lillian, Your hand in all events of my life. —Sabra Ciancanelli

MON
30
"In his hand is the life of every creature and the breath of all mankind." —Job 12:10 (NIV)

It was another beautiful day in Italy. The sky was a rich blue, devoid of clouds, and once again I was taking in the breathless sights of Florence. We'd spent the morning wandering through ancient cloisters, lush gardens, and open markets where I bought fresh bread and bright tangerines. Now my friend and I walked above the city to a small white church on top of a hill. Both of us were tired and sat to rest for a while on the steps of the old building. We were overlooking the city, watching the sun's slow descent over the rust-colored rooftops.

A few steps in front of the church, a small cemetery caught my attention. I walked through the gate and wandered among the marble tombs, statues and colorful flowers. There were pictures encased in glass on most of the stones; one was an old photograph of a woman of thirty-six, her hair tied in a loose bun. I did my best to read the inscription and wondered about the life of this woman who now rested in this beautiful graveyard.

I didn't feel sadness or fear of death as I looked at these memorials. Rather, I found them strangely comforting. *Today I am alive,* I thought as I watched the sky turn pink and violet with the sunset. *One day, in God's good time, someone will come upon my tombstone and wonder about the life I once lived. But today, He's given me life.* And there, with the beauty of Italy before me, I'd never felt so deeply the richness of living it.

Thank You, Lord, for the gift of life and for this magnificent world You've given us to live in. And when the time comes, bring me peacefully home to You. —KAREN VALENTIN

TUE
31

I TRUST IN GOD'S UNFAILING LOVE FOR EVER AND EVER. —*Psalm 52:8 (NIV)*

ON VET'S ORDERS, our cat Nickel was temporarily sporting a brand-new lampshade collar and she was running into trouble negotiating the terrain in the living room. Every time she tried to step from the hardwood floor to her favorite carpet, the bottom of the collar would catch on the rug's edge. One step forward and Nickel was nose-to-carpet, lampshade firmly planted on the ground. She backed up, ready to try again and land facedown, when I gently lifted the collar. A moment later, Nickel was curled in her favorite spot on the rug, gazing at me, trusting and content.

It amazed me that she didn't blame me for her predicament. Our other cat, Antimony, is not so forgiving. But while "Tim" is the family skeptic, Nickel seems to have faith that I'll look out for her.

When I had taken her to the vet a week earlier, even as they had her stretched out on her back for the ultrasound, completely vulnerable and in pain, she looked at me with that same quiet trust. After her operation to remove a bladder stone, she resisted taking her pills and picked at her stitches, but didn't hold it against me that I forced her to swallow the pills and took her back to the vet for new stitches and the lampshade collar.

Soon enough Nickel learned to lift her head when navigating around obstacles and to swallow her pills without too much fuss. Eventually the collar and stitches were gone, but the trust was still there; I am her protector.

Nickel reminds me daily that I'll find comfort and peace in trusting in my Protector. Whatever obstacles I face, even if I feel "nose-to-carpet" and helpless, God is looking out for me.

Heavenly Father, I turn my eyes to You with a trusting gaze. I know You will always guard me and guide me. Amen. —KJERSTIN WILLIAMS

MY WALK WITH GOD

1 _____

2 _____

3 _____

4 _____

5 _____

6 _____

7 _____

8 _____

9 _____

10 _____

11 _____

12 _____

13 _____

14 _____

15 _____

16 _____

17 _____

18 _____

19 _____

20 _____

21 _____

22 _____

23 _____

24 _____

25 _____

26 _____

27 _____

28 _____

29 _____

30 _____

31 _____

August

In his hand are the deep places of the earth: the strength of the hills is his also.

—Psalm 95:4

LESSONS FROM THE JOURNEY
STOP BEFORE YOU DROP

WED
1

But thou, O Lord, art a God full of compassion, and gracious. . . . —Psalm 86:15

I WAS GRIEVING, as usual, over things I hadn't done that day: the clothes I was going to take to the thrift shop, the letter I'd meant to write . . . another day when my good intentions outpaced my energy. Then I remembered a car trip.

It was a route traveled by millions of people in the Middle Ages. Even by car it was a long way, nine hundred miles from Paris to the northwest corner of Spain and the shrine of Santiago de Compostela. For the medieval traveler, intent on receiving the blessing vouchsafed to those who reached the goal, it was a journey of months across mountains, swamps and waterless plains.

Almost at the end of the journey—just seventy-five miles to go—comes the steepest, most difficult stretch of all, the lonely Cantabrian Mountains. The travelers by that time were exhausted, many lame or ill.

As the road began to rise, my husband John and I came to an ancient, almost windowless church in the middle of a weed-grown field, an unimpressive little building but for a weathered wooden door in a side wall. This was *Puerta del Perdon*, the Door of Pardon. Out of pity for those who could go no farther, this spot had been given a special status. To step through this door was to receive the same blessing as those who made it all the way to Compostela.

Many glorious churches have been built along the pilgrim route, but this squat, barren little chapel is the one I think of most often. A door of pardon—what a boon on the lifelong journey too! "You fell short of your ideals," it says. "But it's all right. You're on the right road. I am blessing you right where you are."

Lord of the journey, lift my eyes from my failures to the door forever open to Your grace. —ELIZABETH SHERRILL

THU 2 *THE HEARTFELT COUNSEL OF A FRIEND IS AS SWEET AS PERFUME AND INCENSE.* —*Proverbs 27:9* (NLT)

I'D ALWAYS BEEN A stay-at-home mom, working as time allowed, but when my children were grown, my goal was to get out of the house and become part of the business community. After ten years of working hard from home, I proudly signed my name to a lease for my own office and found myself facing hard decisions in a world completely foreign to me.

I knew I needed help, but where was I going to get it? As a first step, I contacted some successful businesswomen in our town—Lillian, a lawyer; Betty, a bank vice president; Diana, a social worker; Stephanie, a business owner; and Janelle, a real estate broker. I invited them to tea and asked their advice. We had such a good time together that we decided to meet every Thursday for breakfast.

That was eight years ago, and we still meet every Thursday to encourage and support one another. We bring our pains and our triumphs to breakfast; seek advice and share our troubles freely. We wept together when Stephanie developed cancer and died within five short months, and celebrated when Betty, a widow, met a wonderful man and remarried. We laugh together and cry together—often at the same time.

The years have seen many changes in our lives, but what started out as an easy way for me to learn more about being a good businesswoman has evolved into something far more powerful: friendship and a blessing from God.

Thank You, Lord, for the special friends You've brought into my life. May we always continue to be close to You and to one another.
—DEBBIE MACOMBER

FRI 3 *"SAUL AND JONATHAN WERE BELOVED AND PLEASANT IN THEIR LIVES. . . ."* —*II Samuel 1:23* (NKJV)

MY FATHER ED SCHANTZ went to be with the Lord after putting up a strong fight against Alzheimer's disease. At the funeral, we six kids took turns telling the audience the things we enjoyed about him.

"Dad loved children," Bobby noted. "And they loved him too."

"He had such a wonderful, happy laugh," I said.

"He was so innocent, like a little child," Mark added. Others spoke of his childlike faith in God, of fishing trips, of how handsome he was.

Finally, my mother stood up and said, "Let's not forget that first and foremost Ed was a minister of the Gospel who taught and baptized hundreds of converts in his lifetime."

Fair enough, but when it comes right down to it, I think we tend to remember how people were rather than things from their résumé.

Several times this year I have attended funerals, and always I hear the same kinds of remarks about the deceased: "She always had a smile on her face, even when she was in pain." "He was the only school bus driver who never lost his temper." "I liked to be around her, she made me feel so special." "He used to read the *Little House on the Prairie* books to us." "She was everything I always wanted to be: beautiful within and without."

It was a good reminder to me that in this age of overachievers, what I am may be more important than what I do for a living.

I'm glad, Lord, that I can help others just by being myself.

—DANIEL SCHANTZ

SAT

4

AND SHE TIED THE SCARLET CORD IN THE WINDOW.
—*Joshua 2:21* (NIV)

THE DAY OUR SON CHRIS left for a tour of duty in Afghanistan with the Army, my husband Gordon insisted that I buy fifteen yards of ribbon to make a gigantic yellow bow. As I tied the bow around the huge pine tree by the front driveway, I felt a stab of loneliness.

The next morning, as I was picking up the newspaper in the driveway, a neighbor stopped her car and asked about the ribbon. When I told her about Chris, she said, "I'll be praying for him." Soon everyone on the street had noticed the yellow ribbon, and another neighbor called to tell me, "We want to have a cookout to let you know we support your family."

At the cookout a seven-year-old girl named Amanda offered me a gift bag to comfort me. Inside was a dried Play-Doh pot, a thread with several beads on it and a piece of foam with a slit in it. "A ring holder," she told me. A mother brought her two elementary-school boys over to me and each whispered a bit shyly that they were praying for Chris.

The day Chris returned from Afghanistan safe and sound, I got out a ladder and took down the yellow ribbon. By then it was stained from the rain and had pine straw stuck in it. I shook out the bow and took it down to the basement for storage as a reminder of those who comforted us and prayed for us during his absence.

Dear Father, thank You that when I share my personal struggles with others, they support me with Your love. —KAREN BARBER

SUN
5

I WILL SING PRAISE TO THY NAME, O THOU MOST HIGH. —*Psalm 9:2*

MY HUSBAND ROBERT AND I recently attended a weekend program exploring the relationship between dreams and the soul. It's a subject of interest to both of us, since we share our dreams over breakfast and travel together on our spiritual journey.

"I just don't know how to get to my soul," one of the participants told the leader.

"I'll give you the best way I know," he replied. "Take a praise walk in nature. That'll get you there." Then he suggested that we all go outside and take a walk, each one going a separate way, and just *notice and give thanks* for all we see.

The retreat house in southern Colorado is surrounded by wilderness and majestic canyons. I chose to walk eastward on a winding path that took me upward on rocky ground. Looking around, I praised God for the panoramic beauty of the surroundings.

Next, I found a shady place under a canyon overhang and sat down. At first, I just sat quietly, breathing in the beauty of the green grass, yellow-leafed trees, ground-hugging plants, and boulders large and small, unmoved by human "fixing." As I sat there, I thought I heard a bird. The gentle wind seemed to whisper, "Yes, it's hiding in a hole in the canyon wall." Sure enough, within a few minutes a beautiful bird with a black and white tail flew out of its canyon home, soaring above me, filling my heart with birdsong and praise.

Great Creator of all that is, thank You for mountains and rivers and golden leaves, for green grass and tiny ants, and for the "impossible" flight of honey bees. Oh yes, and for canyon birds singing and soaring into listening hearts. —MARILYN MORGAN KING

MON
6

"MY PEOPLE HAVE . . . FORSAKEN ME, THE SPRING OF LIVING WATER. . . ." —*Jeremiah 2:13 (NIV)*

MY SISTER PRISCILLA LIVES on a deep lake. It's not just any lake but the same one I frolicked in as a child, visiting my uncle's cottage. Like the Mole in *The Wind in the Willows*, I had "entered into the joy of running water." But that was a long time ago.

For the past ten summers I've visited the lake. I've sipped tea on the bank. I've dangled my feet from the dock and even donned a swimsuit on occasion. But go for a swim? Return to the waters? Old memories of joy beckoned, but I resisted—water too cold, body too old—until one afternoon this year when Priscilla asked me to keep an eye on her seven-year-old grandson Dylan playing on the dock.

One thing led to another. Priscilla's casual comment—"The water's warmish this year"—prompted me to slip off the dock and inch toward the deep. *Brrr.* Standing in hip-high water, I wasn't ready to take the plunge. Then I looked over at Dylan. The boy I was watching was watching me. I feigned a lunge. I contorted my face. He caught the vision and cheered me on. "Go! Go!" I caught the spirit. "One, two, three. . . ."

After my splash, as I rediscovered the joy of doggie-paddling, I heard Dylan clapping and laughing, sounding, I imagined, like an angel rejoicing "over one sinner who repents" (Luke 15:10, NIV) and returns to the Water of Life.

Lord, bless me with people who will encourage me to enter into the joy of Your spiritual refreshment. —EVELYN BENCE

TUE
7

I HAVE CHOSEN HIM TO BE MY SON, AND I WILL BE HIS FATHER. —I Chronicles 28:6

IT'S 5:40 AM, and I can hear William's alarm. He needs to take an early bus for his job as a counselor at a summer camp. When he was younger and had to wake up early, I would get up with him. I'd fix his breakfast, pack his lunch, see him off. But he's eighteen now, and even if I wished to do those things, he prefers his independence. "You don't need to get up," he said the night before.

From my bed I am aware of his movements—the clank of his spoon against the cereal bowl, the front door opening as he picks up the paper, the water in the sink when he washes the dishes. *His mom will be pleased that he remembered that,* I think. I hear his duffel bag brush the floor. And I start wondering: *Does he have enough money? Did he remember to pack his retainer? Does he have any sunscreen?* Okay, he's a responsible kid, but I miss being needed. I fear that when that door finally slams shut, it's closing on me.

I need to trust that all that Carol and I have done as parents will hold him in good stead. Isn't that the whole point of parenting? If you do a good job, you put yourself out of a job.

I get up and tell him, "Have a good time at camp."

"Bye, Dad." He gives me a hug. Nice to be needed for that. Then the door slams shut, and I hear his footsteps scrambling down the sidewalk as he races to catch his bus.

Be with my child, Lord—Your child—as he steps into the world.

—RICK HAMLIN

WED
8

I HAVE CONSIDERED THE DAYS OF OLD, THE YEARS OF ANCIENT TIMES. —Psalm 77:5

"WE'RE GOING TO PARIS this summer!" we announced to the kids over dinner one fine spring day. Both John and Andy applauded the news. Paris is near the top of almost everyone's vacation list, and the boys knew that Carol and I had fond memories of the nine months we had spent there as graduate students many years before.

A few months later, we found ourselves on French soil. After settling in at our hotel on the Left Bank, we set out to visit our old haunts. "Just wait until you see the Eiffel Tower illuminated at night and hear the bells of Notre Dame and eat a *croque-monsieur* at a sidewalk café," I exclaimed. First, however, we decided to visit our old home, a medieval building in the middle of the city where Carol and I had lived, happy as could be, in a cold, cramped one-room apartment.

As we approached the dim entrance, I anticipated the pleasure of seeing an old friend but discovered instead the sadness of years gone by. We had been so young then, so much in love! As the day went on, and we wandered around Paris, showing the kids the sights, I couldn't shake the feeling of lost youth. The scenery was breathtaking, the coffee and croissants delicious, but I was trapped in sadness. And then Carol broke the spell by saying, "We had a great time here, didn't we? But it's so much better now, being here with our memories *and* our kids."

That was all it took. I realized that although God wants us to remember the past, He wants us to live in the present. I laughed, put my old beret on my head and set out to enjoy our family vacation.

Lord, help me to celebrate the gift of the present moment and to sense there always Your loving presence. —PHILIP ZALESKI

THU
9

IF WE HOLD FAST. . . . —Hebrews 3:6 (NAS)

DISCOURAGEMENT RODE ALONG with me on a steamy August day as I drove to have my hair done some thirty-five miles away. Lately, it seemed impossible to hold on to God and His promises.

When I stopped for a red light, alarm suddenly replaced self-pity as something whizzed into my car through the partially open window. I screamed, and a white-haired man in overalls standing on the street corner called out, "It's only a katydid, lady."

The light turned green, and I took off, quickly opening the windows and the sun roof. The six-legged hitchhiker backed herself resolutely across the passenger's side of the dashboard and hunkered down unflinchingly against a corner of the windshield. I sped up, and wind blew through the car. The katydid only tightened her grip. I had no idea what katydids do. *Will she sting me? Hide in my hair? Crawl into my clothes?* The faster I drove, the more stubbornly Katie held on. I closed the windows and the sun roof and slowed down, keeping my eyes moving from the highway over to Katie. When I applied the brakes suddenly, she put one dainty foot forward to steady herself.

At the hairdresser's, I parked in the shade and decided to leave the windows down and the sun roof open. When I returned forty-five minutes later, there she sat. "You're very determined. I like that," I said softly.

About five miles into our return trip, Katie suddenly bounced up and down like a child who'd finally decided to take off from the diving board. "Wait, Katie!" I said. I pulled off the road, opened the window, swallowed hard and ever so slowly slid a church bulletin in front of her. Amazingly, she put one leg on it, then another, until she'd walked securely onto the paper. Steadily, I inched it over toward the open window. Hesitating a moment, she flew upward. Watching her courageous venture into the unknown, my faith unexpectedly soared skyward too.

Only You, Father, could send encouragement on the wings of a katydid!
—MARION BOND WEST

FRI
10

ATTEND TO MY WORDS; INCLINE THINE EAR UNTO MY SAYINGS. —*Proverbs 4:20*

SERVING OVERSEAS WITH the Army in World War II was a challenge. I survived the heat in the Philippines, the uncomfortable winter in Japan and the drenching spring rains in Korea. My inner strength came from dreaming of returning home to my wife Ruby and to the fourteen-month-old son I had never seen. I was hoping my homecoming would be the warmest and most joyful ever.

In early August 1946 I returned home and rang the doorbell at 1:30 in the morning. Ruby answered, but this was not the Ruby I'd left nineteen months earlier. She seemed cold, angry, distant. All at once I felt a deep sense of abandonment and loss. Ruby took me upstairs to the one little room we were renting. I looked down at our little son and kissed him, but the reception was not what I had dreamed of—not by a long shot. I was a stranger to my own family.

Then one evening on our front porch I shared my feelings with Ruby. She listened patiently and then she told me what she had been through since I'd been gone: the loneliness, the hunger, the lack of money. She and our son were huddled in this one room with no savings and no hope for the future. I listened—really listened—and in my silence, I learned the power of suffering love. That was the beginning of healing. The love that we had for each other returned and has never left us all these years. Listening opened our hearts.

Dear Father, never let me forget to listen. —OSCAR GREENE

SAT
11

*LET YOUR CONDUCT BE WITHOUT COVETOUSNESS; BE
CONTENT WITH SUCH THINGS AS YOU HAVE. . . .*
—Hebrews 13:5 (NKJV)

I THOUGHT I WASN'T hung up on material things, but after a while all the jokes about my tiny black car were beginning to wear on me. "Look, Mommy," a passing child once exclaimed. "That looks like the little car that all the clowns come out of at the circus."

Hardy-har-har, I thought, but I forced a smile at the child.

Add to its diminutive size a manual transmission, a few dents and dings, and a Picasso-esque twisted antenna that I discovered when I came out of the post office one day. I found myself praying, "Just once, God, I wish I had a car that people would envy, not pity." But even with brown-bag lunches for a year, I still wouldn't have the down payment for a new car.

Then last week I was pumping gas, musing over the fact that it had gone from thirty cents to three dollars a gallon in my lifetime, when I heard a deep voice say, "I envy your car."

My head turned to see whom the speaker was talking to. He was talking to me. "You envy *my* car?"

"Yeah. How many miles do you get per gallon?"

"Oh, about thirty."

"And how much does it cost to fill 'er up?"

"*Hmm,* twenty bucks or less."

"Man," he commented, shaking his head as the meter rolled to seventy-something dollars for his fill-up of a sparkling blue SUV, "you're cruisin' down easy street."

I'm not sure exactly what "cruisin' down easy street" means, but I think it has something to do with the smile that crossed my face as I learned to appreciate exactly what I have.

Dear God, today let me see all the blessings I have in life, and then I'll be cruisin' down easy street. —LINDA NEUKRUG

SUN
12

TRUST IN THE LORD FOREVER, FOR THE LORD, THE LORD, IS THE ROCK ETERNAL. —*Isaiah 26:4 (NIV)*

I HAD AN OPPORTUNITY to preach in a church in San Diego last summer, and my wife Rosie and our son Ryan went with me. After the last service we had lunch with the Marshburns, friends who own orchards of oranges, grapefruit and avocados. They insisted we take some back home to Mississippi.

Ryan rode with Mr. Marshburn to pick the fruit. It turned out to be quite an adventure for my son. "Dad, I was scared to death. He drove his truck up and down those hills, and I was sure we were going to flip upside down. When Mr. Marshburn noticed me gripping the door handle and closing my eyes, he said, 'Ryan, it's going to be all right. I've driven these hills many, many times.' I was still nervous and afraid, but I realized I had to trust him."

Ryan brought home a few boxes of oranges, grapefruit and avocados, and more important, a greater trust in the God Who is in control, whether we're on the flatlands of Mississippi or the hills of California.

As I make my way through all the bumpy roads and hills of life, Lord, I need to trust in You, my Savior. —DOLPHUS WEARY

MON
13

A GOOD MAN LEAVETH AN INHERITANCE TO HIS CHILDREN'S CHILDREN. . . . —*Proverbs 13:22*

TO SAY THAT I'M NOT an outdoorsman is an understatement. Born and bred in the city, I'm not comfortable walking unless there's pavement under my feet, the sound of traffic in my ears and a goodly number of fellow pedestrians around me. So you can imagine that I wasn't overjoyed when my wife Julia told me her parents had arranged for us all to go camping last summer.

To be honest, "I wasn't overjoyed" doesn't come close to describing it. I fumed and pouted and grumbled and whined. My mood didn't improve when I saw our cabin. It had a refrigerator and a hot plate, but no running water—showers and toilets were a short walk down the hill. The beds were metal cots with sagging springs and ancient mattresses. That first night I tossed and turned for hours until, imagining that the insect sounds were the hissing of radiators, I managed to fall into a not-very-restful sleep.

After a few days, I started getting used to the routine: swimming, reading, hiking, boating, dinner outdoors and singing around the campfire before bed. I'd still rather have been in the city, but at least I wasn't grousing so loudly about it.

Then one afternoon I took my book and went down to sit on the lakeshore. I'd been reading for about fifteen minutes when a boat glided by and stopped in the middle of the lake. Sitting in the boat were nine-year-old John and his grandfather. John had a fishing rod, and his grandfather was patiently showing him how to cast his line.

Suddenly I was grateful for a week in the great outdoors, where John was learning something he'd never learn in the city and making memories he'd treasure all his life, even if there was no subway station on the corner.

Lord, help me to pass on my strengths to my children and not burden them with my weaknesses. —ANDREW ATTAWAY

TUE
14

WHOSOEVER WILL BE GREAT AMONG YOU, LET HIM BE YOUR MINISTER; AND WHOSOEVER WILL BE CHIEF AMONG YOU, LET HIM BE YOUR SERVANT.
—*Matthew 20:26–27*

THREE DAYS OF OUR TRIP to China were spent on the Yangtze River, traveling through the scenic Three Gorges on our way to the famous dam. I was pleased to cruise the Yangtze, the world's third longest river, and add it to the others I've boated: the Nile, the longest; the Amazon, second; and the Mississippi, fourth. It was important to see this magnificent countryside before it is flooded. When the big dam (over a mile wide and six hundred feet high) is completed in 2009, it will supply one-third of China's power. But it will displace more than a million people and flood many environmentally sensitive areas.

On our way to the dam we made several side trips, including one near Wuhan on a *sampan*. On this excursion we were puzzled to see caskets cradled in the caves of the towering cliffs overhead. My obvious question was *Why?* The answer: to be nearer heaven.

Strange? Maybe not. In Matthew's Gospel, the mother of James and John wanted her sons to be nearer God and asked Jesus if they could be seated on His right- and left-hand sides when He established His kingdom. Afterward Jesus called the twelve apostles together and explained that whoever wants to be great must be a servant and whoever would be first, a slave. That's how to get nearer to heaven.

> *Give us serving hearts, Lord, so we can love.*
> *And serving hands that glorify our God above.*
> —FRED BAUER

READER'S ROOM

WHEN MY WIFE DIED in January 2004 after fifty-four years of marriage, I decided to wait a year before looking for work to see if I could make ends meet. But in August work came looking for me when a friend called. He, too, was retired, working part-time, and they needed more workers. I called the number he gave me, and after we talked, the boss said, "Come to work Monday." Just like that.

Many of my co-workers are widowers like me. We're called "The Happy Seniors." Our conversation is interesting because we have good stories to tell from our long lives. I get up early two days a week, get out of the house, and socialize with other seniors while I work. I'm grateful for a job so late in life. Am I just lucky, or is there a Master Planner in the background? Thanks, God, for unexpected, wonderful happenings.

—*Dave Lambert, Prospect Park, Pennsylvania*

WED
15

"THE LORD DOES NOT SEE AS MAN SEES; FOR MAN LOOKS AT THE OUTWARD APPEARANCE, BUT THE LORD LOOKS AT THE HEART." —I Samuel 16:7 (NKJV)

THE SUN SWELTERED. Sweat ran down my neck. A tall, raw-boned black mule stared from the corner of the corral, his nostrils flared. I stood ten paces away, waiting to catch him. I cooed, "What's wrong, John? I've haltered you a *bazillion* times."

John just snorted.

"John, quit it. You've seen me before."

I stepped toward John. His eyes widened, so I stepped backward. "John, what are you so afraid of?" I knew what I was afraid of: making new friends with Joan, the newly hired cook. When I'd moved, I'd left behind a couple of close friends, for whom my heart ached. *This job is temporary*, I thought. *I might have to move. Why make friends till I'm settled?*

"Rebecca, you forgot your hat!" my cowboy-mentor Snuffy hollered from the porch.

"I don't need it. It's too hot."

Snuffy sauntered over. He leaned his wiry frame on the corral and handed me my black cowboy hat. "John's never seen you without your hat. That's why he's scared."

I put on my hat and watched John. His whole body relaxed and he tipped his head from side to side as if to say, "Is it really you?" I walked into the corner; he sniffed the back of my hand while I slipped the lead rope over his neck and buckled the halter.

As I led John to the hitching rail, I knew that the real reason I didn't want to make friends with Joan was that I was afraid of hurting again. After all, things didn't "look" quite right.

That night I called Joan and we planned lunch. As the summer wore on, we became close friends. And by fall, I did move. I rented the spare bedroom in Joan's house.

God, help me to look into people's hearts, instead of at the circumstances.
—REBECCA ONDOV

GOD-FINDS
FINDING AN OLD FRIEND

THU
16

*"AND YOU WILL SEEK ME AND FIND ME, WHEN YOU
SEARCH FOR ME WITH ALL YOUR HEART."*
—*Jeremiah 29:13 (NAS)*

IT WAS DURING MY early morning Scripture reading that I came upon this verse in Jeremiah. "Today, Lord, help me look for You everywhere . . . and find You," I prayed. But it turned out to be one of those days when I could hardly summon the energy to get through my assignments at the hospital.

Still, something deep within me beckoned. "Where are You hiding, Lord? To whom do You want me to reach out?" I asked again.

After work I stopped by a new store that advertised tremendous bargains. I trudged inside to look for some laundry detergent but headed down the linens aisle by mistake. There I spotted a needlepoint cushion with smiling purple pansies. Its orchid and yellow lettering read, "The best friends are old friends." I immediately thought of Mary, a woman I'd worked with when I first graduated from nursing school three decades before. A senior nurse then, Mary had taken me under her wing, showing me the unwritten rules of the profession.

But the last time I visited Mary in her condo, she had barely known who I was. I argued with the Voice prompting me to purchase the cushion and take it to Mary. "I'll have to tell her all over again who I am, Lord."

Take her the cushion anyway was God's gentle reply. *If need be, tell her a second time who you are. And when you hand her the pillow, tell her how happy you were to find her when you were a new nurse years ago.*

I did just that, and the two of us enjoyed a wonderful visit filled with humorous recollections of nursing days gone by. That day I learned that some of the best God-finds need a divine reminder—this recipient included.

Today, Lord, I will look for You in every person You bring to mind.
—ROBERTA MESSNER

FRI
17

AND AS THY DAYS, SO SHALL THY STRENGTH BE.
—*Deuteronomy 33:25*

MY DAUGHTER GURGLED as I fastened the last pin in her clean diaper. After seven years of waiting for a child, finally ours squirmed on the changing table we'd purchased so long ago. Our baby—*ours!*—so tiny, sweet and beguiling, but also noisy and needy. Feed, change, feed, change, change, change, change! A parent for only two days, I had changed nearly two dozen diapers. *How can I do this for the next two years? Will I have time for anything else? Will I have the stamina?*

Perhaps it's just as well that I didn't know then that I'd be changing diapers not for two years, but for ten. My extended tour of duty would include three children in diapers at the same time and at least five years of laundering cloth diapers before disposables became readily available.

Once I tried to compute the number of diapers I had changed: Five thousand? Ten thousand? More? It was impossible to determine. Yet by the time I changed the last diaper, I felt sad to be giving up the task that I had once dreaded. I missed the special face-to-face time, the song-and-tickle time, the special closeness with my children. To console myself, I invited my closest friends—all mothers, of course—to my Ditch-the-Diaper-Pail party.

Now, twenty-seven years later, I chuckle as I remember how a distasteful task turned special, how my dread turned to smiles. Once again, God gave me strength gift-wrapped with joy.

Help me to remember, dear Lord, that whatever the task, I can do it with You. —GAIL THORELL SCHILLING

SAT
18

AND THE LORD GOD SAID, IT IS NOT GOOD THAT THE MAN SHOULD BE ALONE; I WILL MAKE HIM AN HELP MEET FOR HIM. —*Genesis 2:18*

YOUNG GREG MET the beautiful red-haired Amy on the *Seven Seas Mariner.* They fell in love. The next year, when I boarded the *Seven Seas Voyager* in Singapore, their coming wedding had the ship agog. Our cruise director Jamie Logan had arranged the event. Amy bought her wedding dress in Hong Kong, the galley and the arts-and-crafts group went to work, and all seven hundred passengers, mostly white-haired like me, received formal invitations for the ceremony and reception. The invitation requested "words of wisdom" from all of us older and (presumably) wiser folks. I gave them one word: *forbearance*.

The twilight was iridescent, the waters of the Arabian Sea were calm, the ship's orchestra played "The Last Five Years" (the couple's favorite), and wedding hymns were sung as spectators crowded the decks overlooking the bow festooned with white tulle. The service was reverent as our captain Dag Dvergastein spoke the traditional words, ending with "I now pronounce you man and wife." Then we were off to an immense reception of cake and confetti. Fun it was, but mostly I was moved by the honest responses of the two, innocently spoken before hundreds of men and women.

The newlyweds had dinner with me a week later. They talked about an additional ceremony they would have on shore with their families and about their plans for the future. I asked what they thought of the "words of wisdom," and Amy smiled. "I remember yours," she said. In return, their wedding gave me a word: *hope*.

Be with them, Father, through all the storms of life. —VAN VARNER

SUN
19

YOU MUST HELP US TOO, BY PRAYING FOR US. . . .
—*II Corinthians 1:11 (TLB)*

IN AUGUST 2005, when Hurricane Katrina destroyed most of New Orleans and hundreds of miles of Gulf Coast towns in Louisiana, Mississippi and Alabama, we who live in Florida and worry about hurricanes were stunned as we watched the devastation unfold.

In the following days, after praying for the victims, I found myself becoming more and more depressed. I knew the pittance I'd donated wouldn't make a dent. I wasn't trained as a Red Cross volunteer. And I only have one bed in my condo, so I couldn't take in a family. I continued to pray every day, morning and night, but still I felt depressed.

Then, a week after Katrina struck, the newspaper carried a list of items that the shelters needed desperately. One was can openers. I purchased twenty can openers and tried to deliver them to the City Hall collection center, but when I arrived the doors were locked. The next day when I tried again, the person inside said the truck had already left to deliver the items to New Orleans. The can openers sat in the trunk of my car for a week until I returned them to the store.

I prayed, *Lord, help me to know what I'm supposed to do to help. And let the victims of the hurricane know Your love.*

That Sunday at church, as I added the price of the can openers to the hurricane relief collection, I prayed again. *Father, bless them. Give their spirits a lift. Give them courage.*

I prayed all during church. I continued to pray at home, morning, noon and night. A month later, I was still praying. It finally dawned on me: Studies have shown that people recover faster from any mishap or tragedy when they know that people are praying for them. Prayer is one of the greatest assets a victim can have.

Lord, when I don't know what to give or how to help others in need, let me respond with head bowed and hands folded. —PATRICIA LORENZ

MON
20

FOR WE ARE GOD'S WORKMANSHIP, CREATED IN CHRIST JESUS TO DO GOOD WORKS, WHICH GOD PREPARED IN ADVANCE FOR US TO DO.
—Ephesians 2:10 (NIV)

THERE WAS ONE WEEK of vacation remaining and I was finally free. I had spent the past couple of months doing my assigned reading for the upcoming semester at college, but now I had run out of books. I imagined myself enjoying seven days of long naps and late-night TV reruns. But like countless students on summer vacation, I was only a few hours into the first day of my week off when I felt the restless boredom setting in. What was I going to do for seven whole days?

Going stir-crazy, I walked downstairs to the kitchen to find my mother crying. She was going to have surgery the next day—a routine operation—and my grandparents were supposed to come and stay with us and take care of my little brother and sister while Mom recovered.

"What's wrong?" I asked.

"Your grandparents can't come." My grandfather had just been hospitalized with a small stroke, and there was no way they could make the trip. "I'm worried about your grandfather and my operation, and I don't know who will be able to take care of the children."

"I can do it," I replied.

"But don't you have schoolwork?" she asked.

"Not anymore. I just finished."

It wasn't exactly how I expected to spend the last week of my vacation, but it was the right thing to do. There are a few lessons you can't learn in a textbook.

Lord, thank You for providing in unexpected ways.
—Joshua Sundquist

TUE
21

AND THE SECOND IS LIKE UNTO IT, THOU SHALT LOVE THY NEIGHBOUR AS THYSELF. —*Matthew 22:39*

IT BEGAN TO RAIN as I was on my way back from early morning church one Tuesday. I darted into a tunnel that I knew would take me several blocks to Grand Central Station and the subway. New York is full of tunnels, an invisible network of underground pathways.

I was going against the flow. Everyone else was leaving the station and hurrying intently toward their places of work. Blank, tense faces surged toward me. They so clearly had somewhere important to go, to useful, interesting jobs, I thought. I was unemployed and on my way back to an empty apartment. Self-pity sat like a cloud right over my head. I resented them as they pushed by me. "Thou shalt love thy neighbor as thyself," says the second great commandment. But were these empty faces rushing toward me my neighbors?

A young man in a suit and tie almost ran me down. "Excuse me. I should look where I'm going," he said and smiled as he reached out a hand to steady me.

One smile and he was magically transformed into my neighbor. "No problem," I answered, managing a smile back.

The throng raced on by, but now, under the suits and fashionable raincoats, they were all my neighbors.

*Jesus, help me to remember that You didn't just mean the folks next door when You said, "Love thy neighbor." —*BRIGITTE WEEKS

WED
22

THOU CROWNEST THE YEAR WITH THY BOUNTY; THE TRACKS OF THY CHARIOT DRIP WITH FATNESS.
—*Psalm 65:11 (RSV)*

EVEN WITH ONE HUNDRED YEARS in which to practice, my Aunt Betty will be the first to say she's not perfect. When she recounts her past, I detect certain "memory grooves"—perceptions about people and events in her life that are deeply entrenched in her mind and continually resurface.

There is her irritation: As a minister's daughter whose family was moved every year, she always showed up each October as the "new" kid in school. And she still resents her father for not having kissed her mother good-bye when he boarded the train for chaplain service in World War I.

She's absolutely convinced that her husband's mother wanted her son to marry another Elizabeth, who was a family friend and heiress to an oil fortune. She's never gotten over feeling she was the "wrong" Elizabeth.

On the plus side, Aunt Betty remembers her college roommate Ginny, a wool merchant's daughter, who hid her expensive dresses in the back of the closet so she wouldn't outclass her friends. She tells us how her husband Bill never said a word against anybody. She recalls with pleasure how he, a bass baritone, and she at the piano gave concerts all over China in their missionary years. "I've had a wonderful life," she keeps repeating.

Where will my "memory grooves" be when I am old? What themes will I attach to myself and others? Will resentment or alienation or disappointment kick up like stinging gravel? Or will my life's momentum crest the hill and catch the glow of the setting sun? The time to choose is now.

*Dear God, today's perceptions become tomorrow's memory grooves. Help me to set mine deep in You. —*CAROL KNAPP

THU

23

IF THOU BE KIND TO THIS PEOPLE, AND PLEASE THEM, AND SPEAK GOOD WORDS TO THEM, THEY WILL BE THY SERVANTS FOR EVER. —II *Chronicles 10:7*

SHORTLY AFTER COLLEGE, I was offered a job in Nashville, Tennessee, as a program coordinator at a retirement center. The week I began, the nutritionist who headed the dietary department made what was meant to be a health-friendly decision: Each resident would receive one piece of bacon instead of two with breakfast. Since I arrived on the scene simultaneously with the one-bacon breakfast, word spread like wildfire: "They cut our bacon allowance to hire that young whippersnapper!"

The leaders of the bacon revolt, Mrs. Small and Mr. Taylor, made sure no one showed up for my first activity. A dear lady named Mrs. Estes was the only one to attend. Soon I was pouring out my heart to her.

"Now, honey," she answered, "it's not really about the bacon. Feeling like they're in charge of the folks around here is about all those two have left. If you'll just be kind enough to get to know them, you'll find plenty of good there."

The next morning, Mrs. Estes, Mrs. Small and Mr. Taylor were seated in my office, enjoying sweet rolls and tea. "I need advice," I began, catching the sparkle in Mrs. Estes' eyes. "The three of you stand out as leaders of this community and I was wondering if you would serve as a sort of residents' council to help guide me along."

With the help of that threesome, things were soon humming. Mrs. Small showed real talent in the ceramics class I organized and loved the poetry readings. Mr. Taylor became a champion bingo player and developed a touching relationship with the teenagers I brought in to help with the games. And Mrs. Estes remained everyone's cheerleader.

Father, let me see loneliness for what it is and overcome it with kind ways.
—PAM KIDD

EYES UPON THE RAIL

JOHN SHERRILL and his wife Tib often take trips lasting weeks and even months. But it was on their shortest trip last year that John gained the insights he shares this week.

For his birthday last August, Tib gave John a trip through the Cumbres Pass in the Rockies on a narrow-gauge railroad. The journey by steam train highlighted truths that are also useful on the spiritual journey. For the next seven days John takes us with him on his birthday trip. —THE EDITORS

DAY ONE: THE GIFT OF MEMORY

FRI

24

IF I FORGET THEE, O JERUSALEM, LET MY RIGHT HAND FORGET HER CUNNING. —Psalm 137:5

THE BIG BLACK LOCOMOTIVE—Number 484—stood idling over the ash pit in the Cumbres & Toltec Railroad yard in northern New Mexico. The steam engine had just finished her six-hour run from Antonito, Colorado, over the mountains to this dusty little railhead town of Chama.

Moments earlier my wife Tib and I had checked into the "Parlor Car," a Victorian bed-and-breakfast with bay windows and pressed-tin ceilings, located directly across from the C&T repair shops. While Tib unpacked, I strolled over to look around, listen to the occasional toot as a locomotive switched tracks and brush away flecks of soot.

And suddenly I wasn't in a Southwestern town in the shadow of the Rockies, but in Louisville, Kentucky. With the smell of coal smoke came a flood of memories. For the first time in years, I remembered how as a boy it was my job to shovel the heavy black lumps into the chute at our house—hard work too! I remembered Mother, armed with pail, sponge and indignation, doing battle with the film left on her windows by the soft coal smoke that hung perpetually in the air.

What is it about the sense of smell that can transport us to another time and place? Not particularly pleasant, these memories of life in a soft-coal town, but filled with the vanished places and forgotten voices of childhood. *What a marvel the gift of memory is!* I thought, as I walked back to our bed-and-breakfast.

"God gave us memory," J. M. Barrie wrote, "so that we can have roses in December." And so that we can hold on to the things that give us our identity, as the Jews in exile discovered long ago, rehearsing through the generations the stories of the exodus, the manna in the desert, the Temple in Jerusalem. Without the past, whether it's smoky Louisville or the Promised Land, we know nothing of ourselves or of God.

Thank You, Father, for the gift of memory. —JOHN SHERRILL

DAY TWO: SLOWING DOWN

SAT
25

CONSIDER THE LILIES OF THE FIELD. . . .
—*Matthew 6:28*

EARLY THE FOLLOWING MORNING, Tib and I climbed aboard a sleek new bus. Two trains a day make the trip through the 10,015-foot-high Cumbres Pass, one going north from Chama, the other—the one we would ride—south from Antonito. As our bus sped along Highway 17, I wondered where the legendary pass was. We'd been told there would be an hour's stop for lunch at mid-point on the train trip. Still . . . how could it take six hours to travel a mere sixty-five miles?

But, as I was about to discover, there is a huge difference between the two modes of travel, and the difference is speed. From the beginning the train crew in Antonito encouraged a slow-down attitude. Passengers idled about watching the black cloud from the smokestack rise into the pale blue sky until, around ten, the engineer blew his whistle and we ambled down the track to take our seats. Another toot from the whistle and we were off.

Fourteen miles an hour was our top speed. We clung to cliffs, circled gorges, crept over high wooden trestles, plunged into tunnels blasted from the rock with black powder before the days of dynamite.

There were stops to refill the huge black-bellied boiler at wooden water towers spaced along the route, glimpses of mule deer, elk, hawks, log cabins a hundred years old. There was time to appreciate how the surveyors had worked with the land, following every contour, the tracks curving back on themselves as they climbed, so that the lead cars of the train were often directly above us. The slower pace shifted the emphasis from "getting there" to "enjoying the journey."

Tib has long ago learned to stop and look. I confess that her frequent pausing sometimes irked my let's-get-on-with-it attitude. It took a poke-along train ride to teach me that the best journey is the leisurely one. How can I hear the still, small voice with the wind whistling in my ears?

Stop. Look. Listen, *read the level-grade signs. When I do, Father, I catch sight of You.* —JOHN SHERRILL

DAY THREE: STOKING THE FIRE

SUN
26

SHEPHERDS . . . KEEPING WATCH OVER THEIR FLOCK. . . . —Luke 2:8

THE LUNCH BREAK WAS at the lonely whistle-stop of Osier, high in the Rockies. Waiting for the cafeteria line to shorten, I wandered forward next to the train, where I found a young man in soot-darkened coveralls standing on the platform between the engine and the coal car. His blackened hands and sweat-streaked face suggested that this would be the fireman.

"Want to come up?" he called to me.

Sure! I climbed the ladder as nimbly as my newly implanted metal knee joint allowed, and watched as he demonstrated the single smooth motion with which he shoveled coal from the bunker and threw it into the open firebox. He even let me try a few shovelfuls. He seemed delighted that I was interested in his work.

"People don't talk to the fireman much," he said. "I don't know why. The stoker's the one who keeps the whole show moving. If the water doesn't boil, there's no steam, and without steam you aren't going anywhere." Hunger called me back to the food line. I said good-bye and left the fireman to keep the coal fire burning for me and for the rest of us on the journey.

Thinking about it that night, it seemed to me a perfect picture of the role a pastor plays on the spiritual journey. Day by day, week in, week out, these men and women work to keep the spiritual fires burning. I cannot imagine a harder calling, and I wondered how long it had been since I told my own pastor how much I appreciated his often unseen, unsung labor.

It's so easy, Father, to forget how hard our clergy work for the rest of us, fueling the fires of faith. Let me remember to be thankful.
—JOHN SHERRILL

DAY FOUR: STEAM CLEANING

 MON
27

WHATSOEVER THINGS ARE PURE. . . .
—*Philippians 4:8*

AFTER LUNCH EVERYONE PILED back aboard, and I went to the open flatcar, which let us see the engine, way up ahead, black smoke billowing out of the stack. Suddenly I heard a high-pitched shriek and a tremendous hissing roar. Everyone on the flatcar whirled around to stare as a long jet of white steam shot out over the valley from the side of the locomotive. Later I asked the engineer if it wasn't an awful waste of power to let so much steam escape.

"No," he said. "We do that to *gain* power." There are minerals dissolved in the water used by steam engines, he went on to explain. When the water is heated, the minerals are released, coating the boiler's coils and clogging them so badly that they no longer work properly. "I blast away the scales with a jet of steam," the driver said, "which brings my locomotive back to strength."

There are times when I'm not getting enough power for my journey. A hundred impurities—the scales of worry, wrong priorities, resentments, bitterness—corrode my spirit, stealing strength. How can I blast away these "scales" as our locomotive driver does? There are ways to do just that: the cleansing power of confession, asking for forgiveness from someone I've hurt, getting back to a more disciplined prayer time. The tools await; it's just a matter of taking advantage of them.

Father, show me how to clean my spiritual power system when it begins to clog. —JOHN SHERRILL

DAY FIVE: THE SAFETY VALVE

TUE
28

AND HE WITHDREW HIMSELF INTO THE WILDERNESS. . . . —Luke 5:16

AFTER MY STOP AT the flatcar, before we pulled out, I hurried back to the head of the train to find the engineer standing beside his locomotive, oil can in hand. While he lubricated the dozens of moving rods and gears, I told him about a train accident that had made headlines when I was growing up: The boiler of a locomotive had blown up, scalding many people, one man fatally. Why, I wanted to know—especially after seeing the quantity of coal blazing in the firebox—didn't that happen all the time?

"Because there's a safety valve," said the engineer, straightening up and pointing to a cylinder set on top of the boiler. "If the boiler pressure gets too high, that safety blows!" He drew out a pocket watch. "Time to go." As he climbed into the cab, he added the words that I've since found helpful: "When a boiler explodes, it's probably because the driver's tied down the valve to get extra power. Not a good idea."

We have safety valves too, Tib and I, I thought. *Walks. A dinner date. A game of backgammon.* But don't I sometimes "tie down the safety valve"? When we have tight deadlines or are getting ready for a trip, don't we skip these pressure-relieving outlets, sit at our computers eight hours at a stretch, get to bed late, gulp meals standing in the kitchen? We tell ourselves we need extra power, so we tie down the safety valve and end up tired, drained, sharp with each other . . . in danger of blowing the whole creative engine to pieces.

As I returned to my seat for the second half of our journey, I found myself saying this prayer:

Even Your Son, Father, took breaks from the people and pressures crowding in on Him. Don't let me think I can outperform Him.

—JOHN SHERRILL

DAY SIX: PULLING TOGETHER

WED
29

AFTER THIS THE LORD . . . SENT THEM ON AHEAD OF HIM, TWO BY TWO. . . . —Luke 10:1 (RSV)

WE WERE ON THE last leg of our journey, creeping down the steepest grade of the trip. The Cumbres & Toltec has attracted scores of railroad buffs to Chamas. They come as volunteers to repair cars, rebuild engines, lay tracks, refurbish the rare wooden water tanks. A few also ride the train, answering questions. The young volunteer in our car wore overalls, an old-fashioned striped hat and a neckerchief, and he sported a gold railroad watch. We'd just started down the mountain when he spoke.

"When we come up this grade, we need two engines," he said. "But coupling steam locomotives together is tricky. They can't be synchronized—one locomotive is either pushing or pulling the other.

"Trainmen were always dreaming of a perfect way to match two engines for the tough grades," the volunteer went on. "Well, just that did happen . . . with diesel. Diesels can be linked together perfectly because the engines are coupled electronically. Commands go to both at exactly the same time. One engineer can drive two engines, each smoothly synchronized with the other."

In our personal lives, too, there are grades too steep for one person to manage alone. That's when we look for help. A wife, a friend, business partners, people in church. But far too often quarrels, uneven abilities, misunderstandings keep partnerships from working well together.

Isn't there a lesson to be learned from the diesel engine? If both partners accept directives from the Lord, they become so well matched that they act as one. With Him in control, both partners can use their power to the utmost, never worrying that one is pulling more than his share of the burden.

As I come to the steep grades, Father, thank You for giving me a partner who listens with me for Your directives. —JOHN SHERRILL

DAY SEVEN: BANKING THE FIRE

THU
30

. . . A CONVENIENT SEASON. . . . —*Acts 24:25*

IT WAS THE END of our six-hour trip through the Rockies, and we were once again at the railhead in Chamas. Tib had gone back to our bed-and-breakfast to wash up; we were all sporting soot smudges.

But I couldn't tear myself away from the yard. Our locomotive was standing over the ash pit, her stack puffing quietly. The fireman was still aboard, and I mounted the ladder again, where I found him smoothing out a bed of coals in the firebox.

"How long will it take to get the fire going again tomorrow?" I asked.

"Oh, we never let the fire die!" the stoker said over his shoulder. "We'll damp her down and tomorrow she'll start her own fire from the bed of coals."

I smiled, remembering a technique I learned long ago to avoid a cold start on a day's work. Rather than finish a piece of work, I'll leave it hanging. Then in the morning the fire of creativity is easy to start from the "coals" that have smoldered through the night.

Shouldn't I do the same with my spiritual fires? Tapping power for the journey may well depend on letting this creativity smolder for a bit so that tomorrow it is again ready to blaze.

Thank You, Father, for teaching me once again to "Let go and let God," which is another way of saying I should bank the fires and never let them go out. —JOHN SHERRILL

FRI
31

"*THOSE WHO HARVEST IT WILL EAT IT AND PRAISE THE LORD. . . .*" —*Isaiah 62:9 (NIV)*

IT WAS, QUITE LITERALLY, the last tomato of summer. For weeks my husband's uncle had provided us with delicious tomatoes from his garden. No fertilizers, no pesticides; just tomatoes he had grown from seeds saved from his plants last year. Tomatoes that were huge and firm and wonderfully sweet. And this was the last one.

It sat in a bowl on the kitchen counter. I thought of chopping it into my spaghetti sauce but was afraid the flavor might get lost. A tossed salad perhaps? That seemed too ordinary for this prize. An omelet? Topping a turkey sandwich? Everything seemed too everyday for this last tomato. And then one morning the summer's last tomato was no more. Its top was wrinkled, and its sides puckered and speckled with dark spots. When I tried to pick it up, it was squishy and gave off a slightly acrid smell. I tossed it into the trash. A very ignominious end for the last tomato of summer.

I think of that tomato when I'm tempted to put off lunch with a friend, when I wait for a special occasion to wear my grandmother's cameo, when I promise myself a walk in the woods but never seem to find the time. *Now*—the time is now to act on dreams, to nurture relationships. And, if you have one, to eat the last tomato of summer.

Great Giver of every good gift, let me be a wise—and eager—steward of all Your blessings. —Mary Lou Carney

MY WALK WITH GOD

1 _____

2 _____

3 _____

4 _____

5 _____

6 _____

7 _____

8 _____

9 _____

10 _____

11 _____

12 _____

13 _____

14 _____

15 _____

16 _____

17 _____

18 _____

19 _____

20 _____

21 _____

22 _____

23 _____

24 _____

25 _____

26 _____

27 _____

28 _____

29 _____

30 _____

31 _____

September

The land shall yield her increase, and
the trees of the field shall yield their fruit.

—*Leviticus 26:4*

LESSONS FROM THE JOURNEY
STAY IN TOUCH

SAT
1

THEREFORE I WILL LOOK UNTO THE LORD . . . MY GOD WILL HEAR ME. —*Micah 7:7*

LAST YEAR OUR GRANDSON Andrew attended Monash University in Melbourne, Australia, on the opposite side of the earth from our home in New York. So many miles between us, I thought, places and experiences I couldn't imagine!

So it was a kind of shock—newcomer that I am to the Internet—when an instant message popped up on my computer screen one morning soon after Andrew got there.

"Hi, Gran! I'm loving this place! I've put some photos on my blog."

Blog? Andrew explained that it's short for web log, a kind of journal kept on the Internet, and, sure enough, in a moment I was looking at pictures of him and some new friends . . . the landscape around the school . . . a car trip just the day before. I didn't have to imagine his new setting, I could see it, share it all with him.

Most wondrous of all to me was that as we instant-messaged back and forth, we were in contact *right then.* How different from my efforts to reach my father and mother from Africa in the early 1960s! I had to find a ham radio operator who would patch a call to someone in Egypt to be relayed to another set, and so on until hours later I'd hear the phone ringing in my parents' house in the United States—on the chance that they were home.

Instant messaging, I thought, as Andrew and I chatted electronically across the globe, is much more like the experience of staying in touch with God. *Right now,* wherever I am in my travels over the earth and over the years, I can communicate with Him and receive His reply. Unlike phoning between continents in the 1960s, I know that the Father I want to reach is always there. The only requirement: I must remember to go online.

Lord of the journey, what message do You have for me right now?
—ELIZABETH SHERRILL

SUN
2

TRUST IN THE LORD WITH ALL YOUR HEART, AND
LEAN NOT ON YOUR OWN UNDERSTANDING.
—*Proverbs 3:5 (NKJV)*

SHORTLY AFTER OUR older sons were both driving, we began a family tradition of flying to some remote spot, renting an SUV and exploring the outback areas of North America. Usually our middle son Joel, the most daring of our three, would drive, with Ryan, our eldest, seated beside him navigating.

After a great vacation through Idaho and Wyoming, we found ourselves with a day left for exploring before our 8:00 PM flight home from Salt Lake City. So the boys secured an off-road map of Bridger National Forest, pored over trails and marked a route crisscrossing the Oregon Trail. It wasn't long before the gravel road narrowed to a dirt lane. An hour later, the lane dissolved into a path.

"Joel, are you sure we can get back to civilization before our flight is due to leave?" I asked.

"You bet, Dad. We'll be back on the road in less than six hours."

"Fellows, are you sure you know where we are on the map?"

"Yes, Dad. Remember that last spring we passed? It's right here." Ryan leaned over, pointing to a spot on the map. It looked like we were in a dense part of nowhere.

Joel slowed to a crawl as we dipped down a blind curve. There was a sign: NO SEDANS BEYOND THIS POINT. Was it kidding? How could a regular car have gotten this far? The descending curve ended at the brink of a briskly moving stream. It looked like a fathomless, raging river to me.

"That's it, Joel. We're done. Let's get turned around."

Smiling, Joel looked me square in the eyes. "Dad, where's your power of positive thinking? What would Dr. Peale say?" We forded that stream, with the water rising halfway up the window-wells.

Five hours later, we emerged exuberantly from our back-road adventure within minutes of the city and our flight home.

Thank You, God, for a wonderful trip and a great lesson in faith, trust, courage—and the power of positive thinking! —TED NACE

MON
3

FROM THE FRUIT OF HIS LIPS A MAN IS FILLED WITH GOOD THINGS AS SURELY AS THE WORK OF HIS HANDS REWARDS HIM. —*Proverbs 12:14 (NIV)*

ARE YOU FAMOUS? Maybe president of the company where you work? Do you supervise a couple of hundred people? Are you known throughout your state or country or the world for your accomplishments, for being the best and brightest in your field?

Well, me neither. That's true for most of us. I'm on the job every day and I do good work. But nobody's going to buy my book or pay me tens of thousands of dollars for a speech.

Back when I was in college, I spent one summer working on an assembly line. It was hard, hot, dirty work. One day, during lunch, I turned to a friend and said, "I can't imagine being stuck doing this the rest of my life."

I felt an arm around my shoulder. "Around here, son, the quality of a man is measured by the size of his heart, not his head."

I've heard some famous business leaders speak in the years since then. I've read their books, bought their tapes, gone to their seminars. I've learned some pretty important stuff. Yet nothing has ever had more of an effect on me than one sentence from a career assembly-line worker who knew the true meaning of Labor Day: It isn't about the work you do but the worker doing it.

May the work of my hands, God, honor the gifts and talents You have given me and reflect Your love for the whole world. —JEFF JAPINGA

TUE
4

"*STOP AWHILE AND REST HERE IN THE SHADE OF THIS TREE WHILE I GET WATER TO REFRESH YOUR FEET, AND A BITE TO EAT TO STRENGTHEN YOU. . . .*"
—*Genesis 18:4 (TLB)*

BEFORE THEY MOVED IN, my new neighbor Marie and her husband read a book about what to look for in a neighborhood. Marie said one of the most important things is the "wave factor": If you drive down the street and people wave to you, it's a good thing.

My neighborhood has 193 single-family homes and seven condo complexes, each with twenty-six to sixty units. We all support a lovely clubhouse, two tennis courts, a small playground, a boat dock, fishing pier and a couple of swimming pools that sit along the Intracoastal Waterway just one street away from the Gulf of Mexico. It's a grand neighborhood, with people of all ages, religions, economic and ethnic backgrounds. Best of all, we have a great wave factor. You can't drive or walk three blocks without half a dozen people waving to you from cars, sidewalks, garages or front yards.

I was never much of a waver myself until I moved to Florida. But down here things are different. Whether I'm out for a walk after dinner, scooting around the neighborhood on my Rollerblades, biking to the nearest park or driving home from the grocery, I'll receive and give waves, one after another.

Like a smile that can brighten anyone's day, a friendly wave can mean, "Howdy, neighbor." Or, "You may be a stranger here, but we're a friendly bunch." Or, "If you're lost, slow down and I'll give you directions." And every time I ride my bike past my neighborhood church, I like to think of Jesus standing there, waving me inside for a bit of rest, refreshment and safe harbor.

How's the wave factor in your neighborhood? Could you be the one to start this contagious habit?

Lord, remind me to extend a heartfelt greeting, a welcoming wave, to all I see. —PATRICIA LORENZ

WED
5

"LOOK AT THE BIRDS OF THE AIR, FOR THEY NEITHER SOW NOR REAP NOR GATHER INTO BARNS; YET YOUR HEAVENLY FATHER FEEDS THEM. . . ."
—*Matthew 6:26* (NKJV)

I'VE BEEN A SERIOUS birder ever since I took a college course in ornithology. Dr. Everett Myers, my professor at Bowling Green State, predicted that if anyone studied birds for just a season, "they would fascinate you for the rest of your life." He was right.

Today, I was watching a downy woodpecker on the maple outside our kitchen door. It was hunting for insects. When a woodpecker climbs, it does so with its feet together and its tail feathers beneath. All woodpeckers use their stiff tail for support as they climb up. If they were to head downward, they would lose their footing.

Not so with nuthatches. After the downy left its perch, a white-breasted nuthatch took its place and began foraging for food. The herky-jerky nuthatch first went up the tree and then came down, able to move in either direction at will because of its strong legs and feet. Unlike the woodpecker, it places one foot higher than the other to keep its balance.

Jesus must have been a bird-watcher. He said that not even a common sparrow falls without God's knowledge (Matthew 10:29), and that "foxes have holes and birds of the air have nests, but the Son of Man has no place to lay his head" (Matthew 8:20, NIV). His point in both cases was that our all-knowing heavenly Father is aware of everything that happens. He knows our needs, supplies them and sustains us. But He expects us to do our part. As someone insightfully noted, "God may feed the birds, but He doesn't put food in their nests."

> *We thank You, God, for always being there,*
> *For assuring us daily of Your constant care.*
> —FRED BAUER

THU 6

HE TURNS A WILDERNESS INTO POOLS OF WATER, AND DRY LAND INTO WATERSPRINGS.
—*Psalm 107:35 (NKJV)*

WILL THIS DROUGHT NEVER end, Lord? The farmers have lost everything. Our lawn is Death Valley. The scarlet maples and quaking aspens I set out in spring are yellowed and motionless. I can slide my arm down in the cracks that split our yard from end to end. The thermometer is stuck on one hundred. Just walking to the mailbox makes my skin ache and my eyes burn and my hair feels like it will burst into flames.

Like the earth, I, too, am dry, Lord. I go to work and I come home. I smile politely, but after almost forty years in the classroom, I wonder how long I can keep going back. My dad died in August and now he is with You. I hope You are enjoying him as much as we did, but I wish we had him back. I watch my daughters, working hard on their marriages and putting up with sick children, and it brings back painful memories of my own. Am I just getting old? Solomon said the days would come when "I have no pleasure in them" (Ecclesiastes 12:1, NKJV). Am I there already?

Bring rain, Lord. Let me stand in the yard and watch the heavy clouds racing toward me, rich with liquid relief. I want to feel cool wind in my face and cold drops of water sliding down my arms and chest. I want to take off my shoes and splash through puddles. I want to lie in bed and listen to the drizzle falling softly on the grass.

I know, the rain always returns. It always has and it always will.

Give me my second wind, God. Give me a fresh vision of what can happen in a classroom. Make me laugh and teach me to sing a new song. Amen.

I wait patiently for the sounds of thunder, Lord. —DANIEL SCHANTZ

FRI
7

LISTEN AND HEAR MY VOICE; PAY ATTENTION AND HEAR WHAT I SAY. —Isaiah 28:23 (NIV)

AFTER SEVERAL YEARS of volunteering with the Parents' Association at my children's school, I was asked to be its president. It's a big job: a two-year commitment with frequent meetings and much responsibility, heading up the parent volunteers for kindergarten through twelfth grade. *I don't know if I can do it,* I thought. And when I prayed about it, I didn't feel any urging from God. Just a nudge to ask others what they thought.

My mom was thrilled for me. "That's such an honor! You have to say *yes*." My husband Paul was pleased. "You love volunteering at school," he said. "You could do a lot of good if you were in charge." And my kids thought it was way cool. "You'll get your picture in the yearbook now," they reminded me.

Even with their confidence and support, I still wasn't sure what God wanted me to do. *Is this how I am meant to use my time? Is this the best use of my gifts?* I asked God for an answer but still felt no particular response. Then one day, sitting on my back porch swing (my favorite prayer spot), it finally came to me: *I sent all these people whom you trust, who know you and love you, to give you advice. What more do you need?*

God often speaks through the people in my life. I needed to listen to them. I got up from my porch swing and made a couple of phone calls . . . to accept the job, of course!

Help me, God, to hear You speak in all Your voices.
—GINA BRIDGEMAN

SAT

8

MINE EYES ARE EVER TOWARD THE LORD. . . .
—Psalm 25:15

EARLY IN SEPTEMBER 2005, heart-wrenching stories from survivors of Hurricane Katrina appeared on television. Some victims were barely able to speak; others were openly angry. Many detailed how such a horrific experience might have been avoided. Some placed blame on the lack of preparation and the disorganized response. Their reactions were understandable; after all, they had just lost everything.

Then, on September 8, I watched yet another survivor on television. Her hand rested on her canine companion, a beautiful German shepherd. He sat erect, his eyes fastened on the woman he loved, respected and trusted. The woman didn't seem aware of the microphone the reporter held close to her face. Then he explained that she was blind and had barely escaped with her life and her guide dog. Along with thousands of others, she'd waited for days on a bridge in New Orleans to be evacuated. "How do you feel about all this?" the reporter asked her.

Her face positively glowed. She smiled and, to my amazement, she sang her response to the reporter's question: "Oh, Jesus, oh, Jesus, I know You care! Oh Jesus, oh Jesus, I still trust You. . . ."

Oh, Lord, help me keep my eyes on You, no matter what.
—MARION BOND WEST

SUN
9

*AND HE TOOK THE CHILDREN IN HIS ARMS, PUT
HIS HANDS ON THEM AND BLESSED THEM.*
—*Mark: 10:16 (NIV)*

MY GRANDFATHER DADDY LEE was a striking man: tall, slender, very handsome, very dark, with startlingly blue eyes. There were stories in the family about how strong he was—he had once brought a bucking horse to its knees with one punch—but he was so gentle and considerate that he gave up his precious free time on Saturdays to shuttle neighbors who didn't have cars to the grocery store. He was a hardworking man. Every day he traveled from East St. Louis, Illinois, across the bridge to St. Louis, where he worked in a meat-packing plant. What I remember most, though, isn't the work he did or the help he gave to strangers. What I remember is how safe he made me feel.

When I was a little girl, my family—my mother, father and four brothers—would visit his home each weekend. On Friday nights I'd stand at the front door in the dimming light waiting for my grandfather to come home. When he arrived, I'd watch him quietly open the gate, walk up the sidewalk and open the screen door.

I don't remember us speaking much; he was probably too tired to talk. But I remember resting on his lap, leaning against his chest, safe in his arms. I remember him laughing sometimes with his friends—usually at something I said to them or that they said to me. I remember him stewing rabbit in brown gravy to share with me and teaching me the sweet joy of rock candy dipped in tea. But what I remember most is his quiet, strong, peaceful presence.

God, on this Grandparent's Day I thank You for the foretaste of Your love, which You gave me in my Daddy Lee's arms. —SHARON FOSTER

MON
IO
FOR BY HIM WERE ALL THINGS CREATED, THAT ARE IN HEAVEN, AND THAT ARE IN EARTH, VISIBLE AND INVISIBLE. . . . —Colossians 1:16

THE GREEN FLASH IS something that appears on the horizon at the precise moment that the last of the sun is going down. A fellow passenger on an ocean liner told me about the phenomenon more than fifty years ago. I thought he was joshing me. "Oh no," he said. "Come out on deck and see for yourself." I did, and afterward I still thought he was joshing me. However, enough people I know have seen it and I believe them.

The green flash is a scientific fact, I've learned. Pictures, I'm told, have captured it. All that is well and good, but I've never experienced it. There have been times at sea that I've gotten up hastily from the dining table and rushed outside. Alas, the view was too hazy or clouds have been in the way. Repeatedly I've trained my binoculars on the setting sun and seen nothing. Perhaps my eyes are the reason or I've blinked at the very moment. Oh well, I shall go on trying the next time.

Meanwhile, I content myself with a comforting analogy: Seeing is not necessary to believing. I cannot see God, yet I know He is there.

You are, too, Father, even though I may never see the green flash.
—VAN VARNER

TUE
II
SURELY GOODNESS AND MERCY SHALL FOLLOW ME ALL THE DAYS OF MY LIFE. . . . —Psalm 23:6

IT'S THE MOST ENDURING image I have of life in New York City in those days right after 9/11. The weather, it must be remembered, was gorgeous. Clear, bright and sunny, while smoke rose from a pit downtown. The streets near our offices on 34th Street were almost empty, making it possible for fire engines, ambulances, and emergency vehicles to rush to and from a site newly christened Ground Zero.

Posters were being put up on streetlamps with images of the missing. Little shrines of candles and flowers were assembled in parks and squares. But most of us went to our jobs, trying to do our work. At lunchtime I headed out to pick up a sandwich, and I noticed a stern-looking policeman on the corner of 33rd and Madison. That's how our police officers usually look, brusque and businesslike.

Just then a woman, clearly distraught, bumped into him. At any other time they would have backed away from each other in horror. Instead, the policeman gently put his arms on her shoulders and looked into her eyes as if to say, "Are you all right?" After a minute she nodded: "Yes, I'll be all right." And she went on her way.

It was a reminder to me that the brusque New Yorkers I live with have caring souls. Much of the time you don't know it. People are in a hurry, going about their business. But at that terrible moment we looked into each other's eyes and discovered how much goodness was there.

I shall not forget, Lord, all the goodness You have put in Your people.
—RICK HAMLIN

WED
12

"AND I TOO WILL BE KIND TO YOU BECAUSE OF WHAT YOU HAVE DONE." —II Samuel 2:6 (TLB)

"CAN YOU PICK ME UP at the Co-op Elevator in Montezuma?" my husband Don asked when I answered the phone. "I've got a loaded truck with two flat tires I can't get repaired until tomorrow morning." It was 9:00 PM during September's corn harvest. I'd been late getting home from work, hadn't had supper and wasn't in the mood for a rescue mission that involved a forty-mile round trip.

"I guess," I groused. I hung up the telephone, grabbed a piece of cold pizza and headed out. *At least I'm not the one with flat tires,* I thought.

The pizza took my mind off my stomach, and I began thinking about the times I'd had car trouble. One busy harvest I was the one hauling corn to the grain elevator. When it was finally my turn at the dump, I pulled the power take-off knob to raise the truck bed and somehow pulled out the entire cable. This not only disabled my truck, but blocked every truck behind me. A kind elevator worker told me not to worry, shut the dump door and managed to get the truck bed lowered enough to get me out.

There was the July morning I was to attend an important meeting of the city commission. I was wearing fabric shoes and my best white skirt. Twenty miles from home a tire blew out. While I was struggling to get the jack under the back bumper without getting dirty, a truck driver stopped, changed the tire, phoned the service station so they could have a new tire ready and got me on my way—on time and clean.

Don had rescued me dozens of times, when I overturned a truck, hit a deer, knocked a hole in my radiator, had a flat. By the time I reached Montezuma, my mood had changed. When Don apologized for getting me out so late, I replied, "I'm happy to help."

Lord, thank You for all the people along the road who have been happy to help me. May I always be willing to pass on the kindness in Your name.
—PENNEY SCHWAB

THU
13

AND THE PEACE OF GOD, WHICH PASSETH ALL UNDERSTANDING, SHALL KEEP YOUR HEARTS AND MINDS THROUGH CHRIST JESUS. —Philippians 4:7

AS I BOARDED THE PLANE, I was surprised to find that the passenger behind me was one of my students. Carrie and the rest of the University of Pittsburgh women's soccer team were flying home from a game in Philadelphia. We chatted, then returned to our respective books. I acted calm and collected, which really is an act for me, because I'm a tad fearful of flying. Make that more than a tad.

I hadn't noticed how overcast it was until we climbed into a thick bank of clouds. Despite the weather the flight was smooth and my pulse rate was nearly normal. I thought about trying to sleep and then I looked outside.

It was sunset above the clouds. The sun—ninety-three million miles away but looking mighty close—spilled out like an exploded orange across acres and acres of white, puffy canvas. Here and there little cream-colored waves peeked above the others, frozen in a vermillion ocean. And because we were flying west, the sunset hung in there, suspended, like an encore performance that never really left the stage.

"Carrie," I whispered behind me, "Carrie, look!"

Carrie was already at the window, as awestruck as I. For a moment, we weren't student and teacher; we were both students of good fortune, struck dumb by this amazing treat . . . a divine wonder, which, like the peace of God, "passeth all understanding."

I finally relaxed because I now knew that the firmest, surest support is not visible. We're held aloft by faith, on a long, sometimes worrisome, but always wondrous journey where we're always heading home.

Thank You, Lord, that all of us, all of our lives, are held in place by this ridiculous, ineffable mix of clouds and sun and divine wonder.

—MARK COLLINS

FRI
14

A PERVERSE MAN STIRS UP DISSENSION, AND A GOSSIP SEPARATES CLOSE FRIENDS. —*Proverbs 16:28 (NIV)*

LAST SEPTEMBER I visited Steve, a close friend who lives in Ohio. We met in junior high school there and have remained close friends even though I lived in Colorado for more than thirty years.

We ran in the Hocking Hills Indian Run together, and he took me to an Ohio State football game. But the conversations we had on the way to and from these events meant so much more to me than the events themselves. Somehow, in spite of the miles that separate us, we can talk as if we see each other every day.

On our last evening together I talked to Steve about some members of my family. I say *talked,* but *gossiped* would be more accurate. I thought that Steve would see things from my point of view. Instead, he suggested a solution to the problem. I didn't want a solution; I wanted to complain! It was as if someone (not me, of course!) had somehow sneaked into the room and stirred up dissension between us.

Fortunately, even gossip can't undo forty years of close friendship. But in the future, I'm going to try to control my tongue better. I definitely do not want to say anything that causes two friends to separate, especially when one of the friends is me.

Dear God, thank You for making the bonds of friendship strong enough to withstand words that might weaken them. —TIM WILLIAMS

GOD-FINDS
FINDING A GREAT NEIGHBOR

SAT
15

OPEN MY EYES, THAT I MAY BEHOLD WONDERFUL THINGS. . . . —Psalm 119:18 (NAS)

I COULD SCARCELY CONTAIN my excitement about the plans I had for decorating the garage that's connected to my old log cabin by a screened-in breezeway. I'd been picking up old advertising signs for months at flea markets, planning to evoke the image of a long-ago general store. A large turquoise sign touting Hire's Root Beer and a vibrant red model offering Coca-Cola were sure to stand out against the chocolate-brown stain on my garage.

And stand out they surely did. After my handyman hung a sign advertising feed and seeds, my next-door neighbor promptly paid me a visit. "What's going on here?" he demanded. "Are you planning on putting a feed store next to my nice house?"

That neighbor never did catch my general-store vision, and it wasn't long before a FOR SALE sign appeared in his front yard. "Please send me a neighbor who loves old-timey things, Lord," I prayed.

When my new neighbor moved in, I was the first one there to welcome her. But suddenly, from her stoop, I saw my signs from a neighbor's perspective. I had to admit they were a bit glaring. As I handed her a basket filled with a scented candle, cappuccino mix and mugs, I quickly revised my welcome speech. "I'm Roberta from next door," I explained, then got to the heart of the matter. "If the signs on my garage bother you, I want you to know I'll be happy to take them down."

My new ninety-two-year-old neighbor steadied herself on her aluminum walker, then looked me square in the eye. "*Bother* me?" she answered with a grin spreading across her face. "Why, they're the reason I bought this place. Every time I look over your way, I see something else I love."

My newest God-find lived right next door. And from the looks of things, we were going to get along famously.

Thank You, Lord, for Your divine surprises. —ROBERTA MESSNER

READER'S ROOM

"THIN SPOTS" ARE SITES where the spiritual and temporal worlds seem to be especially close together. My own favorite thin spot in the Texas Hill Country is a ridge twenty miles north of my New Braunfels home, from which one may view the country song's "Miles and Miles of Texas." Along with wind, vast sky and panoramic views, there's occasional muted traffic to keep a visitor's feet on the ground. Near a fence under a scrubby tree is a two-foot, handcrafted cross memorializing "Erin."

No doubt many Guideposts readers have their own favorite thin spots—peaceful places not too far from home. Ironically, mine, the place where, at age seventy-five, I've finally learned to pray to God out loud, is known far and wide as the Devil's Backbone. And I get there by traveling peacefully along rural Purgatory Road.

(The Devil's Backbone in northern Comal County, Texas, is traversed for some five miles by Texas Route 32 from the Hays County line to Farm-to-Market Road 3424. Purgatory Road intersects Route 32 about two and a half miles east of the ridge.)

—*Don Green, New Braunfels, Texas*

SUN
16

HE SHALL GROW UP BEFORE HIM AS A TENDER PLANT, AND AS A ROOT OUT OF A DRY GROUND. . . .
—*Isaiah 53:2*

WHAT A GLORIOUS DAY! I thought to myself as I pulled out of the driveway. The sun burned in a bright blue sky, the air was balmy, and I knew that our morning drive would include some breathtaking New England scenery. When my wife Carol and the kids broke into a traveling song, I should have been radiant with happiness. But instead a cold hand clawed at my heart: We were taking our oldest boy off to college.

Millions of parents go through the same experience; we all want the best for our children and that includes a good education. Carol and I were delighted with John's choice of college and shared his excitement over this new adventure. My own first year at university had been a happy time, filled with new friends and new ideas.

But I couldn't shake my worries. *What if he falls in with the wrong crowd? What if he becomes a stranger to us? Will he stay close to his younger brother?* I said a brief prayer and turned onto the highway.

When John returned home for his first weekend visit, I was thrilled. He dove right into the family routine, helping out with chores, serving at church, joining in our conversations. But something had changed. He had grown a bit, become more mature through his new independence. And perhaps I had grown a little bit too: I'd loosened the apron strings (which, yes, even men wear) and learned that change is sometimes God's way of keeping things on course.

Teach me, Lord, to see the inevitable changes in my family in the light of Your never-ending love. —PHILIP ZALESKI

MON
17

WHEN HE SAW THE CROWDS, HE HAD COMPASSION ON THEM, BECAUSE THEY WERE HARASSED AND HELPLESS, LIKE SHEEP WITHOUT A SHEPHERD.
—*Matthew 9:36* (NIV)

IT WAS NOT A GOOD afternoon. One of my children did something upsetting. In and of itself, the incident probably wasn't all that big a deal. But it was the proverbial straw that sent this camel into emotional overload.

I sat down and cried—sobbed, really—and wept my weary heart out.

Moms aren't supposed to do this. We try to be strong and loving and calm and competent, the ones who hold things together. But I don't think I'm the only one who, once in a blue moon, suddenly breaks down in tears. For me, though, today's tears came as a surprise. They spilled out in amazing profusion. I shooed away the child-who-had-offended and went into my room.

Eventually, I quieted down. I came out and apologized to the child-who-had-offended for my overreaction. My bewildered offspring accepted my apology.

Then my Mary appeared. Mary is my gregarious one, very sociable but not high on the empathy spectrum just yet. She had been elsewhere when my meltdown occurred but now noticed that my eyes were red. Without questioning why I'd been crying, she asked, "Are you feeling better, Mom?" I assured her I'd recovered and that now I was just worn out. She slid into my lap and slipped her thin seven-year-old arm around my shoulders.

"I know how it is, Mom," she said gently. "I'm always tired after I cry too."

I almost cried again, this time for joy.

Lord, compassion is a great thing. Thank You for Mary's—and for Yours.
—JULIA ATTAWAY

TUE
18

"*I LED THEM WITH CORDS OF HUMAN KINDNESS. . . .*"
—*Hosea 11:4 (NIV)*

"MAMA, GUESS WHAT?" Keri said as she rushed through the front door with her two-year-old daughter Abby in tow. "I just signed us up for real estate school."

"What? I didn't say I was going to real estate school!"

"Too late, Mama."

I had to admit it would be fun to earn more money, and I do like a challenge, and Keri did need a partner to help make sure she had plenty of time for Abby.

Real estate school turned out to be more than I bargained for. Studying gobbled up all my free time, and tests turned me into a raving maniac. I fretted through the quiz questions, reading them over again and again. Keri would zip through the pages, hand in her paper and then nervously pace the halls waiting for me to finish. She didn't relax until the teacher told me I'd passed.

Eventually, Keri and I found ourselves working for a Nashville real estate company. We had learned a lot about the principles of real estate but not much about the practice. When our first contract came, we were terrified. What if we made a mistake and spoiled the deal for our client?

"Hey, if you have any questions, call me," Richard, one of our company's top agents, said casually as we were leaving a meeting.

We took him up on his offer, and our first sale went off without a hitch. After that, Richard always had time for us and his kindness extended far beyond business advice.

"Just be yourselves," he'd remind us. "Don't worry about those multimillion-dollar listings people brag about. Remember they sell little houses too. Just be who you are and treat each client as your most important client. You'll do all right."

I was out of real estate school, but as far as kindness was concerned, I was still a student. And that was perfectly okay with me.

Human kindness, Father, leads me on. —PAM KIDD

WED
19

"THE HEAVENS ARE THE WORK OF YOUR HANDS. THEY WILL PERISH, BUT YOU REMAIN; THEY WILL ALL WEAR OUT LIKE A GARMENT. . . . BUT YOU REMAIN THE SAME. . . ." —Psalm 102:25–27 (NIV)

THE OTHER DAY SOMEONE asked me what *bespoke* meant. It brought back a memory.

When I arrived in New York City some twenty-five years ago, I decided I needed a new suit. An acquaintance suggested I get one custom-made—a bespoke suit. That seemed extravagant to me, but my friend was insistent. He knew a place where the cost would be no greater than at a department store and the quality and fit far superior.

I ended up at a little shop on East 62nd Street. After much fussing from the tailor, I chose a houndstooth pattern in Italian wool, which was then fitted to my every dimension. I remember thinking that if anything about me ever changed, I'd have to throw out the suit.

I got many good years from it, including some years at Guideposts; in fact, I wore it for my first interview with then editor-in-chief Van

Varner, who said later that it made an impression. Eventually I retired it, and not long ago, during one of my periodic purges of my closet, I was faced with the prospect of actually throwing out the worn suit.

The urge to put on the suit one last time was irresistible. Would it fit? I was surprised: I'm a little broader in the chest and shoulders, narrower in the waist and hips. The pants seemed a bit too long—they must have stretched because I couldn't possibly have shrunk. Still, there was something so right about it—so *bespoke*.

Sort of like my relationship with God. In those same twenty-five years I've changed, yet God's constancy has remained unchanged. My faith has grown, but it fits me as well as it ever did.

Lord, Your love is unique for each of us. Let me have a bespoke faith.
—EDWARD GRINNAN

THU
20

I AM AMONG YOU AS HE THAT SERVETH. —Luke 22:27

I'M COMING UP RICH taking care of my aunt, and I didn't even know I was on a treasure hunt. I'd come to give companionship and practical help to a one-hundred-year-old woman so she could continue living in her own home, and in the process I discovered the joy of serving.

Recently I read a piece that makes a distinction between helping and serving. Helping conveys an imbalance that says, "I'm coming to your rescue." Serving emanates from mutual respect and equality between individuals. It's my complete person offered to my aunt's complete person.

How does this work between us? I run the tub while she splashes in the bubbles. "It's so dear of you to do this," she thanks me as I bathe her. I reply, "I know how nice it is to feel scrubbed and clean."

I cook the meals and wash the dishes. "You're doing all the work," she fusses. I respond, "You've lived a hundred years. You're entitled to sit and enjoy your coffee."

I am contending with a sore throat, but I keep our nightly ritual of reading aloud from the Bible. "Isn't that exciting!" she exclaims. "Read that again." I swallow painfully and read on.

I sit and rub her feet. "That feels so good," she murmurs, "but I don't want to tire your hands." "These feet need a good rub," I answer. "They've carried you a long way." "Yes," she agrees, "they've been around the world."

Where do this joy and patience and tenderness come from? I ask myself. Jesus answers, "I am among you as he that serveth" (Luke 22:27).

It's taken more than fifty years, but I've finally heard His words.

Father, thank You for the treasure of serving. It is truly Your kingdom come on earth. —CAROL KNAPP

FRI
21

HOLD ON TO THE GOOD. —*I Thessalonians 5:21 (NIV)*

IT HAD BEEN THREE WEEKS since Hurricane Katrina hit and I was in survival mode, monitoring the gas for the generator and driving as little as possible. I was still reeling from this unexpected catastrophe. Bottled water and ice were hard to come by. Debris was piled high along the streets. Parts of the city did not have power, phone, gas or cable. The roads were jammed with utility workers, Red Cross volunteers, extra law enforcement officials, firefighters and the locals who were slowly returning.

I went to the grocery store but barely remembered shopping. I walked through the aisles, picking through the small amount of stock on the shelves and thinking more about the new roof I needed and the big oak tree I'd lost in the storm.

Driving out of the parking lot, I noticed that my favorite café had reopened. What a surprise! I quickly parked. It was all I could do not to run inside.

It was a different world beyond the door. Soft, uplifting music played; the staff was smiling. A family was sitting together, laughing and talking over lunch. A couple was sipping coffee and sharing dessert. I placed my own order, then went to look for a table.

That's when I heard, "Join us!" It was a group of friends from church.

After hugs and hellos, we shared our storm stories. Our stories, though, didn't focus on the devastation. "The tree just missed my house, praise the Lord!" "My electricity is already back on, what a blessing!" "I managed to call my daughter right before the phones went out!"

I left the café, not only full from a wonderful meal but with a renewed sense of gratitude. As one of the ladies said, "It's hard to be stressed when you're feeling so blessed!"

Loving Father, give me the grace to look beyond my difficulties to the blessings in my life. —MELODY BONNETTE

SAT
22

THUS YE BROUGHT AN OFFERING: SHOULD I ACCEPT THIS OF YOUR HAND? . . . —*Malachi 1:13*

READING FROM THE TORAH in the synagogue isn't easy. The Hebrew contains no vowels, which makes pronunciation dicey, and reading involves learning the specific chant that is to accompany the words. It's really more singing than speaking.

Nevertheless, I volunteered to try to learn a Sabbath Torah portion to read in front of the congregation at services. The rabbi sent me a tape and a crib sheet showing the portion with the vowels and chant indicators. I practiced at home until I got it just right. The Wednesday before the Saturday I was to "perform," I went to the synagogue to work with the Torah itself. Alone, without the crib sheet, I did a perfect job.

But on Shabbat in front of the congregation, when I heard the blessing before the Torah reading and the ensuing silence into which I was supposed to chant, the importance of what I was doing crashed in on me. My body and voice shook. The beauty of the reading was lost.

The rabbi congratulated me, but I demurred. "I didn't do as well as I wanted."

"We'll only agree to do a sacred act if we think we can do it better than we really can," he said. "The important thing is to do it and believe that God accepts us as we are."

Teach me, Lord, to come to You even when I can't be perfect at it.
—RHODA BLECKER

SUN
23

The Lord is the One who holds his hand.
—Psalm 37:24 (NAS)

THIS MORNING I WAS reading Psalm 37. The psalmist is wrestling with his own humanity and admitting his share of mistakes. With a wisdom that comes with age, he concludes, "Rest in the Lord and wait patiently for Him. . . . Do not fret, it leads only to evildoing. . . . When he falls, he shall not be hurled headlong; Because the Lord is the One who holds his hand" (Psalm 37:7–8, 24, NAS).

As I read these words, I remembered a moment when I was a small child, walking through a large public market in the Philippines with my father. It was very crowded and people pressed relentlessly against us. Suddenly I became frightened that I would be separated from my father and hopelessly lost. Just then my dad's big hand came down and grasped mine. His grip was so firm that I was sure he wouldn't let go of me, that I was safe because he was with me.

As I've watched my life unfold, I've discovered that no matter how much I fail or how many boneheaded decisions I make, God will never let go of my hand. As King David wrote near the end of his inconsistent life, "Just as a father has compassion on his children, So the Lord has compassion on those who fear Him" (Psalm 103:13, NAS).

Dear God, thank You for being my Father and not letting go of my hand. Amen. —SCOTT WALKER

MON
24

"I, the Lord . . . will take hold of your hand. . . ." —Isaiah 42:6 (NIV)

THE DISTRICT OF COLUMBIA subway system boasts some of the longest escalators in the world. Being afraid of heights, I try to stay away from certain stations. The fear is especially fierce when I'm riding up. On some level the scenario reminds me of the spirit's journey at death: Even though I'm traveling toward the light, I'm venturing precariously farther and farther from the solid ground of the bottom stair.

Last month, when my older sister Alice came to visit, we rode the subway and got off at a stop unfamiliar to me. I saw the escalator and gasped. "Oh, it's too high. I can't."

"Come on," she coaxed. "You're not alone. You can do this."

"Stand in front of me," I said, "so I can see you, and just hold my hand." Which she did, all the way to the top.

This morning a friend asked me, "If you could choose one person to be at your side when you die, who would it be?"

"Alice," I answered quickly—she who knew me from birth, who held my hand in childhood photos, who walked into the hospital with me the morning our dad passed away. "I'd want her to hold one hand." And Jesus the other.

Lord, whether I'm facing life or death, whenever I'm afraid, take my hand.
—EVELYN BENCE

TUE
25

LO, CHILDREN ARE AN HERITAGE OF THE LORD AND THE FRUIT OF THE WOMB IS HIS REWARD.
—*Psalm 127:3*

I WAS VISITING A grade-school classroom recently, talking about prayer and mercy and miracles. A girl raised her hand and said, "Mister, you're talking a lot about miracles, but have you ever seen any?"

I said, "Yes, oh yes. I saw new people emerge from my wife one after another like a circus act, wet and wary. These three people were never in the universe before, and they will never be repeated in the billions of years to come, so, yes, I have seen miracles. Although now I think the miracle would be if my daughter ever let any of the rest of the family use the bathroom, like *that* will happen in a billion years."

Well, they laughed, or at least the boys did—the girls didn't laugh, for some reason—but since that day I've thought a lot about miracles. We swim in an ocean of them, and they are everywhere waiting for us. Pretty much every moment and every breath is a miracle, but the most astonishing miracles of all are children.

Yes, they drive you insane, and the prospect of their being hurt makes you mad with fear, and their education and clothing and feeding and insurance make you poor, and their peculiar music and bizarre dress make you want to live quietly in a desert cave, and their snippy tones and chaotic bedrooms make you want to pull out the few remaining hairs on your pate, but there's nothing more madly miraculous than a child. You know it and I know it, and if my kids ever get out of the bathroom, I will tell them so and hope they know how madly I am in love with them.

Dear Lord, for these wild human mammals in my house, thank You. For their brains and humor and kindness, thank You. For getting my daughter out of the bathroom once before she goes to college, thank You.

—BRIAN DOYLE

WED
26

A FRIEND LOVETH AT ALL TIMES. . . .
—*Proverbs 17:17*

SUMMER WAS GONE and fall was beginning, and I decided to go through last year's Christmas cards before new ones began to arrive. I was surprised by how many I hadn't taken time to read. I put the whole pile on the dining room table, made a cup of tea and sat down.

The first card enclosed a snapshot of two adorable kittens a dear friend had adopted after her older cat died. I remembered the joy in her voice when she called to tell me about them. Another card was from a friend who had moved to Florida when her husband retired and was enjoying the sunny weather. "When are you coming down here?" she wrote. One of the family letters went on for three pages. I savored every picture of the kids and grandkids. "What's going on in your life?" was written at the bottom of the third page, which meant why hadn't they heard from me?

There were more cards and several more letters, and when I finished them I felt as if I had spent the afternoon with loving friends. I went to my desk and began to write the first of many letters I should have written months ago.

This year I'll probably do what I always do with Christmas cards and letters: open them eagerly, glance at them quickly and put them in a pile, because there is so little time during the holidays. But I've started a new tradition. I'll wait until life slows down again and then I'll read all the cards and letters before I answer each and every one of them with all my love.

Friends are among the most wonderful gifts of life. Thank You, Lord, for blessing me with them. Amen. —PHYLLIS HOBE

THU
27

THE LORD WILL TAKE AWAY FROM THEE ALL SICKNESS. . . . —*Deuteronomy 7:15*

"THERE ARE TWO KINDS of people," a friend of mine told me a few years ago as I was approaching my fortieth birthday. "People under the age of forty and people over it."

After forty arrived, I couldn't help but notice that the age really was the milestone it's always made out to be. Almost as if on cue, my knees started bothering me if I jogged for too long, and my hair, graying around the temples for some time, started changing color a little faster. Long taken largely for granted, my body was beginning to assert itself as what, in truth, it always had been: a fragile and temperamental piece of machinery destined ultimately to break down.

This year, I turn forty-five. Over the past couple of years, as I've gotten used to being a member of the second of those two kinds of people, I've started to notice that people over forty can also be divided into two general classes: There are those who are clearly worried about age and all it brings with it, and those who, though perhaps not delighted with the gradual failings of the body, aren't undone by them either. With faith, with the belief that life's end is not really an end at all but only the beginning of another infinitely larger life as yet unknown, gray hair and achy knees are not weighty and terrible events, but markers on a journey far from over—indeed, hardly begun.

Lord, keep me ever mindful of the larger life that lies beyond this one.
—PTOLEMY TOMPKINS

FRI

28

THROUGH FAITH AND PATIENCE INHERIT THE PROMISES. —Hebrews 6:12

THE BIG APPLE TREE in our front yard looked taller than ever as Leo and I began picking its fruit. Was it because I hadn't climbed many trees lately that my courage began to wane as I viewed the apples at the very top? Or was it because I didn't want to fall and create a spectacle for the crew of city workers who were installing new water lines right in front of our house? It was clear that the job would take several days.

Much to my surprise, the minute they saw us picking apples, two of the young city workers sauntered into our yard and began helping.

"Are you sure this won't jeopardize your jobs?" I asked one of them.

"No, we're used to going out on a limb for people," he joked, as he reached up for apples growing on the very top branches. As the baskets began to fill, I had an idea.

"How many men are in your crew?" I asked.

"Let's see. . . ." He began counting on his fingers. "Nine, ten, eleven. Eleven altogether."

"Good! As a thank-you, I'm going to bake apple pie for everybody. Be in our carport on Monday morning around ten for pie and coffee."

I could tell he didn't believe me, so Monday morning when the pies were baked and the coffee percolating, Leo went out to remind the crew of our promise. Before long the roar of heavy equipment grew silent and a line of men in hard hats and orange coveralls walked up our drive-way. As they settled into lawn chairs with their coffee and pie, I counted them . . . eight, nine, ten.

"Isn't there one more?" I asked.

"Yeah, but he wouldn't come. Didn't believe us, I guess. Man, but he doesn't know what he's missing!"

Lord, how many blessings am I missing because I don't trust Your promises? Give me faith to believe that what You say is what You'll do. Amen. —ALMA BARKMAN

SAT
29

IN ALL THY WAYS ACKNOWLEDGE HIM, AND HE SHALL DIRECT THY PATHS. —Proverbs 3:6

I AM NOT VERY GOOD at directions. Okay, the truth is I'm terrible at directions. I get lost in airport terminals and mall parking lots. I shudder every time I stop to ask directions and someone says, "Oh, it's easy. You can't miss it." Because that's exactly what I almost always do: miss it.

So last year, when we bought a new car, my husband asked if I'd like to have a Global Positioning System (GPS) included that would help me navigate. Now I have an electronic pal who speaks to me, telling me where to turn and what lane I need to be in for exits. I have a colorful digital map with a small arrow that is "me," so I can watch as I progress down highways and toward intersections. But before any of this marvelous assistance can take place, I have a screen full of text that comes up every time I start my car. It contains a promise that I must make to drive carefully, obey traffic rules—and not stare too much at the navigational screen. And until I hit the AGREE button, I get no help or guidance.

I thought of that GPS last night when I opened my Bible. It, too, wants to give me direction as I travel the road of life. But first I have to agree to take time to read its words, to apply its wisdom, to surrender to its Author.

I'll probably always be "directionally challenged," but I know that if I use both my GPS and my Bible wisely, I'll be making more right turns in life.

Lead me, Father, down the road that will take me closer to You.

—MARY LOU CARNEY

SUN
30

GOD IS FAITHFUL, BY WHOM YE WERE CALLED UNTO THE FELLOWSHIP OF HIS SON JESUS CHRIST OUR LORD. —*I Corinthians 1:9*

"HAVE YOU GOT EVERYTHING you need?" I asked our daughter Mary. I was taking our seven-year-old to a Sunday afternoon birthday party.

"I've got the present and the card," Mary said. She started for the door and then stopped. "Oh, I forgot Susan!" she said, running back to her room.

Susan. Of all the dolls she has, I thought, *why does she always choose that one?*

Susan came to us when Mary was a baby, a hand-me-down gift to our daughter Elizabeth from a neighbor's daughter. She had been well taken care of in her previous home; her colonial costume was spotless, her hair carefully brushed. A few years later, when Elizabeth was given a brand-new doll of her own, she gave Susan to Mary.

Her time in the Attaway house hadn't been kind to Susan. Her clothes were stained and worn, her limbs displayed the marking-pen skills of the Attaway toddlers, and her hair had never recovered from the shampooing Elizabeth had decided to give it.

Despite all this, Mary loved Susan. She loved her even after her right leg fell off and treatment at the doll hospital proved only temporarily effective; she loved her when we taped her leg back on, and when that, too, proved futile, she loved her with just one leg. When we gave Mary a brand-new doll for Christmas, she was thrilled. But when the newness wore off, Susan was still number one in her heart.

When our tax refund arrived this year, we gave a little spending money to each of the children. Mary's been eyeing a doll catalog; she thinks she's found the perfect wheelchair for Susan.

Lord, let me love like Mary, with a loyal heart. —ANDREW ATTAWAY

MY WALK WITH GOD

1 _____

2 _____

3 _____

4 _____

5 _____

6 _____

7 _____

8 _____

9 _____

10 _____

11 _____

12 _____

13 _____

14 _____

15 _____

16 _____

17 _____

18 _____

19 _____

20 _____

21 _____

22 _____

23 _____

24 _____

25 _____

26 _____

27 _____

28 _____

29 _____

30 _____

October

They that wait upon the Lord shall
renew their strength . . . they shall run,
and not be weary; and they shall walk,
and not faint. —*Isaiah 40:31*

LESSONS FROM THE JOURNEY
EXPECT RIP-OFFS

MON

I

FORGIVE, IF YE HAVE AUGHT AGAINST ANY: THAT YOUR FATHER ALSO WHICH IS IN HEAVEN MAY FORGIVE YOU YOUR TRESPASSES. —Mark 11:25

THEY'D COME TO VISIT us in Normandy, taking a cruise down the Seine from Paris to Le Havre—and they were sputtering with indignation before we got their bags to our car. Driving to our apartment, we heard about the taxi driver who'd taken them the long way around to the pier, the porter who'd overcharged for getting their luggage aboard, the steward who'd demanded a tip for setting up their deck chairs, when tips were supposed to be included. Not a word about one of the loveliest river trips in the world.

After they left, my husband John and I added a new category to any estimate of a trip's expenses: rip-offs. They'd certainly happened to us— the wrong change returned in unfamiliar currency, the mysterious surcharge on a dinner bill—and watching our friends' overreaction reminded us how upset we, too, could get over such things.

To travel is to be the perpetual newcomer, the one who doesn't know the shortest route, the right price, the best deal. Whether it's someone taking advantage of our ignorance or, more often, our own mistakes in new settings, any trip will cost more than it needed to. To build that expectation into our budget has saved us considerable emotional pain over the years and has been a good principle for the day-by-day journey too.

To live is to find myself, like the traveler, forever in new territory. I've never seen this day before. I may be taken advantage of; I'll certainly make mistakes. To live and to travel anger-free, I'm trying to learn, is to practice continual forgiveness of others and of myself. To savor the ever-changing scene from the deck of this swiftly moving boat means expecting, and then forgetting, the little irritations on board.

Lord of the journey, help me accept the worst in others and myself, but go on looking for the best in us all. —ELIZABETH SHERRILL

TUE
2

BUT SAMUEL WAS MINISTERING BEFORE THE LORD—A BOY WEARING A LINEN EPHOD. —I Samuel 2:18 (NIV)

WHEN MY CHILDREN'S FATHER was killed in a motor-cycle accident, we were devastated. Part of our lives died with him. We cried, and then we tried to go on living. I went back to work and my children went back to school: Chase to kindergarten and Lanea to middle school. In that cloud of pain, it was difficult to pray. We retreated to our private places, silently trying to make sense of what was senseless, until Chase rescued us.

One evening after work, I sat in my darkening room. There was a knock on the door and then Chase entered, wearing a hideous plaid jacket. He called it his "comedian jacket."

"What did the penguin say when it fell down the stairs?" Chase said.

"I don't know. What did it say?" I asked, playing straight man.

Chase grinned. "Help! I've fallen and I can't get up!" he answered through missing teeth, clad in that ridiculous coat.

It wasn't much of a joke, but I laughed. I laughed hysterically. I laughed until I cried, and we breathed deeply while we hugged.

It was the only joke Chase knew. He told it to our family over and over again. Night after night, he knocked on my door, wearing the same jacket and telling the same joke. Night after night, until we were com-pletely rescued—until we all regained hope and the courage to live.

Thank You, God, for children who minister to us and make our hearts merry. —SHARON FOSTER

WED
3

THE LORD BLESS THEE, AND KEEP THEE.
                                    —Numbers 6:24

WHAT WOULD I DO for Carol's fiftieth birthday? She made it clear that she didn't want a party, certainly not a surprise party (that was an agreement at our marriage—no surprise par-ties ever). "How about a small dinner with friends?" I asked. "No," she said, "I hate being the center of attention." Still, the milestone had to be marked. I wasn't going to let her get away with a Stouffer's frozen dinner and a movie video, which was all she claimed she wanted.

So I sent a letter to her friends, asking them for photos, poems, notes, cards, letters. "Carol doesn't want a party in person . . . but I'm hoping to give her a party in a book." I bought an album with a friend's advice, and the tributes poured in. For a few minutes at the end of every workday, I would pull out the marking pens and double-sided tape—who knew there were so many scrapbooking items?—and assemble the book, Carol's book. Photos of her in junior high, pictures of us with the boys, original songs, witty verse, fond reminiscences and one haiku in Japanese. It made me grateful for all the years we've had together. The gift wasn't the album, it was the friendship and love she's given to me and to our kids and to all her friends and family. You could read it on every page.

I wrapped it up and took it home. "Happy birthday, sweetie," I said. "It's not a frozen dinner or a video, but it's what you deserve." She cried. She doesn't really like to cry, but I think she likes the book. She's said so many times. And every time I remind her that putting it together was a gift to me.

When I give, I always receive, thanks be to God. —RICK HAMLIN

THU
4

LET NOTHING BE DONE THROUGH STRIFE OR VAINGLORY; BUT IN LOWLINESS OF MIND LET EACH ESTEEM OTHER BETTER THAN THEMSELVES.
—*Philippians 2:3*

I SING TO THE DEAD. I walk regularly through a local cemetery that looks over the Atlantic Ocean, and provided no one is visiting, I sing along with my Walkman.

During the rest of my route I am silent, somber. I don't speak unless spoken to, striding purposefully. Though I love living by the sea, I don't feel comfortable in this new community. I believe the town's wealthy property owners assume I'm from the working-class neighborhoods, while the working-class folk think I'm another wealthy indolent.

One young man, however, has proven difficult to resist. A builder constantly employed in town on new home construction or renovations, he smiles widely and waves generously when I pass his projects. I only nod slightly.

Last week he shocked me out of my arrogance. Planting himself directly in front of me with his merry grin, he said, "I passed you in the cemetery yesterday. If you smiled at the living half as much as you sing to the dead, you might not be alone so much."

To say my feathers were ruffled would be an understatement. I moved around him, fuming at his insolence. As if I didn't want to be alone! As if I was desperate for company! How dare he!

Yet, how dare I? Upon a few days' reflection, that was the better question. I'd presumed with no right or reason. I hadn't listened, looked or sought. I hadn't opened myself to those willing to listen, look and seek. I gave the dead more attention than the living.

I don't expect to change everything today. But singing to the dead, I should definitely start smiling at the living.

Jesus, keep me from the arrogance of studied solitude.
—MARCI ALBORGHETTI

FRI
5

THERE I WAS IN PARADISE, AND HEARD THINGS SO ASTOUNDING THAT THEY ARE BEYOND A MAN'S POWER TO DESCRIBE OR PUT IN WORDS. . . .
—*II Corinthians 12:3–4 (TLB)*

IN 2005, WHEN I went back to Wisconsin to visit, I attended a Big Ten football game, always an exciting event for me because my son Michael is the assistant director of the University of Wisconsin Marching Band. The day before the game, Michael and I were driving around campus.

"Hey, Mom, do you want to see the 'wow room'?"

"The 'wow room'? What's that?"

"You'll see," he said with a chuckle.

In the back of Camp Randall Stadium, we climbed a flight of stairs, then took an elevator to the top floor of the stadium's brand-new luxury boxes. Michael led me down a short hall and opened a door.

I stepped inside. "Wow!" I exclaimed as he ushered me into the outer office of athletic director and head football coach Barry Alvarez. It was dazzling. Floor-to-ceiling windows formed a panorama overlooking the stadium. The huge Rose Bowl and Big Ten championship trophies gleamed from the center of the room. Photos of Wisconsin's proudest football moments and heroes adorned the walls. It was a "wow room" indeed.

That experience made me think about what heaven must be like. Will it cause us to exclaim "Wow!" when we step inside?

Visiting the "wow room" on campus that day helped me get my priorities in order. For instance, rather than worrying about getting my condo into "wow order," I need to polish up my kindness, helpfulness and thoughtfulness skills. I need to concentrate on getting my soul ready for when I get to step into heaven and say, "Here I am, Lord. Oh, wow!"

Father, help me prepare to be dazzled in heaven by making sure I keep my priorities in order down here on earth. —PATRICIA LORENZ

SAT
6

"FEAR NOT, FOR I HAVE REDEEMED YOU; I HAVE SUMMONED YOU BY NAME; YOU ARE MINE."
—*Isaiah 43:1 (NIV)*

BECAUSE OF MY WORK schedule, waking up at home on a Saturday with nothing to do is rare. On one of those mornings, my wife Rosie and I sat and talked, and she said, "Dolphus, there are days that I feel like God is far away and I am all alone."

I realized that this was not a time to talk but a time to listen, and that Rosie was not looking for a solution but a place to share deep feelings. So I listened, which, I have to confess, is hard for me to do.

Rosie told me that a few days earlier she had been feeling lonely and low. She wondered how she could go on in such darkness. Then an amazing thing happened: God brought a song to her heart, "Walking in the Light, Jesus Is the Light." In that moment God gave her strength to move on.

A Scripture also came to mind, Isaiah 43:1. "Dolphus," she said, "as I remembered that beautiful, reassuring verse, my heart felt joyful."

I praise God for songs of remembering and Scriptures of comfort— and for that rare Saturday morning when I had nothing to do but listen to the woman I love.

Lord, when I feel as Rosie did and have my questions, lead me to those things that will enable me to rejoice. —DOLPHUS WEARY

SUN
7

FOR THE BREAD OF GOD IS HE WHICH COMETH DOWN FROM HEAVEN, AND GIVETH LIFE UNTO THE WORLD.
—*John 6:33*

THUMBNAIL CUBES OF BREAD are arranged on a gleaming silver tray. There's a hush in the sanctuary; piano music drifts from the altar as the tray is passed down the rows.

I reach for my own small piece. It is light and feathery in my hand. Silently, I acknowledge my sins before the One Who died for them. Hope flickers in my heart like the flame of the Communion candle. Maybe next time I will be more careful in my choices. For now it is enough to slip the bit of bread in my mouth, remembering the sacrifice of my Savior.

Until last Sunday, this had been my usual Communion experience. What made that day different was, for the first time, I was responsible for preparing the Communion bread. The night before, my husband had brought me two loaves of French bread. I pulled out the cutting board, picked up a knife and began to trim the crusts off the loaves. As I performed this simple task, I became acutely aware of what I was doing and why.

Then I thought about the other things these loaves might have been used for—a party snack dipped in seasoned sour cream, a side order smeared with butter and served with pasta in a restaurant, lunch for ducks on a pond. Instead, this bread would be fed to hearts famished for forgiveness, and longing for God's hope and healing in their lives.

As I watched the bits of bread disappear from the tray at Communion that Sunday, I felt a new awe: God's Son gave His body on the Cross and called it the Bread of Life. Such bread is not to be handled casually.

Lord Jesus, You left us the comforting, sustaining imagery of bread to represent Your broken body. May my reaching for it—and for You—be always genuine and never routine. —CAROL KNAPP

MON

8

MY PEOPLE WILL ABIDE IN A PEACEFUL HABITATION, IN SECURE DWELLINGS, AND IN QUIET RESTING PLACES. —*Isaiah 32:18 (RSV)*

THIS FALL, WE MOVED back to my hometown. Though it's only an hour away from where I've lived for the past ten years, simple things, like picking up the black walnuts scattered over our front yard, bring me back to my childhood.

I close my eyes and smell the olive green husks of the walnuts, and I am seven again, sitting on the side of the dirt road with my best friend Debbie, crushing nuts beneath big stones. We use them to make a pretend stew in a coffee can. Stirring in leaves and handfuls of grass, we daydream about the years to come: the names of our future husbands, the children we will have, the exotic places to which we will travel. With our lives so far in front of us, filled with possibility, we lie in the grass and watch the birds rush through the sky, wishing time could flash by just as quickly, that we could be grown up now, if only for a second.

And now here I stand in the very same spot, fruit from the same tree in my hand, thinking back all those years, back to when I imagined a distant future filled with the mystery of whatever it means to be an adult, never dreaming that I would find myself decades later right where I began.

Lord, thank You for the memories that make my hometown the closest place to heaven I know. —SABRA CIANCANELLI

TUE

9

"SEE, I AM SENDING AN ANGEL AHEAD OF YOU TO GUARD YOU ALONG THE WAY AND TO BRING YOU TO THE PLACE I HAVE PREPARED." —*Exodus 23:20 (NIV)*

MY FATHER WAS DYING, and I was called home from Indiana to North Carolina. The first night at the hospital, my twin sister Debbie and I sat by Daddy's bed, holding vigil as we listened to his raspy breathing.

In the early hours of the morning, I awoke from a fitful sleep. Deb was sitting by the only window in the room. "Come here, Lib," she said. "I want to show you something."

I went around Daddy's bed, and Deb pointed to a framed picture hanging on the wall over the sink. "Can you see the angel in that picture?" she asked.

I had stared at that picture over and over, but until now had noticed nothing unusual. In fact, Deb and I agreed that we didn't particularly like the picture, a wooded scene with red poppies at the bottom and a bird sitting on a branch to one side.

But now, as I glanced at the picture from the angle by the window, I immediately spotted the angel. The sculptured wings and body were clearly made up of the light between the trees and the poppies. The shape was unmistakable.

"I asked God to give me a sign that Daddy would be okay, that he would be at peace," Deb said. "When I looked up, there was the angel. And I thought, *That angel is overlooking red* . . . and I was going to say *poppies,* but then it occurred to me that it was overlooking *Red.*" "Red" was our father's nickname. With a head full of bright red hair, he had been called nothing else since childhood.

Suddenly that picture became the most beautiful thing in the room for all of us, a sign of God's love and divine protection for our father.

Lord, I thank You for signs that assure me that You are present and active in every aspect of my life. —LIBBIE ADAMS

WED
10

CHARITY SUFFERETH LONG, AND IS KIND. . . .
—I Corinthians 13:4

"HEY, GIRLS," A CHEERFUL voice sang across the checkout aisle, "I'm not feeling the love."

A half hour earlier, I had been sulking in my kitchen, trying to recover from a call from a church member who had spent a good fifteen minutes berating me because I was supporting a political candidate she didn't like.

When my husband David appeared in the kitchen, I was past my boiling point. "How in the world am I supposed to love her when I can hardly stand being in the same room with her? It's totally impossible to love everybody!"

"Pam," he said, "I think you need a break. Get in the car and go somewhere."

So here I was in a discount store for some "shopping therapy," not intending to buy anything. But now I was wishing I could buy that happy woman's attitude as she called out again from behind the manager's counter, "Let me feel that love!"

One of the salesclerks left her post to talk with the manager. "I can't do it," she said. "I can't love those people when they're so mean to me. I try hard, Ms. Gibbons, but I just can't find that love you keep talking about."

"Honey," the manager said, "of course you can't always love them. But you can be kind to them. That's the way we win in life, baby. Killing those bad attitudes with kindness. So go on back and practice being kind." She gave the girl an affectionate push toward her register. "I'm already feeling that love!"

I left the store with a lot to think about. I'd been trying to hold myself to an impossible standard. There's just no way I could feel a warm, fuzzy love for everyone who crossed my path. But I didn't have to; I just had to respond with kindness.

Father, let me show Your love by being kind. —PAM KIDD

THU
11

WE CONSIDER BLESSED THOSE WHO HAVE PERSEVERED. . . . *—James 5:11 (NIV)*

WHILE VISITING MY DAUGHTER Lindsay in Southern California recently, I joined her on her brisk daily walk, pushing the stroller and her nine-month-old daughter up and down the hills in her neighborhood. As we walked, she talked about her post-pregnancy diet and exercise. After listening for a few moments, I offered my own reflections on these topics.

"I've decided that I've reached an age where I can quit worrying about fashion and figures," I told her. "I'm going to start wearing loose, comfortable clothes and sensible shoes. I'm not going to worry about how much chocolate I eat anymore or whether I'm holding my stomach in all the time."

I was on a pretty good roll when Lindsay cut me off abruptly. "You can't throw in the towel, Mom!"

"Why not?" I asked.

"Because that means quitting. Giving up. It means you don't care. And you can't care for others when you don't care for yourself."

When I returned home to Colorado a few days later, I brought along Lindsay's "Don't throw in the towel" advice. I even looked up the origin of that phrase. It's a boxing term: a fighter's manager throws in the towel to signal that the fighter is giving up, quitting.

I face lots of temptations to "throw in the towel": on a relationship that feels tedious; on reading through the manual that will tell me how to use my new digital camera; on doing a project on my computer or an exercise program that is sometimes painful. And then I remember Lindsay, persevering with that stroller up those hills, pushing through the hard places. "You can't throw in the towel," I hear her say.

That's why I'm sitting here at my computer . . . and holding my stomach in. Because I can't quit.

Lord, throwing in the towel comes easily for me. Persevering does not. Help me push through the hard places. —CAROL KUYKENDALL

FRI
12

THE SPIRIT OF THE LORD WILL COME UPON YOU IN POWER, AND YOU WILL PROPHESY WITH THEM; AND YOU WILL BE CHANGED INTO A DIFFERENT PERSON.
—*I Samuel 10:6 (NIV)*

I WAS PACKING MY BAGS for a weekend retreat when I heard my wife calling me. "Pablo, it's Denise from Boston on the telephone."

I picked up the phone. "I'm calling you about my brother Charlie," Denise said, her voice low and withdrawn.

It seemed like yesterday when Charlie walked into the Boston church where I ministered on Sunday mornings. He was a thin young man, not much older than I was, nervous, fragile and distraught. He was addicted to drugs and was struggling to get his life on the right track. I prayed with him, asking God to help him break his addiction and give him the courage to start a new life.

In the weeks and months that followed, I helped Charlie through rehab and recovery. We developed a special bond, but we lost touch with each other when I moved to the West Coast. We had reconnected a few months before Denise's phone call, and I'd learned that he was fighting lung cancer.

"Charlie is dying," Denise said. "He's only got a few days. I called you because Charlie loved you and you meant a lot to him. You were always his pastor."

Denise put the telephone by Charlie's ear so that I could say good-bye to him. I took a deep breath and said, "Charlie, I love you. I'll see you soon, my friend. Thank you for your friendship." Two days later, Charlie died.

Whatever I'd been able to do for Charlie was nothing compared to what he had done for me. His victorious struggle with drug and alcohol addiction taught me the power of making the most of a second chance in life through faith in God.

Lord, thank You for putting Charlie in my life. Give me the faith to lend my hand and heart to those who need a second chance. —PABLO DIAZ

SAT

13

DO NOT LET ANY UNWHOLESOME TALK COME OUT OF YOUR MOUTHS, BUT ONLY WHAT IS HELPFUL FOR BUILDING OTHERS UP ACCORDING TO THEIR NEEDS. . . . —Ephesians 4:29 (NIV)

MY TWO OLDEST DAUGHTERS, Faith and Hope, are in high school, so I get to drive them and their friends to football games and the mall and wherever. I have great kids and they have wonderful friends. But spend some time in a minivan with teenagers and your ears will bleed with gossip. Did you know that Kim said that Jordan told her that Abby heard that Brian asked Rachel to the dance even though Brian knows that Rachel is still getting over Steve? He is *such* a jerk.

I shouldn't make fun; I wasn't much different. My high school buddies and I could be just as cutting, just as punishing, just as careless with our comments. It never occurred to us how much those slights could hurt. Or maybe we were scared because we knew the razor-thin edge that separated the ins from the outs, the A-list invitees from those at home on a Saturday night.

This is my apology, my *mea culpa*, to all those I hurt decades ago. I could blame my behavior on lots of things, but I think that I was simply a rookie in the ways of love and I made rookie mistakes. I'm sorry if I ignored your invitation to the prom, if I said something sarcastic when you wanted something else, if I acted . . . well, acted my age.

Lord, I'm older now and out of excuses. Help me to hold my tongue when I should—especially in a minivan full of teenagers. —MARK COLLINS

READER'S ROOM

I HAVE MULTIPLE SCLEROSIS. I don't like it and wish it would go away, but God has seen me through. He sustains me and gives me strength for each day. I know God loves me and is always by my side. What Joy!

Many mornings I "just don't wanna," but then I realize how blessed I am. All these years (over twenty) with MS and I can still walk—not run—but walk, however slow. Praise God! What Joy!

There are many worse off than I am. I am thankful for all I have. If it were all taken from me tomorrow, I hope I can still say, "What Joy!"

—*Margaret McAbee, Portland, Indiana*

SUN

14

WE GIVE THANKS TO GOD ALWAYS FOR YOU ALL. . . .
—*I Thessalonians 1:2*

THE PHONE RANG ON A Sunday afternoon, and I was surprised to hear from the mother of one of my daughter's classmates. She was calling to thank me for driving her children home from school a few days earlier when she had been called out of town for work. I told her it was no trouble at all. "Maybe," she said, "but you really helped me out. I wanted to let you know." Her call made me realize how good it felt to be appreciated. When I thanked her for thinking of me, she told me about her new habit.

"I spend a few minutes every Sunday afternoon calling or writing a note to thank someone who's made my life a little better that week. Just to let them know I appreciate them."

What a great idea, I thought. *I can do that.* I started by writing a note to my sister-in-law for the bouquet of home-grown roses that she'd brought by my house the day before. It quickly turned into a note of gratitude for the many thoughtful things she's done for me over the years, some I'm sure I'd forgotten to thank her for.

I've learned that I never run out of people to appreciate, like the neighbor who loaned my daughter a bike or the librarian who enthusiastically runs our mother-daughter book club. *Forbes* magazine founder B. C. Forbes said, "A word of appreciation often can accomplish what nothing else can accomplish." And what's that? The realization that my life is constantly blessed by the kindness of others and, I hope, their realization of how valuable they are to me.

Lord God, as the Creator of all good things, You deserve my first and greatest thanks. —GINA BRIDGEMAN

MON

15

I KNOW WHAT IT IS TO BE IN NEED, AND I KNOW WHAT IT IS TO HAVE PLENTY. . . . YET IT WAS GOOD OF YOU TO SHARE IN MY TROUBLES.
—*Philippians 4:12, 14 (NIV)*

ONE OF THE MOST COMFORTING, reassuring, hopeful reasons I know to be an active part of a church community is the reassurance that when times get tough someone will be there to support you. Most of us have experienced that.

But what happens when the person who needs the care and support of the church community the most is the one who usually gives it? There was a time not long ago when a pastor friend of mine was in the midst of very difficult circumstances. Despite my own training in care for others, I often found myself tongue-tied around him. What if I said the wrong thing? Of all people, a minister would see through my words in a minute.

That worry had me walking on eggshells for a couple of weeks, until another friend of mine—a rough, gruff former Army sergeant—set me straight. That morning, he marched right up to my pastor friend and in the midst of my careful, well-measured words, poked a finger in his chest and snarled, "What you need is just being normal. You come to my house Monday night and as many Monday nights as you want after that. We'll watch football." As he walked away, he stopped, turned toward me and said, "You too. Might loosen you up."

The Gospel according to Monday Night Football isn't in the Book. Maybe it should be. For it teaches that the greatest gift we can offer a friend in distress is rarely fancy words or pious promises, but simply being there.

Grant, O God, that my life will be both faithful to You and to those whom You love. —JEFF JAPINGA

TUE

16

He was afraid and said, "How awesome is this place! This is none other than the house of God; this is the gate of heaven."
—*Genesis 28:17 (NIV)*

I HURRIEDLY OPENED the trunk of my car to throw in my suitcase, intent on getting to the hospital early enough to catch the doctors who were caring for my elderly father. I groaned as I saw the six short-sleeve shirts I'd taken from Dad's tiny closet at the nursing home. *Those should be taken to Dad's house, but I really don't want to go there,* I thought.

Going up the hill to Dad's empty house was depressing. It was hard to face the fact that he would never be well enough to live there again. I finally forced myself to go inside and ran back to the bedroom closet with the shirts as quickly as I could.

When I passed through the living room on the way out, I looked out the large window. The tree leaves had fallen and I could see Table Rock Mountain turning a golden pink in the early dawn. The rest of the mountain range was a smoky blue-gray, and a white mist curled along the valley below me. A thought formed clearly in my mind: *Sometimes you have to go places you don't want to go to see God's glory.*

There were other difficult places I didn't want to go that day. I didn't want to go to the hospital to deal with doctors and Dad's critical condition or to the nursing home to communicate my concerns about the gaps in Dad's care. But if God could send me up to a house I didn't want to visit to see a sunrise, He could show me His glory in all the other places I don't want to go.

Father, there are places I don't want to go today. But if I must, please show me Your glory there. —KAREN BARBER

GOD-FINDS
FINDING COURAGE IN THE FACE OF FEAR

WED

17

FOR YE HAVE NOT RECEIVED THE SPIRIT OF BONDAGE AGAIN TO FEAR; BUT YE HAVE RECEIVED THE SPIRIT OF ADOPTION, WHEREBY WE CRY, ABBA, FATHER.
—Romans 8:15

I WAS ON MY OWN for the first time since I turned twenty, facing the world after my marriage ended, and with it my dreams. *Whom do I hire to fix this leaky roof, Lord? I can't afford to make a mistake and I sure need a roof over my head. I'm so afraid.*

In my hands I held a nineteenth-century star quilt. The quilter's stitches were steady and even, twelve per inch. This quilt was not simply a bed covering; it was a work of heart. In my mind's eye I could see an Appalachian farm wife who churned her own butter, canned vegetables she grew in stubborn soil, washed clothes with lye soap that roughened her hands. Her spirit came through in the stitches that held the warm cotton batting in place. If I pressed firmly enough into the fabric, I could actually feel the cotton seeds. *There's courage in these stitches, Lord. And resilience.*

But suddenly, I saw the joy in this quilt too. Surely the woman who chose this vibrant red for the stars was in love with life. *Funny, with this quilt in my hands, that roof doesn't seem so insurmountable now, Lord.* First thing the next morning, I'd call that roofer my friend recommended. With God on my side, a friend's vow of trust and the strength of this unseen quilter, I wasn't so afraid after all.

Thank You for the people in our past who pave the way for our present, Lord. —ROBERTA MESSNER

THU

18

His possessions were seven thousand sheep, three thousand camels, five hundred yoke of oxen, five hundred female donkeys, and a very large household. . . . —Job 1:3 (NKJV)

I MAKE NO SECRET of the fact that "FlyLady" has helped me overcome the clutter in my house and get things in order. In fact, I tell practically everyone I meet about Marla Cilley and how she helps me order my life through her Web site www.flylady.org. I especially liked reading about how on their very first date, her husband Robert told her about what he calls "God Breezes." That's when you sit very still and listen closely for what God would like you to do next.

While cleaning out my hall closet, I discovered that I had three sealed cartons of—well, I didn't even know what was in there, though each one was marked TEACHING SUPPLIES. Suddenly I had a wild idea: Why not donate it to a teacher who could use it to decorate a classroom? *Still sealed? Without even looking at it?* The idea was almost horrifying! I sat silently for a few moments. *If I haven't missed it in years, I* thought, *then surely I'll never miss it.*

I phoned the county Board of Education, and they gave me the names of a couple of kindergarten teachers. The first one I phoned came within the hour and picked up armloads of useful stuff. At least that's what she said when she called to thank me later. And I could swear I felt a slight "God Breeze" coming from my new, improved hall closet.

God, is there something I can give up today—some old stuff, an old attitude, an old idea? Let me toss it without a backward glance!

—LINDA NEUKRUG

FRI

19

"Follow me," Jesus told him, and Levi got up and followed him. —Mark 2:14 (NIV)

I USED TO WONDER how Jesus could have had such an impact on the lives of His disciples in the few years He spent with them. But that was before I met Bill, the pastor of the church I attend at college. Young men from my college have been attending Bill's Friday afternoon Bible study for more than two decades—longer than I've been alive.

When I came to the Bible study, I was full of doubts and worries. One Friday afternoon I talked about my struggles, half expecting a stern reprimand from Bill.

"What's the opposite of faith?" Bill asked.

"Doubt," someone said.

"No," said Bill. "The Bible tells us to walk by faith and not by sight, remember? The opposite of faith is sight. Doubt is just a natural part of growing in your faith."

I wrote down those words in a journal in which I've written hundreds of other things that Bill has taught me over these past few years. And it's not just me. On his birthday, at homecoming and during other times throughout the year, men ranging in age from their early twenties to almost forty can be found in Bill's living room, spending time with the man who helped their faith grow roots.

Jesus had a great impact on His disciples. As Bill has shown me, all it takes is the willingness to share your life and your love—and your Friday afternoons.

Lord, thank You for the mentors who have helped me along my spiritual journey. —JOSHUA SUNDQUIST

EDITOR'S NOTE: A month from today, Monday, November 19, is our thirteenth annual Guideposts Thanksgiving Day of Prayer. Please plan to join us in prayer on this very special day. Send your prayer requests (and a picture, if you can) to Guideposts Prayer Fellowship, PO Box 8001, Pawling, New York 12564.

SAT
20

So that your trust may be in the Lord, I have taught you today, even you.
—*Proverbs 22:19 (NAS)*

"MOM, I'M LOSING MY VOICE!" Elizabeth croaked. It was Tuesday. Her next performance of *The Velveteen Rabbit*—in which she had the lead—wasn't until Saturday. Chances were that her voice would recover in time.

Wednesday came and Elizabeth's voice disappeared entirely. That night I got up three times to turn on the shower for steam, in the hopes of lessening the barking cough no syrup could soothe.

On Thursday Elizabeth barely spoke at all and drank lots of licorice tea, and I began heavy-duty prayers. I again got up at night to keep her room steamy.

On Friday Elizabeth chatted with some friends for ten minutes after math class. She came home squeaking. I called our pediatrician, who prescribed a heavy-duty cough suppressant.

That night I was in a quandary. I knew without a shred of doubt that if God wanted to, He could cure Elizabeth's laryngitis. Elizabeth knew it too. The question that weighed on me was *What if He doesn't want to? What if He has some other idea in mind?* I wrestled with what to say to my eleven-year-old. Simply saying, "Trust in God" seemed as if I were promising that He would wave His magic wand and all would be well. Yet, "We'll pray, but we have to accept God's will" seemed feeble and convoluted. I ended up saying nothing.

On Saturday morning Elizabeth got up, wordlessly waved hello and ate her breakfast. We made a trip to the pharmacy for throat lozenges.

Sitting in the audience that afternoon, I was stunned by how good Elizabeth was. Her voice cracked in one of her sad solo songs, but the effect was simply to make the audience teary. I sent up a silent thank-You to God. Evidently my daughter had approached Him with the same confidence she had put into her performance.

Father, whatever the situation, give me confidence in You.

—Julia Attaway

SUN
21

EVEN IN LAUGHTER THE HEART MAY BE IN PAIN. . . .
—*Proverbs 14:13* (NAS)

WHEN I NOTICED the beautiful newcomer at our small church, I hurried over to greet her. Then I realized that we'd met briefly about a year ago. I'd also met her husband, who recently died of cancer. Twenty years ago, I'd lost a husband to cancer. But Dee looked a thousand times better than I had then or did now. Her ivory and beige clothes and jewelry perfectly matched her coloring—blonde hair, porcelain skin. She was an extraordinary artist and had been a nationally known clothing designer. Dee was the most elegant, talented, together-looking woman I'd ever met.

We greeted each other and she accepted my invitation to sit with me. That's when I saw the pain deep in her amber eyes. "Where are you in your grief?" I asked her. "Does it still feel as though you're crawling through broken glass, all alone?"

She grabbed my hand and looked into my eyes. "Yes," she said. "My friends almost seem to be avoiding me. I'm going to make it, but I'm lonely—"

"Dee," I said gently, "I think you scare most people away. You're so—well, beautiful, sophisticated, talented. And you look like you're okay. I mean, if you were a little shabbier, I'd probably invite you to come home with me."

Our giggles cut through my tension and apprehension. Dee and I met for a long lunch the next week. Our brand-new friendship was off and running.

Father, why is it so hard for me to realize that on the inside, we all hurt exactly alike? —MARION BOND WEST

MON
22

THY ROD AND THY STAFF THEY COMFORT ME.
—*Psalm 23:4*

DUSK WAS FALLING ON an autumn afternoon, and I knew it was too late to take my golden retrievers Beau and Muffy out to run. But it had been a long day and I needed the exercise. Hurriedly putting the dogs in the back of my SUV, I took off for the Texas countryside.

When I unloaded Beau and Muffy near a friend's ranch, they exploded with pent-up energy, dashing across a cropped field and soon outdistancing me. The sky grew darker and the temperature dropped, but it was fun to run with the wind at my back, straining to keep the dogs in sight. Soon Beau and Muffy tired from sprinting and dropped back to lope along with me.

It was pitch dark as we reached a gate and turned to retrace our steps. Slowing to a walk, we watched the North Star rise in the sky, illuminating the frosted breath of man and beast. Suddenly the wild howl of coyotes exploded from a distant thicket and my dogs drew closer to me.

Soon they were walking at my heels, finding comfort in the presence of a man they trusted.

I thought of the Twenty-third Psalm: "The Lord is my Shepherd, I shall not want. . . ." How often do I walk in darkness, unable to discern the future stretching before me? Dangers—both real and imagined—lurk in the shadows, and I grow anxious and lonely. Then, like my dogs, I seek the Good Shepherd, slow my relentless pace and settle down to follow Him.

Lord, help me to know that You are with me, that I do not walk alone. Amen. —SCOTT WALKER

TUE
23

IF WE HOPE FOR WHAT WE DO NOT YET HAVE, WE WAIT FOR IT PATIENTLY. —Romans 8:25 (NIV)

THE FIRST TIME I noticed them was on my way to work one morning. Two "chairs" made from large, upright logs sat near the road. Seats and backs had been rough hewn into the wood. *How unusual!* I thought. *Are they set out for the trash?* The next day I looked more closely. They were at the end of a long lane. *Do they have a purpose?* Later that week I saw a father and his young son sitting in them, no doubt waiting for the school bus.

I smiled and gave the chairs no more thought, until the day I noticed a large, hand-lettered sign where the chairs had stood. PLEASE RETURN OUR CHAIRS. THEY ARE NOT TRASH. WE NEED THEM! Weeks went by and the sign stayed in place. Fall rains pelted it, winds made the edges ragged, but still it stayed. *Why don't they just give up and admit that those chairs are long gone?*

Then, one morning almost two months after that sign had appeared, another sign took its place. THANK YOU! And the sign was propped on two chairs made from large, upright logs.

Hope. It's a powerful thing. It can heal broken hearts, provide fresh starts, solve mountain-sized problems and sometimes even bring well-loved objects home.

Forgive me, Father, for giving up too soon. You are tenacious in Your love for us. Let me be tenacious in expecting the best.
—MARY LOU CARNEY

WED
24

FEAR NOT: FOR THEY THAT BE WITH US ARE MORE THAN THEY THAT BE WITH THEM. —II Kings 6:16

HARDLY A DAY GOES BY that I don't hear of violence in the Middle East on the radio or see the carnage on the evening news. So awful, yet mercifully far away. For most of my life I'd managed to block it out and concentrate on stresses closer to home.

Then several years ago my friend Jenny moved to Jerusalem. Suddenly every attack became a threat against her. I scrutinized articles for names of Americans and made myself watch the evening news to see if I would catch a glimpse of Jenny on a stretcher. I prayed for the victims and for world peace, but still felt sick with worry. How could Jenny, who always seemed so sensible, live in such a tormented city?

When she returned stateside to visit her family, I phoned her to find out how she was. Finally I asked, dumbfounded, "How can you live there?"

Jenny seemed strangely calm. "It's my home now."

"But aren't you afraid? Don't you worry about violence?"

"I don't dwell on it, Gail," she said. "When there's an incident, I think of something Mister Rogers used to say about looking for the helpers. There are so many more of them than there are of haters." She knew the mathematics of love.

Now when I learn of violence far away or hear an ambulance wail nearby, I pray for the victims—and the helpers.

Prince of Peace, protect those who help the helpless far and near.
—GAIL THORELL SCHILLING

THU
25

HE WHO BEGAN A GOOD WORK IN YOU WILL PERFECT IT UNTIL THE DAY OF CHRIST JESUS.
—Philippians 1:6 (NAS)

I'D ALWAYS BEEN a devotee of piano music, and I decided that it was time actually to do something about it. So I bought a used piano and signed up for lessons. I imagined myself wowing my teacher and calling my parents to ask why they hadn't recognized my genius in my early years. Soon I'd be entertaining at parties, banging out everything from Rachmaninoff to Ray Charles.

The first lesson was a wake-up call. Every time I touched the keys, the piano let out a terrible groan. Forget Rachmaninoff—I was having enough trouble with "A Tisket, a Tasket" and "Mexican Hat Dance." *Why*, I wondered, *is this so hard?*

It took me months to get through the first volume of the adult beginner's piano book. Then one day my teacher gave me a piece of sheet music: Beethoven's "Moonlight Sonata." Here was my chance to make real music.

After some diligent work, the first line of the Beethoven started to sound recognizable. The next line was tougher, but it felt doable. Still, I was stymied by the last part. No matter how long I worked on it, I couldn't make it sound right. Every day I tried and every day I became more frustrated. I stormed into my next lesson. "Why can't this be easier?" I asked in exasperation.

My ever-patient teacher sat down and played that very passage. Listening to her, I was overcome by the sweetness of it. "Brock," she said, "sometimes the loveliest things in life are the hardest to master. Keep practicing. You'll get it."

I can't say that I have. But I've come to enjoy stretching myself, challenging myself, to meet my goal. I can think of many beautiful things in life that are very hard to master—perfect kindness, generosity, forgiveness, love—but that's no reason why they shouldn't be tried. So I keep practicing. Someday I'll get it right.

Thanks, Father, for Your patience as I practice to be my best.
—BROCK KIDD

FRI

26

GOD HATH MADE ME TO LAUGH, SO THAT ALL THAT HEAR WILL LAUGH WITH ME. —Genesis 21:6

I DISTINCTLY HEARD some autumn leaves laughing at me today.

My leaves—maples and birches—and my neighbors' oaks and ashes
   have married in my backyard
   and they frolicked together while I chased them.
Methinks they think it a game of hide and seek,
   because every time I place them in a pile,
   they conspire with little wind spouts—

I'm tempted to call them dust devils—
to run away, undoing the work I've done.
I believe the red and orange ones taunt the most;
The brown and yellow ones snicker more subtly.
At least it was the colorful ones I heard *ha-ha*-ing
under my wire broom when the wind
merry-go-rounded them in all directions,
including the places I'd just cleaned.
Annoyed, I swung my rake at the teasing twister,
a roundhouse cut of Mickey Mantle proportions,
but I struck out; the invisible imp survived.
"If we had fewer trees," I call to my gardening wife,
"I'd have fewer leaves to rake."
She shouts back, "And less shade in summer,
less warmth in winter, and less clean air!
Thank God for those things too."
"Oh, hickory nuts," I retort.
But she doesn't hear me.
My words are drowned out by the wind
And giggling leaves.

> *Give me a sense of humor, Lord, when I fret;*
> *Wisdom to laugh at myself when I forget.*
>   —FRED BAUER

SAT
27

HOW GOOD AND PLEASANT IT IS WHEN BROTHERS
LIVE TOGETHER IN UNITY! —Psalm 133:1 (NIV)

I HELD MY BREATH. My cousin Jayme was playing in the championship soccer game for girls ages twelve and under. The score was tied 0–0 as the buzzer sounded, signaling the end of the game, and remained scoreless through two overtimes. Now Jayme and nine other girls from her team would be chosen to take penalty kicks. The other team picked their ten kickers, and the twenty girls moved into the middle of the field to prepare themselves for a tense fifteen minutes.

The two soccer teams echoed each other, missing and scoring in tandem, until the final pair of girls moved to the line. Kelly, a teammate of Jayme's, set her ball and backed up. She ran forward, kicked and watched as the goalie dove on top of her shot. Blocked.

My aunt excitedly grabbed Jayme, who had been chosen to kick in the seventh spot, and exclaimed, "Oh, I would've been so nervous if that had been you out there!" Jayme shrugged, still focused on the one kick left that would decide the game's outcome, and replied, "It doesn't matter who kicks first or last, Mom. We win as a team and lose as a team."

The final shot soared past Jayme's goalie and the horn sounded the opposing team's victory, but my aunt never noticed. Tears came to her eyes, not because the team lost a championship, but because Jayme, only eleven, understood that there are more important things in life than scoring goals.

God, thank You for the reminder that my focus belongs on the game, not just the final score. —ASHLEY JOHNSON

SUN
28

LET US NOT LOVE IN WORD, NEITHER IN TONGUE; BUT IN DEED AND IN TRUTH. —*I John 3:18*

DOROTHY WAS ABSENT from church for weeks because of illness. Then our Sunday bulletin stated that she had resigned from her position as president of the senior citizens association. Although she was recognized with warm and caring words, for her this had to be another loss, another letting go.

I wrote Dorothy and thanked her for serving so long and enthusiastically. She understood people and worked hard, always generous with her praise. I also recalled how we had worked in tandem at many funerals, she as lay reader and I as head usher. My duties of lining up ushers, making telephone calls, counting the congregation and communicating with the priests seemed nothing compared to her work as a reader. She never stumbled over a word, always mastered those difficult Old Testament names, and read with dignity and poise.

Dorothy thanked me for my note. She, too, recalled the funerals we had done together. Once again generous in her praise, she remembered things I had done for grieving families that had long escaped me. "I always felt," she said, "that we could do little for the deceased, but we could comfort and support the families. You always did that, Oscar."

So like Dorothy. Even though she had left her official duties, she was still on the job, serving from the sidelines. Caring was her good habit.

From today on, Lord, I will touch the hearts of others. —OSCAR GREENE

MON
29

"I AM WITH YOU AND WILL WATCH OVER YOU WHEREVER YOU GO, AND I WILL BRING YOU BACK TO THIS LAND. . . ." —Genesis 28:15 (NIV)

GROWING UP NEAR THE OCEAN in Southern California, I was often on the beach. I became a shore explorer, collecting treasures—new and mysterious shells, ocean-smoothed glass and driftwood. In the tide pools I counted limpets, urchins and anemones, trying to find more than my big brother could. I felt blessed that God delivered such interesting things to our doorstep.

A couple of years later, deep into graduate school and trying to discover new things in the world of computers and robots, I felt adrift—too far from the tide pools of my childhood. I spent most of my time at school in a windowless subbasement office and rarely found time for the two-hour trip home. I told myself that if I worked hard enough and stayed in my office, I would surely discover something new.

That Christmas, Grandma Nora gave me a fist-sized glass globe filled with bright white sand and some of my favorite shells: a cowry, a limpet, a white spiral snail shell striped with blue, orange and yellow. "It's a piece of home," she said, "for when you feel too far away."

The shells disappeared and new ones emerged with each gentle swirl of the sand, and I remembered my days as an explorer, the delight at the unexpected and unknown, the feeling that God was leading me on the path to discovery. "It's just what I needed," I told Grandma Nora.

The globe looks a little out of place on my desk in that subterranean office, surrounded by robot parts, computers and coffee mugs. But each day I swirl the sand inside to see what's new on that familiar beach and then I set about the job of discovery, full of delight at the unknown.

Father in heaven, today I will venture forth in the spirit of discovery and I will delight in what You show me. Amen. —KJERSTIN WILLIAMS

TUE
30

BUT A SAMARITAN, AS HE JOURNEYED, CAME TO WHERE HE WAS; AND WHEN HE SAW HIM, HE HAD COMPASSION, AND . . . SET HIM ON HIS OWN BEAST AND BROUGHT HIM TO AN INN, AND TOOK CARE OF HIM.
—*Luke 10:33–34 (RSV)*

THE WINDSHIELD WIPERS SWISHED back and forth in hypnotic rhythm as I drove alone through the rain on a two-lane highway in northern New Mexico. I did not realize how tired I'd become until I suddenly snapped awake to find myself headed off the road at high speed. I jerked the wheel to one side, overcompensated and spun down the middle of the road toward oncoming traffic. Overcompensating again, I skidded off the opposite side of the road and slid sideways down a steep embankment. Had the mud not piled up against the right side of my car, I would have overturned.

I thought some of the people in the cars on the road above would stop to help me, but they didn't. Panic set in when I realized I was trapped. The car lay so steeply tilted on its side that I couldn't lift open the driver's door, and the passenger-side door was buried in mud. And the power windows didn't work. For many minutes I yelled at passing cars, but no one noticed.

"Lord, please help me," I prayed over and over, trying to control my mounting fear.

Finally, a truck stopped and two men climbed down to rescue me. They drove me to a nearby town that had a wrecking service and stayed with me until I reached my husband on the phone.

Why do some people go out of their way to help those in trouble while others pass by? I don't know, but the story of the Good Samaritan shows me it's a problem that dates back at least two thousand years.

Lord, please give me the courage and compassion today to help those I see who are in need. Amen. —MADGE HARRAH

WED
31

Unto thee will I cry, O Lord my rock; be not silent to me: lest, if thou be silent to me, I become like them that go down into the pit.
—*Psalm 28:1*

SOME YEARS AGO my wife and I were walking down the street with our baby daughter tucked in the crook of my arm. She was a hundred days old at the time and folded into my elbow like a football. Suddenly she twisted out of my grasp and sailed off into the air. For a chilling second she was falling headfirst between us toward the concrete sidewalk. Without thinking I shot out both hands, juggled her for a second, and clutched her to me in such a spasm of horror and relief that she began to sob and I had to hand her to my wife, who was shaking.

I dreamed about my baby's headlong flight for weeks afterward. I dreamed about it every night. The dream never varied: I was walking down the street with her on my arm, she twisted away and I didn't catch her, and she died.

I talked about this dream to my wife many times. She never lost patience with me. One morning she listened to me recount my nightmare again. After a moment of silence she said, "If you hadn't caught her, we would be in hell," and she was right.

I've thought since that we are often at the lip of hell, and a Hand comes and fends off the fire, and mostly we don't even see, let alone acknowledge, that Hand. But for a minute this morning maybe we should, for there are many hells and they are all too real and there are so many of our brothers and sisters now and in the past seared by evil. So we kneel and pray, and then rise and make ourselves arrows of light against the leering dark.

Dear Lord, two words, and I say them with all my heart and bone and verve and fire: thank You. —BRIAN DOYLE

MY WALK WITH GOD

1 _____

2 _____

3 _____

4 _____

5 _____

6 _____

7 _____

8 _____

9 _____

10 _____

11 _____

12 _____

13 _____

14 _____

15 _____

16 _____

17 _____

18 _____

19 _____

20 _____

21 _____

22 _____

23 _____

24 _____

25 _____

26 _____

27 _____

28 _____

29 _____

30 _____

31 _____

November

O give thanks unto the Lord; call upon his name: make known his deeds among the people. —*Psalm 105:1*

THU
I

NOW THEREFORE YE ARE NO MORE STRANGERS AND FOREIGNERS, BUT FELLOW-CITIZENS WITH THE SAINTS, AND OF THE HOUSEHOLD OF GOD.
—*Ephesians 2:19*

LAST SATURDAY, I TOOK John and Mary to ballet class. I enjoyed seeing the delight they take in their dancing, and meeting some of the parents of their classmates. But mostly, I enjoyed having a chat with Luigi.

Luigi teaches jazz dancing at the ballet studio. He's taught Broadway stars and prima ballerinas, businessmen looking for stress relief and retirees looking to keep limber. He's been teaching for fifty-five years; at eighty-one, he's still going strong.

After serving in the Navy in World War II, Luigi went to Hollywood to dance in the movies. But an auto accident fractured his skull and sent him into a deep coma. As he lay unconscious in his hospital bed, he heard a voice tell him to "never stop moving." And he hasn't, despite the doctors who told him he'd never walk again. Slowly, painfully, he willed himself to move, to walk and then to dance.

Luigi is full of stories of his career as a dancer and teacher, of the stars he's known and the people who've taken his classes. "Do you see that woman?" he'll say, pointing at a robust-looking lady stretching in the corner. "She was recovering from cancer when she came to me, just skin and bones. I don't just teach them to dance, I help them to heal."

Luigi's students greet him with hugs. The love they feel for him, and he for them, is as obvious as the smile on his face, still half-paralyzed from his long-ago accident. "If I hadn't been a dancer, I'd like to have been a saint," Luigi says.

Maybe you have been, Luigi, I think. Maybe you have been.

Lord, thank You for the men and women who have been Your witnesses throughout the ages. And thank You for letting me meet Luigi.
—ANDREW ATTAWAY

LESSONS FROM THE JOURNEY
KNOW WHERE HOME IS

FRI
2

LORD, THOU HAST BEEN OUR DWELLING PLACE IN ALL GENERATIONS. —Psalm 90:1

I THINK I KNOW why my husband John and I have lived in the same house for forty-seven years, paying sky-high school taxes though we haven't had a child in school for more than three decades. It's because we spend so much of each year adjusting to new places.

That's why people travel, of course: to see those new places, meet new people, hear a new language, experience another history. But what a privilege, after all this, to return to a place where we can get to the post office without a street map and find the bathroom in the dark.

I didn't appreciate how important a home base is until I knew people who didn't have one, fugitives from wars or floods or drought or ethnic cleansing. I've come to recognize the lostness in the eyes, the longing in the voice describing the home one can't go back to.

And then I met Marta. A refugee from violence against Christians in the Sudan, she'd wandered from place to place for nearly ten years: to Uganda, where she learned English; then to England as an au pair; to Canada briefly; then back to Uganda. Right now she was in Italy, where we talked as she changed the bed in our hotel room in Venice. She didn't know where she'd go next, just that lacking papers, she could stay in Italy only three months.

And yet there were no complaints, no bemoaning the lost home. "God is so good!" she kept saying as she described the stopgap jobs she'd found.

"What was your work at home?" I asked.

"But," said this undaunted lady, "I *am* home. God is our home, and how can we ever be where He is not?"

If someday John and I have to leave our longtime home, maybe wherever we go I can learn to say with Marta, "I *am* home!"

Lord of the journey, thank You for going ahead of me to every place I can ever be. —ELIZABETH SHERRILL

SAT

3

"TODAY I AM REMINDED OF MY SHORTCOMINGS."
—*Genesis 41:9 (NIV)*

MY SON ROSS WAS preparing for the SAT, searching the house for pencils to take to the college entrance exam. "We must make a lot of mistakes around here," he said, laughing, "because all I can find are pencils with no erasers."

He had a point. I make my share of mistakes and not just when I'm writing. Just last week, angry about a friend's criticism, I spoke too harshly to her. Now the friendship is in trouble. I regretted my words and wondered why I couldn't control my tongue. *What does God do with mistake-makers?* I asked myself.

Turning to the Bible for some sort of answer, I was surprised to see that God puts His mistake-makers to work. For instance, the disciple Peter was devastated by his denying Jesus. But not only did he find forgiveness, he went on to be used by God to bring thousands to Christ. In another passage, the apostle Paul says he wants to do what is good but somehow can't seem to do it. Still, God used him to bring the Gospel to the entire Gentile world.

Maybe I needn't feel so bad about my house full of eraserless pencils. At least they show that we try to correct our mistakes. I needed to do that with my friend: apologize for being so quick-tempered. Maybe my mistake wouldn't mean the end of our friendship.

Mistakes are never the end of the line with You, God. Thank You for Your forgiveness, the ultimate eraser. —GINA BRIDGEMAN

SUN

4

RESTORE UNTO ME THE JOY OF THY SALVATION; AND UPHOLD ME WITH THY FREE SPIRIT. —*Psalm 51:12*

IT'S SUNDAY MORNING, and I'd love to be in church. But my aunt is recovering from an upper respiratory infection. As a child she survived a notorious influenza epidemic. Now, at one hundred years old, she seems to have won another round. She is weak and tired; I don't dare leave her, even for an hour. So feeling shut in, I sit and stare out my bedroom window. A song sparrow bursts into melody in the branches of the Chinese elm.

Quietly, a new awareness comes to me. Hadn't I stepped outside this morning in the predawn to gaze at the night stars? Do the candles in church glow more brightly than these? Hadn't I gone out again when the rising sun tinted the clouds pink? Are stained glass windows more vibrant with color? And this songbird in the tree—will the choir's anthem sing more gloriously to God?

As for missing the Sunday message, didn't Jesus say, "Be ye therefore merciful, as your Father also is merciful" (Luke 6:36)? My aunt needs mercy today. By being here with her, I'm not hearing a sermon, I'm living one.

Lord of life and freedom, when I feel shut in, come to me with Your free-ing presence. —CAROL KNAPP

MON 5

AND LET US NOT BE WEARY IN WELL DOING: FOR IN DUE SEASON WE SHALL REAP, IF WE FAINT NOT.
—*Galatians 6:9*

I HAD ARRIVED IN Baltimore for a visit, and a friend and co-worker I hadn't seen in years picked me up at the airport. Once my student, she is now a teacher. She asked me how things were with me and my children.

"Lanea is working, finishing her degree program. She's very happy and independent. Chase will be a senior next year! Can you believe it?" I told her some stories about my two wonderful offspring. "How about you?"

"We're fine . . . if he survives," she laughingly said of her only son.

"Don't kill him. He's a good kid." We laughed together.

"Yeah," she said. "That's the funny thing. He is."

"You'll make it."

"You just don't understand." She shook her head as she switched lanes.

"Sure, I do. He's not doing his homework, and you think he might fail. And even worse," I tell her, "sometimes he does his homework but still doesn't turn it in, right?"

"How do you know that?"

"It's not just you. I try to tell other moms that it's not personal. I've been through it."

"Not you?"

"Yep."

"Not Chase?"

"Yep. Take a deep breath, be firm, but keep loving him. He'll grow out of it. Reassure him that he'll make it. Remind him of the good things he does, what a good person he is. I think it's adolescence or something. It's just a season. It's not the end of the world. Good things will come."

"Yeah," she said with a laugh, "if we make it through this fall."

Lord, thank You for allowing me to practice patience and unconditional love. Help me to see beyond the moment and put things in perspective, and give me hope for the great things to come. —SHARON FOSTER

TUE

6

"SWING THE SICKLE, FOR THE HARVEST IS RIPE.... FOR THE DAY OF THE LORD IS NEAR IN THE VALLEY OF DECISION." —Joel 3:13, 14 (NIV)

ELECTION DAY ALWAYS FALLS on the first Tuesday after the first Monday in November. The legislators originally chose November because it fell between the busy harvest time and the time of impassable winter roads. They chose Tuesday so the citizens of our new country would not have to travel on Sunday to vote. It's hard to imagine a group of voters so excited by democracy that they were willing to travel to polling places that were more than a day's journey away.

I hope I remember to thank God on this Election Day for the great garden vegetables we picked a few weeks ago. I hope I praise Him for the neatly stacked firewood that will keep us warm all winter. And most of all, when I climb into my climate-controlled vehicle to drive a few short minutes to our polling place, I hope I appreciate the people who struggled so hard so many years ago to do what I can do so easily today.

Dear God, please give us the wisdom to choose leaders whose decisions reflect the courage and endurance of our ancestors. —TIM WILLIAMS

WED

7

AND MY SLEEP WAS SWEET UNTO ME. —*Jeremiah 31:26*

HAVE YOU EVER NOTICED how much press is given to the virtue of early rising?

Maybe the writer of Proverbs started it all with words such as "How long wilt thou sleep, O sluggard?" (Proverbs 6:9). But others quickly jumped on the bandwagon. Is there anyone who hasn't heard "Early to bed and early to rise makes one healthy, wealthy and wise"? Or "The early bird gets the worm"? I have a sweatshirt that proclaims, "She who hoots with the owls at night cannot soar with the eagles in the morning."

My sweatshirt was meant to encourage eaglelike habits. But to be perfectly honest, I'd much rather hoot with the owls. Not that I get to hoot very often. I get up at six o'clock sharp every weekday morning so I can get to work on time, but I'd prefer more lax hours.

Recently, however, I read something that gave me a more positive attitude toward getting up early. Father Edward Hays wrote, "May my rising be a rehearsal for my resurrection from the dead. With gratitude for the wonder of this day, I enter into silent prayer."

Whether you're an owl or an eagle or in between, rise with gratitude for the blessings God gives us each day.

Creator of dawn and sunset, whatever the hour of rising, let us do so with a resurrection attitude of awe. —PENNEY SCHWAB

THU

8

"MY SHEEP RECOGNIZE MY VOICE, AND I KNOW THEM, AND THEY FOLLOW ME." —*John 10:27 (TLB)*

MY DOG SCOOTER was bouncy. Part Border collie and part Lhasa Apso, she had a natural exuberance that put her whole body in motion, especially when she saw me reaching for the leash and knew she was going for a walk.

Taking Scooter for a walk was no easy task. She strained against the leash, gasping, in a desperate effort to pull me through the neighborhood. She was easily diverted, crisscrossing ahead of me. And when we came to a fence with a dog on the other side, Scooter yipped and twirled with excitement.

I asked our veterinarian what to do. "Have you considered talking to her while you're walking?" she asked. "A dog knows its master's voice, and a devoted dog can generally be talked out of many bad behavior patterns."

I decided to put the doctor's advice into practice. "Good dog, Scooter." (I tugged slightly on the leash.) "Heel . . . here." (My hand was pointed down to my feet as we walked along.) As we approached a fence with a barking dog, I said, "Steady, Scooter. Steady, girl." (I rewarded her with a "Good dog!" when she cocked her ears but ignored the barking.)

Scooter responded magnificently. As I watched her grow more obedient, I began to get a better view of myself. I tend to pull against the tug of God's will in my life. I find it easy to be distracted by other voices. Scooter reminded me how important it is to know my Master's voice (through the daily study of His Word), to show my devotion to Him by listening to His leading (through constant prayer), and to put His voice ahead of any other.

Lord and Master of our lives, teach me to listen, to hear, to follow and to obey. —FAY ANGUS

FRI
9

SING TO THE LORD A NEW SONG, FOR HE HAS DONE MARVELOUS THINGS; HIS RIGHT HAND AND HIS HOLY ARM HAVE WORKED SALVATION FOR HIM.
—*Psalm 98:1 (NIV)*

IT'S SEVEN THIRTY AT NIGHT and the fourth time today I've stood in front of the sink, washing dishes. Our dishwasher broke a few weeks ago and has yet to be replaced. Tonight, I'm not only washing the dishes, I'm also grumbling about it.

It feels as if I'm always washing dishes; my hands are wrinkly and dry. And although our family routine is supposed to be "the cook doesn't clean up," I was both chef and maid tonight.

In between cooking and cleaning, I entertained three-year-old Caeli, did some laundry, and put Caeli and her five-year-old sister Corinna to bed. The last thing I want to be doing now is staring at the wall behind the sink again and adding more wrinkles to my already dry hands.

Wait. I always tell the girls that grumbling is a choice, that instead of complaining about the situation, they can choose to sing a new song. One of my favorite hymns, by Charles Wesley (1707–1788), pops into my mind: "And can it be that I should gain an interest in the Savior's blood!/Died he for me? who caused his pain! For me? who him to death pursued?"

Ninety minutes later, I'm still humming that song. Wouldn't you know it? I actually ended up enjoying my quiet time in front of the sink and the rest of my nightly tasks. Funny how a tiny change of heart can change an entire evening.

Father God, thank You for those gentle reminders of what really counts, especially when my own heart wants to grumble. —WENDY WILLARD

SAT
10

THEREFORE SHALL A MAN LEAVE HIS FATHER AND HIS MOTHER, AND SHALL CLEAVE UNTO HIS WIFE: AND THEY SHALL BE ONE FLESH. —Genesis 2:24

THE LIGHT ON THE WATER is gold, the shadows under the bridge a deep purple, the sky a furious pink. "Look at the different colors under the bridge," I say to Carol. My wife stood for a moment beside me next to the Monet.

"Did you see the etching in the other room?" she asks.

"Which one?"

"The view of the Thames. It looks like a Japanese print."

"I'll check it out."

We wander through the exhibition, each of us pursuing our passions. She moves into a room of prints and drawings, and I stare a little longer at the colorful oil of London.

This is the way it often is in our marriage: Some things we do on our own, some things we do together. But even when we're off on our own, we're together.

There are things I want to tell her: "Big Ben looks flat and the arches of the bridge are very abstract. Is there a reason for that?" I'm curious about her reaction. After all, she's the art historian.

I wander through the museum, picking up more points for us to talk about. *Does she still dislike Renoir? How about that little Degas sculp-*

ture? After twenty-three years of marriage, we know each other very well—and yet it seems as if we just met yesterday.

There she is in the last gallery, studying a diminutive drawing. "You know, the colors in that Monet were really amazing," she says.

"Do you still dislike Renoir?" I ask.

Lord, hear my prayer for the differences in life that make each day new.
—RICK HAMLIN

SUN

11

IN EVERY THING GIVE THANKS. . . .
—*I Thessalonians 5:18*

I WAS DRIVING ACROSS the barren plains of west Texas, growing tired as the sun set behind shadowed buttes and flat cattle land. Stopping at a roadside café for a cup of coffee, I settled into a corner booth and glanced at the newspaper headlines. It was Veterans Day, I realized with surprise.

Looking up, I saw an elderly couple sitting quietly at a table in front of me. The man wore a faded jean jacket and a blue baseball cap with gold letters that read, WORLD WAR II VETERAN.

On impulse I walked over and spoke to the man. "I see you were in World War II," I began. "Where did you serve?"

Looking startled, he smiled and replied, "South Pacific. The Philippine Islands, to be exact."

My jaw dropped. "I grew up in the Philippines! My parents were missionaries there. We lived on Luzon, in Baguio. What division did you serve in?"

"The Thirty-second 'Red Arrow' Division. We were on Luzon too."

"I know all about the Thirty-second Division. You were the guys who fought on the Villa Verde Trail. There wasn't fighting any tougher than that!"

Tears sprang to his eyes and a broad grin creased his face. "I can tell you've been there, boy. Not many know about the Villa Verde Trail."

Reaching out my hand, I said, "Let me thank you for fighting that war for me and my family. If it weren't for folks like you, all of us might not be here today."

He squeezed my hand, looking a little bashful, and we said good night. At the cash register, I leaned over and whispered to the waitress, "I want to buy that couple's dinner." Slipping her a few crisp bills, I walked out into the night.

For years I've wanted to express gratitude to my father's generation for fighting for my freedom. I discovered that night that it's never too late to say thank you!

Lord, may I express gratitude to those who have paid a great price for my freedom. Amen. —SCOTT WALKER

MON

12

"YOU SHALL LEAVE THEM FOR THE POOR AND FOR THE STRANGER. . . ." —*Leviticus 23:22 (RSV)*

KEITH AND I don't care about fancy new cell phones. All we want to do is make calls and receive them. No camera phones or text messaging or music downloads for us. So when it came time to renew our cell phone contract, we would have been perfectly happy to keep our old phones.

The cell phone company had other ideas. The salesperson soon realized he couldn't entice us with sexy new features, so he started in on the newer technology: better reception, easier software updating, a faster charger, "and besides, we won't be supporting the older technology much longer."

"What happens to the old phones?" I asked.

"Just throw them away," said the salesperson. That went against my principles—I hate waste. Keith said we would think it over.

For several days we talked about what to do. Then an e-mail arrived from the social action committee at our synagogue: "We are collecting old cell phones for the women's shelter. Battered women can use them to call for help."

We got new phones the next day.

Please always show me, Lord, where I can help those who need my help.
—RHODA BLECKER

TUE
13

I AM LIKE AN EVERGREEN CYPRESS. . . .
—*Hosea 14:8* (RSV)

I BRUSHED MY HAIR over the sink this morning and winced. I'd loosened too many hairs and, yikes, nearly all of them were gray! *A new season of life*, I reminded myself as I walked into my bedroom, where the window gives me visual entrée into the branches of a large maple—now in November looking dead, though it's not.

A few hours later I heard a work crew on the roof, wielding blowers brought in to clear the gutters. This being a large rental complex, I have no maintenance responsibilities more taxing than sweeping my front stoop, so when the workers left I grabbed a broom.

Zealously swishing away dropped decaying leaves, I remembered the last time I'd raked a yard—my father's, peppered with maples, the autumn before he died. What a job! When my back hurt and blisters stung, I stopped to rest at the edge of a clean patch of grass, under a big evergreen, a white pine. Leaning on the rake, I looked at the tree: solid and majestic, not just *being* alive but *looking* alive—staying green—summer, winter, spring and fall, year after year. Yes, it shed cones that had to be picked up eventually—a few today, a few tomorrow. They were a little troublesome, but I didn't mind. I could appreciate their redemptive purpose as seed pods.

Of course, I'd complain if all the trees of the world were conifers. I love those springtime pastels and early autumn golds. But as the seasons of my life change, I feel more secure knowing that Hosea, God's prophet, said that God was like an evergreen, not a leaf-dropper. Constant. Yesterday, today, tomorrow.

Lord, thank You for the constancy of Your being. —EVELYN BENCE

READER'S ROOM

I JUST WANT TO tell you what God has done for me. This is what he has done for me. I was in an abusive home, when God looked down upon me and heard my cry for help. And He rescued me and gave me a good home. If that is not good then I don't know what is.

—*Jenny Jackson, age 12-1/2, Houston, Texas*

WED
14

IF YE HAVE FAITH AS A GRAIN OF MUSTARD SEED . . . NOTHING SHALL BE IMPOSSIBLE UNTO YOU.
—*Matthew 17:20*

I HADN'T HEARD FROM this old friend in years, and here she was on the phone asking for help. "I think I'm an alcoholic."

I'd heard from mutual friends that she'd battled mental and physical problems and professional setbacks. She lived in the Midwest with her husband and eleven-year-old son, but her life was falling apart and I wasn't sure why she had called me or what I could do to help.

"My husband is threatening to leave," she said, "and I'm afraid I can't be a good mom to my son."

"Have you tried AA?" I asked.

"I hate AA. I hate the folding chairs and the musty church basements. All they talk about is that higher power stuff. I don't believe in God. I'll never believe in God."

I said that from what I knew AA wasn't a church or a religious denomination or anything like that. She could believe what she wanted to believe. "All that you have to do is want to stop drinking. Why don't you try it for thirty days? Don't drink. Go to the meetings. If it doesn't work out, well . . ."

"I don't believe in anything," she said quietly. "But I want to stop."

That was the end of our conversation. I had no idea if I'd done her any good or if I'd ever hear from her again.

But I did, a little less than a month later. She'd stopped drinking "for now" and started going to AA meetings "almost every day." "I just wanted you to know I'm trying," she said.

"How's it going with the 'higher power stuff'?"

There was a pause. "Well, I don't *not* believe anymore." Then she was gone with a quick good-bye.

I held the phone in my hand for a long minute. What a lovely word, that *not*.

*Father, we come to You on many paths and some of us can only take the smallest steps. But I know You will be there for my friend and all those like her. They're trying. —*EDWARD GRINNAN

THU
15
LET THE PRIESTS, WHO MINISTER BEFORE THE LORD, WEEP BETWEEN THE TEMPLE PORCH AND THE ALTAR. . . . —*Joel 2:17 (NIV)*

THE DAY AFTER my father died, I dropped my son John off at church for a meeting and decided to escape for a few quiet moments alone in the church sanctuary to sort through my emotions. But when I got to the sanctuary door, lights were blazing and I heard voices and clanging bells. There was a bell choir rehearsal going on.

I stepped outside into the front parking lot and noticed the bungalow on the corner that our church uses for senior citizen gatherings. There on the wide front porch was an old-fashioned porch swing. I hurried to the cottage, sat down on the porch swing, and began to push myself back and forth.

As my body and mind relaxed, I closed my eyes and thought about the last year and a half, when Dad had struggled after a disabling surgery. When he died, I felt relief that his sufferings had finally ended, but there on the porch swing I allowed myself to feel the sorrow of how I would miss him. As tears came to my eyes, I was thankful for the soothing back-and-forth motion that reminded me of being pushed by Dad on our backyard swing set when I was a girl.

All too soon, thirty minutes had passed and it was time to leave. I said a little prayer of thanks for simple places of sanctuary that are there when we most need them.

*God, I need rocking today. Thank You for the quiet places where You take me in Your arms and cradle me. —*KAREN BARBER

FRI

16

EVERYONE WHO HEARD THIS WONDERED ABOUT IT, ASKING, "WHAT THEN IS THIS CHILD GOING TO BE?" . . . *—Luke 1:66 (NIV)*

THREE THINGS YOU DON'T want to overhear your two-year-old saying:

"Yucky! I really need a bath!"

"I think the phone's dry now."

"Hey! I like this olive oil!"

Last week I realized Stephen has officially hit the stage I call perpetual acceleration. Even if I had a full-time maid to clean up after him, the house would still be a disaster. There is no whirlwind to match him, no mind able to foresee what mischief he will get into next. The other day I watched in amazement as he took two fistfuls of baby wipes, snuck up behind Mary, who was reading in an armchair, and threw them into the air and onto her head crowing, "I covering you now, Mary!"

Sometimes I wonder what will come of all this energy. *Where will his ideas take him? What will he become?* There are hints of the future in the present, but I won't know the fullness of Stephen until he's grown. In fact, I may never know what it means for Stephen to be fully Stephen because I'm not my son. It's enough work being Julia.

So when Stephen struts in with a full-body Magic Marker tattoo, or I find forty-two cents worth of change in his diaper, or I hear a gleeful shout of "Wheee! That's slippery!" coming from the kitchen, I focus on being Julia the way God meant me to be: *Deep breath. Laugh. Keep your perspective.* The more I try, the better the chances my son will grow up to be the man God wants him to be.

Jesus, when I focus on You, I become truly myself. —JULIA ATTAWAY

SAT

17

MY FLESH AND MY HEART FAILETH: BUT GOD IS THE STRENGTH OF MY HEART, AND MY PORTION FOR EVER. *—Psalm 73:26*

CHARLES BASKERVILLE WAS a painter of renown long before I knew him. He had a scintillating wit, traveled widely and often, knew the most interesting people, and though he was twenty-five years my senior, we were friends. As Charlie aged into his nineties, he began using a cane. It in no way affected his ramrod bearing. "I use this to throttle the Grim Reaper," he said. "I'll go when God and I are ready."

I began to set aside Saturday lunches for a visit, partly a matter of checking on him—he had no close relatives—but also, truth to tell, for the chance to hear more of his rich life. One day he said, "I haven't painted you. How stupid of me. May I?"

I demurred, of course, but to be in company with such men as India's Prime Minister Nehru and American aviator Charles Lindbergh was too tempting. We began a series of Saturday sittings that were to no avail because, try as he might, he couldn't "get" me. It was a blow to his artist's pride. There was a finality about the way he pushed away the easel.

On a Sunday in November, our friend Dougie invited Charlie and me for brunch at the Plaza Athenée. He appeared briskly, as usual ahead of time, and just as briskly he ate a Cobb salad, lobster (twice—it was a buffet) and finished with a gooey dessert. He couldn't have been jollier. We three left the restaurant in high spirits. Just as I signaled for a cab, I heard the crash of his cane. I turned and Charlie was falling. He was dead before he landed on the sidewalk. He was happy. He was ready.

I have his cane, Father. Let me come to You when it is Your time, as Charlie did. —VAN VARNER

SUN
18

"*FOR WHERE YOUR TREASURE IS, THERE YOUR HEART WILL BE ALSO.*" —*Luke 12:34 (NIV)*

I HAD LUNCH RECENTLY with my friend Sandy O'Donnell. Sandy told me that she'd recently sent her college-age daughter Shannon the Bible Shannon had used as a child. Sandy's eyes twinkled as she confessed, "I put three crisp twenty-dollar bills between the pages of Shannon's old Bible. She doesn't know they're there, and I'm wondering how long it will take her to find them."

Treasures buried in God's Word. I loved it.

I was already a young mother before I discovered the treasures in the Bible. After attending my first Bible study, I came away feeling like the richest woman in the world. That feeling continues to this day. Every time I read the Bible, I find new treasures on each page.

I travel a lot and I'm often in hotel rooms. So I've started a new habit: Inspired by Sandy, I reach for the Gideon Bible, open it, and place a twenty-dollar bill inside. I want whoever finds it to realize that there are other treasures waiting there to be discovered.

Lord, thank You for the treasures of Your Word, precious beyond price.
—DEBBIE MACOMBER

MON
19

"HOLY FATHER, PROTECT THEM BY THE POWER OF YOUR NAME—THE NAME YOU GAVE ME—SO THAT THEY MAY BE ONE AS WE ARE ONE."
—*John 17:11 (NIV)*

THE MEETING OF OUR church elders was tense. At issue were changes to our Sunday worship services. Emotions ran high among those who wanted change and those who didn't. Finally our pastor said, "I'm going to draw names and pair each of you with another elder. Please pray with your partner daily for the next month about resolving this issue."

My prayer partner turned out to be Tom, a very firm supporter of the no-change side. I, on the other hand, was willing to go along with the majority, no matter which way the vote went. But there was one hitch: Tom and I would be traveling extensively before the next meeting, on opposite ends of the country, three hours' time difference apart, and we weren't sure how our schedules would mesh.

"Let's pray by e-mail," I suggested. Tom agreed.

So each day I sent Tom an e-mail prayer and he e-mailed his prayer to me. And little by little, those prayers changed. We began to pray about other concerns at our church, including finances and outreach. Our requests expanded to cover local and national concerns. And there were prayers for our personal needs too.

We were many miles apart, not hearing each other's voices as we prayed together, but in our e-mails Tom and I found ourselves together in God's presence.

Lord, thank You for the unity You give us when we pray for each other.
—HAROLD HOSTETLER

EDITOR'S NOTE: Join us today for our annual Thanksgiving Day of Prayer. On every working day, Guideposts Prayer Ministry prays for your prayer requests by name and need. Visit us online at www.dailyguideposts.com, where you can request prayer, volunteer to pray for others or help support our ministry.

TUE
20

WITH GOD ALL THINGS ARE POSSIBLE.
—*Matthew 19:26*

AS AN EDITOR AT Guideposts, one of my chief jobs is finding ways to tell long, often complicated stories in as short and efficient a way as possible. The average story in our magazines is about fifteen hundred words. That's not a lot of room to move around in.

I think that constant quest for compression is one reason I'm so fascinated by stories in which the narrator has a close brush with death. Perhaps a fisherman gets pulled underwater in a storm, or a climber gets caught overnight on a mountaintop and almost freezes. Whatever the specifics, there always comes a moment when the narrator realizes he or she really is about to die. That's when, in story after story, I've encountered the line, "My whole life flashed in front of my eyes."

It's a cliché, of course, that when we're on the verge of death we see our lives go by like a movie on a screen. But if you talk to enough people who have actually experienced this phenomenon—as my job has given me the chance to do—you develop a respect for the amazing reality behind that cliché. These people don't get some vague, abstract glimmer of the life they've lived. They really and truly *see everything that ever happened to them.* All the good and all the bad; all the beauty and all the pain. Every last bit of their journey through life appears before them, in a manner so vivid, so unbelievably lifelike, that they remember the moment forever after.

How can such a wondrous thing be? That's a question I've worked at Guideposts long enough not to bother asking. After all, it was answered long ago with the Scripture that starts this devotional.

Lord, thank You for the miracles and mysteries scattered everywhere throughout my life. —PTOLEMY TOMPKINS

WED
21

My brethren, count it all joy when you fall into various trials, knowing that the testing of your faith produces patience.
—*James 1:2–3 (NKJV)*

THERE IS AN eighty-year-old violin repairman in Paris named Etienne Vatelot. Yehudi Menuhin, Pablo Casals and Isaac Stern were just a few of his clients. Though Vatelot says that his hands are no longer steady enough to fine-tune instruments, his ear is still uncanny, able to diagnose problems—damaged wood, uneven fingerboards or the angle of a bridge, for example—for his trainees to fix.

I remember once visiting the shop of an old violin maker in New York City. He told me that there were two elements that went into the making of a fine violin. The first was the wood. Fine instruments are made of north-side-of-the-mountain trees, he explained. "They have stood firm against winds and cold, and the bad weather has made them strong."

"And the second?" I asked.

"The touch of the master's hand," he answered with a smile.

People of faith, I've noticed, have often been seasoned by north-side-of-the-mountain trials and made stronger by their tests. And they, too, have been touched by the Master's hand.

> *Teach us Lord, not to ask for lighter loads,*
> *But greater faith for steep and rocky roads.*
> —FRED BAUER

THU
22

Giving thanks always for all things. . . .
—*Ephesians 5:20*

ONE DAY LAST SPRING, I found myself in a grouchy mood. I inflicted my grumbling on family and friends until at last someone at the office challenged me to spend one full day giving thanks to God for *everything*.

It should be easy to give God thanks, I thought. *Just do it!*

The next morning I got up, put on my bathrobe and started down for coffee. But what was that all over the window and on the walls in the foyer? Swirling . . . writhing . . .

Tiny insects—thousands of them. The front door had been left open a crack and the bugs swarmed in, attracted by the light we leave on at night. For two hours my wife Tib and I swept, shooed, swatted, vacuumed until the last bug vanished. But so had my morning. Remembering my promise, though, I said a shallow, "Thank You, God."

And that was just the beginning. The car battery was dead: *Thank You, God*. A story disappeared into the innards of my computer: *Thank You*. Tib got stuck in a massive traffic tie-up and missed the doctor's appointment she'd waited months for. *Thank You, God*. Each *Thank You* was a bit less spontaneous.

At least these were minor mishaps. Suppose they'd been serious. Could I thank God no matter what happened? When someone was sick? When a company folded? When relationships soured?

Perhaps so, because as the day went on, despite the hassles, I found I was immersed in an atmosphere of thanksgiving that was beginning— just beginning—to be independent of circumstances. How wonderful if I could live this way all the time!

Thanksgiving takes us beyond the circumstances to the Father Who stands beside us in the circumstances. I can always thank Him for being a loving God. A forgiving God. A guiding God . . . and even, I thought as I looked back over the annoying mishaps of the day, a God Whom I distinctly heard chuckling.

Thank You, Father, for all things. —JOHN SHERRILL

GOD-FINDS
FINDING SOMEONE LESS
FORTUNATE THAN I

FRI
23

GOD LOVETH A CHEERFUL GIVER.
—*II Corinthians 9:7*

THIS PAST YEAR, Jimmy joined our family for Thanksgiving. Jimmy is on a very limited budget, so I was surprised when he handed back the bag of goodies I'd fixed for him to take home. "I heard you say you were taking that homeless man

Thanksgiving dinner," Jimmy explained. "I want him to have my bag. He needs it more than I do."

Jimmy's attitude really got me to thinking, especially since I knew he'd spotted the giant candy bar in his sack. I explained that I'd also prepared a bag of goodies for our homeless friend, but Jimmy, beaming, insisted that I take him both bags.

Jimmy's gesture taught me that no matter what circumstance I find myself in, there's always an "others" focus that can take the spotlight off my problems. Did someone cut in front of me in traffic? I'll motion for a driver more harried than I to cut ahead of me in the long line at the stoplight. Did a shopper grab the last of the Granny Smith apples at the market? When I find them at another store, I'll buy twice as many as I need and make an extra pie for that neighbor whose daughter was in an auto accident.

And you know what? Just like Jimmy, I'm beaming. There's nothing, I'm learning, like the transforming power of giving.

Help me to find small ways, Lord, to share Your gifts every day.
—ROBERTA MESSNER

SAT
24

BE VERY CAREFUL, THEN, HOW YOU LIVE—NOT AS UNWISE BUT AS WISE, MAKING THE MOST OF EVERY OPPORTUNITY. . . . —*Ephesians 5:15–16 (NIV)*

BOTH OF MY CHILDREN played sports in school, and one of the things that I noticed was that their best coaches weren't the ones who knew the game best, they were the ones who knew life best. They knew that they weren't simply coaching a forward pass or a jump shot, but how to deal with adversity and success and disappointment.

I like that, but I don't often see it. That's why I was so struck by something I read in the newspaper one day from Randy Walker, the football coach at my alma mater, Northwestern. Walker had put a player on the bench for a few games, but then, following some injuries to other team members, he needed to put that player back on the field. "Here's a guy who was a starter at the beginning of the season and then found himself in a backup role. His attitude stayed positive, but I'm sure he wasn't happy about it. Well, it's amazing how that door swings both ways. And just when you think it's slammed shut and there's no opportunity, it opens up wide again."

That's a coach and a player who understand life. And though I'll never be a football coach, I think there's a profound life-lesson here about being ready—and staying ready—for the opportunities God places in our lives. Will I be known as a person who stayed positive in adversity, who was ready when God opened the door for me? I hope so.

I don't know what tomorrow holds for me, God, except for this: the hope that whatever I do will honor You. —JEFF JAPINGA

SUN 25

I CAN DO ALL THINGS THROUGH CHRIST WHICH STRENGTHENETH ME. —*Philippians 4:13*

IT WAS 7:30 ON Sunday morning, and I was at church to play the piano for our worship band. I was rehearsing with them, struggling as I usually do, when our music director had an idea.

"Dave, I want you to play like this," he said and then *doo-dah-dahed.* I gave him a deer-in-the-headlights look.

"Here, watch." He sat down and showed me. "I want you to do it alone before the band comes in, right at the beginning of the first song."

That's way too complicated, I thought. *I'll blow it!* "I don't think I can do that," I said.

"Yes, you can."

Rehearsal ended just as morning worshippers filed in. There was only a minute left before the service started. *Now's my chance,* I thought. *I have to tell him I need him to cut out my intro.* But just as I stood up to go over to him, one of the pastors caught up with him to discuss the service.

I sat at the piano and stared at the keys. *Oh, God, please don't let me blow it and look like a fool.* As I looked up, I caught the eye of one of the singers onstage with me. She must have read my posture because, without saying anything else, she mouthed these words: "Own it."

Suddenly I was ready to tackle the piece because I knew that I was somehow called by God to be here at this moment, sitting on this piano bench. Therefore, my duty was to knock it out of the park. And if I didn't, I was to go down swinging.

So I played the intro, unafraid. It wasn't perfect, but it was mine.

Lord, that piece was mine only because it was Yours. Strengthen me to meet any challenge in Your service. —DAVE FRANCO

MON

26

THE WORD IS VERY NEAR YOU; IT IS IN YOUR MOUTH AND IN YOUR HEART. . . . —Deuteronomy 30:14 (NIV)

FOR AS LONG AS I can remember, I've loved words. I'm especially fond of little sayings, quotes that form the backbone of my personal and spiritual life. That's why I put a large piece of glass on my desk and promptly began to stick words underneath.

On any day, without even moving my chair, I can be motivated by these words, printed in black on a faded piece of yellow paper: "You are going to do something great today!" Victor Hugo offers me advice for tough times: "Have courage for the great sorrows of life and patience for the small ones." James 1:17 (NIV) reminds me that "Every good and perfect gift is from above." A cute piece of Mary Englebreit artwork encourages me to "Do Good. Avoid Evil." Mother Teresa, ever the model of Christian charity, tells me that "Love is a fruit in season at all times and within reach of every hand." And when I'm tempted to skip lunch, Kobi Yamada's question jars me into making better choices: "Be good to yourself. If you don't take care of your body, where will you live?"

I'm grateful for the power of words in my life. I'm especially grateful for the Word that became flesh and dwelt among us, inspiring and challenging us. And I'm grateful, too, for the wisdom and humor that words bring me.

Which reminds me, did I mention my favorite quote? "All a girl really needs is the right pair of shoes." Advice from (who else?) Cinderella.

Today and every day, Lord, let my words be inspired and directed by You.
—MARY LOU CARNEY

TUE

27

A MAN CANNOT TELL WHAT SHALL BE; AND WHAT SHALL BE AFTER HIM, WHO CAN TELL HIM?
—Ecclesiastes 10:14

DIGITAL PHOTOGRAPHY IS AMAZING. I have no idea how it works, but I know that it does. The other day I found that I had 115 photographs of my grandson on my computer—and he was only seven weeks old!

His father wanted to compare them with baby pictures of himself, and the battered albums of my children's babyhoods were brought out.

We played the "He looks just like . . ." game. It's lots of fun linking the generations, even if the resemblance is mostly imaginary.

There is only one photograph of me as a child: a very small, black-and-white picture taken when I was maybe three or four. My children can't understand that; they want to see the others. There are no others. Life was very different in the England of the 1950s as we struggled to recover from five years of war. Food was still rationed—oranges were an exotic luxury—and photography wasn't thought of.

We've come from black-and-white to living color. I've come from a small English village where I hoarded food coupons to New York City, one of the largest and most complex places in the world, with restaurants from almost any country you can name. How will digital photographs strike this baby when he's middle-aged? My imagination can't stretch that far.

Change is a part of every life, Lord. Let me greet it with an open mind and an open heart. —BRIGITTE WEEKS

WED
28

YOU SHALL HAVE A SONG AS IN THE NIGHT WHEN A HOLY FEAST IS KEPT; AND GLADNESS OF HEART. . . .
—*Isaiah 30:29* (RSV)

I STOOD LOOKING OUT of the open bedroom window of my sister's home in Virginia. The beauty of the Shenandoah Valley sunset should have filled me with peace. But I was too worried about events back home in Louisiana to appreciate the scene before me.

My son Christopher was enlisting in the Army. Tomorrow was the day that he would report to the Military Entrance Processing Station, where he would be assigned a job and sworn in. I was feeling anxious, wishing I was close to him. This trip to visit my sister had been planned long before I knew he would be joining.

Dear Lord, I prayed, *take care of Christopher. Touch the people who will be helping him decide on his career in the Army. And, Lord, give me peace.*

I turned to walk away from the window but stopped short. A bugle was sounding outside the bedroom window. It was a familiar tune, but I didn't recognize it at first. Then it came to me. Someone was playing "Taps"! The music drew me closer to the window. I knelt down and placed my arms on the windowsill. As I closed my eyes and listened to the melody, I felt my anxiety leave me.

The next morning at breakfast I said to my sister, "Sandi, I know this sounds crazy. But last night I heard 'Taps' playing outside my window."

"Oh, I forgot to tell you!" she exclaimed. "The Massanutten Military Academy is across the street. Every evening the recruits gather on the campus and the bugler plays 'Taps.'"

The next day I checked my e-mail. I had a message from a fellow history teacher. It began: "Just thought you might be interested in this:

> Day is done,
> Gone the sun,
> From the lakes,
> From the hills,
> From the sky.
> All is well.
> Safely rest.
> God is nigh."

It was the words to "Taps."

Dear Lord, You are my strength, my wisdom, my peace.
—MELODY BONNETTE

THU
29

ENTER HIS GATES WITH THANKSGIVING AND HIS COURTS WITH PRAISE; GIVE THANKS TO HIM AND PRAISE HIS NAME. —*Psalm 100:4 (NIV)*

IT WAS THE ONLY brand-new car I ever had—a bright red Toyota Tercel wagon, small enough to handle easily but big enough, with the seats down, to haul my son's drum set to band contests and to transport my kids and all their possessions to college dorms and apartments. I put 192,000 miles on that car and kept it for seventeen years.

Before I moved to Florida, my dad, brother and friends all said, "You have to get rid of it. The air-conditioning hasn't worked for ten years. You *cannot* take that car to Florida."

I argued, whined and cajoled, but finally gave in and sold it to a young man for 750 dollars. I took his picture standing next to my little red car, walked into the house and cried when he drove away.

When I flew down to Florida, the first thing I had to do was find a car. I prayed about it, knowing that I had to find something very inexpensive.

"My son Joseph has a car for sale," my new friend Jack told me. He drove me over to see it.

There, in the driveway, was another little red car just like my old one, only this was a sports car, six years newer, with a CD player, a sun roof and air-conditioning! I climbed in and saw that it was a stick shift. *Wow, I haven't driven a manual transmission in years! This'll be fun!*

I turned the key, drove it around the block and wrote Joseph a check.

I've learned that when I'm down and out about losing something I love, God comes through with something better, something I never even imagined. Who'd have thought God wanted me in a sports car . . . and a little red one to boot? With a sun roof, no less!

Father, You continue to amaze me with Your surprising goodness in taking care of all my needs. Thank You for my little red car.
— PATRICIA LORENZ

FRI
30

FOR HE SHALL GIVE HIS ANGELS CHARGE OVER THEE, TO KEEP THEE IN ALL THY WAYS. —*Psalm 91:11*

I'M A WORRIER; I always have been. Unfortunately, I seem to have passed on this trait to my three-year-old son. Solomon fears monsters. Scary things live in his closet, and gorillas lurk in the attic, behind the couch or in his bedroom.

"They're in there, Mom," he says, pointing to his room. "Gorillas." The first time he announced the arrival of the primates, his big eyes were so intense, his tone so serious that I checked his room as much for myself as for him.

Each night we go through the same ritual. "Come with me," I say, entering his room. "See. There's nothing here. Just us."

Together we look in the closet. "Nope, no monsters." I look under the bed, behind the dresser. No gorillas.

His little head nods in agreement. "Nope, Mama. No gorillas in here."

One night I said, "See, Solomon, you're safe. There's no one in the house, but Mommy and Daddy and you."

"And the angels," he said.

"The angels?" I asked.

"The angels who keep the monsters and gorillas away."

Often when I'm in bed, my thoughts shift to the usual worries about things at the office, finances and the future, but then I find myself thinking about Solomon's monsters. Aren't my worries the same? Fear of things that are for the most part figments of my imagination? As I close my eyes, I can feel the angels taking away the weight of my anxiety.

Lord, when worries are lurking in the dark corners of my mind, remind me that You are always with me—and so are Your angels.

—SABRA CIANCANELLI

MY WALK WITH GOD

1 _____

2 _____

3 _____

4 _____

5 _____

6 _____

7 _____

8 _____

9 _____

10 _____

11 _____

12 _____

13 _____

14 _____

15 _____

16 _____

17 _____

18 _____

19 _____

20 _____

21 _____

22 _____

23 _____

24 _____

25 _____

26 _____

27 _____

28 _____

29 _____

30 _____

December

And the Word was made flesh, and dwelt among us.... —*John 1:14*

LESSONS FROM THE JOURNEY
FINISH WITH A FLOURISH

SAT

I

I HAVE FINISHED MY COURSE. . . . —II Timothy 4:7

FOR ME, THE HARDEST part of any trip is the ending. Over already, when there was so much more I wanted to do! And the exhaustion at trip's end: packing (How could I have bought so many books?), then the long flight or car trip back. The secret for me here is to focus on the next day, when I'll wake up and be home—more than one room to live in, friends, clothes I haven't been living in for weeks.

I didn't see how any of this applied to the end of my life's journey until I met John Eaves. He came to New York in the fall of 2001, as director of Hephzibah House, a ministry to international students. It was an answer to prayer for the ministry and for John, the fulfillment of a lifelong dream.

Then early in 2003, John began to have abdominal pains. A colonoscopy revealed stage-four colon cancer, giving him less than a year to live. A trip cut short indeed! So much he wanted to do. And the exhaustion of a terminal illness . . . chemotherapy, visits to oncologists and medical centers. The dreary end of a fifty-year journey.

Not for John. For him it was the beginning of an exciting new one. So exhilarating were the discoveries he was making along the way— about himself, God, the Bible, the ministry opportunities from "chair number eight" in the treatment room—that he began sending friends an e-mail record of it all. We in turn forwarded them around the world, a travel diary shared with thousands.

And when on February 22, 2004, he woke up at home, what a joy it must have been to explore that many-roomed mansion, to see friends, to change worn clothes for new ones.

Lord of the journey, help me to end my little earthly trips the way I want to end the longest one: looking ahead to the best of homecomings.

—ELIZABETH SHERRILL

A SAVIOR IN THE STRAW

THIS MONTH, as we make our annual Advent journey to Christmas, we've asked Daniel Schantz to show us how some of the little things we sometimes take for granted played important parts in the story of the world's most extraordinary birth. —THE EDITORS

FIRST SUNDAY IN ADVENT: EVERYDAY DUTIES

SUN
2

THERE WENT OUT A DECREE FROM CAESAR AUGUSTUS, THAT ALL THE WORLD SHOULD BE TAXED.
—*Luke 2:1*

AS A BOY, I WAS captivated by the Christmas story, especially by the miracles. Now that I'm older, I'm even more intrigued by the very ordinary things God wove into the tapestry of Nativity.

Take taxes, for example. Is there anything less Christmasy than income taxes? Yet it was a tax census that started the wheels of Christmas turning, getting Mary and Joseph to the prophesied birthplace, Bethlehem.

The trip was likely worse than the bill. This was a painful pilgrimage seventy miles south along a mountain range, through unfriendly Samaritan territory and across several rivers. It ended with standing in long lines, paperwork and bills. The ultimate insult was having to stay in a grungy stable. But here it was that the very hope of the world was born.

No one escapes distasteful duties, not even at Christmas. Harried shopping trips, maxed-out credit cards, long flights—all take a bite out of Christmas cheer. Yet who knows what blessings are hidden in those obligations, waiting to be discovered? Shopping for that hard-to-please brother-in-law might draw you closer to him. Balancing the bank statement might lead to a very positive New Year's resolution. And during that long holdover at Denver International, who knows whom you might meet?

Okay, maybe I'm being too optimistic. But I remember a student of mine who desperately wanted to marry. One day she took some groceries to an elderly woman in her apartment complex who was ill, and while there she met the woman's grandson, who is now her husband.

Teach me, Lord, to see Your hand at work in everyday duties.
—DANIEL SCHANTZ

MON
3

BUT BE TRANSFORMED BY THE RENEWING OF YOUR MIND. . . . —Romans 12:2 (NAS)

AT A SMALL DINNER PARTY recently, I found myself listening intently to the beautiful music coming from the entertainment center. Our hosts explained that they had satellite radio.

Andy Hines, a computer genius sitting next to me, asked, "Do you want one?"

"Sure," I answered, "but I'd never be able to figure out which one to buy, much less hook it up and subscribe."

"No problem," Andy said. "I'll get it and set it up for you. How about tomorrow?"

The next evening, a satellite radio sat on the old library table in our living room. Andy explained that I could choose from more than a hundred channels. "I only want music from the forties," I said, thinking of the music that I'd loved so much as a child. He punched a button, handed me the remote and said good night. My husband Gene went to bed.

All alone in the living room, I pushed the PLAY button. As the first words to "Dance, Ballerina, Dance" floated out of the radio, I saw myself as a child, carefully placing one of my mother's big seventy-eight records on the record player. The music had been scratchy and marvelous. I would dance all alone to such songs as "Harbor Lights," "Till the End of Time," "The White Cliffs of Dover". . . .

Unable to stop smiling, I kicked off my shoes and danced all over our living room. Sweet memories of my childhood came alive; I was in the small three-room house on Myrtle Street in Elberton, Georgia. My mother hummed in the kitchen and my cat Josephine watched me wide-eyed.

I dance often now, alone in my living room. It's powerful exercise, physical and emotional. Joy springs up in me and lingers long after I've turned off the music.

Father, thank You for renewing my mind, my heart, my soul.

—MARION BOND WEST

TUE

4

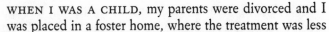

HAPPY IS HE THAT CONDEMNETH NOT HIMSELF IN THAT THING WHICH HE ALLOWETH. —*Romans 14:22*

WHEN I WAS A CHILD, my parents were divorced and I was placed in a foster home, where the treatment was less than kind. Mother was miles away working as a domestic to earn enough for my care. I was so unhappy and lonely that I began to develop a seriously upset stomach every morning before school. Finally a doctor was called. He suggested that I be removed from school and be sent to a warmer climate.

But how? My father was out of the picture, and my mother was already doing all she could. That's when Aunt Lillian came to my rescue. She worked as a live-in domestic in nearby North Adams, Massachusetts, earning less than ten dollars a week. But she didn't hesitate to quit her job and use her meager savings to take me to her sister's home in Charleston, South Carolina. For five months she stayed with me while I frolicked over the fields and enjoyed delicious meals prepared at hearthside. My health returned and so did my demeanor. We returned to North Adams, and I lived with Aunt Lillian for several years until my mother remarried.

Looking back, I can't remember thanking Aunt Lillian for her sacrifice and her love. She died in 1945, while I was stationed at the Jure Naval Base on Honshu, Japan. I couldn't even go to the funeral. Since then I often wondered how I could repay Aunt Lillian. Then I stumbled upon these words of John Ruskin: "There is only one power, the power to save someone. And there is only one honor, the honor to help someone."

By phone, through letters, in visits, I've tried to help others. Most of those people have never known that I do it for Aunt Lillian.

Good Shepherd, I received life. Let me serve in Your name.

—OSCAR GREENE

WED
5

IT WAS NOT WITH PERISHABLE THINGS SUCH AS SILVER OR GOLD THAT YOU WERE REDEEMED . . . BUT WITH THE PRECIOUS BLOOD OF CHRIST. . . .
—*I Peter 1:18–19 (NIV)*

I WAS WALKING TO the subway station in a daze, weighed down with anxiety about my future. Life seemed fragile and uncertain, as if the concrete sidewalk under me would crack at any second and swallow me whole.

I reached the subway stairs and began fishing through my bag for my fare card. "Great!" I growled under my breath. My card was gone, and I wasn't sure if I had enough money to get home. I slowly climbed down the stairs, collecting the coins in my purse. As I did, I made brief eye contact with a woman standing at the bottom who looked as if she was waiting for someone.

I stopped midway and counted the quarters and dimes. *Not enough!* I continued walking, digging deeper to find twenty more cents. When I reached the bottom of the stairs, the woman approached me. "Do you need a fare card?" she asked.

"Excuse me?" I said, snapping out of my daze.

"It's an unlimited pass," she said. "It's valid through midnight."

I dropped the coins back in my bag and took her card with my first smile of the day. "Thank you so much!"

I slid the card through the reader. GO, it said in bright green lights. "Thank You, Lord," I whispered as I went through the turnstile.

I had been worrying about my life, panicking about my future, wondering if I had enough to get through. *Let it go,* I felt God saying. *You'll never have enough. But I do, and I've already paid the way.*

Lord, never let me forget the price You paid for me.
—KAREN VALENTIN

THU
6

O TASTE AND SEE THAT THE LORD IS GOOD....
—*Psalm 34:8*

IT'S BEEN A YEAR since my back surgery, and my legs are still weak. My doctor referred me to a neurologist, who did an electrical test and told me that some of the nerves to my legs are damaged beyond repair. Because I have frequent falls, he suggested I get a walking stick. I've been strongly resisting this for some time. I guess it's vanity; I want to continue to be told I look younger than my age.

But today my friend Nancy offered me a cane she no longer needs. I thanked her and accepted it, with some reluctance. My husband Robert and I have been eagerly looking forward to a trip to Greece next May. There will be lots of walking and some climbing. *Will I have to give up the trip?* Such discouraging thoughts continue to inhabit my mind.

I recently received a letter from my friend Sarah, whose brother was killed in a freak accident in New York City a short time ago. He was only fifty-four years old. "It was a terrible shock," Sarah wrote, "and it's been tough."

Sarah's home now, and she told me about the three women who waited with Tom until the ambulance came. One of the women lives in Denver, just a two-hour drive from here, so Sarah drove there to thank her. "I think we're going to become friends," she told me. Then she added, "Life is sweet, even in its pain."

My weak leg problem suddenly seems trivial. To be able to embrace one's pain and still say "Life is sweet" is, to me, the epitome of acceptance. Sarah is a great model for me.

Now I can say, "My legs may never be strong, but I'll use Nancy's cane. Life is sweet."

Creator God, thank You for the joy of living in Your stunningly beautiful world, where pain and joy coexist and life is sweet.
—MARILYN MORGAN KING

FRI
7
ABRAM SAID TO LOT, "PLEASE LET THERE BE NO STRIFE BETWEEN YOU AND ME, AND BETWEEN MY HERDSMEN AND YOUR HERDSMEN; FOR WE ARE BRETHREN." —Genesis 13:8 (NKJV)

I WAS PERPLEXED when my friend Donna said to me, "My family's going to have a 'Bob Hope Christmas' this year!"

"What on earth is a 'Bob Hope Christmas'?"

"You know how Bob Hope was always away from his family on Christmas, entertaining the troops? Well, what about his own family celebration? When did he do that?"

"I never really thought about that. Whenever he got back, I guess. Whenever he could . . ."

"You see!" she said triumphantly. "That's a 'Bob Hope Christmas.' When I first got married, there was so much hustle and bustle seeing both families—each in a different city—that it took the joy out of celebrating. And then after the kids came along, it became really hectic. Sometimes we had to spend the whole day traveling. And we occasionally had *two* turkey dinners!

"So I decided that when my kids had kids, we'd have a 'Bob Hope Christmas.' It's important to their in-laws that the children spend the twenty-fifth with them, so I tell my kids that we'll do Christmas whenever it's convenient.

"I go to church on the day itself," Donna explained, "but as for the rest of the celebration—"

"A Bob Hope Christmas," I mused. "Sounds like a great new tradition."

Dear God, let me do what I can to assure that holidays are a time for restoring and reinforcing relationships, not hurt feelings and petty squabbles. —LINDA NEUKRUG

SAT
8
MAY YOUR UNFAILING LOVE BE MY COMFORT. . . .
—Psalm 119:76 (NIV)

I HAVE A CONFESSION to make: I have a need for affirmation. That's surely not a godly trait, especially if I look to others for it. So I often express my need by turning it into a joke.

For instance, for years I told my children that I'd like to host my own funeral—early—while I'm still healthy. "I'd like to hear what people say. That way, I'll be able to make any necessary personality adjustments while I still have time."

Guess what? They sort of took me up on the idea. On a recent birthday, my husband Lynn and I, our three children and their spouses, and three grandchildren gathered at a cabin by a lake in Idaho. The gathering alone was gift enough! But they had more in store for the celebration. When it came time to open gifts, they presented me with a DVD, which they slipped into the player. For the next half hour, I watched a rerun of my life, complete with background music and comments from family and friends: a brother, my sister and sister-in-law, my pastor, my boss. I was stunned by their words of affirmation. For the rest of my life, I will be nurtured by this gift.

That birthday celebration showed me how God uses other people to deliver His love. I was the receiver that day, but I can also be the deliverer. The words of affirmation that are often saved for a funeral should be delivered during a lifetime. And I have lots of words to deliver.

Father, I know we find our ultimate affirmation in You. May I be Your instrument of love as I pass affirming words on to others.
—CAROL KUYKENDALL

A SAVIOR IN THE STRAW
SECOND SUNDAY IN ADVENT: A GOOD DAY'S WORK

SUN
9

"HE HAS PUT DOWN THE MIGHTY FROM THEIR THRONES, AND EXALTED THE LOWLY."
—*Luke* 1:52 (NKJV)

THE MAN GOD CHOSE to watch over His Son was a blue-collar laborer. Carpenters in those days made everything from furniture and houses to plows and yokes, and they also did excavations and stonemasonry.

It's uncanny how often carpenters figure into the story of the Gospels. Carpenters made the stable where Jesus was born and the synagogue where He went to school. They made the boat He used as a pulpit and the upper room where Jesus staged the Last Supper. They even made the Cross and the tomb from which He emerged, alive and triumphant. No wonder Jesus referred to so many everyday laborers in His parables.

I grew up in the heartland and spent a lot of time watching people at work. I loitered at the lumberyard, observing a cabinetmaker put together custom cabinets. I studied a boat maker as he polished a mahogany sailboat with rottenstone and rouge till it shone like glass. My favorite hangout was the corner garage, where I stood for hours, hypnotized by mechanics who tuned car engines and changed tires. Although I learned many skills from watching these workers, I also picked up qualities of character, such as patience and economy, industry and carefulness.

Don't look now, but little eyes are watching you. Someone is watching me when I shovel the snow. A little one is mimicking your talent for basting a turkey or washing dishes. What these youngsters see, they will never forget.

Lord, make me worthy of those who are watching me at work.
—DANIEL SCHANTZ

MON
10

AND THE GLORY OF THE LORD SHONE AROUND THEM. . . . —Luke 2:9 (NAS)

EVERY YEAR MY HUSBAND Rick and I argue about the same thing: how to decorate for Christmas. I'm the get-it-done-quickly type, and he's a man of detail. I love simplicity, using things from nature, while Rick likes figurines, sparkly ornaments, and a train that toots and whistles its way around the Christmas tree.

So when he announced another new idea, I wasn't too thrilled. "Why don't we buy ornaments and write the names of family and friends on them?"

"Think how expensive that will be," I said. "And can you imagine the time it's going to take to do it?"

"Just go to the store and pick out plenty of silver balls," Rick said. "Get green, blue and gold markers. I'll help you write."

To avoid another Christmas argument, I went along with him. I found the decorating items the next day.

"Let's get started," he said, breaking open the packages.

"Can I ask you one question?" I said. "Why are we doing this? Who's going to notice? All these people won't be visiting us this Christmas."

Carefully, Rick began writing names on the ornaments: *Marion, Jennifer, Jon, Jeremy, Gene*—my mother, my sister, my brothers and my stepfather. Then he answered me. "We're going to pray for every person on our tree this year."

After writing all our family names, we began with our friends, our pastor and even the country's president. And every night during the Christmas season, instead of watching the endless holiday TV shows, we stood together by the tree and prayed.

Father, thank You. As we pray, Your glory shines around us.

—JULIE GARMON

TUE
11

"YOUR NAME WILL NO LONGER BE JACOB, BUT ISRAEL, BECAUSE YOU HAVE STRUGGLED WITH GOD AND WITH MEN AND HAVE OVERCOME." —Genesis 32:28 (NIV)

MY BACK ACHED. I had spent the afternoon teaching a four-year-old to skate. We went around and around the rink as I skated behind her, guiding, steering and supporting as best I could. She gripped my hands tightly, squeezing my fingers as we slowly made the turns. Her feet moved frantically, scuffling along as she attempted to balance herself, clinging to me all the while.

We battled for a few laps before she asked for a break. Sitting on the side of the rink, we watched as the big kids skated by with ease. She panted softly, brushing her hair from her eyes. "Just trust me," I said. "You'll be okay."

After watching for five minutes, she announced, "Let's go. I can do it this time." She grabbed my hands and off we went, continuing just as we had left off—death grip, shaky feet and wobbly trust that my hands around her waist would hold her up. Then, after the first curve, she began to relax in my arms, slowly gaining her balance and understanding what she needed to do to support herself. "I can do it!" she said.

Yes, I thought, *when you don't hold on so tight, when you don't try to make it happen, when you relax and trust*—just what I needed to do in my relationship with God.

God, thank You for being the strong arm in my life and never letting go, even when I struggle and think I can do it all on my own.

—ASHLEY JOHNSON

WED

12

"FOR NOTHING IS IMPOSSIBLE WITH GOD."
—*Luke 1:37 (NIV)*

A FEW YEARS AGO I was feeling trapped and helpless, facing issues that I couldn't resolve. I decided to visit an older friend, Tom Parrish, and glean his life-earned wisdom.

As we talked in his study, Tom walked to his bookshelf, thumbed through a small book and handed it to me. "Read this page," he said.

Glancing at the cover of the well-worn book, I saw it was *Gitanjali,* a collection by the Indian poet Rabindranath Tagore. As I read the opened page, printed words became an epiphany:

I thought that my voyage had come to its end at the last limit of my power—that the path before me was closed, that provisions were exhausted and the time come to take shelter in a silent obscurity.

But I find that thy will knows no end in me. And when old words die out on the tongue, new melodies break forth from the heart; and where the old tracks are lost, new country is revealed with its wonders.

Suddenly I knew that while I might be powerless, God is not. And though my vision might be limited, God sees beyond the horizon of the universe.

Advent is the season that calls us to reflect on the incarnation of this age-old truth: "Nothing is impossible with God!" The birth of Jesus reveals for all time that God is with us. And as the Apostle Paul wrote, "If God is for us, who can be against us?" (Romans 8:31, NIV).

Father, give me the faith to believe that "when old tracks are lost, new country is revealed." Amen. —SCOTT WALKER

THU
13

LET US NOW GO EVEN UNTO BETHLEHEM, AND SEE THIS THING WHICH IS COME TO PASS. . . . —*Luke 2:15*

IN A FIT OF MADNESS this year, I decided that the best way to teach four-year-old Maggie the Christmas story was to organize a neighborhood pageant. I made arrangements for space at the chapel around the corner, then sent an announcement to our community e-mail list to round up some kids.

I was so laid back about the project that I completely forgot about the first of three rehearsals. On my second try two dozen kids showed up, most of them preschoolers. Hearing my description of the adventurous rehearsal later, my husband Andrew looked at me oddly and commented that I seemed awfully mellow.

At the next rehearsal I remembered to bring the script for the narrator but forgot Baby Jesus. The kids were okay with that. So was I. What mattered to me was that the children got the basics of the Christmas story and learned a few carols. On the way out one of the moms murmured, "Better you than me!"

The day of the pageant arrived. The chapel filled with shepherds in bathrobes and angels in oversized white T-shirts. I quieted the babbling horde and chatted with them briefly. "Remember, this is a real story. It's not a cartoon. We're not here to make people laugh, but to honor Baby Jesus and teach others about Him." They all nodded and looked remarkably serious.

Much to my delight, the angel Gabriel didn't gallop up to meet the Virgin Mary, the shepherds didn't bean each other with their crooks, the heavenly host came out on cue without trampling the shepherds, the Magi looked regal as they processed to the crib. Children sang, parents glowed, people applauded. Everyone asked if we could do it again next year.

I don't see why not. It's not as if it's stressful or anything.

Jesus, help me to remember that Your birthday isn't supposed to be about stress. —JULIA ATTAWAY

—————

FRI
14

WITH EVERLASTING KINDNESS WILL I HAVE MERCY ON THEE. . . . —*Isaiah 54:8*

THE DEATH OF A FRIEND turned my world gray. To add to my loneliness, our daughter Keri was studying in China. Now Christmas was fast approaching.

"Hey, Mom," my son Brock called one day, "my lunch appointment just canceled. Come meet me at the mall."

The mall was shiny and bright with Christmas cheer. I felt like a dreary fog dampening the merriment. "Excuse me," someone said, "I believe you dropped this." A smiling girl handed me my glove.

A few steps more and I was engulfed in hugs. It was Virgie, who lives at our church's home for people with disabilities. Up ahead, I spotted Brock, his eyes crinkled in delight at Virgie's onslaught.

We ate a quick lunch, then strolled through the mall and talked. "Look at that poor tree, Brock," I said as we passed the Christmas Store. "It looks like the Grinch's tree." Its slightly bent trunk pointed toward the sky, but its branches were irregular and spaced far apart.

A quick hug later, Brock was on his way back to work. As I walked to my car, I passed a little girl singing "Jingle Bells." At the door to the parking lot, a teenager rushed ahead of me and opened the door. "Have a happy Christmas," he said.

Sitting in the car, I mentally retraced my steps: the fetched glove, the hearty hugs, Brock's attention, the child's song, the boy at the door. Without even knowing it, each one of those people had done something that mattered to me.

The tiniest kindness really does matter, I thought to myself.

I had errands to run, and it was growing dark by the time I neared home. When I turned into the driveway, I noticed something on our front porch. It was the tree I'd seen at the mall. There was a note attached: "Merry Christmas from the Grinch."

Father, Your everlasting kindness offers Christmas hope to us all. Thank You. —PAM KIDD

SAT
15

HOPE WE HAVE AS AN ANCHOR OF THE SOUL, BOTH SURE AND STEADFAST. . . . —Hebrews 6:19

ONE HUNDRED TULIP BULBS shipped from a gardening company in the Midwest. Ever since I ordered those first hundred bulbs a couple of years ago, the company has had my number. They send me catalogs every fall and then a reminder in the form of a postcard that asks, "Have you ordered your spring bulbs yet?" I fill out the card and send it in. The bulbs, they promise, will arrive at the seasonally and regionally appropriate moment for planting.

I leave them in the refrigerator for a couple of weeks, making sure that Indian summer has passed. Then, on a bitter December day when others are putting up wreaths and hanging lights, I put in my bulbs. In the weak sunlight, with dead leaves blowing past, I dig into the cold earth and think about where the purple, yellow and scarlet-tinged flowers will look best. I can see them in my mind's eye, just like the photo in the catalog, even though the box hedge is bare and the hydrangeas are sticks. The Christmas carols will be sung and the stockings hung, but I'll be thinking about my bulbs. They give me hope through the snow and ice and frozen mud. Beneath it new life is growing.

I don't mind waiting for things—good dinners with friends, a new book by a favorite author, a movie with an unbeatable cast—as long as I know they're coming. I say the prayers of Advent and think of my tulips. I can weather any winter storm as long as I've made that down payment on spring.

Lord, I trust You with my hopes. May they grow. —RICK HAMLIN

READER'S ROOM

WHEN MY HUSBAND passed away, I moved to a smaller apartment. As I began unpacking things, I noticed a small "to and from" Christmas tag. On the back of this tiny card, in my husband's handwriting, was the message: "Arline, with the deepest love a man can have for a woman, I have for you. Fred." I was very touched, and I tucked the message in the side of a framed picture above my desk.

About a week before Christmas, I looked up at my husband's note for some comfort, but what I saw was a picture of the crèche. I stared, wondering why my love note was gone. Then the strangest feeling came upon me. When I gave my life to Christ, I recall the Lord telling me that He wanted me to put Him first in my life. What a joy I felt in my heart for the true meaning of Christmas and all of life. God's love is eternal.

P.S. The card had been turned around, revealing the picture of the crèche on the other side!

—Arline K. Foster, Chicago, Illinois

A SAVIOR IN THE STRAW
THIRD SUNDAY IN ADVENT: SMALL IS BEAUTIFUL

SUN
16

So Rehoboam dwelt in Jerusalem, and built cities for defense in Judah. And he built Bethlehem. . . . —II Chronicles 11:5 (NKJV)

TO THE CASUAL EYE, Bethlehem was an odd choice for the birthplace of a messiah. It was just another ho-hum dot on the map, yet it had a rich, romantic history that made it a shoo-in for a king's birth.

All my life has been spent in small towns. Only someone who has lived in these little villages can appreciate their genius. The city dude, passing through, doesn't "get" it, but a small town is a perfect slice of life. There is one of every kind of person in a small town. Most important, you actually know these people. You sit with them in the library and worship with them in church. You talk to them at the gas pump and in the hardware store.

Moberly, Missouri, where I live and work as a college teacher, is a town of thirteen thousand. "There's nothing to do here," my students complain, but that's the beauty of it. Here children learn to entertain themselves without pricey theme parks and museums. The more leisurely pace of the small town is conducive to reflection, and spiritual instincts are fed by close contact with nature. When I say my prayers, I can lie on the grass under a tree and breathe in a sweet breeze and listen to the sound of bees. Try that on Wall Street.

My wife Sharon has spent a lifetime reading about American presidents. "Did you know that most of our presidents came from small towns?" she points out. Maybe she's on to something, something God knew when He chose the little villages of Nazareth and Bethlehem to cradle His Deliverer.

Truth is, God can use me wherever I live, as long as I am available.

Lord, help me to be great right here, where You have planted me.
—DANIEL SCHANTZ

GOD-FINDS
FINDING A NEW LIFE

MON
17

THIS IS THE DAY WHICH THE LORD HAS MADE; LET US REJOICE AND BE GLAD IN IT. —*Psalm 118:24 (NAS)*

I WAS AT THE BANK, standing in line at the teller's window. As the gentleman ahead of me finished up his business, the teller said, "Have a nice day!"

The smiling gentleman, grandson in tow, answered, "I always say, 'Make it a nice day!'"

Make it a nice day! Is it truly in my power to do such a thing? I wondered for the rest of that Monday. *Can I really fashion a day to my liking? Well, at least I can try.*

My process of "making a nice day" began in tiny increments, starting with jotting in my journal just what I thought a nice day would be. It would certainly begin with ample prayer time, so that evening I set my alarm clock for a half hour earlier. And that new vanilla coffee I'd spotted at the supermarket too; I added that to my shopping list. The living room cleaned up before going to bed would surely be nice come morning, so I made a new ritual of counting off ten things that I would put away before retiring. Soon I was having such a good time that I increased it to twenty things. Before a month was out, I was getting a handle on the papers that cluttered my life. And before I knew it, I'd reshaped my life, one choice at a time.

Won't you join me in *making* this day—this life—a great one?

I give You my life, Lord, one day at a time. —Roberta Messner

TUE
18

For unto you is born this day in the city of David a Saviour, which is Christ the Lord.
—*Luke 2:11*

It so happened that I asked two friends to join me for the Christmas show at Radio City Music Hall. They refused. "That's for tourists," said Marcia. "Why waste good money on corn?" said Kevin. Embarrassed, I bought a ticket anyway. I hadn't been there since they offered a movie along with the show.

Nostalgia hit me right off the bat when I entered the enormous lobby with its grand staircase. It made me think of the movie palaces—cathedrals, some called them—like the late-lamented Roxy Theatre nearby or the Loews in Louisville, Kentucky, with its altocumulus clouds moving across the ceiling.

I went to my seat in the orchestra and was awestruck all over again by the size of the dome and the three balconies where three thousand of us spectators waited impatiently.

Two musicians thundered away on Wurlitzer organs to warm us up. The lights dimmed, the huge orchestra rose from below on a sliding ramp for the overture, then moved away as ninety minutes of 3-D spectacles, ice skaters and fun-makers whirled onstage. The Rockettes, an institution since 1933, kicked their way once for us, then came back again to perform their famous, meticulously timed wooden soldier routine. The extravaganza moved me to applaud repeatedly. I was brought to near tears by the evening's high point, the homage to the Christ Child.

Corny? Touristy? So what. Every year the Living Nativity has been the same, with Mother and Child, wise men, shepherds, camels, sheep, donkeys, familiar hymns—every year the same. Who wants it any different?

I felt Your presence there, Father, especially close. —Van Varner

WED

19

WE HAVE DIFFERENT GIFTS, ACCORDING TO THE GRACE GIVEN US. . . . —Romans 12:6 (NIV)

WHILE MY BOYS WERE in college, they struggled with what to buy their grandparents for Christmas. They wanted my mom and dad to know how much they loved them, but finding a gift within their price range became more of a challenge each year.

Then one Thanksgiving, my father casually mentioned how much he had loved decorating the house with lights every Christmas. He couldn't any longer and that saddened him.

Shortly afterward, Ted and Dale came to me with an idea. As their Christmas gift to their grandparents, they wanted to make the three-hour drive to their house and decorate it for Christmas.

I pitched in and purchased the necessary supplies, and the boys spent two days stringing up lights and boughs all around the outside of the house. Every bush, plant and tree trunk was wrapped in lights. My dad beamed with pride that his house was the most brilliantly lit home in the neighborhood.

Ted and Dale had such a good time with my parents, and each other, that they returned every couple of months and completed necessary tasks around the house that my father could no longer manage. My parents treasured this special gift more than anything the boys could have purchased.

I learned something valuable from my sons that year: An extra toy under the tree for the grandchildren won't mean half as much as playing a game with them or holding a special tea party complete with fancy hats and gloves. The gift of my time will be remembered long after they have outgrown their toys.

Lord Jesus, at the first Christmas You gave us the gift of Yourself. Help me to make myself a gift to others. —DEBBIE MACOMBER

THU
20

NOW YOU ARE LIGHT IN THE LORD; WALK AS CHILDREN OF LIGHT. —*Ephesians 5:8* (RSV)

WHEN ANDY, OUR ten-year-old, announced early in the Christmas season that he wanted to sign up for yo-yo classes, I said *yes,* even though driving him to his lessons put another strain on my busy schedule. After all, yo-yos appeal to almost everyone. They're simple and silly and a lot of fun. *Anyway,* I thought, *he'll lose interest in a few weeks.* How much could you do with a toy that goes up and down, up and down?

Our house soon filled with metal, wooden and plastic yo-yos, many with high-tech bearings and sleek designs. Grandma Jean stumbled over one and almost hurt herself, several Christmas ornaments shattered from misplaced swings, and Andy was dotted with minibruises from tricks that had gone awry. Meanwhile, I was driving Andy to his lessons three times a week, losing an hour of work each time. Maybe it was time to cut the string on yo-yos.

I was just about to announce my decision when Andy gathered his mother and me into the living room, declared that he had just passed the first level on his way to yo-yo mastery, and gave us a demonstration of his skills. I watched amazed as his yo-yo glided through the air, looping forward and backward, the string working into fantastic shapes—a motorcycle handlebar, an angel's wings, the Eiffel Tower—while the body spun on its axis for an impossibly long time, as if dizzy with joy.

The only thing more beautiful than the arcing of the toy was the smile on Andy's face.

A broken ornament can be replaced, I said to myself, *but a grin like that is what Christmas is all about.*

Teach me, heavenly Father, to cherish the innocence of children and to learn from it what really matters. —PHILIP ZALESKI

FRI
21

FOR THOU WILT LIGHT MY CANDLE: THE LORD MY GOD WILL ENLIGHTEN MY DARKNESS. —Psalm 18:28

IT HAS BEEN A YEAR of loss for me on many levels. So when I find out that our church will be hosting the "Longest Night Service" for grieving people in our community, I drop my hectic pre-Christmas schedule and attend.

The sanctuary is quiet and dimly lit. Teal green silk drapes several long tables that fill the platform behind the altar. White pillar candles are nestled into its folds; red poinsettias rest against its skirt. Trees with white lights line the baptistery. Nearby, the Advent wreath stands ready for fresh flames. Hope. Peace. Joy. Love. Slowly, the room fills with people, hurting people who have covered their grief with suit coats and holiday sweaters.

The service begins. We sing a carol. Psalms are read. A meditation is given. And then we begin to file forward, toward two big red tubs of sand sitting on the Communion table. Between them a single pillar candle burns and a pile of tapers waits. "Light a candle to commemorate your loss," the leader says. And we do, sticking our candles deep into the sand. One by one, our flames illumine those tubs, each hurt transformed into brightness and warmth. Tears fall freely and then, after a few sighs, shoulders straighten. The piano begins a bright melody. The room is filled with light.

And, suddenly, the truth is all around us: Darkness and death do not win. Not ever. Not even on this, the longest night of the year.

I praise You, Father, because You are present in the midst of whatever darkness I am experiencing. You are Light! —MARY LOU CARNEY

SAT
22
Joseph also went up from Galilee, from the city of Nazareth, to Judea, the city of David, which is called Bethlehem. . . . —Luke 2:4 (RSV)

ONE YEAR I FOUND Christmas at a fast-food restaurant in the Orlando International Airport. Or perhaps more accurately, Christmas found me.

Actually, it was Hakim who found me—sort of. All he really wanted was a place to sit for himself and his wife, who was obviously tired and even more obviously pregnant. I was occupying one seat of a four-person booth, nursing the last of my onion rings and feeling enormously sorry for myself because I was missing a Christmas program back home.

"May we sit down here?"

"Of course." Feeling awkward in the silence, I ventured, "Going home?"

Hakim nodded and then, looking at his wife, added, "To have the baby. And raise him."

"Where is home?" I asked. And he might as well have said the moon, so taken aback I was with his reply.

"Bethlehem," he said, eyeing me seriously. "Do you know of it?"

Do I know of Bethlehem? I did, I told him, but as we talked I learned about the real Bethlehem—how dangerous a place it was in Jesus' day and how dangerous it remains today. And yet Hakim said, "The God of the universe continues to touch a most ordinary place of our world in a most extraordinary way—and through it touches us all."

Once, a baby born in Bethlehem changed the world. That year in a fast-food restaurant, a baby about to be born in Bethlehem changed me.

Grant me, O God, ears to hear and eyes to see the wonder of Your presence this holiday season, in the ordinary places of my life.

—JEFF JAPINGA

A SAVIOR IN THE STRAW
FOURTH SUNDAY IN ADVENT:
A CHILD SHALL LEAD THEM

SUN

23

She bore a male Child who was to rule all nations with a rod of iron. . . .
—*Revelation 12:5 (NKJV)*

WHEN I WAS ATTENDING the University of Missouri, a Chinese man sat next to me in Educational Foundations class. He struggled to understand our language, so after class I would go over the notes with him. He was baffled by many of our customs and expressions.

One day he asked me, "What does it mean when you say, 'The hand that rocks the cradle rules the world'?"

I smiled. "Well, Chang, I think it means that if you take good care of babies, they may grow up to be presidents and kings, justices and queens."

"Ah," he lit up. "I like that. It is full of much wisdom."

I suppose there are other forms Jesus could have taken when He came to earth. How nice that He made his entry the same way all of us do, as a helpless baby.

"Christmas is for children," people say. Sometimes I forget how thrilling it is to them—the manger mystique, the charm of angels and wise men, "Jingle Bells" and candy, and opening presents with squeals of delight.

Sometimes I tire of Christmas, after celebrating sixty-three of them, but children do not. How I treat them may well determine the state of the world in fifty years. What a wonderful honor it is to rock the cradle and thereby rule the world.

Now I lay me down to sleep; I pray the Lord my soul to keep.
—DANIEL SCHANTZ

A SAVIOR IN THE STRAW
CHRISTMAS EVE: LIGHT IN THE DARKNESS

MON
24

EVEN THE NIGHT SHALL BE LIGHT ABOUT ME.
—*Psalm 139:11 (NKJV)*

IT'S NOT HOW I would have done it. If I had news as big as the Gospel, I would have called simultaneous news conferences at high noon, in Athens and Alexandria, in Jerusalem and Rome. But when God announced the birth of His Son, He did so at night, in a rural pasture. Jealous kings and picky Pharisees were slumbering then, but receptive shepherds were watching the sky when it exploded with the glory of God.

Darkness is not my favorite time. Since childhood I have needed a night-light to make it to sunrise. I also own thirty-eight flashlights. It seems like everything gets worse at night: aches and pains, anxieties, regrets. At times I can't tell the difference between my nightmares and reality until my wife Sharon nudges me and asks, "Are you okay, hon?"

Yet, even I welcome darkness at Christmas. Without it, I could not enjoy the necklaces of light that grace the trees and homes of our neighborhood. Without darkness, I could not see the flickering candles of the carolers coming up our sidewalk. Without darkness, I couldn't enjoy our traditional candlelight Christmas supper.

Spiritual darkness can settle over a person at any season. Even at Christmas, things go wrong with marriage and health. Temptations sneak up on you, just when you're supposed to be singing "Joy to the World." At such times, it's good to step outdoors and look up at the stars. The night sky is filled with a trillion eyes, the eyes of angels, watching over us, longing to help us find our way back to the light.

Thank You, Father, for not leaving me in the dark. —DANIEL SCHANTZ

A SAVIOR IN THE STRAW
CHRISTMAS: SIMPLY A SAVIOR

TUE
25

"THE FIRSTBORN OF THE POOR WILL FEED, AND THE NEEDY WILL LIE DOWN IN SAFETY. . . ."
—*Isaiah 14:30 (NKJV)*

I'VE HEARD THAT America's favorite Christmas carol is "Away in a Manger." Little wonder! To think that a simple wooden box filled with hay was all God needed to incubate the Savior of the world!

To me, the message of the manger is simplicity. I am, frankly, astonished that today it takes a whole team of doctors and millions of dollars worth of equipment to bring a baby into the world. The Son of God Himself was delivered without health insurance, anesthesia, antibiotics, LPNs or MDs.

The manger provided just what Mary needed: privacy, shelter from the elements, and—most importantly—economy, for Mary was poor.

Simplicity holds sway over me and never more so than at Christmas. I have been to many Christmas pageants, and every year they seem to get more affluent and elaborate, with professional actors, wire-borne angels and camels clopping around the stage. I saw a magazine cartoon that pictured one of these extravaganzas getting ready to start and the narrator began by saying, "And now, the *simple* story of Christmas."

The Christmas program that is forever burned in my heart is the one that took place in our living room when I was a boy. The six of us kids sat 'round the tree, singing "Silent Night," while Mom and Dad snuggled on the couch. We breathed in the fragrance of pine and chocolate as my handsome father opened his Bible and slowly read the Christmas story in his rich baritone voice and ended with a prayer of thanks for Jesus. Then we exchanged gifts.

Christmas doesn't get any better than that.

Lord, thank You for making Christmas so simple. —DANIEL SCHANTZ

WED

26

AND SUDDENLY THERE WAS WITH THE ANGEL A MULTITUDE OF THE HEAVENLY HOST PRAISING GOD, AND SAYING, GLORY TO GOD IN THE HIGHEST, AND ON EARTH PEACE, GOOD WILL TOWARD MEN.
—*Luke 2:13–14*

IT'S NO SECRET THAT my husband is an optimist. Charlie sees the good side of just about everything, occasionally to the exasperation of the perennial pessimist he lives with. I'm constantly talking myself out of fears, irritations and moods, while he always starts on the right track. He never even has a bad dream.

I look at him and wonder how he does it. How does he maintain such a good attitude? I badger him for answers, thinking if I can figure out his secret, I can be like him. He always puts off my questions by saying with a grin, "Good genes."

Last Christmas, we bundled up and headed out into the cold Connecticut night for a carol sing at church. As excited as I get about this holiday, I couldn't resist complaining about the cold night, the bad weather forecast. But the church was cozy, and soon I got into the spirit, caroling out the beautiful old songs with Charlie at my side. We came to "O Little Town of Bethlehem." At the words, "The hopes and fears of all the years are met in thee tonight," I heard Charlie sing, "The hopes and *dreams* of all the years are met in thee tonight." I looked up swiftly to see if he'd realized his mistake. He sang on blithely, innocently. It never occurred to him that "fears" could describe the world at Jesus' birth; to him it could only be "dreams."

Tears of joy came into my eyes as I looked at Charlie. Maybe I can't be like him, but I sure can learn from him.

Sweet Jesus, in the season of Your birth, help me to focus on dreams and not fears. —MARCI ALBORGHETTI

THU

27

MINE EYES HAVE SEEN THY SALVATION . . . A LIGHT TO LIGHTEN THE GENTILES, AND THE GLORY OF THY PEOPLE ISRAEL. —*Luke 2:30, 32*

AFTER PEARL HARBOR, my mother and I were among the civilians interned by the Japanese at Yangchow, China. Christmas was bleak. No tree, no tinsel, no cookies nor flaming plum pudding and, worst of all for us kids, no presents. Then someone came up with the bright idea of a pageant. A ripple of joy spread through the camp. "Mary can borrow my nightgown . . . my teddy could be Baby Jesus . . ." We kids jostled for the parts we wanted to play, and my heart soared when I was put into the angel chorus. Volunteers offered to cut bits off their mosquito nets to be made into wings for the angels.

Rehearsals began. "Speak the words in unison, loud and clear, with smiles. 'Glory to God in the highest, and on earth peace and goodwill toward men.'" Being small, I was in front.

Suddenly the lady directing us pulled me forward. "Fay," she said, "I want you to play the part of the high priest Simeon. You get to hold Baby Jesus and have an important speech."

My joy imploded. I was snatched out of angelic heaven and fell to earth with a sobbing thud. No beautiful net wings; instead I would be dressed as an old man. I held up Baby Jesus, a bundle made from a rolled up sweater, and said the lines. "For mine eyes have seen Thy salvation . . . a light to lighten the Gentiles and the glory of Thy people Israel."

Those words so reluctantly learned as a disappointed child were to become the cadence of my life. Salvation. Light. Glory. Hallelujah, the Lord is come.

This holy Christmas season, open the eyes of our hearts to see and receive the salvation You have given us in Christ, O Lord. May the glory of His light shine in and through us, now and forevermore. —FAY ANGUS

FRI
28

A CHEERFUL HEART IS GOOD MEDICINE. . . .
—*Proverbs 17:22 (NIV)*

LAST YEAR I SPENT a couple of months skiing at Mount Hood in Oregon. There was an attractive girl about my age whom I had seen skiing a few times and was hoping for an opportunity to meet. One day as I waited in line to board the ski lift, I spotted her just a few yards in front of me. I brainstormed about something to say to catch her attention.

But before I could muster the confidence to do anything, she reached the front of the line and sat down on the chairlift. Just then our eyes met and we held each other's gaze momentarily. Unfortunately, at precisely that moment, my ski slipped on the snow and I toppled headfirst off the four-foot-high embankment at the edge of the lift line. I couldn't free myself until several other skiers came to my aid. By the time I was back upright, the girl had floated far out of sight.

That experience has brought laughter to many conversations in the months since. And now, whenever I want to meet a girl, I remind myself that things couldn't possibly go worse than they did on that day. As for the girl on the chairlift, I never did meet her. But if I ever see her again, I'm hoping to begin our relationship on more solid ground—and with a laugh!

Lord, don't let me take myself too seriously. —JOSHUA SUNDQUIST

SAT
29

BUT MARY KEPT ALL THESE THINGS, AND PONDERED THEM IN HER HEART. —Luke 2:19

I'M MOVING AGAIN. I tear off a length of packing tape and seal another box, gazing at eighteen years' worth of family souvenirs crammed into the garage.

How many times have I packed and hauled these silly mementos: the bashed-in straw hat with plastic orchids that Greg, then five, snapped up at a yard sale for my birthday; the two-pound ceramic candy dishes lovingly engraved and glazed by Trina in sixth grade; or the jelly bean holder made from a concave slab of cement? Booties, ABC books, baptismal outfits, wooden blocks—what good are they now with my youngest almost in college? Yet to toss them feels like betrayal.

But toss I must. Within two weeks I need to move two thousand miles, and all my keepsakes have to fit in a small storage unit or in a tiny trailer hitched to the car. I wonder how Mary and Joseph decided what to take when they fled to Egypt. I'll bet they didn't haul souvenirs. Of course not; Mary treasured the miracles of Jesus' birth and baby-hood in her *heart*.

I look with renewed wonder at Trina's penmanship papers, dated 1994. Such lovely Ws. I toss out the papers. Then her math facts: 9+4=13. I smile and throw them out too. Here's Tom's bewildering Sunday school drawing of a camouflage tank under the heading MY FAMILY. He draws on the computer now, but this tank is a keeper.

Sorting, celebrating and tossing, the garage empties while my heart fills.

Lord, may my heart always be fuller than my storage unit.
—GAIL THORELL SCHILLING

SUN
30

GIVE UNTO THE LORD THE GLORY DUE UNTO HIS NAME: BRING AN OFFERING, AND COME INTO HIS COURTS.
—*Psalm 96:8*

THE SERVICE AT OUR church offers few attractions for a four-year-old, and just sitting still for an hour, even with a picture book to leaf through during the sermon, is an exercise in heroic virtue for as lively a little girl as our daughter Maggie.

But sitting still seemed to be way beyond Maggie's ability today. When we stood to sing or pray, she wanted to be picked up, which was fine, and to stand on the back of the pew in front of us, which wasn't. When we were sitting, she wanted to snuggle with me or crawl over her sisters to cuddle with Mommy, arousing the jealous wrath of two-year-old Stephen. I did the best I could to keep her still, regretting that we were sitting in the middle of the pew, where an unobtrusive exit was impossible.

But there was one point in the service when Maggie paid attention: the collection. When the ushers began to head up the aisles, she took our offering envelope, stood on the kneeler and held on to the back of the pew in front of her. As the usher reached us, she bounced up and down, waving the envelope, and finally dropped it triumphantly into the basket. Then, a big grin on her face, she settled back down (if only temporarily) in the pew.

As she grows up, Maggie will be able to participate more and more in church. She'll be able to sing the hymns, understand the Scripture readings, follow the sermon and join in the prayers. And I hope she'll always have a smile on her face when she puts her envelope in the basket, because that offering helps make it possible for four-year-olds to fidget and fuss on Sunday mornings to the glory of God.

Lord, in the coming year, give me Maggie's joy in giving.
—ANDREW ATTAWAY

MON
31
LAY NOT UP FOR YOURSELVES TREASURES UPON EARTH, WHERE MOTH AND RUST DOTH CORRUPT, AND WHERE THIEVES BREAK THROUGH AND STEAL: BUT LAY UP FOR YOURSELVES TREASURES IN HEAVEN . . . FOR WHERE YOUR TREASURE IS, THERE WILL YOUR HEART BE ALSO. —*Matthew 6:19–21*

UNLIKE THE DAYS of my misspent youth, my holiday celebrations are low-key. I'm really hoping that this year's festivities will be better than last year's: While we were away, someone was back at our place lifting my wife Sandee's purse—cash, cards, keys, etc. Happy New Year to us.

The usual headache followed: police reports, insurance calls, tallying up our losses. Our youngest daughter Grace had been away at a sleepover and missed the excitement. I picked her up and told her the sad news. Grace was surprisingly stoic; she's only nine, so perhaps she didn't understand what had happened.

Or so I thought.

I stopped at the bank to cancel Sandee's checking account. Grace came with me, then suddenly returned to the car. She opened the trunk and put her treasured stuffed Pooh Bear inside it. "That way no one will take it," she said.

"Nothing that grieves us can be called little," Mark Twain said. "By the eternal laws of proportion a child's loss of a doll and a king's loss of a crown are events of the same size." I thought our new year had been ruined; no chance. We still had Pooh Bear and we still had each other.

This year, I hope all that you treasure remains safe. Don't spend your time worrying about cars and keys—they're nothing but the usual headache. Instead, focus on what you pull close to your heart at night, what comforts you when you're sick or hurt. Everything else is just etc.

This year, Lord, help me to know what my treasure truly is.
—MARK COLLINS

MY WALK WITH GOD

1 _____

2 _____

3 _____

4 _____

5 _____

6 _____

7 _____

8 _____

9 _____

10 _____

11 _____

12 _____

13 _____

14 _____

15 _____

16 _____

17 _____

18 _____

19 _____

20 _____

21 _____

22 _____

23 _____

24 _____

25 _____

26 _____

27 _____

28 _____

29 _____

30 _____

31 _____

LIBBIE ADAMS of Berne, Indiana, writes, "It's hard to believe that Larry and I have been in Indiana for more than two years now. Life passes so quickly. We love our respective jobs—mine as news editor of the local paper and Larry's as a cabinetmaker. The major disadvantage for both of us is being so far from our family in North Carolina. Our son Greg and his wife Kim had another baby last fall—a little boy they named Gregory Landon. Now we have a total of six grandchildren, all of whom are special and dear to us in ways we could never have imagined. We've also faced profound sadness this past year. My father died in the spring, and I'm learning that while grief is an ongoing process, God's grace is always sufficient. I'm thankful to be a part of this unique *Daily Guideposts* family, and appreciate the kind letters and cards I receive from readers."

This has truly been a year of journeys for *MARCI ALBORGHETTI* of New London, Connecticut, and her husband Charlie. There has been the frightening and exciting journey into a new way of life as Charlie retires from the lobbying/government world and explores other alternatives. There have been physical journeys from their home base to Key West and northern California, where they plan to live for at least part of every year. There have been emotional journeys as Marci continues to work with a new doctor on nurturing God's gift of health. And there have been journeys into the world of God's work as they support local soup kitchens and agencies for the homeless. "All these journeys require strength, courage and the capacity to embrace joy," says Marci. "Qualities that Charlie possesses abundantly and I continue faithfully to seek."

FAY ANGUS of Sierra Madre, California, writes, "This has been a year of great contentment and gratitude. An angiogram and the implant of a stent to clear a blocked artery suddenly brought into focus the fragility of the mortal coils that make us tick. The reality that at any time the Lord can call us home in a wink makes each new day a gift. The grass is greener, the flowers brighter, birdsong sweeter, and the prayers and steadfast love from family and friends more precious than ever. Daily I call with St. Patrick for 'God's strength to direct me, His power to sustain me, His wisdom to guide me, His hand to uphold me and His pathway before me' my whole journey through."

"For me, every year of life's journey seems to go more quickly than the one before," writes *Daily Guideposts* editor *ANDREW ATTAWAY* of New York City. "It's hard to believe how fast the children are growing: At 12—almost a teenager—Elizabeth remains devoted to math; John, 10, has worked hard at writing, ballet and being the world's best big brother; 8-year-old Mary has blossomed as a performer and a lover of poetry; at 5, Maggie is reading up a storm; while 3-year-old Stephen loves to tell us stories." Andrew has been busy preparing titles for the new GuidepostsBooks imprint as well as editing his eleventh *Daily Guideposts*. "Even when the road's been a bit bumpy, God has provided me with an abundance of strength—in His Word, the church, the prayers and shared faith of the *Daily Guideposts* family, and most especially, Julia and our children."

"For a family that tries to lead a quiet life, we sure spent a lot of time on stage last year!" writes *JULIA ATTAWAY* of New York City. Elizabeth and Mary performed in several shows at the local children's theater, and in between ballet classes and performances John joined them in *The Tempest*. Maggie continued to be dramatic in her own way. Stephen was content to watch it all. "It was definitely a year where I had to look each and every day for strength. One great thing about having had too much to do was that I had to focus almost exclusively on the daily tasks set before me. That meant thinking and praying about what specific things God was placing on my to-do list for the day . . . and making sure that everything else fit around them."

"This past year Gordon and I saw our sons off to new adventures," writes *KAREN BARBER* of Alpharetta, Georgia. "Our oldest, Jeff, received his MBA from Duke University and helped start a faith-based clothing company called Messenger Apparel. Our middle, Chris, continued his active Army service at Fort Bragg, North Carolina. And our youngest, John, got his driver's license. I launched in a brand-new direction myself, creating a video series called *Personal Prayer Power*. As I wrote the scripts, I realized that some of the difficulties I mentioned in my devotionals this year—my father's illness and death and my sister's house fire—had challenged my usual way of praying. I learned that not only does prayer give strength for the journey, but the journey gives us strength and opportunity to draw closer to God by learning new ways to reach out to Him in prayer."

"I am thankful that God has thus far given us strength for the journey, but with several decades of life behind us, Leo and I are trying to slow down a bit," writes *ALMA BARKMAN* of Winnipeg, Manitoba, Canada. "'Too soon old and too late smart,' we finally got around to starting a perennial flowerbed behind our big vegetable garden. My biggest project this year has been the compilation of an autobiographical book about my childhood that I've entitled *Peeking through the Knothole and Other Stories of the 1940s*, which contains sixty-five vignettes, some humorous, others poignant, each written from a faith perspective. With family scattered across Canada, phone calls and e-mails continue to flow back and forth. Leo and I both celebrated milestone birthdays this year, and to mark the occasion the family gifted us with a surprise train trip. We now have the pleasant task of deciding when and where we will 'ride the rails.'"

FRED BAUER says, "We don't discover God's true strength in good times, but when the going gets tough. When King David faced adversity—some of his own making—and fell short of his heavenly Father's expectations, he was a good example of God's powerful presence and forgiveness. The truth is God never breaks our hearts or forsakes us. That's His promise, and He keeps His promises." Fred and his wife Shirley divide their time between Englewood Beach, Florida, when the thermometer dips, and the mountains of State College, Pennsylvania, to see the seasons change. They recently took nine of their children, mates and grandchildren on a trip to China. Church work, volunteering and hugging their grandkids occupy most of their free time.

"This past spring I led a quiet day at my church," says *EVELYN BENCE* of Arlington, Virginia, "urging participants to delve into two 'watery' stories from the Gospel of John: Jesus' conversation with the woman at the well and His turning water into wine. After the session, a participant gave me a small electrified fountain for my home office. The sound of the flowing water is a daily reminder of God's sustaining and strengthening presence. This fall I'm taking on a new responsibility at my church as a chalice bearer. I feel humbled and honored to bring the cup of blessing to friends and strangers who worship with me and come to the altar to receive the Eucharist's strength for the journey."

"The journey has been a difficult one this year," says *RHODA BLECKER*, "but it has also been filled with blessings. Keith retired, we bought a new home, sold our old home, lost one of the dogs (poor Jessif had to be put down), and moved out of Los Angeles with only Hobo and the two cats, Tau and Chi. The new home in Bellingham, Washington, was being remodeled when we moved in, and we had to live in the basement for several months until things upstairs were ready. While we were still living downstairs, I had to have an angioplasty and a stent. And while I was recovering, Keith had to have knee surgery. Through it all, we have been privileged to laugh and recognize God's upholding hand in our lives."

MELODY BONNETTE of Mandeville, Louisiana, writes, "The day after Hurricane Katrina, I prayed, 'Dear God, give me strength.' And, as always, He did. He gave me the stamina to walk for three hours to retrieve our only car that survived the storm. He gave me the faith to use my limited supply of gas to drive to work to help locate missing employees, instead of saving it for the generator. He gave me a generous spirit that allowed me to open my home to others who had lost theirs. And in my weariest moment, He gave me the gift of awe. At a local shelter designated only for evacuees on life support, I watched selfless caregivers minister to strangers. I left there with a renewed sense of wonder at the indomitable strength of the human spirit, which has, in turn, strengthened me throughout my journey to rebuild after the storm."

For GINA BRIDGEMAN of Scottsdale, Arizona, strength for any journey comes from counting God's many blessings. "When I begin to worry too much, I reverse direction and start itemizing every wonderful thing God has given us, such as good health, happy children and the fun times we've spent together." Those times are more precious as son Ross graduates from high school and starts college in the fall. "We know he's headed in a musical direction, whatever it might be. Meanwhile, Maria, a sixth-grader, dances up a storm, everything from ballet and jazz to hip-hop. My husband Paul is still teaching theater, this year adding directing to his résumé. And I spend most of my time volunteering at school, another blessing. My own kids are always glad to see me, and I draw strength from knowing I'm making a difference not only for them, but for so many children."

It's been an eventful year for MARY LOU CARNEY and her family in Chesterton, Indiana. For starters, there was the birth of her second grandson, Brock, who joined his two-year-old brother Drake. "Now our lives are twice as blessed!" says Mary Lou. Daughter Amy Jo and her husband Kirk enjoy living close to

Nana and Paw-Paw. Son Brett married his longtime sweetheart Stacy last spring. Gary and Mary Lou remodeled their thirty-year-old home. "I got so used to drywall dust I almost missed it when the project was completed. Almost!" Gary continues to do excavation work for new homes, and Mary Lou still edits Guideposts' magazine for teen girls, *Sweet 16*. "It's been pretty smooth traveling for our family this year . . . which means we're probably due for a few potholes in the road soon! But knowing God is directing our journey makes me eager to face every new day."

"This year has been an exciting one," says *SABRA CIANCANELLI* of Tivoli, New York. "We finally moved into the old farmhouse we've been renovating, and though we're still completing the finishing touches, most of the dust has settled and we're looking forward to our first Christmas in our new house. My grandmother always said, 'New house, new baby,' and there must be some truth in that because we had our second child this spring, Henry. We're thrilled at all the new blessings! Most especially, our son Solomon loves that his new house is so close to his grandma's that he can join her each morning for tea and chocolate chip cookies." Sabra serves as Web Editor for Guideposts Online.

"My favorite saying these days," says *MARK COLLINS* of Pittsburgh, Pennsylvania, "is 'If you understand, things are just as they are. If you do *not* understand, things are just as they are.' I feel that way as a parent. One day I'll feel as if I really understand what's going on, then the kids change and I'm back to square one. Or if I don't understand, it doesn't matter because my kids will still grow up whether I figure them out or not. Sometimes it's frustrating, sometimes it's a wonderful puzzle." Mark has a passel of puzzles to figure out. He and Sandee have Faith, 15, Hope, 14, and Grace, 10. "I think God gave me just enough smarts to let me figure out how clueless I really am," Mark muses. "It's a blessing, really—otherwise the puzzles wouldn't be as much fun to solve."

"It's been a wonderful year for our family," says *PABLO DIAZ* of Carmel, New York. "My daughter Christine and I organized a party for my wife Elba's fiftieth birthday. It was a great fiesta with authentic Mexican food and music, a piñata, sombreros, maracas, and lots of dancing. Elba is enjoying this new and exciting stage of life. She considers herself blessed to work with seniors at the Senior Housing Development where she is the site manager. Christine and her mom, who are best friends, enjoy kick-boxing classes. Our son Paul is delighted with college life. In the midst of his busy schedule, he finds time to call us and occasionally comes home for his mother's Puerto Rican cooking. I continue to enjoy my ministry at Guideposts Outreach, traveling across the country to meet with military chaplains, prayer volunteers, knitters and all our partners who do so much for others."

"*Hmm*, strength for the journey," says *BRIAN DOYLE* of Portland, Oregon. "Well, my daily breads are my children, all music, sunlight in whatever dosage, my wife's grin, the puppy making that sound like a creaky door (I don't know how she does it), e-mails from my dad, comics in the newspaper, towels hot from the dryer . . . and crows. Between you and me, I think maybe crows run the world and are laughing all the time among themselves about it." Brian is the editor of *Portland Magazine* at the University of Portland and the author of six books, most recently *The Wet Engine*, about "the magic and muddle and mangle and miracle and music of hearts." He is a contributing essayist to *The Age* newspaper and *Eureka Street* magazine in Melbourne, Australia.

"'You and me against the world' is a line from a song made popular in the seventies by singer Helen Reddy," says *SHARON FOSTER* of Durham, North Carolina. "I sang the song over and over again to my daughter Lanea when there was just the two of us. Recently, the song came to mind and I asked her if she remembered it. She smiled, 'No, Mommy.' She's 30 now, and my son Chase is 22. It makes me realize that I haven't sung the song in more than twenty years. More importantly, I have not felt that way—alone in the world—in many, many years. These days, I'm singing much more joyful songs. God has blessed us, covered us, and we are surrounded by His love and the love of many others. Now we sing songs of gratitude." Sharon's latest book, *Abraham's Well*, is due out in the fall.

"I have the great fortune to be surrounded by such derring-do Christians," writes *DAVE FRANCO*, "in my family, my church family and my friends around the country. I receive such strength when I see so many of them give of themselves to people they don't know, sacrificing their own wants, sometimes even sacrificing their own safety. Last year when we were down to our last penny, we received a check from a client who owed us a small sum. As soon as we received it, my wife Nicole told me to start checking around to see if anyone we knew needed a little financial help. Who but someone truly touched by the Gospel would think to do that?" Dave and Nicole and their son and daughter live in Solana Beach, California.

"I'm finally becoming less of a control freak," writes *JULIE GARMON* of Monroe, Georgia. "Being ultra-responsible, the oldest of four children, I grew up thinking I could control my siblings and the rest of the world. Silly me! I thought I did a nice job of holding things together—for a while. Then the world stopped cooperating with me. Our daughters each turned eighteen and wildly rebelled. But their rebellion did something remarkable in my life: It broke me, revealed what a weakling I really am and brought me to my knees—literally. Now I begin each morning by admitting my weaknesses. I know how small I am without God's help. Daily I whisper, 'God, I can't make it on my own. Will You help me? Today is Yours. So are the people in my life.'"

For *OSCAR GREENE* of West Medford, Massachusetts, most of the year was filled with enjoyable projects and with the helping of others, until November. Then came emergency heart surgery and a convalescence that prevented Oscar from attending church, driving his car, shopping and completing needed chores. "Instantly, others appeared and helped," he says. "I was overjoyed, but accepting this kindness was difficult because I felt I was imposing. Then I noted the joy and enthusiasm others radiated while helping me. Slowly I realized that giving and receiving are equal gifts from above, and life requires that we experience both. From this journey through helplessness to recovery has come strength and insight that will last a lifetime."

EDWARD GRINNAN is in his twenty-first year at *Guideposts* magazine and his eighth year as editor-in-chief and vice president. "My first interview with Van Varner (then editor-in-chief) left me thinking that Guideposts might be a nice place to spend a year or two. But like a lot of people who come here thinking it's a nice place to catch your breath professionally, I found myself loving the quality of the air. I stayed. I couldn't be happier." Edward lives in New York City with his wife Julee Cruise and their elderly but still plucky and strong-willed cocker spaniel Sally. "Sally is really an inspiration to me. These days in the morning she is usually stiff (especially her hips), but as soon as she sees me with her leash she gets up, slowly, with her stubby tail wagging at the prospect of greeting the day with a walk. And I can swear she's smiling. If that's not strength for the journey, I don't know what is!"

"'Two teen-aged boys,' people say to us, 'that must be hard!' I have to disagree," writes *RICK HAMLIN* of New York City. "William is almost 20 and Tim is 16, and they're funny, kind, rambunctious and smart. I give Carol all the credit. She just finished her master's in art history and has a couple of writing projects to keep her busy. We both still sing in a choir together every Sunday, then I teach the fifth- and sixth-graders (who keep me on my toes). I have a novel that's just come out, *Reading Between the Lines* (Howard Publishing). It's a romance about the power of a prayer . . . and I assure you it has a happy ending. The rest you can read between the lines!"

MADGE HARRAH of Albuquerque, New Mexico, writes, "When our daughter was stressing out over a difficult divorce, a demanding job and the care of her toddler, she said to me one day, 'Mom, I don't know what I'd do without God's support. How do people cope who have no faith?' Our daughter is now happily remarried, her job is going well and her child is entering the teenage years. Her faith gave her strength for the journey that has led her to this point in her life. Larry and I have moved on too: retirement for Larry, new projects for me and the completion of our observatory near our cabin in Platoro, Colorado, where we view the moons of Jupiter, the rings of Saturn, the purple glow of the Orion Nebula. We've faced our own challenges along the way, but God's support remains steadfast. We look forward to the journey that lies ahead."

"I grew up as a city kid," writes *PHYLLIS HOBE* of East Greenville, Pennsylvania, "but all my life I dreamed of living in the country. Well, now I do, and I've loved it for many years. Yet a lot of other people felt the same attraction, and as they moved in we were beginning to feel crowded. And then some of these new folks began to speak up about what's good about our region—the spaciousness, the beauty of the land, the way people care about each other. With the help of county and state groups, they've been able to preserve farmland that might have been overdeveloped, and old unused railroad routes and neglected open spaces, turning them into hiking and bike trails and family parks. I have to admit, this has been a time of learning for me. And I'm grateful to all these newcomers for teaching me how to hold on to the things I love."

"There are many advantages to living in Southern California," says *HAL HOSTETLER* of Vista, California, "but a big disadvantage for my wife Carol and me is that we're so far from most of our relatives. Our daughter Laurel and granddaughter Kaila live only two miles from us, but almost everyone else is back East. Our visit with our daughter Kristal and her family in New York's Hudson Valley was confined to two weeks in the fall, and it's been a while since we saw our relatives in western Pennsylvania. Carol's sister Lynn and family from Virginia met us in Las Vegas over the Thanksgiving weekend for the marriage of her son Bryan and his bride Molly. Kaila was thrilled to be able to play with her cousins again. At home I've just concluded my second three-year term as an elder at our church, where Carol and I both taught adult studies and served on the discipleship committee."

"You can come home again." At least, that's what *JEFF JAPINGA* says he learned after last year's return from a twenty-year *Daily Guideposts* hiatus. "Common bonds must be made of an incredibly strong material," he says, "because they sure last a long time." He's been saying the same thing to his son Mark after experiencing the household emptiness that comes with sending off a first child to college. Mark is a political science major at Grinnell College, 422 miles from home in Holland, Michigan. Wife Lynn continues to teach at Hope College, even as she works on her next book. The most nerve-wracking part of life? Being the parent of soccer goalie/basketball forward/volleyball spiker teenaged daughter Annie. Amid all this, Jeff continues to devote significant energy to his work for the Reformed Church in America, as assistant to the general secretary, focusing on organizational enhancement.

Last year brought many challenges and changes for *ASHLEY JOHNSON*. She graduated from college, returned to Florence, Alabama, and began working as a travel writer. "With each new turn," Ashley says, "I encounter new adventures and chances for exploration. As a recent college graduate, I pray daily for strength and wisdom in my life. I've embraced the motto 'joy in the journey,' because, as far as I can tell, my destination in this world is still unknown."

BROCK KIDD of Nashville, Tennessee, writes, "This year I discovered that my son Harrison, who recently turned 6, already has his life planned out. 'Dadda, I'm going to be everything when I grow up, but mostly I'll keep a zoo at our house. God and me are gonna gather all of the plant eaters, and God and you can gather up the meat eaters that bite.' This past year my family has been blessed with more ups than downs, and I'm particularly thankful for a bright 6-year-old who gives me more strength for the journey by his faith in our Father and for me to handle the 'meat eaters' that life brings my way."

"Offering kindness when I can't radiate love has proved to be a renewable energy source for life's journey," says *PAM KIDD* of Nashville, Tennessee, "especially considering that my daughter Keri has led me kicking and screaming into the real estate business! Our son-in-law Ben has joined a dental practice in nearby Dickson and has never been happier. He and Keri have produced daughter Abby to rave reviews. Our son Brock continues to excel in his work. In a recent citywide poll he was named one of Nashville's best role models. That makes me almost as proud as when I see Brock with his son Harrison. Our family's commitment to our projects in Zimbabwe remains a major priority, and my husband David's work at Hillsboro Presbyterian continues to attract national recognition. Herb and Arlene Hester, my mother and stepfather, continue to travel about the country, with my mother asking everyone she meets, 'Do you happen to read *Daily Guideposts*?'"

MARILYN MORGAN KING of Green Mountain Falls, Colorado, says, "I've learned that as the body ages and begins to deteriorate, grace allows the spirit new growing space! This is the time I've been waiting for—a time for silence and solitude, a time for being alive to God's gift of sitting with a loved one in front of the fire on a snowy night, of waking to a fresh new day with its pink and gold newness shining through stained glass, of intimate conversations with grown children who have traveled many miles to be with an aging parent. My husband Robert and I found our spiritual lives blossoming as we participated in a workshop for teachers of Christian meditation in Tucson, Arizona, and attended a workshop on soul growth through dreams. Sure, there have been times of physical pain and personal loss, but I've found that embedded in each trial is a jewel for the growth and strengthening of the spirit. So I give thanks for life, with all its pain, inseparable from its many graces."

"Joy is precious," says CAROL KNAPP of Lakeville, Minnesota. "I've found mine in surprising places: building a valentine snowman with a red paper heart, seeing a new songbird, a brown thrasher, speaking hope to my neighbor's one-and-a-half-pound son in intensive care (Paul made it!), climbing ninety-six steps to my college fiction and poetry class, welcoming Brenda's new son Daniel (my eighth grandchild in seven years!), cruising down a scenic Alaska highway with my son Phil in his new truck, music blasting, living in California as caregiver for my 100-year-old Aunt Betty Blackstone. Recently, she enfolded me in her arms and said, 'You are a precious morsel in the Lord's hands.' Now, that is some full-strength encouragement for my life's journey!"

CAROL KUYKENDALL of Boulder, Colorado, writes, "The word *cancer* entered our lives this year when my husband Lynn was diagnosed with a malignant brain tumor in October. Amazingly, six weeks later I, too, was diagnosed with Stage 4 ovarian cancer. Our strength for the journey comes from the hope we have in Jesus, regardless of our circumstances. We also gain strength from the many expressions of joy that surround us, even in our most difficult moments. Our three granddaughters, ages 1 to 3, are like sunbeams on our cloudy days. Our daughter Lindsay and her husband Jeff moved back to Colorado from San Diego this year, and all our children now live close enough to have spontaneous family dinner parties on many weekends."

PATRICIA LORENZ of Largo, Florida, made the move after twenty-four years in Wisconsin. "I simply had to follow my dreams while I was still awake," she says. "It wasn't easy leaving my six-bedroom house, but my four children were grown and gone, and those long winters did me in. I mustered up strength for the journey by holding on to my deep faith that God would be with me every step of the way. I sold or gave away half of everything I owned and bought a lovely condo across the street from a huge heated pool, three feet from the Intracoastal Waterway and one street from the Gulf of Mexico. I'm in swimmers' paradise. Since the move, I celebrated my 60th birthday, wrote my sixth and seventh books, and am finishing up my eighth, *The Five Things We Need to Be Happy*. My journey has just begun!"

"'It was the best of times, it was the worst of times,'" says *DEBBIE MACOMBER* of Port Orchard, Washington, "but God's grace has sustained and strengthened me through the journey." In March, Debbie lost her mother, a short thirteen months after losing her father. At the same time, her career has continued to thrive, with a number of *New York Times* best sellers and the inaugural Quill Award for excellence in romance fiction. She proudly advocates the efforts of the Warm Up America! Foundation and serves on its board of directors. She is also part of the Guideposts National Advisory Cabinet. "My favorite hours are those spent with family and friends, and I treasure those singular moments of grace when I can sit and talk with my grandkids and receive those precious hugs and kisses."

ROBERTA MESSNER of Huntington, West Virginia, finds it's the little things that give her strength for the journey. "I've been decluttering my life this year," she says, "one drawer, one closet at a time." The vintage log cabin she calls home, like most of its era, is short on storage, so Roberta has been busy finding new homes for things that no longer fit her simpler lifestyle. "It's amazing how freeing it is to have a lighter load. The Gospel is powerful in its simplicity, so why not our lives too?" One thing she'll never think of parting with, though, is her beloved dog Spanky, "the stray who came to stay" whom God brought into her life in 1995.

As *TED NACE* and his wife Kathy of Poughquag, New York, have entered the latter years of their sixth decade of life, they've found "strength for the journey" through some of God's most special gifts: their children and grandchildren. "For almost twenty-five years," Ted writes, "a hand-painted school slate has hung in our upstairs foyer: THREE WAYS WE KNOW GOD'S GREATNESS—RYAN, JOEL, KYLE. Then a few Christmases ago, I gave Kathy an engraved music box that reads, OUR GRANDCHILDREN—WAYS WE KNOW GOD'S GREATNESS: AMANDA AND JIM, AUSTIN AND CONNER." Watching his grandchildren grow and develop, Ted finds incredible strength, refreshment and joy. "Add the thrill of traveling across the continent to visit with many members of the Guideposts family as vice president of stewardship and special gifts, and I don't believe life can get much better than this!"

LINDA NEUKRUG of Walnut Creek, California, says, "Just as hikers gain strength for the journey by being prepared, I strap on a backpack every morning. My backpack includes thoughts of family and friends who have encouraged me (when I was critical of myself, a friend said, 'I wish you could see yourself through my eyes'), mental pictures of my smiling nephews in their soccer uniforms, images of friends who are removed through distance or death but are still close to my heart, and a Bible quote that reminds me I don't have to do it alone: 'God is my strength and power' (II Samuel 22:33). Just as any journey includes glorious peaks and deep valleys, so does our journey through life. I try to enjoy the view from both vantage points, and when the going seems rough, I reach into my backpack."

Daily Guideposts newcomer *REBECCA ONDOV* writes, "The afterbirth of my mule baby reminded me of my past year. I'd gone through a divorce and found myself a middle-aged woman, alone (I'd never had children), with no 'real skills' with which to support myself financially. Tears of trepidation, fear and loneliness stained my cheeks. Then Wind Dancer shimmied between my arm and body. I hugged her and asked, 'How could something as beautiful as you come from something as awful as that?' I shook my head. I could focus on the afterbirth of my life—my divorce and the poor decisions I'd made—or I could *choose* to build a productive new life. A couple months later I took a job as a lumber broker (no, I didn't have any experience), and moved my three horses, two mules, two cats and one dog to Hamilton, Montana, where I am chiseling a new place for myself in the world."

RUTH STAFFORD PEALE of Pawling, New York, writes, "My journey has been a long one—101 years as of September 10! So my need for strength has indeed been great. Now I find myself very thankful for family, friends and colleagues who make my days pleasant and who have helped me countless times. Really, whenever I think about the word *strength*, a Bible verse comes to mind that has meant a lot to me, Psalm 121:1. 'I will lift up mine eyes unto the hills, from whence cometh my help. My help cometh from the Lord.' This is my prayer. Lifting up my eyes, lifting up my heart to the One Who is always there, available to give strength for each day."

ROBERTA ROGERS of New Market, Virginia, writes, "What wonderful strength the Lord gave our family this past year! It began with great gulps of sad and worrisome events, but it ended with the total joy of 1-year-old grandson Jack's face-splitting grin, hand-clapping and high-fives. This new year finds our sons on the move: Peter moving ahead with his FAA career, and David and his wife Matti moving on when his Army commitment ends. Tom, his wife Susan and Jack—and a new grandbaby—will move into a new home in Marietta, Georgia, and John plans to move over into the valley, which will put him closer to Bill and me. We are moving into our fifth decade of marriage. Bill bought me a basic elliptical machine to keep us both moving, literally! We send you blessings and the encouragement that the Lord's strength is never-ending and always trustworthy."

DANIEL SCHANTZ's father passed away in August 2004, and Dan's mother-in-law joined him the following May. "As I watched Sharon's mother fading in strength," Dan says, "I wanted to cheer her, so on my way to the hospital I stopped and picked one of the peonies that grow along her driveway. I picked the largest one, which also had a big bud artfully attached to the stem. She loved the peony, and as her strength continued to diminish, the peony yellowed and the petals fell off. But on the night that she left us, I noticed that the bud had finally opened into a beautiful new peony, prettier than the first one. I felt that God had given us an object lesson to illustrate how the old Ruth had left a world of weakness and ugliness, but now she was blooming in a new world of evergreen beauty." Dan is beginning his fortieth year as a teacher at Central Christian College in Moberly, Missouri.

GAIL THORELL SCHILLING shortened her sixty-minute commute to six minutes by moving to Concord, New Hampshire, where she teaches and daughter Trina attends classes at New Hampshire Technical Institute. "Many of my students are refugees from war-ravaged countries: Rwanda, Uganda, Sudan, Moldova, Bosnia," says Gail. "I am humbled by their resilience as they rebuild their lives in a new culture. Stories of their journeys inspired me to volunteer in resettlement services, and I now teach English to Susanna from Liberia. Both of us love our grandkids, cooking and gardening. Following a death in her family, she wept and assured me, 'It will be all right. God is here.' I teach reading, but she teaches faith." After graduating from Massachusetts Institute of Technology, son Tom heads to Santa Cruz, California, for graduate studies, where he'll be closer to his brother Greg. "My girls still live close enough for impromptu suppers—only now Tess does the cooking, not me!"

"Genesis 12:9—'Then Abram journeyed by stages to the Negev'—has held special meaning for me this year," says *PENNEY SCHWAB* of Copeland, Kansas. "Looking back over twenty years as executive director of United Methodist Mexican-American Ministries, a social service and medical agency in southwest Kansas, I'm convinced that God leads us at a pace we're able to go. His grace strengthens and guides as we take each small step." Penney and husband Don still live on their farm and spend their free time traveling to their grandchildren's sports and music activities. "Ryan is now 17, David, 15, Mark and Caleb, 12, Olivia, 8, and Caden, 4, so there's always something going on."

This December, *ELIZABETH (TIB) SHERRILL* of Chappaqua, New York, and her husband John will celebrate sixty years of marriage. "Marriage is a journey with the delights and hazards of any trip," says Tib. "John and I have traversed a lot of treacherous terrain—the clash of very different backgrounds, the tensions of careers in the same field, financial crises, mental and physical illness, and more. But each rough road has brought us closer to each other and to God. The daily adventure of getting to know more of Him and more of each other is the best part of the journey."

Because *Guideposts* Roving Editor *JOHN SHERRILL* and his wife Tib are on the road half the time, mail piles up at home. "It's not a problem for me," says John, who's learned the art of the gracious three-line reply. "For Tib it's different. She makes a project out of every letter." Hoping it would streamline communication for her, John set up a Web site in her name, www.ElizabethSherrill.com. "I've had to learn a whole new language. Not just new words like *bytes* and *kilobytes*, but new definitions for words I thought I knew—*site, visitor, page, link, live, host.*" John's wiser, but is Tib better off? "It's too soon to know," he says. "Right now it's a battle between her desire to reach out and her resistance to anything and everything technological."

"Last fall I completed another semester of college," says *JOSHUA SUNDQUIST* of Harrisonburg, Virginia, "and in the spring I moved to Colorado to ski race full time. It was a lot of fun. I got to race in the United States, Canada, Austria and Switzerland. I almost ran out of money a few times, but God always provided. In other news, my younger brother just started his freshman year at a college in Boston, and I recently bought some really cool polo shirts!"

"The theme of this year's *Daily Guideposts* is a particularly apt one for me," says *PTOLEMY TOMPKINS* of New York City. "In addition to the pieces I wrote here, it seems to me that I've been writing about the journey aspect of life in a lot of other places too. Last spring, for example, I wrote a piece about C. S. Lewis's *Narnia* books for *Guideposts* ('A World Discovered,' March 2006) that got me thinking about the way one's youth and one's adulthood can connect in surprising ways. The next step, I've decided, is for me finally to get down to reading Dante's *Divine Comedy*, the all-time Christian classic of life-as-journey. I've been meaning to for years. I hope that by the time I report in here next year, I will have done so!"

"I have a great passion for travel," says *KAREN VALENTIN* of New York City. "You learn more about your own life and culture while experiencing someone else's. When I lived abroad for a year, God went beyond giving me strength for my journey. He taught me the meaning of strength, understanding and appreciation for life. He gave me a new way of looking at His creation, and the view was spectacular. Wherever God leads you, He will give you what you need to get through. But what I find even more amazing about God are the extra blessings He surprises us with along the way."

VAN VARNER writes from New York City: "'BlackBerry,' the young girl said. 'It's all the rage.' My nephew tried to explain it to me as a handheld computer. I simply shrugged. It annoyed me, and I started thinking about all the technology products that have appeared in recent years that I didn't understand: eBay, iPods, cell phones, DVDs. Along about this time a friend gave me the assignment of writing a piece about Ruth Stafford Peale, who turned 100 last year. I had been a Guideposts employee and a friend for more than fifty years. She was the one, not the good Dr. Norman Vincent Peale, who insisted years ago that *Guideposts* should move into the computer age. She was forward in her thinking. Ruth is the principal reason that I have a new widescreen HDTV set in my living room and why I'm struggling to understand today's world."

"This has been a year of positive and exciting transitions in my family," says *SCOTT WALKER*. "Our oldest son Drew spent ten weeks in Thailand, teaching history in a university, and is now in law school. Luke is a junior at Samford University. And Jodi has graduated from high school and is a freshman at Furman University. Beth and I are adjusting to the 'empty nest' syndrome and our golden retrievers Beau and Muffy are receiving much more attention. Beth continues to work with international students at Baylor University. Recently she took a dozen Baylor students for a study abroad experience in Hong Kong, Cambodia and Thailand. I'm enjoying my fourteenth year as pastor of First Baptist Church in Waco, Texas, and I'm working on several book projects. Sharing life with others through reading and writing is one of the greatest gifts God has given me."

DOLPHUS WEARY of Richland, Mississippi, writes, "This has been a great and challenging year for Rosie and me as our son Ryan began his second year at Belhaven Christian College. One of the major decisions we made was that Rosie would travel more with with me as I attend meetings around the country or go on speaking trips." Dolphus serves on three national boards: the Evangelical Council for Financial Accountability, World Vision and the Wheaton College Board of Visitors. He also serves on several local boards, including Belhaven Christian College. His daughter Danita is a pediatrician in Natchez, Mississippi. Rosie is getting more and more comfortable serving as the executive director of R.E.A.L. Christian Foundation, and Dolphus now serves as the president of Mission Mississippi, a statewide movement that seeks to bring about racial healing by working through the Christian community. They spend a lot of time with their grandson Little Reggie, who is a joy.

"I've started over professionally several times in my career—and it is hard to do," says *BRIGITTE WEEKS* of New York City. "But this year I've taken on an exciting challenge as editorial director of a new literary prize called The Cadmus Award. Its aim is to encourage fiction writers, young and old, who find it hard, if not impossible, to get their work published. So it is a new journey and a fascinating one. There's also been a new arrival in the family: another grandson. His name is Hugo, and he's fourteen months younger than his cousin Benjamin. Time for some girls in our family? As always, I've been hearing from Guideposts knitters working tirelessly on their sweaters coast to coast. Now I'm knitting for both our two babies *and* the Guideposts Knit for Kids project, so that's keeping me very busy."

"I wish I'd learned decades ago that our thoughts create our emotions," says *MARION BOND WEST* of Watkinsville, Georgia. "This year I've made a deliberate effort to supervise my thinking. Many thoughts I welcome, others must be instantly refused entrance. I'm attempting to envision happy scenarios, no matter what may loom ahead. While walking, I've started meditating on favorite hymns like 'Great Is Thy Faithfulness.' I've recalled cherished Christmas memories and my mother's perfume. Another favorite exercise is quoting poems I memorized in high school. I especially like 'Abou Ben Adhem,' 'Myself' and William Shakespeare's Sonnet CXVI. Because of my constant need for God's strength in my daily journey, I've posted this Scripture outside the door to my mind: 'Finally, brethren, whatever is true . . . honorable . . . right . . . pure . . . lovely . . . of good repute, if there is any excellence and if anything worthy of praise, dwell on these things' (Philippians 4:8, NAS)."

"This year has been overflowing with changes for our family of four," writes WENDY WILLARD of Bel Air, Maryland. "After spending twelve years in places like California, Massachusetts and Maine, I've finally returned to my hometown, just one street away from my sister and her family. My husband Wyeth has settled into life here quite well, even though he's a true Mainer (or 'Maine-ah,' as they say up there). Corinna, 7, and Caeli, 4, say they miss the snow, but we don't miss shoveling it! Wyeth returned to the full-time workforce as a computer analyst, while I left my full-time job to stay home with our youngest, and freelance as a writer and graphic designer. I've also had the opportunity to complete the third edition of my book *HTML: A Beginner's Guide*. Even though some of the year's changes were unexpected and a bit confusing to us, we're blessed to catch a few glimpses here and there of how this all fits into God's great plan."

It was a whirlwind year for KJERSTIN (EASTON) WILLIAMS and her new husband Travis. They were delighted that so many family and friends could come to their long-anticipated wedding at Kjerstin's home church in Dana Point, California. Travis finished his PhD in chemistry at Stanford University and is now a postdoctoral fellow at Caltech in Pasadena, where Kjerstin is finishing her dissertation on multirobot systems. On the home front, Kjerstin is delighted to report that her two cats have welcomed Travis to the family;

he's their new favorite piece of furniture. Kjerstin still loves to sing at every opportunity, but when she's not onstage or parked in front of her computer, she and Travis enjoy cycling together and volunteering with their local Boy Scout troop.

TIM WILLIAMS of Durango, Colorado, writes, "Our son Patrick got married last July, but he and his wife are now having a more formal wedding to please their friends, her parents and us. They want me to perform the ceremony. Dianne and I didn't really pressure them; we just sighed a lot and talked constantly about other wedding ceremonies we had enjoyed. The guests will include Patrick's brother (whom we adopted), my wife's ex-husband (Patrick's biological father), Patrick's sister (the daughter of another ex-wife of his father and her ex-husband), and another brother (the son of Patrick's father and the other ex-wife). What a strange journey for someone like me, whose seven brothers and sisters have the same mother and father! I feel so blessed that God has not only given me the strength to marry two people who are already married, but has also allowed me to look forward to such an unusual reunion."

ISABEL WOLSELEY writes, "Recently our church staff, knowing of my interest in missions and Wycliffe Bible Translators (my older son is with this organization), asked my husband and me to represent our church at the dedication of a New Testament. The translation into a never-before-written language had taken a Wycliffe missionary more than twenty-three years. The jubilant, dramatic celebration on a remote rain forested island in southeast Asia was exhilarating, yet not without danger. But my pharmacist-husband handled medications for all in attendance, and God's guardian angels were ever present. I was mentally prepared for the lack of normal amenities like electricity and plumbing, but not for the extreme heat and high humidity, making it the most physically demanding—and rewarding—trip I've ever been on." Isabel, a newspaper columnist for more than thirty years, and her husband Lawrence Torrey live in Syracuse, New York.

"This year has been a blend of change and continuity," says *PHILIP ZALESKI* of Northampton, Massachusetts. "Our oldest son John went off to college in northern New England, where he is studying religion and classics and enjoying the snowy landscapes. Sometimes the house seems a bit empty without him, but not for long, as our younger boy Andy keeps things lively with his piano-playing, yo-yoing and happy, inventive spirit. Carol and I celebrated our thirtieth wedding anniversary in customary fashion, by sitting down with our children for a joyful family dinner. This year we also celebrated the publication of our latest book, a history of prayer that took us several years to research and write. Now we look forward to new opportunities and challenges, knowing that our loving family and our faith in God will give us the strength we need to carry on."

SCRIPTURE REFERENCE INDEX

A Note from the Editors

DAILY GUIDEPOSTS is created each year by the Books and Inspirational Media Division of Guideposts, the world's leading inspirational publisher. Founded in 1945 by Dr. Norman Vincent Peale and his wife Ruth Stafford Peale, Guideposts helps people from all walks of life achieve their maximum personal and spiritual potential. Guideposts is committed to communicating positive, faith-filled principles for people everywhere to use in successful daily living.

Our publications include award-winning magazines like *Guideposts, Angels on Earth, Sweet 16* and *Positive Thinking*, best-selling books, and outreach services that demonstrate what can happen when faith and positive thinking are applied to day-to-day life.

For more information, visit us online at www.guideposts.org, call (800) 431-2344 or write Guideposts, 39 Seminary Hill Road, Carmel, New York 10512.